Thematic Guide to the
AMERICAN NOVEL

Lynda G. Adamson

GREENWOOD PRESS
Westport, Connecticut • London

In honor of Bill and for Frank, Frank III, and Gregory

Library of Congress Cataloging-in-Publication Data

Adamson, Lynda G.
    Thematic guide to the American novel / by Lynda G. Adamson.
        p.   cm.
    Includes index.
    ISBN 0–313–31194–3 (alk. paper)
        1. American fiction—Themes, motives—Handbooks, manuals, etc.   2. American
    fiction—Outlines, syllabi, etc.   I. Title.
    PS373.A33   2002
    813.009—dc21   2001040565

British Library Cataloguing in Publication Data is available.

Library of Congress Catalog Card Number: 2001040565
ISBN: 0–313–31194–3

First published in 2002

Greenwood Press, 88 Post Road West, Westport, CT 06881
An imprint of Greenwood Publishing Group, Inc.
www.greenwood.com

Printed in the United States of America

The paper used in this book complies with the
Permanent Paper Standard issued by the National
Information Standards Organization (Z39.48–1984).

10 9 8 7 6 5 4 3 2 1

Contents

Acknowledgments

When I was a college sophomore many years ago, Dr. James Ellis stunned me with his enthusiasm about a mere book—*Moby-Dick*—and hooked me on American Literature. Dr. Ellis and another extraordinary American Literature professor, my dear friend and colleague, Dr. William A. Fry, have shared their love of literature with me and made this collection of thematic essays possible. More recently, editors at Greenwood Press have offered guidance and advice. Lynn Malloy, Acquisitions Editor for Greenwood Press's Broad Reference Program, suggested the project and proposed a selection of titles outside the traditional American literary canon that dramatically improved and deepened the development of the chosen themes. Maureen Melino gave logical guidance as Editorial Coordinator, and Liz Leiba has been a thorough and thoughtful production editor. I thank them all.

Introduction

To discuss themes in American novels most often read in high school and college literature courses, one must first select the appropriate novels and identify their central themes to be examined. Three sources especially valuable for identifying novels most often studied in high school English classes are Arthur N. Applebee's *A Study of Book-Length Works Taught in the High School English Courses* (Albany, NY: Center for the Learning and Teaching of Literature, 1989), Sandra Stotsky, Philip Anderson, and D. Beierl's *Variety and Individualism in the English Class: Teacher-Recommended Lists of Reading for Grades 7–12* (Boston: New England Association of Teachers of English, 1989), and Marjorie Lewis's edition of the Young Adult Library Services Association (Yalsa)'s *Outstanding Books for the College Bound: Choices for a Generation* (Chicago: American Library Association, 1996). I also consulted many high school and college American literature survey course syllabi. From a list of between 200 and 300 novels, I chose 150 novels appropriate for readers during the last two years of high school and the first two years of college. Although the reading level of some of the novels is accessible to the lower grades, their thematic content is appropriate for older readers.

In literature, the term "theme" is usually associated with the author's purpose for writing the work. Unlike a short story, for which the theme can be defined in a single complete sentence, the novel rarely contains only one theme. A good synonym for theme in a novel is "motif." Like a musical phrase or motif, a theme appears and reappears throughout the novel in different guises as it affects different characters and situations. To choose the themes, I collected lists of themes from a variety of sources including appendices and tables of content in texts arranged thematically. I compiled a list of over 200 themes, and as I read each novel, I identified several themes that appeared in it. After I completed the novels, I culled the list of themes to fifty, limiting the choices to themes prevalent in at least three of the novels. In Appendix A, I have listed an additional fifteen themes that appear in some of the 150 novels included in the essays. An instructor may also want to explore these additional themes during a class discussion of a novel.

After identifying themes and novels, I then selected three novels to discuss in terms of each of the fifty themes. I chose diverse novels as a way to emphasize different cultural perspectives and different time frames in either setting or literary history. The selection underscores the universality of the themes. For example, for the theme of cultural conflict, I chose novels with different cultural backgrounds—*Goodbye, Columbus, How the Garcia Girls Lost Their Accents*, and *Tar Baby*—to illustrate that similar conflict occurs within different cultures. Another theme, that of family, occurs in almost all the novels since families often influence the choices that a character makes. I chose *The Grapes of Wrath, The Sound and the Fury*, and *A Tree Grows in Brooklyn* because the theme of family is central to each novel, while the relationships within the family differ in each novel. The nuclear family in *The Grapes of Wrath* survives because its members work together during the Great Depression. Only the maid Dilsey holds the dysfunctional Compson family together in *The Sound and the Fury*, and it completely disintegrates when Quentin commits suicide. In *A Tree Grows in Brooklyn*, Francie's father dies, leaving her with her brother and expectant mother, but their extended family of aunts and uncles gives them additional emotional support during their economic struggles.

Each essay follows the same format, beginning with an introductory quotation focusing on the theme under discussion. The first paragraph presents a general statement about the theme, identifies the other novels discussed in the text that address the theme, and cites other novels presented in the body of the essay. The second paragraph defines the theme according to *The Oxford English Dictionary*, the definitive dictionary in English. Since many of the themes are terms that have several definitions, this paragraph sets the parameters for the interpretation of the theme within the essay. Additional quotes from literature with a similar thematic interpretation furnish a brief literary history of the term. The body of the essay includes a discussion of three novels, each with a brief plot summary, important critical aspects of the novel, and an interpretation of the theme appropriate to the novel. Because of the difference in the content of the novels, this section varies according to the theme and the novels under discussion. The final paragraph is a brief summary of the novels and their relationship to the theme. For further reading, a carefully selected list of additional novels that relate to the theme discussed follows each essay.

In the essays, I use literary terms as necessary to describe style and content. One of the most important aspects of a novel is its point of view, whether first person, limited omniscient, or omniscient. Some critics refer to limited omniscient as "third person"; I prefer the term "limited omniscient." When the reader is privy to the thoughts of more than one character, the author has written the novel in an omniscient point of view. Some of the novels shift point of view between third and first person. Those novels are basically omniscient, although more complex. Another device is stream of consciousness where the author relays the thoughts of the character without designating time, place, or subject so that the reader must piece together clues in the text to anchor the information. Benjy's narrative in *The Sound and the Fury* illustrates this stylistic approach.

Two appendices contain further information to help readers explore themes in American novels. Appendix A includes fifteen additional themes and topics with a list of American novels incorporating them. For example, African Americans and Native Americans are not themes but rather topics of interest to readers. Novels with these topics appear under the appropriate headings in the appendix. A second category is one that describes form rather than content in a novel. A bildungsroman or "coming of age" novel follows a particular process. In these novels characters grow frustrated with the parameters of their world. At an early age, they leave home to get an education in the larger world. But during the separation from home, they often regret the loss of innocence that connected them to childhood. Other bildungsroman novels are also listed under the appropriate category in Appendix A.

Since all novels explore multiple secondary themes in addition to a central theme, a guide to these is provided in Appendix B. This guide alphabetically organizes the titles of the 150 novels discussed in the text. Each title is followed by a suggested list of themes, including those discussed in the essays (marked by an asterisk) as well as additional appropriate themes for possible discussion.

The purpose of this book is for readers to examine American literature through its themes. Those themes define the character of America and its people from the beginning of its literary heritage through the present time. Incorporating the information in the appendices with the discussions in the text should allow readers to experience the marvelous variety that fills the cornucopia of American literature.

Abandonment

How can you abandon your own flesh and blood?
—Daniel Defoe, *History of the Plague* (1722)

To be abandoned by a loved one is a human fear. For a family member to intentionally part from another can cause such strong feelings of loneliness that the abandoned one has difficulty surviving. In *The Adventures of Huckleberry Finn*, Huck finds solace in his friendship with Tom Sawyer and Jim during his father's disappearances. Jim Loney's father in *The Death of Jim Loney* refuses to acknowledge the existence of either Jim or his sister. In *Middle Passage*, Rutherford remains angry at his father who disappears one day and never returns. Parents abandon, either physically or emotionally, five young Native Americans in *Reservation Blues*. And in *The Women of Brewster Place*, a son abandons his loving mother. Three additional novels, *Dinner at the Homesick Restaurant*, *Memoirs of a Geisha*, and *Maggie: A Girl of the Streets*, also illustrate situations in which family members find themselves abandoned.

In essence, the term "abandonment" means "to give up absolutely." *The Oxford English Dictionary* notes that "abandon" appeared in literature before 1490 as meaning to "forsake, leave, or desert . . . without one's presence, help, or support." In 1671, John Milton refers to a character "as one past hope, abandoned, And by himself given over" (*Samson*). In 1879, M. E. Braddon said, "I felt myself abandoned and alone in the world" (*Vixen*). Based on these definitions, characters in these three novels, *Dinner at the Homesick Restaurant*, *Memoirs of a Geisha*, and *Maggie: A Girl of the Streets*, suffer abandonment because someone deserts them, leaving them without support.

Dinner at the Homesick Restaurant by Anne Tyler

In Anne Tyler's *Dinner at the Homesick Restaurant* (1982), members of the Tull family abandon others and are themselves abandoned. The first chapter, set in 1979, introduces the mother Pearl preparing to die at eighty-five and realizing that, by dying, she will never know what happens to her family. She laments that "questions you have asked will go unanswered forever." In the next eight chapters before her death, members of the family except the father, Beck, tell their stories, slowly revealing the events that have formed their attitudes.

---

* Future references to *The Oxford English Dictionary* in the text will appear as *OED*.

As she ages, Pearl loses her sight, and Ezra, her unmarried son, describes photographs to her and reads her diary aloud. As he details facial features and clothes, she identifies the person and the moment. When he mentions a middy blouse, she remembers Cousin Elsa, and Pearl "hear[ing] their fluid voices, feel[ing] the crisp ruching of the ladies' shirtwaists, smell[ing] their pomades and lavender water and the sharp-scented bottle of crystals that sickly Cousin Bertha had carried to ward off fainting spells." She also recalls Beck Tull at the Charity Baptist Church when she was an unmarried orphan of thirty who had refused money to attend college; he was twenty-four and a salesman. She felt that he was "her reward for attending with the Baptists. . . . She became a member . . . just so her reward would not be snatched away." When her first child was born, she worried that something would happen to him so she had a second, and then a third, but found that all were individuals, impossible to replace. Beck stayed until their oldest son, Cody, was fourteen. When he left, Beck said he would not visit the children, and "Pearl felt . . . like someone given a stomach punch." Pearl told the children he had gone on a long journey, and, to support the children, she started working as a cashier in Sweeney's Grocery while gradually ceasing her attendance at the Baptist church.

The oldest child, Cody, remembers the family's poverty and Pearl's special love for his younger brother Ezra. He tells friends that his father is "missing in action" and silently asks the absent Beck why he left: "was it something I said? Was it something I did? Was it something I didn't do, that made you go away?" All during his childhood, Cody goads and teases Ezra, and after Beck's departure, he recalls Pearl's frustrated exclamation, " 'Parasites . . . I wish you'd all die, and let me go free. I wish I'd find you dead in your beds.' " During college, Cody brings his girlfriends home, and, to his dismay, they all fall in love with Ezra. But when many years later, Ezra announces his engagement to Ruth, a much younger woman, Cody retaliates and temporarily assuages his animosity by wooing and winning her. Later Cody worries that Ezra will steal their son, Luke, and thus makes excuses not to visit.

Jenny, the middle child, also responds to her abandonment. She dreams that Pearl "laughed a witch's shrieking laugh . . . [and] told her . . . that she was raising Jenny to eat her." Jenny attends college and, just before medical school, meets and immediately marries Harley Baines. She returns home the next summer, unhappy with his rigidity and feels "safe at last, in the only place where people knew exactly who she was and loved her anyhow." After a second failed marriage, Jenny becomes a pediatrician and marries Joe, a man whose wife has left him with six children. Jenny, as a child whose own parent left without saying "goodbye," aids Joe's children as they try to understand their mother's desertion. In her adulthood, Jenny begins to understand Pearl's comment that " 'life is a continual shoring up . . . against one thing and another just eroding and rumbling away."

Ezra, always Pearl's favorite, bears the guilt of not doing what she wants—attend college and become a teacher. Ezra instead works for Mrs.

Scarlatti, a restaurant owner who "rescue[d] him . . . and [taught] him all she knew . . . [and] depended on him." Before her death, Mrs. Scarlatti tells Ezra that she has willed the restaurant to him, and he begins to renovate while she lies ill in the hospital. She sees his additions and asks him to change the restaurant's name. He calls it the Homesick Restaurant where he serves food that "people felt homesick for." Soon he loses Ruth, his cook and fiancée, to Cody. Later he refuses to go to the doctor when he finds a lump in his thigh because the theme of his life has always been "*Let it be.*" He, however, does not abandon Pearl. He stays with her and finally finds the one passage of importance to her in her diary.

Early this morning . . . I went out behind the house to weed. Was kneeling in the dirt by the stable with my pinafore a mess and the perspiration rolling down my back, wiped my face on my sleeve, reached for the trowel, and all at once thought, Why I believe that at just this moment I am absolutely happy. . . . The Bedloe girl's piano scales were floating out her window . . . and a bottle fly was buzzing in the grass, and I saw that I was kneeling on such a beautiful green little planet. I don't care what else might come about, I have had this moment. It belongs to me.

Only after Pearl is dead do the children reunite with the father. Ezra invites him to her funeral, and, for the first time, the family finishes a meal in Ezra's restaurant. Cody, shocked to see the jovial, approving Beck, lashes out at him. "You think we're some jolly, situation-comedy family when we're in particles, torn apart, torn all over the place, and our mother was a witch." Cody had spent his life wanting his father's recognition and approval. He discovers from Beck that Beck had desired the same from Pearl, but, incapable, Pearl had admitted the need for "a whole separate language . . . for words that are truer than other words—for perfect, absolute truth. . . . She did not understand him [Beck], and she never would." Because no one in the family could truly appreciate another, they abandoned relationships and, in turn, had to endure abandonment themselves.

Memoirs of a Geisha by Arthur Golden

In *Memoirs of a Geisha* (1997), Chiyo is a child of nine in Yoriodo on the Sea of Japan when her elderly fisherman father sells her and her sister to become either a geisha or a prostitute in Kyoto. The book, from Chiyo's first-person point of view, begins with a convincing translator's note, making the reader think that the contents are truth rather than fiction. Chiyo remembers meeting the man who arranged her purchase and thinks that the day was both the worst and the best in her life. From that time, she rapidly learns to hide any emotions. As a woman "recalling" her life, she says "I long ago developed a very practiced smile, which I call my 'Noh smile' because it resembles a Noh mask whose features are frozen." In the *okiya* (geisha house) where she lives, Granny and Mother approve of her and her beautiful gray eyes. Chiyo tries to escape further abandonment by fulfilling the requirements to become a geisha, but the *okiya*'s geisha Hatsumomo instantly dislikes her and lies about her.

The geisha world reveals itself to be highly structured, attempting to adapt the titles and attitudes of a family, and when an *okiya* thinks a geisha will earn fame and money, it adopts her so that it will receive all of her earnings. Auntie directs Chiyo's life at home, and, at first, she attends school for geishas. After she discovers her biological sister was sold into prostitution, she sneaks out to see her, and they decide to escape. Discovered, however, Chiyo is relegated to maid with no hope of attaining geisha status. She must also repay all the expenses of her keep before she can ever leave. She muses, "I believed my life would never have been a struggle if Mr. Tanaka hadn't torn me away from my tipsy house." Mameha, one of the most revered geishas in the district, eventually offers to be Chiyo's "Older Sister" and convinces Chiyo's "family" to let her re-enroll in school. And although many of the geishas begin training at three years and three days, Chiyo starts at twelve. She learns that "Gei" of "geisha" means "arts" so she has to become an "artisan." She learns to sing in the back of her throat, dance, and play instruments including the *fue* (flute), the shamisen, and different types of drums—*tsutsumi* (drums resting on the shoulder), the *okawa* (drums resting on thigh), the *taiko* (drums struck with sticks from a standing position). She also studies the tea ceremony.

Chiyo learns that being successful involves lessons and many rituals. After she has studied and become more poised, Mameha and a fortune teller examine an almanac to decide when she will officially become Mameha's Little Sister. They arrange the ceremony and choose the name of Sayuri for Chiyo, a name indicating that she understands "balance." Then Mameha creates a bidding war between Dr. Crab and Nobu, a wealthy disfigured owner of Iwamura Electric whom Sayuri likes but finds physically repulsive, for Sayuri's *mizuage*, her first sexual encounter. Mameha manipulates Dr. Crab so that he offers the most money since Sayuri would prefer him for this "eel going into a cave" event. After the "ceremony," Sayuri wears her hair differently to symbolize her changed status. Throughout her early geisha days, Sayuri must foil the jealous Hatsumomo in her *okiya*. She finally discovers how to combat Hatsumomo after hearing an admiral say, "I never seek to defeat the man I am fighting. I seek to defeat his confidence. A mind troubled by doubt cannot focus on the course to victory. Two men are equals—*true* equals—only when they both have equal confidence."

While battling Hatsumomo, Sayuri must also worry about appealing to men, knowing that "a true geisha will never soil her reputation by making herself available to men on a nightly basis." She also has to find a suitable *danna*, a man who will support her by agreeing to pay certain fees and go through a ceremony formalizing the relationship. "The real money in Gion comes from having a *danna*, and a geisha without one—such as Hatsumomo—is like a stray cat on the street without a master to feed it." As World War II begins, General Tottori becomes Sayuri's *danna* and supplies her *okiya* with food unavailable elsewhere. Throughout her early experiences, however, Sayuri remembers a man who kindly gave her his handkerchief and money for an ice cream outside a theater after she had been demoted to maid. She meets him again with Nobu, discovering that he is the Chairman of Iwamura Electric and Nobu's close friend. He tells her "friendship is a precious thing. . . . One musn't throw it away." Not until Nobu finally rejects her can the Chairman express his desire for her, and then he reveals that he initially asked Mameha to become her Older Sister. In essence, the Chairman gave her the opportunity to become a geisha.

Throughout her life, Sayuri fears abandonment, but she learns to adjust. She surmises during World War II that "adversity is like a strong wind. I don't mean just that it holds us back from places we might otherwise go. It also tears away from us all but the things that cannot be torn so that afterward we see ourselves as we really are, and not merely as we might like to be." She remembers her family whom she never saw again, and she dreams about the Chairman after his death. She realizes that even in abandonment, "all the people I'd ever known who had died or left me had not in fact gone away, but continued to live on inside me."

Maggie: A Girl of the Streets by Stephen Crane

Using omniscient point of view, Stephen Crane shows how Maggie Johnson's family abandoned her in his novel demonstrating naturalism, *Maggie: A Girl of the Streets* (1893). Literary naturalism, a philosophical term, reveals a biological or environmental determinism, and either the traits inherited or the environment determines a protagonist's life. Maggie lives with her brother Jimmie and alcoholic parents who scream and fight and seem unconcerned when the baby Tommie dies. "[Tommie] went away in a white, insignificant coffin, his small waxen hand clutching a flower that the girl, Maggie, had stolen from an Italian." Her father is despicable enough to appropriate a pail of beer that Jimmie has purchased for an old woman in their tenement with her money. Jimmie feels anonymous and imposed upon when "he was held liable by the police for anything that might occur in the streets, and was the common prey of all energetic officials." And to Maggie, employed in the collar and cuff factory, "the earth was composed of hardships and insults."

Pete, Jimmie's friend, introduces Maggie to some of the possibilities available in the world beyond the tenement. He "disdained the strength of a world full of fists. . . . He was a knight" to her, and she begins to accompany him to different places. She admires his attitude that "Oh, ev'ryt'ing goes." She wonders if she, "a girl who lived in a tenement house and worked in a shirt factory," could become refined like the heroines of the melodramas they view. After their first date, Maggie refuses to kiss Pete, but he finally gains control of the relationship when she agrees to go home with him. Horrified at Maggie's behavior, Jimmie finds Pete at work and fights him. Maggie, however, decides that "her life was Pete's and she considered him worthy of her charge. She would be disturbed by no particular apprehensions, so long as Pete adored her as he now said he did. She did not feel like a bad woman. To her knowledge she had never seen any better."

Maggie becomes a conversation topic in her neighborhood. Her own mother is shocked that she has "gone bad." Maggie's morals disgust Jimmie, but although calling her disgraceful to his friends in order to "appear on a higher social plane . . . he once almost came to a conclusion that his sister would have been more firmly good had she better known why." Maggie becomes more dependent on Pete, but when he leaves a bar with Nellie, Maggie returns home. Her family refuses to let her stay because they do not want the neighbors to think they might harbor a "fallen woman." Pete does not understand their attitude. He comments "What deh hell do dey wanna' raise such a smoke about it fer?' . . . He saw no necessity for anyone's losing their equilibrium merely because their sister or their daughter had stayed away from home."

For once, Pete is correct. The family's moralistic attitude toward Maggie's sexual behavior belies their despicable habits of drink and disrespect. Maggie's attitude seems more moral than any of the rest. They and others from whom she seeks help, including the priest, can only make themselves seem more acceptable to society by damning her than by accepting her and her mistakes. Instead, they force her to leave home, abandoning her, with amoralistic and false values, typical of novels illustrating naturalism. She solves her loneliness by jumping into the river and drowning.

Abandonment by a family member is the theme that unites these three novels, *Dinner at the Homesick Restaurant*, *Memoirs of a Geisha*, and *Maggie: A Girl of the Streets*. Beck abandons his family physically while Pearl abandons it emotionally in *Dinner at the Homesick Restaurant*. In *Memoirs of a Geisha*, a father unable to support his children, abandons them to the harshness of the world where they must create their own lives despite the adults they encounter. And in *Maggie: A Girl of the Streets*, the entire family abandons Maggie both emotionally and physically; her world of "hardships and insults" ends only with her death. To survive the severing of family ties, a character must find a source of strength. As Sayuri realizes in *Memoirs of a Geisha*, "We lead our lives like water flowing down a hill, going more or less in one direction until we splash into something that forces us to find a new course." And abandonment by family is one of those experiences that may either create or crush the person abandoned.

Additional Related Novels

Alexie, Sherman. *Reservation Blues.*
Johnson, Charles. *Middle Passage.*
Morrison, Toni. *Tar Baby.*

Naylor, Gloria. *The Women of Brewster Place.*
Rowson, Susanna. *Charlotte Temple.*
Twain, Mark. *The Adventures of Huckleberry Finn.*
Welch, James. *The Death of Jim Loney.*
Wilson, Harriet E. *Our Nig.*

Absurdity of War

Each of the wars to end wars has set the stage for the next war.
—Walter Lippmann (1967)

That humans want to destroy another's home or to murder someone during a war as a means to personal happiness seems contradictory and absurd. In *A Bell for Adano*, the insensitivity of a general who hates traffic almost destroys a town's livelihood. Hank Morgan, the protagonist of *A Connecticut Yankee in King Arthur's Court*, time travels into the Middle Ages and discovers that the nobility kill without care. In *Fahrenheit 451*, firemen burn books and kill those noncompliant with the book ban. In *Fallen Angels*, the men worry about sacrificing their lives for an officer's career advancement. Similar incongruities fill three other war novels, *Catch-22*, *Going after Cacciato*, and *Slaughterhouse-Five*.

In assessing how war can be absurd, one needs to define both "absurd" and "war." The *OED* states that "absurd" is the "opposition to obvious reason or truth; folly . . . a logical contraction; a foolish error." Sir Thomas More said in his *Heresyes* (1528) that the "argument hath . . . much inconuenience [inconvenience] and absurdite [absurdity]." "War" as part of written English since 1154 has meant "hostile contention by means of armed forces, carried on between nations, states, or rulers, or between parties in the same nation or state." The three novels, two set in World War II, *Catch-22* and *Slaughterhouse-Five*, and the third, *Going after Cacciato*, set in Vietnam, reveal hostilities that oppose reason and truth and illustrate the absurdity of war.

Catch-22 by Joseph Heller

In *Catch-22* (1955), Joseph Heller uses omniscient point of view to expose the military maze with its disorganization and waste as officers seek career advancement rather than safety for their men. Throughout the novel, normal avenues for survival do not exist, and the men try to devise ways to outlive the war. The exchange between Yossarian, the protagonist, and Doc Daneeka contain the essence of the novel and the absurdity of war. Yossarian says:

"You mean there's a catch?"

"Sure there's a catch," Doc Daneeka replied. "Catch-22. Anyone wants to get out of combat duty isn't really crazy."

Catch-22 . . . specified that a concern for one's own safety in the face of dangers that were real and immediate was the process of a rational mind. Orr [Yossarian's tent mate] was crazy and could be grounded. All he had to do was ask; and as soon as he did, he would no longer be crazy and would have to fly more missions. Orr would be crazy to fly more missions and sane if he didn't, but if he was sane he had to fly them. If he flew them he was crazy and didn't have to; but if he didn't want to he was sane and had to. Yossarian was moved very deeply by the absolute simplicity of this clause of Catch-22.

Yossarian arranges to be safely hospitalized at the beginning of the novel, where he censors letters by deleting modifiers one day and articles the next. When completely bored, he signs the letters as "Washington Irving" or "Irving Washington." After his release, Yossarian swears he will not fly to Bologna, and Dr. Stubbs says, "That crazy bastard may be the only sane one left." Irritated at his superiors, Yossarian exclaims, "am I supposed to get my ass shot off just because the colonel wants to be a general?" At the same time, Yossarian exhibits bravery and gets a medal (stripping off all his clothes to feign insanity just before it is to be pinned on his uniform) and a promotion to captain for bombing Po on his second attempt. Later, Yossarian orchestrates another hospital admission. Then a doctor covers him in bandages so he can pretend to be the dead Italian soldier from New York whose father, mother, and brother have arrived to prevent his dying alone. After the enemy shoots out Snowden's internal organs on the Avignon mission, and Yossarian tries unsuccessfully to save him, Yossarian mentally disintegrates. He hears that Orr has rowed to neutral Sweden, and he decides to follow. He scornfully responds to Danby's accusation that he is deserting his responsibilities that he is "running *to* them. There's nothing negative about running away to save my life. You know who the escapists are. . . Not me and Orr."

Military life is no less threatening to other characters. Doc Daneeka hates flying but needs extra flight pay for his family; therefore, he signs up to fly but never boards the plane. When the pilot DeWatt tries to impress his friends on the beach with his antics and, swooping low, inadvertently slices through a friend, he crashes himself into a mountain. Since Doc Daneeka is supposedly in the plane, his wife gets his life insurance and moves their children, leaving no forwarding address. Major Major discovers that his father named him Major Major Major. When he is promoted, he is Major Major Major Major. In parodies of lines from Edgar Arlington Robinson's poem "Miniver Cheevy" and Shakespeare's *Twelfth Night*, Heller describes him. "Major Major had been born too late and too mediocre. Some men are born mediocre, some men achieve mediocrity, and some men have mediocrity thrust upon them." Major Major does everything he is told, thus men disapprove of him "because he was such a flagrant nonconformist." After unexpectedly being named squadron commander, a position he does not want, Major Major begins signing documents with "Washington Irving" and then "John Milton" or "Milton John" as Yossarian had done.

Still others have desires to advance their rank, make money, or enjoy military trappings. Captain Black, wanting to be squadron commander, resents Major Major and starts the Glorious Loyalty Oath Campaign, hoping to be featured in *Life* magazine. Captain Cathcart volunteers his fliers for extra missions, and, after DeWatt crashes, Cathcart agrees to more missions. Lieutenant Scheisskopf loves rules and parades, finding any excuse to support either. Sargeant Whitcomb glows when his report of men killed in combat contains high numbers because they might interest the *Saturday Evening Post*. Lieutenant Milo Minderbinder realizes the lucrative aspects of moving merchandise from people who have it to people who want it and creates a syndicate for which he flies around the area making deals on merchandise and promising that all will profit. He even contracts to bomb his own men with their own planes, an especially profitable plan.

Throughout the novel, the men who must fight the war, not the officers who are trying to better their positions, heroically try to save each other and themselves. When having to cope with the inefficiencies of the military establishment, their individual efforts shine. The novel has broader thematic implications than the absurdity of war, especially the labyrinth of modern life with its frustrations and dilemmas, but Heller's satire softens the sting of reality.

Going after Cacciato by Tim O'Brien

Rather than ending with a desertion like *Catch-22*, *Going after Cacciato* (1978) begins with one. Cacciato ("the hunter" in Italian) announces that he is walking 8,600 miles to Paris, and Spec Four Paul Berlin along with Third Squad men, Stink, Eddie, Oscar, Harold, and Doc, must find and return him to the battlefront in Vietnam. Throughout, Tim O'Brien uses a surrealistic technique of juxtaposing unexpected images of war and peace. Cacciato gains several days of travel before Lieutenant Corson discovers his absence, but he leaves maps as clues to his path. Surprised with this seeming oversight, Paul thinks that Cacciato has erred. "Open-faced and naïve and plump, Cacciato lacked the fine detail, the refinements and final touches, that maturity ordinarily marks on a boy of seventeen years."

Berlin has his own difficulties as well, both before and while preparing to arrest Cacciato. He remembers his first day in Vietnam when the corporal spent a silent hour with the fifty recruits before saying they had just had their first lecture on how to survive. When others call him names, Berlin thinks "Paul Berlin was not a twirp." He feels "much abused, to hear such nonsense—twirp, creepo, butter-brain. It wasn't right. He was a straightforward, honest, decent sort of guy. He was not dumb. He was not small or weak or ugly. True, the war scared him silly, but this was something he hoped to bring under control." While the men search for Cacciato, Stink gratuitously kills a water buffalo, and when the women start crying about its death, Paul meets Sarkin Aung Wan, a Vietnamese girl who speaks English and French and wants to go to Paris. She becomes part of the group, functioning in some ways as its guide.

In this picaresque progression, unrelated events occur. The men capture Cacciato very quickly, but he bites one of them and escapes. The men then fall into a hole, but instead of finding a rabbit like Alice, they encounter a Vietcong, Li Van Hgoc. He says the tunnel has no exit, and he tells them that "a man's spirit is in the land, where his ancestors rest and where the rice grows. The land is your enemy." Sarkin Aung finds an exit to the tunnel in Mandalay where Paul sees Cacciato dressed as a monk arriving for *Cao Dai* (evening prayers). Cacciato escapes to a train, but when the group searches for him on the Delhi express, they find only his empty bag. In Delhi, the lieutenant falls in love with Jolly (Hamijolli Chand), a woman who has visited Baltimore. He begins to eat regularly and recovers from an unspecified illness.When a newspaper picture shows Cacciato boarding a train for Kabul, Afghanistan, the group must depart, but the lieutenant wants to stay in Delhi with Jolly. The African-American Oscar disagrees with the others by refusing the lieutenant's request. He tells the men, "You don' never leave your wounded behind. It ain't done." They then reach Tehran in time to celebrate Christmas, see a young Iranian soldier beheaded for desertion, and be arrested. During their eight days in jail, a revolution occurs, and Cacciato frees them before disappearing. Throughout these events, Paul and Sarkin develop their friendship.

To escape and to continue their search, the men use a variety of vehicles. They steal a car and drive through the Turkish border while the guards sleep. On the coast, they find a boat going to Athens, and throughout Paul remembers Cacciato saying they would be "home" if they reached Athens. From Athens, they take a bus north to Zagreb where they meet a revolutionary Californian with a van whose superficial understanding of their situation annoys them. They seize her van, but when it breaks down in Fulda, they continue to Paris's Gare du Nord via train. When gendarmes accuse them of desertion, they must locate Cacciato to prove they are on a mission. Before they find him in Les Halles, Berlin begins wondering why he must return to the front.

Throughout this long journey filled with improbable but possible situations, Berlin considers the war and its meaning to his own life. His "only goal was to live long enough to establish goals worth living for." Berlin knows that "each soldier . . . has a different war. Even if it is the same war it is a different war." And he knows that each stays in the war "because we're afraid of what'll happen to our reputations. Our own egos. Self-respect, that's what keeps us on the line." But he never reconciles the situation in his own mind. He recalls

the textures of things familiar: decency, cleanliness, high literacy and low mortality, the pursuit of learning in heated schools, science, art, industry bearing fruit through smokestacks. . . . Weren't these the valued things? Wasn't freedom worth pursuing? . . . Hadn't wars been fought for these very promises? Even in Vietnam—wasn't the intent to restrain forces of incivility? The *intent.* Wasn't it to impede tyranny, aggression, repression? To promote some vision of goodness? Oh, something had gone terribly wrong. But the aims, the purposes, the ends-weren't they right?

Thus Berlin's entire dream focuses on the misunderstandings of war and the way people treat others during its stresses, the absurdity of reality when imagination disappears.

Slaughterhouse-Five by Kurt Vonnegut

For *Slaughterhouse-Five* (1968), Kurt Vonnegut uses the subtitle *The Children's Crusade: A Duty Dance with Death.* The actual Children's Crusade "started in 1213 . . . [when] two monks got the idea of raising armies of children in Germany and France, and selling them to North Africa as slaves. Thirty thousand children volunteered, thinking they were going to Palestine." Vonnegut intimates that modern war is no different. Very young men go to war, but, in Lieutenant Martin's terms from *Going after Cacciato*, do not know why and often are unaware that they have "the absence of a common purpose." The narrator (Vonnegut) returns to Dresden with a colleague who had been a prisoner of war with him during World War II. The narrator hopes to stop the absurdity of war by writing about Dresden, but a friend suggests that a book about stopping glaciers might have a similar effect. In his book, the narrator introduces Billy Pilgrim, a wealthy optometrist who saw Dresden bombed. Pilgrim fights absurdity by time traveling to Tralfamadore at significant moments in his life, including the Battle of the Bulge, where he escaped death, a situation similar to Paul Berlin's imaginary Paris trip in *Going after Cacciato* and Yossarian's trips to the hospital in *Catch-22.*

In Tralfamadore, Billy Pilgrim is able to see his own future. Its citizens tell him that "there is no beginning, no middle, no end, no suspense, no moral, no causes, no effects. What we love in our books are the depths of many marvelous moments seen all at one time." They often repeat the phrase "so it goes," a reference to dead people avoiding the finality of death. They think for humans that death does not exist because they are "bugs trapped in amber." They suggest that "Earthlings might learn . . . if they tried hard enough: Ignore the awful times, and concentrate on the good ones." Tralfamadorians rate Charles Darwin as the most interesting Earthling, one "who taught that those who die are meant to die, that corpses are improvements. So it goes."

Juxtaposed to Pilgrim's time travels are his experiences during the war and after. He meets a misfit, Roland Weary, who tries to bully him when they become prisoners of war, and when Roland gets gangrene from raw feet ruined by ill-fitting shoes, he blames Pilgrim. Weary's buddy, little Paul Lazzaro, announces he will kill Billy (Lazzaro once fed a dog steak with razor blades in it). Billy himself discovers an impresario coat with a fur collar that keeps him warm, and inside the outlandish garment later finds a two-carat diamond. Billy thinks Dresden is beautiful (like Oz) when they arrive, but the next night, the Americans firebomb the city, and 130,000 people die. Dresden becomes a desolate moonscape. After Pilgrim and his fellow prisoners escape, the absurdity of their situation crystallizes in the figure of the older soldier Edgar Derby; guards shoot him for taking a teapot from a ruined home. Much later in life, Pilgrim meets the official air force historian, Bertram Copeland Rumfoord, who initially doubts that Pilgrim was in Dresden. Rumfoord believes that the military *had* to destroy Dresden, and Billy believes him. In the Tralfamadorian way, Rumfoord espouses that what was and what is *is* what should be. Billy Pilgrim does not have the intelligence to protest what *is*; he accepts it and encourages his son to fight in Vietnam rather than to protest against it and other injustices. The scene in the hospital with Rumfoord stands as the climax of the novel because prior events in the novel are cyclical and similar to a stream of consciousness progression with images repeated, including "tears in the eyes" and "feet of blue and ivory."

Heller, O'Brien, and Vonnegut, according to some critics, have with these novels investigated the process of writing, how humans use imagination and memory as a method of survival. Heller's imagination creates the elderly Italian in *Catch-22* who says "You [Americans] put so much stock in *winning* wars. . . . The real trick lies in *losing* wars. . . . Victory gave us such insane delusions of grandeur that we are losing again, everything has taken a turn for the better, and we will certainly come out on top again if we succeed in being defeated." In *Going after Cacciato*, Berlin imagines Sarkin saying to him, "For just as happiness is more than the absence of sadness, so is peace infinitely more than the absence of war. Even the refugee must do more than flee. He must arrive." And imagination has Pilgrim in *Slaughterhouse-Five* marveling that the fictional Kilgore Trout's novel, *The Gospel from Outer Space*, "made a serious study of Christianity, to learn, if he could, why Christians found it so easy to be cruel. He concluded that at least part of the trouble was slipshod storytelling in the New Testament. He supposed that the intent of the Gospels was to teach people, among other things, to be merciful, even to the lowest of the low." Yet, simultaneously, memory allows all three of these authors to examine the destruction and meaningless death that they observed while serving in the military during either World War II or Vietnam in their fiction. Pretending to be crazy, time traveling to Tralfamador, or marching to Paris helped each of their protagonists endure the absurdity of war.

Additional Related Novels

Alvarez, Julia. *In the Time of the Butterflies.*
Bradbury, Ray. *Fahrenheit 451.*
Cooper, James Fenimore. *The Last of the Mohicans.*
Crane, Stephen. *The Red Badge of Courage.*
Fast, Howard. *April Morning.*
Foote, Shelby. *Shiloh.*

Frazier, Charles. *Cold Mountain.*
Golden, Arthur. *Memoirs of a Geisha.*
Hemingway, Ernest. *A Farewell to Arms; For Whom the Bell Tolls.*
Hersey, John. *A Bell for Adano.*
Kingsolver, Barbara. *The Poisonwood Bible.*
Meyers, Walter Dean. *Fallen Angels.*
O'Brien, Tim. *The Things They Carried.*
Saroyan, William. *The Human Comedy.*
Shaara, Michael. *The Killer Angels.*
Tan, Amy. *The Joy Luck Club.*
Twain, Mark. *A Connecticut Yankee in King Arthur's Court.*
Welch, James. *Fools Crow.*

Alienation

"Alienation": the notion that in modern capitalistic society man is estranged or alienated from what are properly his functions and creations and that instead of controlling them he is controlled by them.
—E. Kaneka (1962)

Many novels explore the condition of alienation in contemporary society. Humans feel separated from each other and from core values that have seemed to disappear from their lives. In *The Assistant*, Frank Alpine wants acceptance so desperately that he becomes a Jew. Holden Caulfield in *The Catcher in the Rye* feels separate from everyone, even his sister Phoebe. In *The Heart Is a Lonely Hunter*, unable to hear or speak, John Singer Is physically alienated from all others. Nearly all the characters in *Ragtime* live in singular worlds. And in *The Day of the Locust*, the lack of love in Hollywood symbolizes alienation. Alienation is a basic theme in three other novels as well, *After the First Death*, *Foxfire*, and *The Moviegoer*.

Since 1388, alienation has been recognized as a human condition referring to the "state of estrangement in feeling or affection" (*OED*). *The Listener* (1958) notes that "[Karl] Marx, or at any rate the early Marx, has used a concept, Hegelian in origin, which Berdyaev found immensely fruitful for his own discussion of the idea of objectivity: the concept of 'alienation.' Men turn or are turned into impoverished things, dependent on power outside themselves." In the three novels discussed here, *After the First Death*, *Foxfire*, and *The Moviegoer*, the state of alienation does make people feel psychologically or emotionally dependent on something outside themselves. One protagonist commits suicide, another forms a support group, and the third acquiesces to a relative's requests.

After the First Death by Robert Cormier

In *After the First Death* (1991), each of the three main characters feels alienated from at least one other person. Robert Cormier begins the novel with Ben waiting for his parents to appear at his boarding school two weeks before Christmas, approximately three months after he functioned as the messenger for the Inner Delta secret force to terrorist hijackers. Of the twelve chapters, some are flashbacks about the relationship between Ben and his father, using first-person point of view. The others, in present tense, disclose the process of the hijacking with a few relevant flashbacks. These chapters, in omniscient point of view, reveal the thoughts of Kate Forrester, the substitute bus driver, and Miro Shantas, an orphaned refugee trained as terrorist and attempting to commit his first murder. Usually omniscient point of view tempers the suspense of a novel, but, in this story, the reader can never anticipate what Miro's actions will be because he does not react like an American. The climax of the novel occurs in chapter ten, but surprises continue through the last two chapters. A simple plot belies the complex psychological undercurrents. Terrorists hijack a bus carrying sixteen children, and the general heading a secret military group asks his son Ben to negotiate with the terrorists. Ben reveals information when they begin to torture him.

On the bus, the characters slowly confess their insecurities. Kate worries whether she has any ability other than cheerleader, flirt, actress, or female with a weak bladder. She discovers, as the situation unfolds and she offers to die in place of five-year-old Raymond who, remembering his mother's prohibition of sweets, refused to eat the drugged candy that killed one of the other children, a surprising strength. Although Miro refuses her request, Kate looks after the other children, glad that she enjoys them, unlike her uncle who drives the bus only for money. Kate feels alienated from herself and from others because of the façade behind which she hides.

Miro never knew his parents, has never seen his homeland, and cannot remember his real name. He is alone, totally alienated from society because Artkin, the terrorist leader, has trained Miro to forget self. His identity will come with his first kill—a woman whose face reveals revulsion toward him but for whom he feels a sexual attraction. When the Inner Delta force attacks, Miro grabs Kate as his shield but neglects to warn Artkin, and soldiers kill him. When Kate then suggests that Artkin was Miro's father, Miro shoots her, unable to accept that Artkin might have lied to him about his childhood.

The complications in the novel heighten in the relationship of Ben with his father. General Marchand chooses Ben to talk to the terrorists because he knows that Ben will break under the torture and tell them what he saw his father write on a sheet of paper in his office. When Ben's father asks him to come to his office, Ben has never before known anything about his father's work. Ben remembers the time of day his father wrote and tells the terrorists, not comprehending that he is telling them the incorrect time, just as his father knew he would. Ben's role in the hijacking is to deliver a stone to the hijackers showing that Sedeete, their leader, has been shot and captured. When Ben arrives, Artkin tortures him for additional information. Atkin knows that Ben's father has sacrificed him and that the general is either a patriot or a fool.

The novel never clarifies whether Ben committed suicide after the highjacking or if he waited until his father arrived at their mutual school, Castleton Prep. Ben says that he would do nothing before his father came to the school, but then Ben says that he took pills, and that "I am a skeleton rattling my bones, a ghost laughing hollow up the sleeve of my shroud, and a scarecrow whose straw is soaked with blood." On the other hand, Ben may have committed suicide earlier. His father might be having both sides of the conversation—what he imagines Ben to say and his own responses. The general, however, seems to have become schizophrenic, unable to understand how he could have sacrificed his son just to fulfill his pledge for making the death of a friend at Iwo Jima worthwhile.

Foxfire: Confessions of a Girl Gang by Joyce Carol Oates

In *Foxfire: Confessions of a Girl Gang* (1993), parents divorced, alcoholic, or dead plus poverty have alienated the protagonists from society. Maddy-Monkey (Madeline Faith Wirtz) records the activities of the group Foxfire in her notebook so that someone will "record things as they truly were." Since a child, Maddy thought that "a certain talismanic power resided in handwriting: *in knowing how to write.*" Although she is the diarist, the omniscient point of view allows readers to understand what Legs (Margaret Ann Sadovsky) also thought. After Legs leaves her grandmother and moves in with Maddy, she decides to create a group, and on January 1, 1953, in Hammond, New York, Foxfire holds its initiation. Four girls, Legs, Maddy, Betty Siefried (Goldie), and Elizabeth O'Hagan (Rita), pledge their lives by mixing blood, drinking, and baring their breasts. To them, "Foxfire was a true blood-sisterhood, our bond forged in loyalty, fidelity, trust, *love.*" They proclaim "FOXFIRE IS YOUR HEART!" and later wear "flamey-orange" scarves and identical gold stud earrings to show their bond. The value of the gang to Maddy is "*knowing now I would never be alone again never lonely again as in those years God allowed me to be thus as if He did not exist forcing onto me the bitter knowledge that He did not exist in truth or if He did His existence touched in no way upon my own.*"

Each of the girls has had difficulties with males, and the group focuses on getting revenge. Males who "were too ashamed, or too cowardly, to come forward to complain" are their victims. The first is the ninth-grade math teacher, Buttinger, who detained Rita after school so he could rub against her breasts. Foxfire writes a sign on the passenger side of his car referring to his sexual interests, and he has to retire after he has unknowingly driven the sign around town. They beat up "Uncle Wimpy" who decides Maddy must pay for a typewriter she wants that he had thrown into the trash. He raises the cost each time she appears with money but offers to give the typewriter to her if she will touch his penis. She refuses. Then they [FOXFIRE] picket outside a pet store because the owners are abusing the dogs; their sign reads *"The oppressed of the Earth, rising, make their own law."* After they initiate Violet Kahn (Snow White) in the second year, Legs "kidnaps" a new Buick, races with the police, and ends up in the Red Bank State Correctional Facility for Girls.

Legs's experiences in prison lead to many of her later decisions about Foxfire. At first, she refuses to follow prison rules, but after days in solitary confinement, she decides that being a model prisoner may make her life easier. She even joins a Big Sister–Little Sister Christian Girls program and meets Marianne Kellogg. After her release, Legs works in the country and discovers a house for the girls to buy. To support themselves, they pretend to be prostitutes, but they, instead of performing, beat up and take wallets from the men they dupe. Legs observes Yetta, a dwarf-woman, in the yard of a house during the day, and, one night, Legs peeks into a back window and sees that someone has chained Yetta to a bed and that men are raping her. Legs discovers that Yetta's brother has enslaved her; to combat the horror Legs feels, she burns down the house.

Discord comes into the group when Legs decides that only by kidnaping someone for ransom will they obtain the money to keep their house. When Legs visits Marianne in her home, *Windward*, she decides to kidnap Marianne's father, Whitney Kellogg. Maddy disagrees with this plan. She also disapproves of newer members of Foxfire who seem to enjoy hurting people contrary to Foxfire's original intent. Legs asks Maddy to leave, and Maddy moves out before the kidnaping. The captured Whitney Kellogg refuses to tell his wife he is alive, and one of the girls accidentally shoots him. But instead of letting him die, Legs calls an ambulance. Then she disappears, never to be seen again. Many years later, when Rita and Maddy unexpectedly meet, Rita shows Maddy a newspaper picture of a woman in Cuba with Fidel Castro. Both think she might be Legs. Thus, the girls of Foxfire remain alienated from society and, after a while, from each other.

The Moviegoer by Walker Percy

In *The Moviegoer* (1961), twenty-nine-year-old John Bickerson Bolling, called Jack or Binx, feels alienated from everything. He notes, "I have discovered that most people have no one to talk to, no one, that is, who really wants to listen." During the week of Mardi Gras in New Orleans, his Aunt Emily wants to know about his future. Jack is only interested in girls and the movies; "I spend my entire time working, making money, going to movies and seeking the company of women." He has dated all the secretaries at the branch office of his uncle's brokerage firm in Gentilly (a suburb of New Orleans) where he has been working for four years—Marcis, Linda, and now Sharon Kincaid. He also admits, "I am quite happy in a movie, even a bad movie." He especially likes movies offering him "certification" because "if he sees a movie which shows his very neighborhood, it becomes possible for him to live, for a time at least, as a person who is Somewhere and not Anywhere." For his landlady, Mrs. Shexnaydre (a fireman's widow), he gloats, "I am a model tenant and a model citizen and take pleasure in doing all that is expected of me. My wallet is full of identity cards, library cards, credit cards." Jack has become an object and allowed routine to inauthenticate him, traits that Walker Percy thought damned modern humans.

Jack's interaction with his family is only slightly more personal. He tries to help his cousin Kate escape her suicidal depression, and he enjoys the company of his crippled younger half-brother Lonnie. Jack's physician father died on Crete in the "wine-dark sea" after joining the Canadian Royal Air Force in World War II. His brother Scotty died from pneumonia when Jack was eight, and his mother remarried a man named "Smith," and bore six other children, including one who drowned the previous summer and Lonnie. Aunt Emily raised Jack and says, "I did my best for you, son. I gave you all I had. More than anything I wanted to pass on to you the one heritage of the men of our family, a certain quality of spirit, a gaiety, a sense of duty, a nobility worn lightly, a sweetness, a gentleness with women—the only good things the South ever had and the only things that really matter in this life."

Unlike Jack, other members of the household and friends are socially oriented. His aunt's husband is Jules Cutrer, and Jack says about him, "For the world he lives in, the city of Man, is so pleasant that the City of God must hold little in store for him." Walter, Kate's fiancé, wants Jack to join his *krewe* in the Mardi Gras parade, but Jack refuses, even though they belonged to the same college fraternity. "It is distracting, and not for five minutes will I be distracted from the wonder." As Kate becomes more depressed, Jack tries to help her. She announces that the happiest day of her life was when her first fiancé, Lyell, died in an accident. When she takes an overdose of phenobarbital, she and Jack flee to Chicago. Since neither remembered to tell Aunt Emily of their plans, they contritely return the following night, and Kate announces that she and Jack will marry. Jack agrees and declares that he will attend medical school as well.

In an epilogue, Jack reveals that he has married, started medical school, sold his inherited estate for a large sum, and that his favorite brother Lonnie has died. Life does not yet absorb him, but Kate makes him feel less alienated, and he offers her emotional stablity. He concludes, "There is only one thing I can do: listen to people, see how they stick themselves into the world, hand them along a ways in their dark journey and be handed along, and for good and selfish reasons."

All the novels illustrate the state of humans when they experience alienation or estrangement from others. Ben in *After the First Death* feels guilty for breaking under the torture and dismayed that his father expected his behavior. In *Foxfire*, Legs's father falsely accuses her of prostitution, and Maddy's family is nonexistent. Jack drifts aimlessly in *The Moviegoer*, long refusing to commit himself to other humans. He admits early in the novel, "Before, I wandered as a diversion. Now I wander seriously and sit and read as a diversion." Perhaps his comment best defines the alienated—people who "wander seriously" trying to find someone who will validate their being by creating a "diversion."

Additional Related Novels

Alexie, Sherman. *Reservation Blues.*
Bellow, Saul. *Henderson, the Rain King; Seize the Day.*
Doctorow, E. L. *Ragtime.*
Ellison, Ralph. *Invisible Man.*
Faulkner, William. *Light in August.*
Fitzgerald, F. Scott. *The Great Gatsby.*
Gaines, Ernest J. *A Gathering of Old Men.*
Kerouac, Jack. *On the Road.*
Lewis, Sinclair. *Main Street.*
Malamud, Bernard. *The Assistant.*
McCullers, Carson. *The Heart Is a Lonely Hunter; A Member of the Wedding.*
Salinger, J. D. *The Catcher in the Rye.*
Sinclair, Upton. *The Jungle.*
Updike, John. *Rabbit, Run.*
Vonnegut, Kurt. *Slaughterhouse-Five.*
Welch, James. *The Death of Jim Loney.*
West, Nathanael. *The Day of the Locust.*
Wharton, Edith. *House of Mirth.*
Wideman, John Edgar. *The Hiding Place.*
Wright, Richard. *Native Son.*

American Dream

The American Dream, the reasonable expectations of Americans, are by tradition that all men shall be equal.
—*The Observer* (1960)

Almost every adult who has lived in the United States understands the elusive concept of the American Dream—one can be wealthy if one works hard. Money, however, rarely brings happiness, and this dichotomy between what is and what should be causes discontent among Americans who fiercely follow the dream. Many American novels in some way address the American Dream, some about established natives and others about pioneers or immigrants. The family from *In the Time of the Butterflies* comes to America from the Dominican Republic to escape the tyranny of dictatorship. Swedish immigrants settle in Nebraska in *O Pioneers!*, where they break the soil and often their backs, because in America they can own land. *Main Street* presents the stereotypically shallow American town in which the wealthy shun the poor and deprive themselves of valuable friendships. Esperanza equates the American Dream with a house having a yard and trees and three washrooms in *The House on Mango Street*. And in *On the Road*, the protagonist journeys around the country always searching for something better with no concept as to what *it* is. The American Dream serves as one of the major themes in three other novels, *The Rise of David Levinsky*, *The Great Gatsby*, and *Ragtime*.

One of the difficulties in defining what the American Dream means is understanding what an "American" is. The *OED* defines American as "belonging to the continent of America . . . or pertaining to its inhabitants." The earliest use of "American" was in 1598, just as people were beginning to explore the country. A broad interpretation allows anyone who has lived in America to be considered an American. The *OED* defines "American dream" as "the ideal of a democratic and prosperous society which is the traditional aim of the American people; a catch-phrase used to symbolize American social or material values in general." Thus the American Dream is social and material, not emotional or spiritual. An article in *Rolling Stone* (1977) stated, "When they die-cast the fins on the 1959 Cadillac, part of the American Dream blossomed." David Abrahansen expressed a contentious viewpoint that "the American dream is, in part, responsible for a great deal of crime and violence because people feel that the country owes them not only a living but a good living" (*San Francisco Examiner & Chronicle*, 1975). An assessment of Bruce Springsteen in one of his short biographies is that "his songs draw their inspiration from small towns and the Midwestern industrial heartland, expounding working-class themes and exploring the effects of a decaying American dream." William J. Brennan, associate justice, U.S. Supreme Court, stated for the majority in 1979 that a plan to reserve places for African Americans in a training program was not illegal reverse discrimination because the law "intended to improve the lot of those who had 'been excluded from the American dream for so long.'" The protagonists in *The Rise of David Levinsky*, *The Great Gatsby*, and *Ragtime* all strive for their share of the American dream.

The Rise of David Levinsky by Abraham Cahan

In Abraham Cahan's *The Rise of David Levinsky* (1917), the protagonist arrives in America, ready to begin his quest of the American Dream. In the first of fourteen chapters, the reader discovers that the protagonist David has become wealthy; therefore, the difficulties he encounters throughout his early life are less threatening. David's father died when he was three, and his mother struggled to support them. They lived in one corner of a large room with three families filling the other corners and sharing a large cookstove in the center. David's illiterate mother, determined that he should read, encourages country relatives to pay for his schooling. His intelligence earns him a spot in a free Talmudic seminary when he is thirteen, and after graduating at sixteen, he enters the Preacher's Synagogue where he enjoys discussing the Talmud with Reb Sender, "a dreamer with a noble imagination, with a soul of beauty . . . one of the most quick-witted, nimble-minded scholars in town." Levinsky remembers during his study that "I loved Him [God] as one does a woman." But gentiles attack David on the way home one day, and, as she had done throughout his childhood, his mother goes to complain. She returns with a split skull, and after David has received visitors for seven days of mourning, he hears about America and loses interest in God.

Throughout his life, David falls in love with unattainable women. Some, instead of marrying him, help him survive. His first love is the divorced daughter of a wealthy woman who kisses him and gives him the money to go to America. He arrives in America "with four cents in my pocket," and says that "the half-hour that followed is one of the worst I experienced in all the thirty-odd years of my life in this country." A kind man sees him, gives him clothes, feeds him, rents him a room for a month, and tells him to buy dry goods and begin peddling. A second woman he loves is his married landlady. Then he falls in love with the wife of a friend after they have welcomed him into their home as a boarder. He vacillates in love, becomes engaged, and breaks his engagement.

Finally, he finds himself unmarried at forty because no woman he has chosen could make him a happy husband.

David makes mistakes in business but learns from the people he meets. After arriving in America, Levinsky cuts his hair to erase his Orthodox identity and chooses American garments. One man suggests that he take up cloakmaking, and, although he hates the work, he devises ways to make coats more quickly. After studying English at night, he decides to go into business with a talented designer. When a man tells him to emphasize the value of the product rather than belittle his competition, he changes his methods. Another business acquaintance instructs him on behavior in a fine restaurant. He incorporates this information into his persona and becomes respected in the cloak industry. But he realizes after he has two million dollars and no family that "I had no creed. I had no ideals. The only thing I believed in was the cold, drab theory of the struggle for survival of the fittest." Levinsky's view of Americans themselves emphasizes the emptiness of the American Dream. He reflects: "Here I found a peculiar kind of smile that was not a smile. It would flash up into a lifeless flame and forthwith go out again, leaving the face cold and stiff." The American Dream has given him money and prestige, but "I can never forget the days of my misery. I cannot escape from my old self. My past and present do not comport well. David, the poor lad swinging over a Talmud volume at the Preacher's Synagogue, seems to have more in common with my inner identity than David Levinsky, the well-known cloak manufacturer."

Ragtime by E. L. Doctorow

In *Ragtime* (1975), E. L. Doctorow explores through omniscient point of view the desire for the American Dream in the lives of many people—Harry Houdini, Henry Ford, J. P. Morgan, Emma Goldman, Evelyn Nesbit, Booker T. Washington, Sigmund Freud, and three family groups. Neither the wealthy family nor the immigrant family has a proper name. The wealthy are Father, Mother, Mother's Younger Brother, the Boy, and Grandfather. The immigrant family contains Tateh and the Little Girl; Tateh leaves Mameh after she brings home extra money from working late for her employer. Father travels with Peary to the Arctic while Mother looks after the family's fireworks and banner business. One day she finds a black child in the garden, locates the child's mother Sarah, and shelters them in the attic. Mother's Younger Brother follows Evelyn Nesbit around New York, having fallen in love with her. "Evelyn Nesbit had caused the death of one man and wrecked the life of another and from that he deduced that there was nothing in life worth having, worth wanting, but the embrace of her thin arms." One Sunday, Coalhouse Walker, father of the black child, comes to visit Sarah, but she refuses to see him. He returns each Sunday, and, finally, Mother invites him to tea. Sarah hears him play Scott Joplin's songs on the piano, eventually decides to talk with him, and finally agrees to marriage.

Each of these characters encounters the others in unexpected ways as they separately search for happiness and their share of the American Dream. Harry Houdini, who adores his mother, meets Father and hears about the Arctic trip. He laments the public's lack of appreciation for his skills, and after his mother dies while he is abroad, constantly investigates ways to communicate with her. J. P. Morgan asks to meet Henry Ford because Ford looks like Seti I, and J. P. Morgan believes that reincarnation will save him. Henry Ford created the assembly line because he "believed that most human beings were too dumb to make a good living." He "established the final proposition of the theory of industrial manufacture—not only that the parts of the finished product be interchangeable, but that the men who build the products be themselves interchangeable parts." Emma Goldman preaches her anarchism, and, through her, Mother's Younger Brother finally meets Evelyn Nesbit. Booker T. Washington advises Coalhouse Walker after he breaks into Morgan's house and threatens to destroy Morgan's library because firemen who desecrated his car have not returned it in pristine condition. Walker disagrees with Washington. Evelyn Nesbit happens to see Tateh cutting his silhouette pictures in the slums and falls in love with the Little Girl's beauty. She returns every day and buys the pictures. When Nesbit and Tateh go to hear Goldman speak, Goldman points to her, and Tateh disappears, distressed that women in his life are prostitutes. Goldman's accusations of Nesbit give insight into the American Dream, "I bet it would shock you to know how free I've been, in what freedom I've lived my life. Because like all whores you value propriety. You are a creature of capitalism, the ethics of which are so totally corrupt and hypocritical that your beauty is no more than the beauty of gold, which is to say false and cold and useless."

Each of the characters discovers that others have unexpected traits. Mother's independence surprises Father after his return from the North. Mother's Younger Brother invents the cherry bomb after Nesbit leaves him, and he throws her silhouette pictures in the trash. The Boy retrieves the pictures because he "treasured anything discarded," including his grandfather. "Grandfather's stories proposed to him that the forms of life were volatile and that everything in the world could easily be something else." Coalhouse demands the return of his property, refusing to marry Sarah until compensated. But Sarah tries to appeal to the vice president visiting nearby, is apprehended, and dies of pneumonia in several days. Mother's Younger Brother admires Coalhouse's strength and decides to offer his newly improved weapons to the cause. After Coalhouse dies, Mother's Younger Brother leaves to fight for Zapata in Mexico, taking Goldman's advice that "there is only one struggle throughout the world, there is only the flame of freedom trying to light the hideous darkness of life on earth." Mother and Father vacation in Atlantic City, and Mother enjoys the company of Baron Ashkenazy (Tateh) and his lovely daughter. Tateh has sold his idea of a movie book to the Franklin Novelty Company, become wealthy with his inventions, and created a new identity for himself. After Father drowns when the *Lusitania* sinks in 1915, Mother marries Tateh, who tells her he is a Jew from Latvia, and they move their three children, one black, to Hollywood and the movies. Of all the characters, the two true to themselves, Mother and Tateh, are the only ones who do not seek an elusive American Dream. Even though Tateh becomes wealthy, he sacrifices neither his spiritual self nor his family.

The Great Gatsby by F. Scott Fitzgerald

Most literary critics think F. Scott Fitzgerald's novel, *The Great Gatsby* (1925), to be the quintessential representation of the American Dream. Jay Gatsby's quest, the wealthy Daisy, represents the emptiness of an American society focused on money, a sordid but accurate view of the American Dream. Both Jay Gatsby and Nick Carraway come from the Midwest to the East (a reversal of the pursuit of the American Dream in "Go West, young man"), and unknowingly take houses near each other in West Egg on Long Island Sound. Gatsby entertains hundreds of party-goers, few of whom he knows, at his mansion. Across the water in East Egg lives Daisy Buchanan, Nick's cousin, with her husband Tom. Nick, the narrator, tells the reader in the beginning, "I'm inclined to reserve all judgments, a habit that has opened up many curious natures to me and also made me the victim of not a few veteran bores." He soon admits to one "cardinal virtue." He unreservedly announces, "I am one of the few honest people that I have ever known."

The plot of the novel covers the summer of 1922 after Nick has lunch with Daisy and Tom and their friend, professional golfer Jordan Baker, whom Nick later finds to be "incurably dishonest." At this gathering, Tom reveals his bigoted attitude, his concern that "the white race will be—will be utterly submerged." As one of the "dominant race," Tom asserts that all of them at the meal must "watch out or these other races will have control of things.'" Daisy confides her disillusionment to Jordan when she remarks about her daughter, "I hope she'll be a fool—that's the best thing a girl can be in this world, a beautiful little fool." Later Tom reveals to Nick that he is having an affair with Myrtle Wilson, the wife of George, a garage owner on the route into New York City. Nick discovers from Daisy that Tom has always pursued other women (usually from a lower economic class like the chambermaid Tom propositioned just after he and Daisy married). Tom takes Myrtle and Nick into New York one afternoon where he keeps an apartment for her on 158th Street and breaks her nose in front of company when she mentions Daisy's name.

Nick's introduction to Jay Gatsby follows rumors that Gatsby is a murderer, a spy, an army veteran, a bootlegger, and "nephew to Von Hindenburg and second cousin to the devil." When Nick spots Gatsby raising his hands toward the green light on the end of Daisy's dock, he realizes that Gatsby is more complex. Gatsby tells Nick that he went to Oxford and grew up in the Middle West, in San Francisco [*sic*]. He adds that he wants to reunite with Daisy whom he first met in 1917 in Louisville and with whom he fell in love before going to fight in World War I. Nick arranges for Daisy to have tea with Gatsby, and Gatsby thinks his American Dream is in hand. What Nick discovers about Gatsby after George Wilson shoots Gatsby, thinking he ran over Myrtle when Daisy was actually driving the car, is very different. "Jay Gatsby of West Egg, Long Island, sprang from his Platonic conception of himself. He was a son of God . . . [who] must be about His Father's business, the service of a vast, vulgar, and meretricious beauty. So he invented just the sort of Jay Gatsby that a seventeen-year-old boy would be likely to invent, and to this conception he was faithful to the end." James Gatz, at seventeen, had begun to work for a wealthy man, and when he did not receive the money willed to him at Cody's death, he found other means to attract Daisy, whose "voice is full of money." He became involved in illegal stock market deals, collecting enough to buy a mansion with a view of Daisy's dock.

Tom sees Daisy tell Gatsby that she loves him while they all eat lunch together, and on that afternoon Gatsby's dream ends. On their return from this unsatisfactory trip to New York in the heat, Daisy drives Gatsby's car, the car Tom had driven into New York. Myrtle sees the car, assumes that Tom is driving, runs onto the highway in front of the symbolic eyes staring down from Dr. T.J. Eckleburg's billboard, and Daisy hits her. Before Tom leaves town, he tells George that the car belongs to Gatsby, and George assumes that Gatsby was the driver. George kills Gatsby and then himself. Nick observes firsthand what happens to those who pursue the American Dream and those who seem to be born with it.

I couldn't forgive him [Tom] or like him, but I saw that what he had done was, to him, entirely justified. . . . They were careless people, Tom and Daisy—they smashed up things and creatures and then retreated back into their money or their vast carelessness, or whatever it was that kept them together, and let other people clean up the mess they had made.

Although written at different times, each of the books is set in approximately the same time period, soon after large numbers of immigrants had entered the United States and many pioneers had ventured westward. Coalhouse Walker in *Ragtime* and Levinsky in *The Rise of David Levinsky* both resemble Gatsby in *The Great Gatsby* because they think the American Dream hovering over the horizon will cure their ills. Cars, money, and the fiction of a beautiful woman gain their trust. The American Dream is no more than the myth of American capitalism. Nick sees that "Gatsby believed in the green light, the orgiastic future that year by year recedes before us. It eluded us then, but that's no matter—tomorrow we will run faster, stretch out our arms farther. . . . And one fine morning—So we beat on, boats against the current, borne back ceaselessly into the past." But while many continue to strive for the allusion, Emma Goldman's comment in *Ragtime* may be the best antidote. She tells Mother's

Young Brother, "In this room tonight you saw my present lover but also two of my former lovers. We are all good friends. Friendship is what endures. Shared ideals, respect for the whole character of a human being. Why can't you accept your own freedom? Why do you have to cling to someone in order to live?" Those who focus on the American Dream are always shackled to something beyond themselves, something outside of love, embodied in the illusions of materialism and superficial social status.

Additional Related Novels

Alvarez, Julia. *In the Time of the Butterflies.*
Cather, Willa. *My Ántonia; O Pioneers!*
Cisneros, Sandra. *The House on Mango Street.*
Dreiser, Theodore. *Sister Carrie.*
Ellison, Ralph. *Invisible Man.*
Johnson, Charles. *Middle Passage.*
Kerouac, Jack. *On the Road.*
Kingston, Maxine Hong. *The Woman Warrior.*
Lewis, Sinclair. *Main Street.*
Potok, Chaim. *The Chosen.*
Rölvaag, O. E. *Giants in the Earth.*
Sinclair, Upton. *The Jungle.*
Steinbeck, John. *The Grapes of Wrath.*
Updike, John. *Rabbit, Run.*
Wharton, Edith. *House of Mirth.*

Battered Women

The common characteristics of a battered wife [include] her inability to leave despite such constant beatings; her "learned helplessness"; her lack of anywhere to go; her feeling that if she tried to leave, she would be subjected to even more merciless treatment; her belief in the omnipotence of her battering husband; and sometimes her hope that her husband will change his ways.

—Robert N. Wilentz (1984)

In real life, husbands may abuse their wives. Some literature has tried to incorporate this behavior, suggesting positive ways to counter it. Battering a wife usually refers to physical harm, but psychological battering may be even more damaging in many circumstances. In *The Poisonwood Bible*, missionary Nathan Price relocates his four daughters and his wife to the Congo, refusing to acknowledge any dissent from any of them at any time. In *Tell Me a Riddle*, the protagonist's husband has belittled her love of books and pirated her privacy, only allowing her to do as he wishes. Janie's first two husbands in *Their Eyes Were Watching God* think her either a farm laborer or a jewel to sparkle while remaining silent. Rabbit deserts his wife and child in *Rabbit, Run*, leaving them without his support. In *The Kitchen God's Wife*, *The Color Purple*, and *Black and Blue*, the protagonists have real reasons to fear their husbands' abuses.

Although mention of a man abusing his wife appears in 1756, "battered" entered literature earlier, in 1592, to refer to someone "bruised and shattered by repeated blows; worn and defaced by rough or hard usage" (*OED*). Later specifics of "battered wife" include "a woman who has been repeatedly injured or otherwise ill-treated by her partner." The "battered wife" syndrome is "a pattern of signs and symptoms commonly appearing in women who are physically and mentally abused over an extended period by a husband or other dominant male figure. Characteristics of this syndrome are helplessness, constant fear, and a perceived inability to escape" (*American Heritage Dictionary*, 1996). In the late 1970s and 1980s, courts began to debate a wife's rights in battering cases. The New Jersey Supreme Court argued in 1985 as to whether "expert testimony about the battered-woman's syndrome is admissible to help establish a claim of self-defense in a homicide case." Since the battering of wives usually occurs behind the closed doors of a home, few can protect the woman except herself. Even then, she has no assurance that a husband will not pursue her after she has left. These novels, *The Kitchen God's Wife*, *The Color Purple*, and *Black and Blue*, illustrate three ways that husbands have battered their wives in contemporary society.

The Kitchen God's Wife by Amy Tan

As Jiang Weili (Winnie) relates her history to her grown daughter, Pearl, she names Pearl's real father and describes his vicious treatment of her before she could escape to America from China in Amy Tan's *The Kitchen God's Wife* (1991). Winnie's experience discloses that wife battering occurs in Eastern cultures as well as in America and England. Underlying the story is the legend of a virtuous wife who saves her husband Zhang, a selfish and weak man who left her for someone else. To escape her, he jumps into a fire. He becomes known as the kitchen god, responsible for informing the Jade Emperor about everyone's behavior during the previous year. As her terrible marriage continued, Winnie had come to identify with the kitchen god's wife.

These two women, mother and daughter, think they know each other, with Pearl disdaining what she interprets as Winnie's simple past. Pearl says that Winnie "drives me crazy, listening to her various hypotheses, the way religion, medicine, and superstitions all merge with her own beliefs." Pearl's middle-class American life has isolated her from her Chinese heritage. Her marriage to an American pathologist, not Chinese, and her position as a speech and language clinician have given her money and prestige beyond what her mother has known in America. Pearl also hides from Winnie that she has multiple sclerosis. Pearl, however, has assumed herself to be an expert on events about which she has only superficial knowledge. When Auntie Helen announces that she will tell Pearl the secrets of China, Winnie knows that she must reveal her real past. At one point before she hears her mother's story, Pearl admits that "apparently, there's a lot I don't know about my mother and Auntie Helen."

Pearl only knows her mother as Winnie Louie, but as Winnie (Weili) recalls her life in China, surviving a terrible marriage and the invasion of an enemy before a Chinese-American soldier rescues her, Pearl observes a complex woman whom she has never actually understood. Weili's mother, the beautiful concubine of a wealthy Shanghai man, had abandoned her when she was six to the home of an uncle in the country. There the lonely Weili had lived with a wealthy family and played with her cousin Peanut. Then the family had married her to Wen Fu, a man they disliked personally but whose social standing made him desirable. This man used his dead brother's diplomas as credentials to gain a position in the Nationalist Air Force, but deserted his fellow pilots when they encountered Japanese aircraft. Weili's first baby is stillborn; Wen Fu repeatedly hits the second, and she soon dies because Wen Fu would not leave a mahjong game to summon a doctor to stop her diarrhea. Wen Fu then publicly blames Weili for the child's death. When Weili arrives home from the hospital with Danru, her third, Wen Fu has brought a concubine into the house. After the woman becomes pregnant, he evicts her. He then accuses Weili of being a prostitute and makes her confess her unsubstantiated crimes to others. Weili aborts her further pregnancies, refusing to have another of Wen Fu's children. Although she actually meets Jimmie Louie (the man Pearl thinks is her father) while still married to Wen Fu, she does not see him again for five years.

Wen Fu's elevated social position deters anyone from accusing him of lying or cheating or cowardice. When Weili first tries to escape from Wen Fu, her friends Hulan (later Auntie Helen in America) and Auntie Du (the woman whose funeral Pearl attends in the initial chapter of the book) tell Wen Fu where she has gone. Weili additionally discovers that her own father is a traitor, informing the Japanese and betraying his country as he did his daughter. When Weili's father finally gives her money to run away, Wen Fu finds the money, accuses Weili of theft, and takes her to prison. Weili refuses to leave prison, remaining to teach other women to read and write, but her cousin Peanut, who runs a Communist shelter for battered wives, easily rescues her because the Chinese government has become fearful of Communist retribution. Peanut confides that a dead friend's mother now helps women escape from horrible marriages as expiation for not aiding her own daughter before she committed suicide. Yet Weili's troubles last until the day before her flight from Shanghai, eleven days before the Communists arrive, because Wen Fu finds her and rapes her.

The most startling information that Winnie offers Pearl, therefore, is that her own father is not Jimmie Louie, the man who treated her as his own until his death when Pearl was fourteen, but the evil Wen Fu, the sexual sadist who delighted in humiliating his wife. Pearl's conception resulted when Wen Fu raped Weili (Winnie). At the time Winnie tells her story to Pearl, Winnie has just discovered that Wen Fu has died in China, surrounded by loved ones, never punished for his evil deeds, while her own honorable Jimmie Louie had died young and poor.

Pearl's discoveries awaken her to the vagaries of truth. Wen Fu could divorce her mother by making her sign a paper, but if he decided to tear up the paper proclaiming the divorce, then they would remain married. As Pearl hears her mother's version and Auntie Helen's version of their lives, they are seemingly different but the same, and she realizes "I watch them continue to argue, although perhaps it is not arguing. They are remembering together, dreaming together." Winnie tells Pearl, "I have told you about the early days of my marriage so you can understand why I became strong and weak at the same time. Maybe according to your American mind, you cannot be both, that would be a contradiction. But according to my life, I had to be both." Pearl learns the horrors her mother endured as a battered wife and can only appreciate the immeasurable strength of her mother's seeming timidity.

The Color Purple by Alice Walker

In *The Color Purple* (1982), Alice Walker allows Celie, who endures years of abuse at the hands of her father and then from her husband before Shug helps her, to tell her own story in an epistolary novel, a series of letters to God. Celie's father Alfonso (later identified as her stepfather) rapes her when she is fourteen, but Celie refuses to tell her mother the identity of her children's father. Then Alfonso takes away the children, but Celie later sees them in town living with another family. Celie's determination to protect her sister Nettie from Alfonso leads her to ask Alfonso to abuse her sexually instead of Nettie. He does, but he beats Celie first. Alfonso's friend Albert decides to marry Celie to look after his three children when Celie's father offers a cow as part of the deal, although Albert prefers the prettier sister Nettie. "She [Celie] ugly. He [Alfonso] say. But she ain't no stranger to hard work. And she clean. And God done fixed her. You can do everything just like you want to and she ain't gonna make you feed it or clothe it." Celie considers marriage as becoming a man's piece of property. When Albert's children misbehave, he beats Celie. When Sofia, Albert's son Harpo's girlfriend, does not obey Harpo, Celie says "wives is like children. You have to let 'em know who got the upper hand. Nothing can do that better than a good sound beating." But when Sofia mauls Harpo instead, her assertiveness surprises Celie. Sofia confronts Celie, and after Celie admits that she is jealous of Sofia and Harpo, they become friends. Albert's sisters offer Celie clothes, and she requests purple but must settle for the blue they own. They advise her about Albert and his children, "You got to fight them, Celie. . . . I can't do it for you. You got to fight them for yourself."

Nettie also wants Celie to escape, but Celie says "I don't know how to fight. All I know how to do is stay alive." In these letters, Celie explores her thoughts and eventually becomes more aware of her inner self. Many years after Nettie disappears, Celie discovers that Albert has hidden Nettie's letters from Africa in revenge for Nettie having rejected him. Furious at God, Celie stops writing to him and begins writing Nettie instead. After Celie loses faith in her god, Shug convinces her to accept a different god. She says, "God is inside you and inside everybody else. You come into the world with God. But only them that search for it inside find it." Shug has a unique theology: "God love admiration. . . . I think it pisses God off if you walk by the color purple in a field somewhere and don't notice it." Celie responds, "You mean it [God] want to be loved, just like the bible say. Shug replies, "Everything want to be loved." Celie experiences her sexuality with Shug, begins wearing pants, and starts her own business. When Celie returns from living with Shug in Memphis, she and Albert have both lost Shug to a young man. With Celie gone, Albert discovered that he enjoyed keeping a clean house and that he liked to sew. He discards the male role he has had to play throughout his life when he begins helping Celie design shirts to accompany the pants she sells. Finally Nettie returns as the stepmother of Celie's children, with her story of Africa. Celie could not have escaped from being a battered wife without the help and encouragement of independent women who helped her find an inner strength.

Black and Blue by Anna Quindlen

In *Black and Blue* (1998), Anna Quindlen introduces Fran Benedetto, a nurse who leaves her abusive spouse, takes the name of Beth Crenshaw, and moves with her nine-year-old son to Florida. After Fran's husband Bobby, a New York City policeman, breaks her jaw, she decides to leave him. "It was my first broken bone; I think maybe that scared him. But I knew he'd try again, and again, and yet again to wipe that look off my face, that reflection of himself in my eyes." She understands that he thought she was more physically attractive after he had beaten her. Peggy Bancroft, a woman affiliated with a battered wife telephone hotline, promises Fran a new identity and gives her the nerve to leave.

Although their lives are outwardly normal, Fran (Beth) and Robert have difficulty with their relocation. Beth takes Robert to Florida where she becomes a home visiting nurse, and he attends the local elementary school. As they follow a daily routine in their small apartment, Beth becomes attached to her patients, one with multiple sclerosis, another needing a liver transplant, and a stroke victim, Mr. Levitt, who lives with his wife of forty-eight years. She meets Robert's physical education teacher, Mike O'Riordan, and begins running with him every day for her exercise. Throughout, she worries that somehow Bobby will trace them. Soon she begins dating Mike but refuses to become seriously involved. When Mr. Levitt dies, his wife recounts the day he liberated her after World War II, a contrast to the bonds Bobby has tried to tie around Fran.

Two events help Bobby locate them. As a nurse, Beth accompanies a school group to a carnival. One of the fathers irritates the adults by videotaping everything his son does, and his camera whirs when children fall off a Ferris wheel. Beth runs to help the children, and the videotape of the accident illustrates national television news accounts. Soon after, Robert telephones his father, upset when another child calls his new friend a "Spic." When Beth becomes angry at him, Robert accuses her of lying about his father and keeping him away. She tells him, "I didn't lie about anything, Robert. You did something really foolish tonight." Bobby appears at Beth's door while Robert is camping one night with a friend. He has carefully traced them and has been secretly watching their movements. Prepared for the pain of his fists, Beth recalls, "I came up hard against him, surprised him, almost knocked him over." He retaliates. "That's it, he said . . . grabbing me around the throat. And then I saw points of color against black, like the fireworks we watched every year on the Fourth from the Coney Island boardwalk. That's it. That's the last thing I remember."

In the final chapter, Beth has uneasily adjusted to a new reality. She is married to Mike and has a daughter Grace. She has not seen Robert for four years and had only one telephone message; he has disappeared. Sometimes she gets calls where she hears breathing on the other end, and she thinks they might be Robert. Mike has searched for him, but Beth never knows if she made the right choice to change her life. "There's not a day when I haven't wondered whether I did the right thing, leaving Bobby. But of course if I hadn't, there would have been no Mike. And therefore no Grace Ann. Your children make it impossible to regret your past. They're its finest fruits. Sometimes its only ones."

Thus, one of the heinous crimes of humanity is physically, psychologically, or emotionally hurting a loved one. In all three of these novels, the male spouse has considered himself superior to the female and tried to destroy her by either publicly humiliating her or beating her. In fiction, the woman can survive, but not always in reality. In *The Kitchen God's Wife*, Weili might have died if the invading Japanese had not swarmed around her and someone had not finally realized how arranged marriages degrade females. Celie lives an inward life in *The Color Purple*, enduring the beatings and the loss of her children, until a strong woman convinces her to accept her own identity. And in *Black and Blue*, a modern woman saves herself only because a group of other women realize the dangers when a husband beats his wife and act to prevent her death. What all three do when they escape the bonds of battering is accept themselves, as Beth notes in *Black and Blue*, "The thing you took into a new life with you was yourself."

Additional Related Novels

Baldwin, James. *Go Tell It on the Mountain*.
Flagg, Fannie. *Fried Green Tomatoes at the Whistle Stop Café*.
Gibbons, Kaye. *Ellen Foster*.
Hurston, Zora Neale. *Their Eyes Were Watching God*.
Naylor, Gloria. *Linden Hills*.

Being and Becoming

Our life is a "becoming" rather than a simple "being."
—Edward B. Pusey, *The Minor Prophets* (1860)

In life, a desire to be different often conflicts many people. They want to be more attractive or more intelligent or more social. Few are satisfied with the present, concerning themselves instead with a future. They remain unsatisfied with the choices they or someone else has made for them. In *The Awakening*, unhappy with her marriage and her social staleness, Edna Pontellier decides to move into her own abode, but when she cannot establish the "being" that she desires, she commits suicide. Sal Paradise in *On the Road* remains in a state of "becoming" while wandering across the United States on whatever vehicle happens to be available. George Willard leaves his small town for the city in *Winesburg, Ohio*, and the town becomes the "background on which to paint the dreams of his manhood" and his concept of the future. In the novels, *The Shipping News*, *As I Lay Dying*, and *Henderson, the Rain King*, the protagonists are each in a state of "becoming," aspiring for an acceptable "being."

In definitions of existentialism, "being" and "becoming" refer to specific states. "Being" defines the permanence of each person's existence. It is all stages of existing, but "being" only has meaning if the individuals have made choices for themselves rather than accepted the choices of others for them. "Becoming" is the "willing" to choose in a series of conscious events. As a philosophical term, "becoming" is "that which is coming into existence." In *Institutes of Metaphysic*, James F. Ferrier refers to "becoming" as "inchoate existence." While "becoming" implies movement from one place to another, "being" implies a momentary arrival or stasis, "the fact of belonging to the universe of things material or immaterial." It is the "essential substance, essence" (*OED*). However, in existentialist terms, existence precedes essence only in humans. No one can define the essence of another human prior to his or her existence. Philosophically, "being" is "that which exists or is conceived as existing . . . the widest term applicable to all objects of sense or thought, material or immaterial." Hegel complicates the term in *Lectures on Historical Philosophy*, when he determines that "two different states must be distinguished. The first is what is known as capacity, power, what I call being-in-itself . . . the second principle is that of being-for-itself, actuality. . . .

Being-in-self and being-for-self are the moments present in action" (E.S. Haldane trans., 1892). And in *Logic*, Hegel says that "the readiest instance of Being-for-self is found in the 'I.' We know ourselves as existents" (W. Wallace, trans., 1892). In "being-for-self," no split between the mind and the body occurs—they are completely integrated as one. Something or someone outside one's body ("others") do not control it. Thus "being" and "becoming" are metaphysical as well as physical states, and the protagonists in *The Shipping News, As I Lay Dying*, and *Henderson, the Rain King* must deal with these states in themselves.

The Shipping News by E. Annie Proulx

Quoyle in E. Annie Proulx's *The Shipping News* (1993) does not find the essence of himself and reach a state of authentic being until he has left Mockingburg, New York, for Newfoundland with his Aunt Agnis and his two daughters. Before, others have controlled his concept of self, and his name, Quoyle, designates a rope designed "so that it may be walked on if necessary." His parents have ignored him, his favored brother has tormented him, and he feels ugly, with "a giant's chin. As a child he invented stratagems to deflect stares; a smile, downcast gaze, the right hand darting up to cover the chin." After leaving college, he meets Partridge, the one man who recognizes his innate goodness, in a laundromat, and Partridge introduces him to Ed Punch at the local newspaper. Punch hires Quoyle but fires him when his children return home for summer employment and rehires him when they leave. Quoyle views his pitiful life in imaginary headlines such as "Stupid Man Does Wrong Thing Once More." Quoyle marries Petal Bear because she flatters him, not knowing beforehand that she pursues every man she meets. Even after bearing two daughters, Bunny and Sunshine, she continues her unfaithfulness. When the older child, Bunny, is six, Petal Bear sells the children to a pornographic photographer and leaves with one of her lovers before conveniently dying in an automobile accident. Quoyle rescues his adored children, and his newly found Aunt Agnis emancipates him in turn by suggesting they use Petal's insurance money to move to the Quoyle family's abandoned property in Newfoundland.

Once in Newfoundland, Quoyle begins defining his "being," his essence, a change that occurs gradually and remains within his character. Never having known his Aunt Agnis because his father and she rarely communicated, he forges a relationship with her after his telephone call announcing his parents' deaths. (They left a message on Quoyle's answering machine saying that they were committing suicide.) He and Agnis begin renovating the house, and Partridge's recommendation obtains a job for Quoyle on *The Gammy News*, where he covers car wrecks and the shipping news. He fears himself incapable of success, but Agnis demurs. "Of course you can do the job. We face up to awful things because we can't go around them, or forget them. The sooner you get it over with, the sooner you say 'Yes, it happened, and there's nothing I can do about it,' the sooner you can get on with your own life. You've got children to bring up. So you've got to get over it. What we have to get over, somehow we do. Even the worst things." Quoyle does succeed when he listens to himself. He writes an article about one of the luxury yachts docking nearby that once belonged to Hitler. The editor, Jack Buggit, likes and publishes it. Then Buggit assigns a regular column to Quoyle and orders a computer for him. Quoyle thinks "thirty-six years old and this was the first time anybody ever said he'd done it right." He enjoys the people with whom he works and begins to offer rides to the widow Wavey Prowse and her Down's syndrome son when he passes them walking to the library.

The omniscient point of view allows us to learn about Quoyle's aunt, Agnis Hamm, and her strengths. After her arrival in Newfoundland, Agnis disposes of her brother's ashes by pouring them into the outhouse hole. Then she "hoisted her skirts and sat down. The urine splattered. The thought that she, that his own son and grandchildren, would daily void their bodily wastes on his remains a thing that only she would know." She remembers her brother's actions during her childhood, and the reader realizes that he raped her; however, Quoyle only discovers this secret when a crazy cousin, Nolan Quoyle, tells him that the impregnated Agnis had aborted the child. Agnis also reveals that her dear friend Warren who died in 1979 and for whom she named her beloved dog was a female. Agnis has suffered, but she has survived and thrived as a skillful upholsterer of ship interiors, much in demand by wealthy yacht owners, a fact Quoyle discovers not from Agnis but from townspeople. When Agnis confers with Quoyle about Bunny, she reveals her own insecurities. "I agree with you that she's different, you might say she is a bit strange sometimes, but you know, we're all different though we may pretend otherwise. We're all strange inside. We learn how to disguise our differentness as we grow up. Bunny doesn't do that yet."

Throughout his metamorphosis in Killick-Claw, Quoyle begins to make decisions for himself and instead of merely "becoming," to create a "being" that he likes. He appreciates the value of others and tries not to hurt them. When Wavey speaks of a husband who belittled her and also philandered, Quoyle does not accuse but acknowledges her attempts to make life better for her afflicted son and for others like him. He does not condemn Jack Buggit for preying on his reporters' fears by assigning accidents to Quoyle, sexual assaults to Nutbeem (abused by a teacher and older students in boarding school), and love affairs to the old bachelor, Billy Pretty. The essence that Quoyle creates for himself allows him to think after admitting his love for Wavey, that "it may be that love sometimes occurs without pain or misery," and when a storm blows the family home into the sea, Quoyle survives as a man who accepts who he has become.

As I Lay Dying by William Faulkner

Unlike Quoyle, who is trying to live, Addie in William Faulkner's *As I Lay Dying* (1930) is trying to die. She comments in the chapter she narrates, "I could just remember how my father used to say that the reason for living was to get ready to stay dead a long time." After Darl, her second son, is born, Addie wants revenge, and she makes her husband Anse "promise to take me back to Jefferson when I died, because I knew that father had been right, even when he couldn't have known he was right any more than I could have known I was wrong." In Addie's situation, her determination to be buried in Jefferson indicates that she will reach a state of "being" only with her death. Except for the one time she allowed herself to "be," a brief affair with the minister Whitfield during which she conceived Jewel, she is, throughout her life, continually "becoming." After she bears two more children for Anse, she notes "then I could get ready to die." From the title, *As I Lay Dying*, the reader expects Addie to confide her own feelings throughout, but, ironically, Faulkner relies on the perceptions of others to describe this time in Addie's life. The reader cannot dismiss the idea, however, that Faulkner intentionally uses the "I" to refer to each individual narrator.

The novel, composed of fifty-nine interior monologues, shifts the point of view with each narrator's stream of consciousness. Faulkner devotes nineteen chapters to Darl; ten to Vardaman; six to Tull; five to Cash; three to Cora, Dewey Dell, and Anse; two to Peabody; and one to Jewel, Samson, Whitfield, Armstid, Moseley, MacGowan, and Addie herself. As each persons adds a perspective, the plot develops. Addie's family prepares for her death and to fulfill her desire to be buried forty miles away. Her son Cash builds the coffin while she watches from a window. Darl, the second son, watches Cash as he works, and notes "he muses as though from beyond time, upon the ultimate outrage." Darl thinks his father Anse will die if he sweats; describes his younger brother Jewel's "pale wooden eyes" that are "two bleached chips"; knows why his sister Dewey Dell needs to go to town; senses the moment Addie dies even though he is not with her; and grasps that Addie loves Jewel the most. Jewel, Addie's favorite, seems tired all day, but no one knows that he is paying for a horse by working nights to clear its owner's fields. Vardaman, the youngest boy, resembles Benjie in *The Sound and the Fury* with his disjointed observations. He thinks that Peabody, the doctor, killed Addie when he arrived too late to save her, and he retaliates by releasing Peabody's horses. Vardaman sees Dewey Dell cutting a fish, thinks it is his mother, and announces: "My mother is a fish." After Addie is sealed in the coffin wearing her wedding dress, Vardaman thinks she needs air so he cuts holes in the top and gores her face.

The core of the novel is the journey to Jefferson to bury Addie. After intense rains wash away the closer bridges, to cross the river (Styx?), the family must find a narrow spot for the mules to swim while hitched to the wagon. As Darl watches Vernon, Anse, Dewey Dell, and Vardaman across the river, he thinks, "It is as though the space between us were time: an irrevocable quality. It is as though time, no longer running straight before us like a diminishing line, now runs parallel between us like a looping string, the distance being the doubling accretion of the thread and not the interval between." While they cross the ford, a log upends the wagon, Addie's coffin drifts off, Cash's tools disappear, and the mules drown. The accident breaks Cash's leg, but Jewel and Vernon recover his cherished tools. The stench from Addie's decomposing body in the recover coffin repels nonfamily members and attracts buzzards. Darl sets fire to a barn where they have placed Addie for the night and will not help Jewel rescue her body. Anse then appropriates Cash's money and sells Jewel's spotted horse to buy a team of horses from Snopes to continue the journey. Darl encases Cash's broken leg in concrete, but gangrene sets in, and they must chip off the cement after the exposed foot turns black. When the family finally arrives in Jefferson, Anse has forgotten a spade and must borrow one to dig Addie's grave. Anse then gets both new teeth and a new wife. Dewey Dell exchanges sex for abortion pills with the unscrupulous pharmacist and then comprehends that the pills will probably not work. Thus, Addie enters her state of "being," no longer "becoming," and the others, except for Darl, meet the new Mrs. Bundren. Darl stays in Jefferson, locked up in the mental hospital for burning the barn, but perhaps he remains the only sane member of the family.

Other characters from the community comment on the family's attitudes and choices. The self-righteous Cora, who forbids her husband Vernon to wear overalls in town, thinks her "Christian duty" is to help the Bundrens, although she disapproves of Addie's request to be buried in Jefferson. Cora dislikes Jewel, "a Bundren through and through, loving nobody, caring for nothing except how to get something with the least amount of work." Her husband stores Cash's carpentry tools to deter Anse from selling them and reports Uncle Billy's comment about Anse taking Addie to Jefferson. "It's like a man that's let everything slide all his life to get set on something that will make the most trouble for everybody he knows." Peabody arrives too late to save Addie but expects she did not want to recover. He muses, "She has been dead these ten days. I suppose it's having been a part of Anse for so long that she cannot even make that change, if change it be. I can remember how when I was young I believed death to be a phenomenon of the body; now I know it to be merely a function of the mind—and that of the minds of the ones who suffer the bereavement. The nihilists say it is the end; the fundamentalists, the beginning; when in reality it is no more than a single tenant or family moving out of a tenement or a town." And Vernon thinks, "Wherever she went, she has her reward in being free of Anse Bundren." The reader must agree with both that Addie seems to have finally achieved "being" with her death.

Henderson, the Rain King by Saul Bellow

Although the very wealthy Gene Henderson in Saul Bellow's *Henderson, the Rain King* (1958) loves beauty and intellect, he can make himself neither act acceptably in his society nor define himself appropriately. Henderson is unfaithful to his wives, rude to the neighbors, and an irresponsible citizen who nearly kills his former tenant's cat ("almost a deadly sin"). Married twice and father of five children including twins from his second marriage, he notes, "I always have some real basic motivation, and how I go so wrong, I can never understand." After he returns with a Purple Heart from World War II, he tries to communicate with his dead father, estranged from him since his brother's death when Gene was sixteen. Gene is certain that his father wishes he had died instead of his brother, and Gene thinks that he will find the answer after he reaches his "father by playing on his violin" (and thus perhaps symbolically reaching God). Throughout his life, Henderson hears a voice saying "I want . . . I want." He acknowledges "that some people found satisfaction in *being* . . . *Being*. Others were taken up with *becoming*. Being people have all the breaks. Becoming people are very unlucky, always in a tizzy. The Becoming people are always having to make explanations or offer justifications to the Being people." And Henderson sees himself as one of the "Becoming people" who must do something because the grave awaits them. He believes that "death will annihilate you and nothing will remain, and there will be nothing left but junk. Because nothing will have been and so nothing will be left. While something still *is—now!* For the sake of all, get out." He wants to understand himself and his life so he searches for his "being" on a journey to Africa with his friend, Charlie Albert, and Charlie's new wife.

In Africa, Henderson's adventures continue. He leaves Charlie and his bride soon after arrival and hires a guide, Romilayu. He first visits the gentle Arnewi, but embarrassed that he has no gifts, lights and burns a bush to honor them. During his stay with Prince Itelo and his queen Willatale ("to me she was typical of a certain class of elderly lady . . . the flesh of her arm overlapped the elbow"), the queen's sister Mtalba falls in love with him and sends him gifts. Then Itelo informs Henderson that he expects his guests to wrestle with him. By winning, Henderson gains enormous respect, and the people allow him to help them save their cows. Although their cows have been dying from thirst, the people will not give them water from a cistern contaminated with frogs. When Henderson attempts to bomb the frogs out of the water, he destroys their cistern. In frustration, he exiles himself. "Thus I had once again the conviction that I filled a place in existence which should be filled properly by someone else."

The Wariri tribe, the next group Henderson encounters, contains warriors and a tradition of killing kings who disappoint them. The scholar king and schoolmate of the Arnewi's Itelo, Dahfu, says that his life will end when he can no longer satisfy his forty wives and if he cannot capture the soul of his dead father in a living lion. When Dahfu asks Henderson who he is, Henderson answers that he is a traveler. Dahfu wants to know what kind of traveler. Gene responds, "Oh . . . that depends. I don't know yet. It remains to be seen." In a later conversation after the two men have become friends, Dahfu comments that perhaps Henderson "rush[es] through the world too hard." Henderson continues to see himself as a "displaced person," occupying a "place that belongs to another by rights." He adds, "King, I am a Becomer. . . . You are a Be-er. I've just got to stop Becoming. Jesus Christ, when am I going to Be?" Henderson laments that he has waited his entire life and still remains unsatisfied. However, Henderson thrives during his conversations with Dahfu and his feats of strength with other Wariri. During a contest, he moves a very fat man twenty feet and gains the name of Sungo. Then, when Dahfu refuses to capture the baby lion of his father Gmilo, choosing instead to befriend it, he must die, and Gene, unhappily selected as king, escapes with the lion cub and returns home.

A thoughtful man, Henderson never feels a sense of belonging or acceptance until Dahfu befriends him. Dahfu enjoys Henderson's entertaining imagination and relishes his company and conversation. No one in his tribe has Dahfu's intellect or inquisitive mind, and he considers Henderson "a godsend." Henderson's decision to bring the cub home with him underscores his new beliefs. Instead of hunting and killing the lion, Henderson now understands that humans can only relate to nature and its creatures by nurturing them. He once nearly killed a cat, but in his new found maturity, he rescues one. While aloft and communing with the lion cub, he achieves the state of "being" that he has so desired. He remembers his wife Lily's sayings: "Like one should live for this and not for that; not evil but good, not death but life . . ." and realizes the transient clouds outside the airplane window "aren't eternal, that's the whole thing; they are seen once and never seen again, being figures and not abiding realities; Dahfu will never be seen again, and presently I will never be seen again; but every one is given the components to see: the water, the sun, the air, the earth."

The existentialist philosophy guarantees no easy path from "becoming" to "being." Painful choices made in solitude cause loneliness. But if one accepts the concept of choosing responsibly without concern for the extremes of the existentialist, one can contentedly "be" without self-imposed isolations. All these protagonists want a place to "be," rather than to continue "becoming." Only after his experiences in another world can Henderson understand that he must make reasonable rather than extreme choices. Quoyle, in *The Shipping News*, learns to value himself and to examine positive options. And Addie, in *As I Lay Dying*, satisfied to find her "being" in death, welcomes it as more desirable than living. Thus individuals must carefully measure the differences they desire to be sure that they have chosen the one representing a unification of their body and mind rather than one selected by the "others."

Additional Related Novels

Anaya, Rudolfo. *Bless Me, Ultima.*
Anderson, Sherwood. *Winesburg, Ohio.*
Chopin, Kate. *The Awakening.*
Dreiser, Theodore. *Sister Carrie.*
Ellison, Ralph. *Invisible Man.*
Hawthorne, Nathaniel. *The Scarlet Letter.*
Kerouac, Jack. *On the Road.*
Warren, Robert Penn. *All the King's Men.*
Wharton, Edith. *Ethan Frome.*

Bereavement

The accident . . . had bereaved the father of his child.
—Isaac D'Israeli, *Amenities of Literature* (1841)

When one loses a family member—parent, sibling, child—or a dear friend, one's life changes. If the loss is a parent, one may become an orphan or must adjust to having only a father or a mother. If the oldest child in a family is the same sex as the deceased parent, that child may suddenly become the surrogate father or mother for brothers and sisters. If the loss is a sibling, the birth order to which one has acclimated loses its relevance. The second born may become the oldest living child, or one may suddenly become the family's youngest. Because the death of a child means that a parent loses something created with his or her own body, a parent's bereavement may be especially severe and impact the lives of surviving children. And the death of a close friend often terminates a valuable source of comfort or conversation outside one's family. Some people are so shocked by a death that the bereavement process delays for many years as it does for the narrator in *A Death in the Family*. Sarah in *These Is My Words* grieves for many of the people she meets and loses through her life from her father to her child to her husband, but she suppresses her pain and successfully comforts those around her. Others, however, are unable to function constructively. Esther Greenwood's bereavement for her father's death in *The Bell Jar* continues until she is nineteen when she swallows a bottle of sleeping pills. In three other novels, *The Accidental Tourist*, *The Catcher in the Rye*, and *Ordinary People*, the protagonists all lose family members and must endure the bereavement.

The *OED* defines "bereavement" as the "deprivation or stripping of a possession from a person." Since 1650, "bereavement" has often referred to the loss of relatives by death. In 888, King Ælfred mentioned being "bereaved" (*Boethius De Consolatione Philosophiae*). "Grief," in modern times, is a companion condition and refers to a loss causing a "deep or violent sorrow" and "a keen or bitter feeling of regret for something lost" (*OED*). The Roman orator Cicero commented that "Griefe is a disease which vexeth the mind." Caxton in 1483 printed in *The Pilgrimage of the Soul* (1413) "how may myn eyen . . . Restreyne them for to shewen by wepyng Myn hertes greef" [men cannot restrain from showing their heart's grief with weeping]. In 1603, Davison refers to "my grief-dull'd heart." Ouida, in *Wanda I* (1883), relays that "their father died of grief for his eldest son." By 1965, J. Pollitt in *Depression and Its Treatment* gives a clinical definition that "bereavement occurring during a depressive illness is not followed by the normal process of forgetting, the patient remaining grief-stricken." The protagonists in these novels, *The Accidental Tourist, The Catcher in the Rye,* and *Ordinary People,* exhibit unusual behaviors that professionals might label "depression," and, although the actions differ, each one detaches himself in some way from other humans.

The Accidental Tourist by Anne Tyler

In *The Accidental Tourist* (1985), parents Macon and Sarah Leary grieve for their son. When Ethan Leary first goes to camp at twelve, he and his roommate slip out of the grounds to get a hamburger at a Burger Bonanza, and someone shoots him. Neither Macon nor Sarah can function normally following his death. After twenty years of marriage and a year after Ethan's death, Sarah shocks Macon by asking for a divorce. Sarah reminds Macon that in response to her question if there were any point in life, "you said, 'Honey, to tell the truth, it never seemed to me there was all that much point to begin with.' Those were your exact words." Sarah must find something for which to live, and she cannot find it with Macon. Since Macon works at home, he remains there, and Sarah moves out. Macon superficially copes because he writes travel books for businessmen who hate to travel. He also hates to travel unless he must go on a fact-finding trip for one of his books. However, " he loved the writing. . . . he spent pleasurable hours dithering over questions of punctuation. Righteously, mercilessly, he weeded out the passive voice." Macon's behavior, however, becomes even more compulsive while living alone. He notices that the walls echo in places and that he holds his arms close to his body, walking past furniture sideways, "as if he imagined the house could barely accommodate him. He felt too tall. His long, clumsy feet seemed unusually distant. He ducked his head in doorways." He sleeps in a folded sheet that functions like a body bag (symbolizing his death in life) so that he never has to sleep on dirty sheets.

Throughout his life, Macon has had to temper his reactions to his own family. His mother Alicia, a "silly, vain, and annoying" war widow, sent the four children to live with her parents in Baltimore when she remarried and continued to pursue her "careless" life. Macon, therefore, is determined to live a "careful" one. But after Sarah leaves, Macon breaks his leg and returns to the family home where his sister Rose has alphabetized the kitchen and cooks the favorite meal of baked potatoes for the three males and herself. To keep his leg cast clean, Macon paints it with white shoe polish. Macon continues to live in a cocoon here as well, refusing to answer the telephone and not telling anyone where he is. However, none of the four has a sense of direction outside the house; they have "geographic dyslexia," and Sarah disparages their propensity to "cruise hardware stores." Each one of the male siblings has returned home in times of stress to the surrogate mother Rose, a woman who feels appreciated only if she can organize kitchens or files or offices.

After Macon encounters dog trainer Muriel Prichett when he deposits his disobedient dog Edward at the Meow Bow Animal Hospital to stay while he journeys to London on a research trip, his life begins to change. She telephones and persuades him to let her teach dog manners to Edward. Eventually Macon moves in with Muriel and her son Alexander. Macon helps Alexander contend with the bullying of his peers and selects appropriate clothes for him, unlike his cloying mother. When Macon becomes attached to the boy, he realizes that "he was forced to worry once again about nuclear war and the future of the planet," those concerns he had felt with Ethan's birth. Macon's family disapproves of his relationship because Muriel has few of the refinements that the family appreciates, from grammar to social class to youth. His brother Charles says Macon has changed, but Macon understands that for the first time with Muriel and Alexander, "I'm more myself than I've been my whole life long." Even though Macon returns to Sarah after Rose and Julian (Macon's publisher) marry, focusing on the past with her tires him, and Muriel charms him back. The unpredictable Muriel helps Macon begin to heal from his bereavement by propelling him from his solitary and solid winged armchair. When Macon dreams that his grandfather accuses him of having lost the center of his life, he eventually understands that through accepting and enjoying Muriel's eccentricities, he can regain it and assuage his grief over Ethan's death.

The Catcher in the Rye by J. D. Salinger

In J.D. Salinger's *The Catcher in the Rye* (1951), Holden Caulfield cloaks his grief for his brother Allie by mistrusting others, accusing them of being liars and phonies. Holden recalls incidents involving Allie as he recounts experiences before he had a mental breakdown. After redheaded Allie, two years younger, died from leukemia, Holden knocked out window panes with his fist and regretted not having allowed Allie to join him and a friend on a bicycle trip because Allie was too young. Holden seems to compare himself and Allie with a reference to Jesus and his followers. "Take the Disciples, for instance. They annoy the hell out of me, if you want to know the truth. They were all right after Jesus was dead and all, but while He was alive, they were about as much use to Him as a hole in the head. All they did was keep letting Him down." Because Holden knows that he disappointed the living Allie when he refused to allow him to play with him, Holden appeals to the dead Allie to save him. Fearful that he will disappear before reaching the other side of the street, Holden notes, "I'd say to him, 'Allie, don't let me disappear. Allie, don't let me disappear. Allie, don't let me disappear. Please, Allie.' And then when I'd reach the other side of the street without disappearing, I'd *thank* him." In essence, appealing to Allie helps Holden save himself, but simultaneously, recollecting Allie's death prolongs Holden's intense pain.

Holden remembers visiting Allie's grave.

It was awful. It rained on his lousy tombstone, and it rained on the grass on his stomach. . . . All the visitors that were visiting the cemetery started running like hell over to their cars. All the visitors could . . . go someplace nice for dinner—everybody except Allie. I couldn't stand it. I know it's only his body and all that's in the cemetery, and his soul's in Heaven and all that crap, but I couldn't stand it anyway. I just wish he wasn't there. You didn't know him.

Holden has idealized Allie, the child who wrote poems on his baseball glove. Because he cherishes the glove, Holden only shows it to Jane Gallagher, his friend with an abusive father and an unhappy family. When Holden's roommate Stradlater announces that he has a date with Jane and commands Holden to write an English essay for him while they are gone, Holden writes about the glove. Stradlater, unappreciative of Jane's interests and Holden's memories, hates the narrative. This insensitivity verifies to Holden the disinterest of others in the things in life that matter and directly leads to his breakdown.

During the three days after being expelled from Prency Prep, Holden participates in an archetypal journey during which he actually "falls" into hell and rises from it. After he leaves school and returns to New York City, the places where he seeks respite do not offer him peace. His favorite teacher, Mr. Antolini, gives Holden unsolicited and unwanted advice before patting his head in the middle of the night, causing Holden to rush out of the apartment. The bench in Grand Central Station where he spends the rest of the night offers no comfort. When he makes a deal with a hotel elevator man to meet a prostitute, he loses interest in sex and becomes angry when charged five dollars more than agreed. He encounters a friend of his older brother, a screenwriter and World War II veteran, who invites him to join her and her date. He refuses and instead buys drinks for three tourists, silently accusing them of pretentiousness (one of his foibles) and disdaining their interest in Radio City Music Hall. Then he calls his friend Sally, makes a date, and takes her to the same place. Finally he returns to his family's apartment to see Phoebe, his younger sister, while his parents are socializing elsewhere. He convinces the fearful Phoebe that his father will not "kill" him for being dismissed from school.

The next day, he reveals his continued obsession with death by tarrying with the mummies in the Natural History Museum while he waits for Phoebe. (On his history examination, he had ignored all questions except the one about mummies.) Later when he visits the men's room, falls, and briefly passes out, he seems to have made his symbolic journey into hell. He recovers, relieved to be alive. He meets Phoebe, tells her he wants to save children, "to catch everybody if they start to go over the cliff . . . I'd just be the catcher in the rye. . . . that's the only thing I'd really like to be." He wants to cleanse the world so that children will not see foul language displayed in public places. But as he watches

Phoebe play, he understands that children must have a chance to fail. "The thing with kids is, if they want to grab for the gold ring, you have to let them do it, and not say anything. If they fall off, they fall off." Even though Holden must still go through a difficult recovery after he makes this observation (an initiation), he has begun the process. He has to face reality, a state that includes Allie's death, in order to function adequately in a world that he neither created nor chose. In a way he begins to act on the advice from Mr. Antolini quoted from Wilhelm Stekel, "The mark of the immature man is that he wants to die nobly for a cause while the mark of the mature man is that he wants to live humbly for one."

Ordinary People by Judith Guest

While Holden only thinks about suicide in *The Catcher in the Rye*, Conrad Jarrett in *Ordinary People* (1976) actually tries it. Severely depressed after his older brother drowns in a boating accident, Conrad cannot escape his grief and slits his wrists. His attempt alerts his father to his condition, but Conrad's perfectionist mother accuses him of trying to punish her. She is unwilling to accept that her living son needs her compassion and understanding. "Everything had to be perfect, never mind the impossible hardship it worked on her, on them all; never mind the utter lack of meaning in such perfection, weighed as it was against the endless repetition of days, weeks, months. . . . Certain things drove her to the point of madness: dirt tracked in on a freshly scrubbed floor; water-spotted shower stalls." The point of view shifts between Conrad and his father, and his voiceless mother Beth detaches herself from Conrad and then her husband when she leaves him after twenty-one years of marriage.

Talking to different people helps Conrad eventually contain his grief. Cal, Conrad's father, wants to help Conrad, and he asks him to see Berger, an analyst recommended by friends. Grudgingly, Conrad appears in the doctor's office and discovers a man who will neither sympathize nor coerce. After many discussions, Berger helps Conrad to determine that he was not responsible for his brother's death, but he *is* responsible for his own survival. Conrad visits with Karen, a girl he met in the hospital, and when he hears that she has committed suicide, he rushes to Berger who supports him in his bereavement. "Tears of grief this time *Not fair not fair!* No, but life is not fair always, or sane, or good, or anything. It just *is*." After dating Jeannine, a young woman he has met while singing tenor in the school chorus, Conrad appreciates her confiding in him about her own anger at her mother's dating after her finalized divorce from Jeannine's father. Although a painful process, Conrad must discard what no longer fits in his life, such as racing on the swimming team, and accept what works, playing golf with his former best friend Lazenby. He successfully wrestles with his grief and ends his bereavement.

The protagonists in these novels are either professionals or the sons of professionals. Neither wealth nor social class protects one from bereavement. All endure loss of family or friends at some time, and grieving constructively may be almost impossible. But finding that one is not alone may make the process more bearable. In *The Accidental Tourist*, "it seemed to him [Macon] as he sank back into his dreams, that she [Muriel] had as good as spoken aloud. *About your son*, she seemed to be saying: *Just put your hand here. I'm scarred, too. We're all scarred. You are not the only one.*" And Antolini in *The Catcher in the Rye* functions like Muriel by telling Holden "You are not the first one who was ever confused and frightened and even sickened by human behavior. You're by no means alone." Berger instructs Conrad in *Ordinary People*: "Geez, if I could get through to you, kiddy, that depression is not sobbing and crying and *giving vent*, it is plain and simple *reduction of feeling*. Reduction, see? Of all feeling. People who keep stiff upper lips find that it's damn hard to smile." By learning that others suffer, bereavement will not be less painful, but perhaps it will be less lonely.

Additional Related Novels

Agee, James. *A Death in the Family.*
Flagg, Fannie. *Fried Green Tomatoes at the Whistle Stop Café.*
O'Brien, Tim. *The Things They Carried.*
Plath, Sylvia. *The Bell Jar.*
Turner, Nancy E. *These Is My Words.*
Updike, John. *Rabbit, Run.*

Betrayal

Once a traitor, thou betray'st no more.
—Homer, *The Iliad* (Alexander Pope, trans., 1718)

When people discover that someone trusted has revealed a secret or reneged on a promise, they feel reviled and betrayed. Many novelists incorporate this theme in their characters. Jimmy Blevins in *All the Pretty Horses* blames John Grady and Lacey Rawlins for a crime that he committed, forcing Grady to kill a man before Mexican police will free him from prison. Carrie thinks she has married Hurstwood in *Sister Carrie*, but she discovers later that he is someone else's husband and a father. The protagonist of *Invisible Man* unwittingly carries Dr. Bledsoe's letter of recommendation to those from whom he seeks employment only to find from one of them that the letter warns them not to hire him. Men often betray women as does Morris Townsend in *Washington Square*. But men betray men (Cody woos away his brother Ezra's fiancée in *Dinner at the Homesick Restaurant*), and women betray women as Sula does when she seduces her friend Nel's husband in *Sula*. Tom's owner betrays his loyal service by selling Tom to a slave trader in *Uncle Tom's Cabin*. In *The Natural*, Roy Hobbs betrays both himself and a woman who trusts him. Two other novels, *Charlotte Temple* and *Rabbit, Run*, disclose what can happen when a man betrays a woman who loves him.

Since the late 1200s, people have understood "betrayal" to show disloyalty toward another or to disappoint someone's hopes or expectations. "Betrayal" has also meant to "lead astray or into error, as a false guide; to mislead, seduce, deceive (the trustful)" (*OED*). In 1766, Sir Oliver Goldsmith used the term in reference to a woman surrendering her chastity to a man who seduced her with false promises. "When lovely Woman stoops to folly, And finds too late that men betray," she suffers. In the twentieth century, the term has retained these meanings. Jack Black's *You Can't Win* recounts another coping with rejection. "Betrayed and deserted, she stole enough of her father's money to take her to the city and into a hospital where her baby was born" (1926). Characters in *The Natural*, *Charlott Temple*, and *Rabbin, Run* either betray others are themselves betrayed.

The Natural by Bernard Malamud

In Bernard Malamud's *The Natural* (1952), Roy Hobbs, a talented baseball player, leaves home to become a star in the major leagues. When he meets

Harriet Bird on the train, his life changes. She "tests" his worth, and since he wants only fame and money, he fails, first on the train, and then in her hotel. When she summons him to her room, she asks him a second time what he wants, and when his response is again unsatisfactory, she shoots and wounds him. In this story, Hobbs represents Sir Parzival, the knight who has the charge of finding and restoring health to the Fisher King in the Wasteland. Parzival fails because he does not ask the right questions to fulfill his duty. Hobbs disappears for fifteen years. Then a talent scout sees Hobbs playing at age thirty-five and offers him a contract. Hobbs enters the major leagues as an unknown rookie on the losing New York Knights team with his specially crafted bat, "Wonderboy." Some critics think that Malamud's characters attempt to transcend themselves through their desire to change their lives, but Hobbs fails. Roy Hobbs tries to change his luck, but unlike characters in some of Malamud's other books, Hobbs's lack of character betrays not only himself but also the ideal woman, Iris Lemmon, and his team manager Pop Fisher, the symbolic Fisher King.

Roy Hobbs represents the anti-hero, the protagonist who attempts greatness but allows his humanness to prevail. Using omniscient point of view, Malamud allows the reader to sense that Hobbs could be a hero. One of the coaches calls Roy "a natural" because he "naturally connects with anything that gets in [his] way." Iris Lemmon addresses his potential for being the hero. Roy asks her, "Ever see me play—before the other night?" She responds that she has seen him twice. He asks why she came to the ball game the first time. She thoughtfully answers, "Because I hate to see a hero fail. There are so few of them. . . . Without heroes we're all plain people and don't know how far we can go." The sportswriter, Max Mercy, senses a different Hobbs, a man whose unknown past might reveal a weak future, and he searches for clues as Hobbs raises his batting statistics with hit after hit.

Roy has several difficulties, physical and mental, to overcome if he is to be the perfect "knight," winning the right woman and releasing the Fisher King. Unfortunately, he cannot learn from his mistakes. Iris Lemmon tells him, "We have two lives, Roy, the life we learn with and the life we live with after that. Suffering is what brings us toward happiness." But Roy continues to gratify only himself, not using the information he has learned to live a satisfying life. He becomes enamored with Memo Paris, a woman interested only in money. After impregnating Iris, he abandons her for Pop's materialistic niece, Memo. Parallel to Hobbs' weakness for self-gratification is his weak body. It betrays him during an early celebration of the season's successes that the team manager Pop had not wanted to occur before the team's last game. Roy becomes ill as a result of his enlarged "athlete's heart" and high blood pressure. In the game for which Hobbs has accepted a bribe of $35,000 to "throw," his foul ball knocks out Iris. Then his bat breaks. "Wonderboy lay on the ground split lengthwise, one half pointing to first, the other to third." Along with Iris and Pop, he betrays the public. After the game, he grasps that Memo does not love him, and he rejects the money. He is overcome with "self-hatred. In each stinking wave of it he remembered some disgusting happening of his life. He thought, I never did learn anything out of my past life, now I have to suffer again." On the street, he meets a paper boy who asks if the rumor that he has "sold out" is true. "When Roy looked into the boy's eyes he wanted to say it wasn't but couldn't, and he lifted his hands to his face and wept many bitter tears." Roy, the Knight, has destroyed his sword (Wonderboy), neglected to free the Fisher King, and lost the ideal woman who could have given him new life.

Charlotte Temple by Susanna Rowson

Charlotte Temple in Susanna Rowson's novel, *Charlotte Temple* (1794), also betrays others after she has been betrayed. Miss LaRue, her French teacher in boarding school, first lies to Charlotte when Charlotte is fifteen. Charlotte then betrays her parents by leaving home without their knowledge. Finally, Lieutenant Montraville, the man who has enticed her to accompany him to America with a promise of marriage, abandons her after they arrive in New York. Later Belcour, former lover of Miss LaRue and friend of Montraville, betrays both Montraville and Charlotte. Throughout the novel, Charlotte regrets her initial decision, but she cannot undo it.

Rowson establishes the basis of love in Charlotte's family by devoting an early chapter to events leading to the marriage of Charlotte's parents. A Captain Eldridge refuses to give his daughter Lucy to his son George's friend Lewis in marriage. Lewis demands immediate repayment of money lent to Eldridge for George's military commission. Since Eldridge cannot pay, he goes to debtor's prison. George challenges Lewis to a duel, and after Lewis kills George, Mrs. Eldridge dies. Henry Temple discovers the problem, helps Eldridge, and meets Lucy. Then he decides to forfeit a large inheritance rather than marry Miss Weatherby, the woman to whom his father promised him. Temple says, "Her form lovely as nature could make it, but her mind uncultivated, her heart unfeeling, her passions impetuous, and her brain almost turned with flattery, dissipation, and pleasure." The elder Henry Temple, a widower, then himself marries Miss Weatherby and cuts off his son's inheritance. Eldridge says about Temple, "When the heart has will the hands can soon find means to execute a good action." And because Temple has demonstrated his goodness, Eldridge happily gives him Lucy, even though Temple is no longer wealthy.

Rowson uses omniscient point of view, but she allows the narrator to personally address the reader nine times in the novel's thirty-five chapters. The narrator condemns Charlotte's decision to leave her parents. "No woman can be run away with contrary to her own inclination." But the narrator also comments that Charlotte's parents sheltered her and did not prepare her for the seductive nature of a thoughtless, handsome man. In other asides, the narrator admits that a young girl might be weak who does not realize that a man is insincere, especially if her parents have not cautioned her about the possibility. The reader knows that Montraville is a cad when he says about himself and Charlotte, "I never think of the future . . . but am determined to make the most of the present, and would willingly compound with any kind Familiar who would inform me who the girl is and how I might be likely to obtain an interview." He has no concern for her or her family and, once he determines that her family has no money, knows that he cannot marry her.

Montraville's father cautions him about ever marrying someone without a dowry. He says, "Your happiness will always be dear to me, and I wish to warn you of a rock on which the peace of many an honest fellow has been wrecked; for believe me the difficulties and dangers of the longest winter campaign are much easier to be borne than the pangs that would seize your heart when you beheld the woman of your choice, the children of your affection, involved in penury and distress, and reflected that it was your own folly and precipitancy had been the prime cause of their sufferings." Yet Montraville ignores the advice and treats Charlotte, his rejected lover, in just this way. After he leaves her, marries, and no longer sends her money because Belcour has not allowed Charlotte's letters reach him, Charlotte bears her and Montraville's child "in penury and distress" because of his "own folly and precipitancy." Only Mrs. Beauchamp befriends Charlotte, and, without her support, Charlotte probably would not have survived as long as she does.

Throughout the story, Charlotte remains trusting, unaware of the duplicity of those whom she has supposedly befriended rather than those who are concerned only about her livelihood. Miss LaRue first tells Charlotte that they are going to see Miss LaRue's brother while taking a walk near the school. In truth, Miss LaRue had planned to meet Belcour who was bringing his friend, Montraville. After meeting Charlotte, Montraville promises that he will marry her upon their arrival in America, knowing fully that he will not honor his word. On the other hand, Charlotte disappears without telling anyone, even though her parents have remained devoted to her. She writes to them after she is on the ship, but Montraville throws her letters overboard. Thus her family hears nothing from her and worries constantly about her condition. After Montraville meets the lovely Julia and becomes engaged to her, Belcour tries to seduce Charlotte. Belcour bribes the mailman to deliver Charlotte's letters to him instead of Montraville; therefore, Montraville is unaware of her penury. When Charlotte rebuffs Belcour, he tells Montraville that she has accepted his advances, and Montraville spurns her. In New York, Miss LaRue, as the wife of the wealthy widower Crayton (Mrs. Beauchamp's father), refuses to admit the freezing Charlotte into her home, denying that she knows her. When Montraville discovers that he too is a victim of betrayal, he begins to suffer the consequences of his actions and remains melancholy until his death.

That Charlotte's parents could be so loving and forgiving in response to the pain she has inflicted on them remains believable because of their early history

of suffering and deciding that love was the most important part of life. Charlotte's father finally hears from her and comes to America as soon as possible to
help her and her child. He arrives after Charlotte's daughter Lucy is born, and
when Charlotte dies within days, he returns home with the child in place of his
beloved Charlotte. He also forgives Montraville. He tells him, "If thou wert
the seducer of my child, thy own reflections be thy punishment. I wrest not the
power from the hand of omnipotence. Look on that little heap of earth, there
hast thou buried the only joy of a fond father. Look at it often; and may thy
heart feel that true sorrow as shall merit the mercy of heaven." Later when Mrs.
Croydon (Miss LaRue) appears destitute and diseased on the Temple doorstep, Henry Temple takes her to a hospital. Throughout, Temple remains a
man who helps others and forgives them, no matter how they have wronged
him or his family.

Rabbit, Run by John Updike

Rabbit betrays his wife, the pregnant Janice, and Ruth, the woman he impregnates while separated from Janice in John Updike's *Rabbit, Run* (1991).
Using omniscient point of view and present tense, Updike shows Harry "Rabbit" Angstrom, who, like Montraville, has concern only for the present when
he is very young, realizing at twenty-six that he has no future selling
Magi-peelers in the local dimestore. As a star high school athlete with no college, Rabbit has not prepared himself for the emptiness he feels. His wife no
longer worries about her appearance or cleaning the apartment, and his only
diversions are shooting a few basketball goals on the way home from work with
the neighborhood teenagers or watching television. He lacks spiritual resources, not seeming to know what Jimmie on television's *Mickey Mouse Club*
means when he discusses "Know thyself," and his inadequate intelligence prevents him from inventing creative ways to sell the Magi-peelers.

Rabbit flees from his responsibilities—job and family. One night, when he
stops at his parents' home to retrieve his son Nelson, he sees them eating dinner through the window and decides to keep going. He drives into the night,
but, after stopping for fuel, comprehends that he has nothing in common with
the people he has met. After returning to town, he visits his former coach
Tothero, separated from his wife and living at the Athletic Club. Rabbit sleeps
the next day, and he and Tothero take prostitutes to dinner. Rabbit goes home
with his date, Ruth, and stays for several days. When he asks her if she is a
"whore," she wonders aloud if he is a "rat." He at least acknowledges that he
has shirked his obligations by answering "in a way." When he appears at home
to retrieve his clothes, he encounters Eccles, the minister his family has asked
to help find him. Eccles questions, "Do clean clothes mean so much to you?
Why cling to that decency if trampling on the others is so easy?"

Rabbit meets with Eccles several times over the next weeks while he remains
with Ruth. He discusses religion with both of them. Rabbit asks Ruth, "Well

now if God doesn't exist, why does anything?" Eccles says that he understands hell "as Jesus describes it. As separation from God." Rabbit thinks everyone is in hell, but Eccles disagrees. "I don't think even the blackest atheist has an idea of what real separation will be. Outer darkness. What we live in you might call inner darkness." Eccles later elaborates while they play golf. "Christianity isn't looking for a rainbow. If it were what you think it is we'd pass out opium at services. We're trying to *serve* God, not *be* God.'" Eventually Eccles accuses Rabbit of his faults, by noting, "You're monstrously selfish. You're a coward. You don't care about right or wrong; you worship nothing except your own worst instincts."

After Eccles telephones Rabbit in the middle of the night at Ruth's to say that Janice is in the hospital to have their daughter, Rabbit goes to see Janice, tells her he loves her, and returns home. He begins working for Janice's father, but Janice soon starts drinking and makes Rabbit restless. His interest in Janice is limited to his own physical pleasure. She denies him, saying, "Why don't you look outside your own pretty skin once in a while?" He leaves, goes to Ruth, and discovers that she is also pregnant. He gallantly tells Ruth to keep the baby, and then he abandons her. While drinking, Janice bathes the baby and drowns her. (Although the drowning is accidental, it resembles Jiang Weili's deliberate drowning of her son in *The Kitchen God's Wife*.) Rabbit remains with Janice afterward but offers no assurance that he will stay.

Once someone decides to betray another, he or she will always be a traitor, never to be trusted again. In *The Natural*, Roy Hobbs denies the good in himself, in Pop, and in Iris Lemmon by finding the attractive, unattainable, and insincere Memo Paris fascinating. Instead he loses everything—respect, love, and money. Charlotte Temple is both victim and victimizer, betrayed and betrayer. Although she immediately regrets her decision to leave home, she must endure the knowledge that parents who adored her will never again enjoy her company. In his complete selfishness, Rabbit betrays everyone except Mrs. Smith, the woman for whom he becomes a gardener after Eccles recommends him. Mrs. Smith, lonely for her son who died fifteen years before in World War II, thanks Rabbit and gives him advice that would be appropriate for both Roy and Charlotte. She says, "You kept me alive, Harry; it's the truth; you did. All winter I was fighting the grave and then in April I looked out the window and here was this tall young man burning my old stalks and I knew life hadn't left me. That's what you have, Harry: life. It's a strange gift and I don't know how we're supposed to use it but I know it's the only gift we get and it's a good one." Unfortunately, none of the protagonists has understood the gift of life and the value of using it wisely by accepting responsibility for themselves and for their relationships with others.

Additional Related Novels

Alexie, Sherman. *Reservation Blues.*

Alvarez, Julia. *In the Time of the Butterflies.*
Cormier, Robert. *After the First Death; I Am the Cheese.*
Crichton, Michael. *The Great Train Robbery.*
Dreiser, Theodore. *Sister Carrie.*
Ellison, Ralph. *Invisible Man.*
Hawthorne, Nathaniel. *The House of the Seven Gables.*
Hemingway, Ernest. *The Sun Also Rises.*
James, Henry. *Washington Square.*
Kesey, Ken. *One Flew Over the Cuckoo's Nest.*
McCarthy, Cormac. *All the Pretty Horses.*
Morrison, Toni. *Sula.*
Stegner, Wallace. *Angle of Repose.*
Steinbeck, John. *The Grapes of Wrath.*
Stowe, Harriet Beecher. *Uncle Tom's Cabin.*
Tyler, Anne. *Dinner at the Homesick Restaurant.*
Warren, Robert Penn. *All the King's Men.*
Wharton, Edith. *House of Mirth.*

Community

The ability to think straight, some knowledge of the past, some vision of the future, some skill to do useful service, some urge to fit that service into the well-being of the community—these are the most vital things education must try to produce.
—Virginia Gildersleeve, *Many a Good Crusade* (1954)

Since Europeans first settled America, they have revered the individual. Adults who made the arduous transatlantic crossing thought they would find a better life for themselves and their families—economically, politically, or spiritually. To survive, however, they had to join others in their communities for such basic activities as finding food and building shelter. Thomas Jefferson and his colleagues set forth in the Constitution that all people "are created equal . . . with inherent and inalienable rights," and this belief has sometimes hindered the ability of groups to work together. Because of this American attitude that the individual has rights beyond the good of the group, some Americans have felt isolated from or unable to function effectively with others. But many have discovered and appreciate the value of being included in a community. The gang of girls in *Foxfire* depend on each other for friendship and support. Mark Brian arrives in Kingcome, British Columbia, and discovers that the members of the Isawataineuk tribe need each other for survival in *I Heard the Owl Call My Name*. In *The Human Comedy*, many people in the small California town offer both condolences and congratulations during the difficult days of World War II. And the community around Miranda in *Mama Day* knows that she will help them face unexpected burdens. In *Love Medicine*, *A Gathering of Old Men*, and *Waiting to Exhale*, the protagonists' communities help them accept themselves and their decisions.

A community is something with a "common character" or identity. It may refer to people of the same economic class or social state, or a group living in the same locale. Persons in a community have common interests. J. R. Seeley said that "there are . . . three ties by which states are held together, community of race, community of religion, community of interest" (1883). In literature since 1375, the term has referred to a group having "common or equal rights or rank" (*OED*). And Arthur Golding notes in his translation of Mornay's *Work Concerning the Trewnesse of the Christian Religion* that "Men . . . ought . . . naturally to be united, by the community of their kind" (1587). And in 1711,

Sir Richard Steele referred in *The Spectator* to "those little communities . . . we express by the word Neighbourhoods." During World War II, Julian S. Huxley said when writing about the Tennessee Valley Authority that "a real community spirit has developed in the new town." In these three novels, *Love Medicine*, *A Gathering of Old Men*, and *Waiting to Exhale*, protagonists find solace in the community spirit.

Love Medicine by Louise Erdrich

In Louise Erdrich's *Love Medicine* (1984), the community *is* the protagonist. One might argue for Lipsha Morrissey as the main focus because his witch doctoring inadvertently unites wife and husband's lover in friendship, but one would be forgetting the roles of Marie Lazarre Kashpaw, Lulu Nanapush Lamartine, or June Kashpaw. Erdrich presents the story in fourteen chapters covering fifty years with six different first-person narratives and limited omniscient point of view to reveal aspects of five other characters. William Bevis asserts in *Recovering the Word* (1987) that mainstream American novels are "leaving" novels with plots pointing toward freedom and independence outside the original home; they reveal competitive individualism as a way to Caucasian success. He contrasts Native-American novels with "homing" plots in which individuals find fulfillment and personal growth within the tribe—family, clan, or community. The Native American finds happiness when unified with native society and cultural past. In *Love Medicine*, only Albertine Johnson, granddaughter of Marie Kashpaw, finds contentment away from her Chippewa tribe on the Pine Ridge Reservation. Albertine goes to Fargo and, after graduating from nursing school, pursues her medical degree.

Others also leave, but unsuccessfully. Henry Lamartine, Jr. (Lulu's son) becomes a prisoner of war in Vietnam, and when he returns, his brother Lyman can barely interest him in the car they purchased before Henry left. Henry soon walks into the river and drowns himself. Lyman remembers that "drowning was the worst death for a Chippewa to experience. By all accounts, the drowned weren't allowed into the next life but forced to wander forever, broken, cold, sore, and ragged. There was no place for the drowned in heaven or anywhere on earth." Howard King, Gordie and June Kashpaw's son, marries a white woman and moves to Minneapolis but never outgrows his boorish, selfish ways. When June dies, he uses her insurance money to buy a red sports car. His wife Lynette notes, "His mom gave him the money . . . because she wanted him to have responsibility. . . . She wanted him to take care of his family." He calls himself "King," lies that he fought in Vietnam, nearly drowns his wife, and fights with his father when he returns to the reservation, breaking pies his grandmother and aunts have carefully baked for the family gathering. Albertine comments, "Once they smash there is no way to put them right." When Albertine visits her grandfather, she compares him to King. "His great-grandson, King Junior, was happy because he hadn't yet acquired a memory, while perhaps Grandpa's happiness was in losing his." Lulu's son, Gerry Nanapush, also must leave Pine Ridge. Nanapush lives by his own set of rules, and the white world puts him in prison after a barroom brawl with a white cowboy. His tribe admires his exploits, however, because he is, according to his son Lipsha, a "dangerous armed criminal, judo expert, escape artist, charismatic member of the American Indian Movement . . . suave, grand, gigantic . . . enormous, gentle." Gerry only wants to be with his family and his friends, but the white world refuses. He remarks, "We got dealt our hand before we were even born, and as we grow, we have to play as best we can."

Others remain on the reservation where the strong women guide the weaker men, emasculated by God and government. Lipsha verbalizes the situation of those who stay: "Was there any sense relying on a God whose ears was stopped? Just like the government? I says then, right off, maybe we got nothing but ourselves. And that's not much, just personally speaking." Marie Lazarre encounters Nector Kashpaw in 1934 while fleeing the Sacred Heart convent where she had expected "the black hem of [Sister Leopolda's] garment would help [her] rise." Instead, Sister Leopolda burns her with a poker and pours boiling water on her. Years after she and Nector have married, Marie, who has raised two daughters and June, her dead sister Lucille's child, says about Nector, "He is what he is because I made him." She had nominated him to be tribal leader and then had kept him sober for meetings. His lover, Lulu, admits that through her two marriages and his one, she has always loved him. She says, "All that mattered was his greed. And the odd thing was, I loved him for it. We were two of a kind. There is no getting around that. We took our pleasure without asking or thinking further than a touch. We were so deeply sunk in the land of our greed it took the court action of the tribe and a house on fire to pull us out." Nector realizes his good fortune because he has never had to do much other than enjoy his women and many readings of *Moby-Dick*.

Lipsha Morrisey does not discover his true parentage until 1984, after he has unsuccessfully tried to reunite Marie and Nector with love medicine (he asks them to eat turkey hearts after failing to obtain hearts from geese mated for life, and Nector chokes to death on his). His mother was Aunt June, not Marie, and her affair with Gerry Nanapush produced him. About the child June, Marie commented, "There was a sadness I couldn't touch there. It was a hurt place, it was deep, it was with her all the time like a broke rib that stabbed when she breathed." And Lipsha also seems unfocused until told about June. He, "the biggest waste on the reservation," has been "training for all my life . . . to wait. Sitting there and sitting there was no hardship on me." Knowing does not bring him success, but, for the first time, he can identify some of his father's strength in himself and accept Lulu as his real grandmother. His actions unexpectedly unite Lulu and Marie after Nector's death because, alone in the world, Lulu needs help after an operation. Marie joins her at the Senior Citizens and puts drops in her eyes. Without the community, even at its worst, they could not have survived.

A Gathering of Old Men by Ernest J. Gaines

Although not identified as a "homing" plot, the black community of Bayonne, Louisiana, in *A Gathering of Old Men* (1983), functions best when united. In this novel, Ernest J. Gaines has first-person narrators relay the words and actions of the main characters—Candy, Mathu, and Charlie. Thus the story becomes a story of the community rather than the white Candy or the black Charlie. On the Marshall plantation, land has been leased to the Cajun Beau Boutan rather than the blacks who have always worked it. After someone murders Beau in front of old Mathu's cabin, the white Candy asks young Snookum to spread the news and tell people to gather at Mathu's. They all know that Beau's father Fix and his gang will come for retribution.

Since Mathu has often disagreed with Beau, the whites think Mathu killed him, but they discover otherwise. When Sheriff Mapes arrives, he encounters several men holding recently fired shotguns and Candy Marshall, the woman orphaned at five but now thirty-one who Mathu and the white Miss Merle raised. All of the men as well as Candy claim to have murdered Beau Boutan. However, Mapes thinks that only Mathu would have had the courage to commit such a crime. Yet as he listens to each person's declaration of guilt, he hears good reasons for each of them to have killed Beau. Mat remembers his son Oliver dying after being denied hospital treatment as a black; he also did it for "the times I done come home drunk and beat [my wife] for no reason at all." Uncle Billy says he killed Beau because Beau beat all the senses out of his son. Johnny Paul remembers that Beau destroyed the beautiful flowers his brother grew by plowing them. "I did it 'cuse that tractor is getting closer and closer to that graveyard, and I was scared if I didn't do it, one day that tractor was go'n come in there and plow up them graves, getting rid of all proof that we ever was." Yank says no one remembers what a good horse breaker he was after farm machinery became commonplace. Gable recalls a boy electrocuted in 1932 after a white girl who seduced everyone accused him of raping her, and no white person cared. Coot appears wearing his uniform, a man who returned from World War I with a medal only to face whites who condemned blacks who had killed whites (even though they were enemy Germans). The actual murderer is Charlie, the weakest, who at first asks old Mathu to take the blame. But after all the men have confessed, Charlie returns and takes responsibility. His demeanor changes, and, for the first time in his life, the white sheriff calls him "Mr. Biggs."

While Mapes questions the men, the Boutans plan their revenge. The complication arises when Gil Boutan, summoned from Louisiana State, reminds them that he must play a football game the following day. He and a black running back are the core of the team, called Salt and Pepper, and by working together they hope to be named All-Americans. Gil asks his father Fix not to cause racial violence, and Fix angrily tells him not to return home. One of the family's associates, Luke Will, becomes Fix's surrogate, and, with his accomplices, he goes to Mathu's home. Shocked to discover a group of men holding loaded shotguns, the whites open fire and the blacks respond. Charlie stands outside the cabin to face the whites like a man, and as someone shoots him, he kills Luke Will. In the end, a new community of black, Cajun, and white together infiltrates the segregated Bayonne, but the changes could not have begun if these individuals, the blacks and Candy in front of Mathu's house and Gil and his teammate, had not banded together to support their beliefs.

Waiting to Exhale by Terry McMillan

In *Waiting to Exhale* (1992), Terry McMillan does not develop a "homing" plot in the sense that Bevis uses it, but she does create characters who know that a community gives them more support than pursuing their goals alone. Two characters, Savannah Jackson and Robin Stokes, narrate their first-person stories while limited omniscient point of view reveals those of Bernardine Harris and Gloria Matthews. Simultaneously, Bernardine and Gloria's stories communicate information about Savannah and Robin that the two would not willingly disclose. The four forge a close friendship based on their African-American background and their affiliation with Black Women on the Move, a group that raises money for scholarships, legal fees, and medical advice; holds workshops on financial planning and sexual harassment; and offers achievement awards.

The four women, each with different credentials, meet in Phoenix after Savannah moves from Denver. Savannah wants "peace of mind; a place I can call home; feeling important to somebody, and just trying to live a meaningful, significant, and positive life." She admits, however, that black men are "getting away with murder when it comes to women. And *we* let them." In Phoenix she reunites with her friend Bernardine whose wealthy husband John has begun a relationship with his young white "Barbie doll" bookkeeper. Robin has helped Bernadine persevere in her marriage to John while living in an unfriendly white upper-class neighborhood, sending her children to white schools, and staying at home neglecting her career, following "the blueprint of *his* life." Robin works in a large insurance agency and wants to marry Russell, a handsome liar. "I don't think I'll be satisfied until I get Russell, even though in my heart I know he's a dog." Gloria, an astute businesswoman, owns Oasis Hair, "one of the few black shops in Phoenix that had a consistent reputation for keeping up with all the latest hairstyles and techniques," and is raising Tarik as a single mother. Her goal for Tarik echoes what the other three women seem to think about black males in general. "I've tried to raise him so he won't grow up to be as trifling and irresponsible as some of these fools running around out here parading as grown men."

As they meet each other for casual dinners, birthdays, and other events, they tend to focus on one topic—men—but by listening to each other's honest opinions, however, they eventually realize that they are extremely attractive, capable women who do not need a man to define their identities. They have been succumbing to the existential idea of the "other" to make their choices. Savannah sees herself as "thirty-six years old and still childless and single" rather than as a creator of new programming for a Phoenix television station. She helps her mother with government aid while her brothers do nothing. Bernadine first worries about "who's gonna want me?" when John leaves, but after she sells all of his possessions for one dollar each, including a valuable car he has rebuilt, she begins to like herself enough to start an affair. Lawyers discover tax evasion and methods John has used to hide his real assets from her, and a huge divorce settlement allowing her to open her own shop makes her especially happy. Although having gotten a raise and added responsibility, Robin blames herself for looking older than twenty-four and despairs that black men "think white girls epitomize beauty and femininity." She then becomes pregnant with Russell's child after he has married someone else and decides to have the child, while refusing to take him back. She says, "I'm going to have to learn how to stand on my own two feet. . . . The answer to everything is inside me." When Gloria discovers that Tarik has a white girlfriend, she wonders, "Did white women have something we didn't?" But even at sixty pounds overweight, she still attracts the new neighbor across the street, a widower. Gloria has a heart attack, an event during which the women proclaim their community. They all arrive at the hospital, introducing themselves as family members and continue to support each other, even when they know each other's defects and weaknesses.

Being part of a community allows each of these groups to function. The individuals seem less judgmental of others than of themselves. Lulu comments in *Love Medicine*, "All through my life I never did believe in human measurement. Numbers, time, inches, feet. All are just ploys for cutting nature down to size. I know the grand scheme of the world is beyond our brains to fathom, so I don't try, just let it in. I don't believe in numbering God's creatures." In *A Gathering of Old Men*, the men have symbolically murdered Beau for the maltreatment of blacks by whites and Cajuns throughout the history of Bayonne; their assertion of themselves allows them all, in their seventies and eighties, to finally stand proud. And in *Waiting to Exhale*, only by helping each other can the four women begin to accept their own worthiness. Savannah finally admits to Gloria, "Don't ever think a man would have that much power over me that I'd stop caring about my friends." By caring about her community, she is finally "able to exhale."

Additional Related Novels

Burns, Olive Ann. *Cold Sassy Tree.*
Cather, Willa. *O Pioneers!*
Cooper, James Fenimore. *The Last of the Mohicans.*
Craven, Margaret. *I Heard the Owl Call My Name.*
Flagg, Fannie. *Fried Green Tomatoes at the Whistle Stop Café.*
Guterson, David. *Snow Falling on Cedars.*

Hersey, John. *A Bell for Adano.*
Kesey, Ken. *One Flew Over the Cuckoo's Nest.*
Lewis, Sinclair. *Main Street.*
McCullers, Carson. *The Heart Is a Lonely Hunter.*
McMillan, Terry. *Mama.*
Naylor, Gloria. *Mama Day.*
Ng, Fae Myenne. *Bone.*
Oates, Joyce Carol. *Foxfire.*
Proulx, E. Annie. *The Shipping News.*
Rölvaag, O. E. *Giants in the Earth.*
Saroyan, William. *The Human Comedy.*
Steinbeck, John. *The Pearl.*
Twain, Mark. *The Adventures of Huckleberry Finn.*
Warren, Robert Penn. *All the King's Men.*
Welch, James. *Fools Crow.*

Compassion

I believe that man will not merely endure. He will prevail. He is immortal, not because he alone among creatures has an inexhaustible voice, but because he has a soul, a spirit capable of compassion and sacrifice and endurance.

—William Faulkner, Nobel Prize speech (1949)

Throughout history, some people have eased the burdens of daily existence for others. Concerned about problems, they have listened and commiserated and, when able, offered appropriate assistance. Oliver Ward in *Angle of Repose* always treats those around him with kindness, supporting them even when he jeopardizes his own position. In *The Age of Innocence*, Ellen's concern for May's innocence restricts her love affair with May's fiancé, Newland Archer. When Billy Budd of *Billy Budd* comes aboard the *Rights of Man*, "a virtue went out of him, sugaring the sour ones." In *The Catcher in the Rye*, Holden has unlimited compassion for children, wanting to protect them from the evils of adulthood. And in *Cold Mountain*, Inman walks hundreds of miles home during the Civil War and serves those along the way who suffer. Certainly Idgie's compassion in *Fried Green Tomatoes at the Whistle Stop Café* improves the lives of her acquaintances. In *A Bell for Adano, I Heard the Owl Call My Name*, and *The Old Man and the Sea*, the protagonists see that those around them have needs, and they express their compassion by trying to fulfill them as best they can.

Compassion is "the feeling or emotion, when a person is moved by the suffering or distress of another, and by the desire to relieve it; pity that inclines one to spare or to succor" (*OED*). Chaucer in the prologue to the *Legend of Good Women* (1385) speaks of compassion for the poor. In *The Fable of the Bees*, Bernard Mandeville suggests that "humanity bids us have compassion with the sufferings of others" (1714). Abraham Joshua Heschel identified the spiritual connection in the world when he wrote in the *New York Journal*, "A religious man is a person who holds God and man in one thought at one time, at all times, who suffers harm done to others, whose greatest passion is compassion, whose greatest strength is love and defiance of despair" (1963). And Eric Hoffer agrees by noting that "compassion alone stands apart from the continuous traffic between good and evil proceeding within us" (*Christian Science Monitor*, 1980). In these three novels, *A Bell for Adano, I Heard the Owl Call*

My Name, and *The Old Man and the Sea*, the protagonists confirm their compassion.

A Bell for Adano by John Hersey

John Hersey based *A Bell for Adano* (1944) on a newspaper article about American Major Frank E. Toscani, son of Italian immigrants, after he took control of Licata during World War II. Acting as a foil to an egotistical general, the army officer in the small Sicilian town of Adano tries to help the people recover their lost treasure, a 700-year-old bell that the "big shot" Mussolini stole and melted for scrap metal. In the novel, Major Victor Joppolo tries to obtain the trust of the townspeople by asking what they want most. And more than food, they want the bell. The local businessman Cacopardo explains that "the spirit is more important than the stomach. The bell was of our spirit. It was of our history." Joppolo then begins his search. The ill-mannered General Marvin (a character resembling General Patton) soon comes to town in his armored car and becomes annoyed at a man asleep in his donkey cart blocking the road. The general's aides kill the donkey and dump the cart and the man into the ditch. Marvin then declares that no mule-drawn carts can enter the town. Such a decree means that the people will have neither food nor water. Joppolo, ignoring the order, later asks Captain Purvis, head of the military police, to write a letter to Marvin requesting that he rescind his command. Lieutenant Trapani, Purvis's deputy, conveniently loses the memo by mixing it with papers that will not reach Marvin because he knows the message will jeopardize Joppolo's career.

Joppolo further shows his compassion in his relationships with the townspeople, although his assistant, Leonard Borth, unsuccessfully tries to change him. Borth "was an American citizen and an enlisted man by choice. To him the whole war was a cynical joke, and he considered his job in the war to make people take themselves less seriously." Joppolo asks Tomasino, a local fisherman, to resume work and become the head fisherman. Tomasino refuses; he says, "I would be a man of authority. I would be the thing I have hated all my life. The other fisherman would laugh at me for becoming the thing I had always hated most." Yet Tomasino respects Joppolo and appreciates his goodwill enough to invite him for a taste of his daughter's *torrone* (dessert). Later, Joppolo reprimands some of the soldiers for breaking family heirlooms where they are billeted; he says they must treat these houses as if their own mothers owned them. He enjoys his moments as a judge because he likes to watch the people's response to real justice. "Major Joppolo's trials were impressive, because he managed, by trickery, by moral pressure and by persuasion, to make the truth seem something really beautiful and necessary."

Since he believes in justice and compassion for all, Joppolo works for the people. The citizens have called the police chief "Two Hands" because of his illegal activity and have had to listen to Radio Roma under the dictatorship.

Joppolo informs them, "Democracy is that the men of the government are no longer the masters of the people. They are the servants of the people. . . . You too must behave now as servants, not as masters. You must behave as the servant of the man without shoes just as much as of the baron." When Mayor Nasta tries to convince the inhabitants that Americans are bad, the townspeople arrest him and jail him in a prisoner-of-war cage. After the Germans rescue him, he runs away. Everyone informs Joppolo and Borth of the escape. "Sergeant Borth got out of the jeep and went out onto the fields. He did not hurry, because Mayor Nasta was running in circles, wishing to run away from himself more than anything else." After Borth catches Nasta, Joppolo sends him to Africa. But throughout, Joppolo searches for a bell. He eventually meets an American navy officer who offers a ship's bell, and the day the bell arrives, the whole town has a party. To thank him, the people give Joppolo a portrait of himself that the local artist Lojocano has painted in secret. The next day, Borth informs Joppolo that General Martin has transferred him to Algiers. They both cry, Borth changed by the compassionate Joppolo's efforts.

I Heard the Owl Call My Name by Margaret Craven

Also compassionate is Mark Brian, an Anglican priest, in *I Heard the Owl Call My Name* (1973). Sent by his bishop Caleb to the remote British Columbian village of the Kwakiutl Indians, Mark has a fatal disease and only three years to live; however, no one has told him. Caleb knows that Mark needs to find "enough of the meaning of life to be ready to die." Margaret Craven uses omniscient point of view in the four parts of the novel to reveal the ways of the people and how Mark gains their trust with his patience and understanding. Mark realizes that he is entering a different world as he watches his escort Jim, one of Caleb's former students, on the boat trip to the village. "There was pride in his eyes without arrogance. Behind the pride was a sadness so deep it seemed to stretch back into ancient mysteries."

Mark focuses on learning the customs and expectations of the people. Caleb has warned him that they are not cannibals even though associated with the *hamatsa*, a dance during which a young man, crazed by the cannibal spirit, supposedly runs through the village with a body stolen from a grave tree. Immediately after his arrival, Mark observes the tribal attitude about death. A young boy's body waits for the Canadian Royal Mounted Police to come and certify his natural death. After Mark performs the Anglican ceremony, he realizes at the rite's end that the people want him to leave, and he does. The people appreciate his actions; "Did you notice that at the graveside he left quietly and asked no questions? . . . He respected our customs." He soon discovers that the people place their dead in open caskets and hoist them into the trees so that birds may eat bits of flesh. Thus when the bird (often a raven) dies, the airborne body will have a chance for rebirth. Later, tribal elders, concerned that some of the graves have fallen from the trees, ask Mark's advice, and he suggests a communal burial area, an idea happily accepted. When a woman of forty-six dies at the birth of her sixth child, "It seemed to him [Mark] that the ugliness of death was as unimportant here as the fir needles which made the path soft beneath his feet, or last year's windfall in the thick underbrush." The village's social ranks also surprise Mark since some villagers function as slaves. "Sam was descended from slaves and in the old days to be a slave was to be worse than a nothing. He had no pride. His boats burned under him. When he reached the fishing grounds, the fish had not come yet, or they had seen him and fled." Mark also sees the attitudes toward disgraced tribal members when his young friend Keetah and her family leave the tribe after her sister's white fiancé purchases a valuable mask for less than its worth, takes her and the mask back to Vancouver, and disappears, leaving her to die from a drug overdose.

The importance of nature's cycles in everything becomes obvious as Mark learns the language, comprehends the humor, and begins to feel welcome. He understands that the village defines itself in terms of myths, wind, rain, the river, killer whales, seals, bluejays, and that "the village is the talking bird, the owl, who calls the name of the man who is going to die." But of all the associations, their most important is the salmon, the "swimmer." After Mark watches the humpback salmon going to spawn, knowing that in its "desperate urgency" it moves toward death, he and Keetah discuss its life. He says, "It isn't [sad]. The whole life of the swimmer is one of courage and adventure. All of it builds to a climax and the end. When the swimmer dies he has spent himself completely for the end for which he was made, and this is not sadness. It is triumph." In March, the tribe prepares its rituals for the coming of the óolachon (the candlefish). That children leave and do not return disrupts the cycle, distressing the tribe's older members. When Mark finally tells his friend Marta, "on the bank of the river I heard the owl call my name," she merely acknowledges his statement because she has watched his illness progress. The village returns Mark's compassion by asking the vicar to allow Mark to remain with them rather than seek medical treatment elsewhere. He agrees, but Mark soon unexpectedly (and mercifully) dies in a mud slide while boating on the river. "Past the village flowed the river, like time, like life itself, waiting for the swimmer to come again on his way to the climax of his adventurous life, and to the end for which he had been made."

The Old Man and the Sea by Ernest Hemingway

In Ernest Hemingway's *The Old Man and the Sea* (1952), the old man Santiago shows reverence and compassion for the boy Manolin and for the creatures he must kill for his own strength and livelihood. In turn, Manolin realizes Santiago's true value and treats him with compassion when Santiago returns from the sea hauling only the skeleton of a huge marlin. The limited omniscient narrative reveals the relationships of Santiago to Manolin, to the sea, to the marlin, and to the sharks. After forty days (perhaps symbolizing Jesus' time in the desert) of unsuccessful fishing with Santiago, Manolin moves to another boat because his parents want him to have a master who catches fish. Santiago's unlucky stretch continues for forty-four more days following Manolin's departure. When Santiago begins his final fishing trip, "everything about him was old except his eyes and they were the same color as the sea and were cheerful and undefeated."

Santiago has compassion for the sea and its inhabitants. He feels guilty about killing turtles "because a turtle's heart will beat for hours after he has been cut up and butchered." But simultaneously, he compares himself to the turtle because "I have such a heart too and my feet and hands are like theirs." To gain the strength necessary to catch the big fish in September and October, Santiago eats the turtle's white eggs in May. While at sea, Santiago reluctantly catches a large tuna, knowing that he must eat it before it spoils. He thinks, "I wish I could feed the fish. . . . He is my brother. But I must kill him and keep strong to do it. Slowly and conscientiously he ate all of the wedge-shaped strips of fish." He feels his loneliness, thinking "no one should be alone in their old age. . . . But it is unavoidable," and he keeps saying, "I wish I had the boy." He remembers the sadness of a male marlin jumping near his boat to see the female Santiago had caught on a prior fishing trip. After he actually hooks the marlin on this trip, and it drags him away from shore, Santiago ruminates, "You are killing me fish . . . but you have a right to. Never have I seen a greater, or more beautiful, or a calmer or more noble thing than you, brother. Come on and kill me. I do not care who kills who."

During the hours while battling the marlin on his hook, Santiago reveals his loving nature and fortitude. He finally kills the 1,500-pound fish after two days and nights and thinks, "I am sorry that I killed the fish," even though "Man is not made for defeat. A man can be destroyed but not defeated." Throughout his ordeal, he imagines himself the fish and prays for it and himself. He remembers his former strength as a hand-wrestling champion and compares the fish's efforts to his own. Even when the sharks smell the carcass, he thinks, "Everything kills everything else in some way." But after the sharks eat the entire fish, he realizes "It is easy when you are beaten. . . . I never knew how easy it was. And what beat you, he thought. 'Nothing,' he said aloud. 'I went out too far.'" He does not lament his fate; he accepts the reality of his situation and remains unconquered. And lastly, the old Santiago admits his love for the boy because thinking of the boy "keeps me alive." Santiago's compassion for living things continues, but his body finally becomes tired, and the turtle eggs that he once ate for strength to fight "the truly big fish" do not help him.

Although Manolin no longer fishes with Santiago, he has learned enormously from his experience. He apologizes to Santiago for having to leave and wants to return because the two did catch a few fish before the eighty-four-day unlucky streak. "It was papa made me leave. I am a boy and I must obey him." Santiago responds, "I know you did not leave me because you doubted," and

reassures Manolin that his father's concern "is quite normal." Manolin, however, appreciates Santiago's respect for him. Manolin remembers that Santiago
carried the gear himself. "He never wants anyone to carry anything" or be bur-
dened unnecessarily. Santiago does not mind sacrificing himself for his worker.
On the other hand, Manolin says of his new master, "I do not like for him to
waken me. It is as though I were inferior." Manolin knows that the new master
simply uses him to make money whereas Santiago actually taught him how to
fish and wanted him on the boat because he enjoyed his company. Santiago
treated him compassionately, like an equal. And because of Santiago's kindness, Manolin comforts Santiago after the sharks eat his huge marlin. Later,
Manolin sees the exhausted Santiago in bed, and he cries. Mandolin then
watches over Santiago while he sleeps. The reader discovers that Santiago is
"dreaming about lions," the animals that he had recalled earlier, "play[ing]
like young cats in the dusk and he loved them as he loved the boy." Santiago
admires the beauty of nature and of other humans, but as he prepares to die, he
can no longer re-create the strength of the lion in his own body

   These three novels, *A Bell for Adano, I Heard the Owl Call My Name*, and
The Old Man and the Sea, present protagonists who have compassion for their
fellow humans. Major Joppolo prepares the townspeople of Adano for living in
a democracy where all are equal. After Mark earns the tribe's trust, the villagers
offer to help him rebuild the dilapidated vicarage that he has attempted to
patch and paint as a sign of their appreciation. Bishop Caleb responds to
Mark's request for a prefabricated house; "You suffered with them, and now
you are theirs, and nothing will ever be the same again." Santiago offers his
kindness and knowledge to Manolin, and, when he lies dying, Manolin remains with him so that the old man will never again face loneliness. These characters all demonstrate that helping others can fulfill one's own life.

Additional Related Novels

Anaya, Rudulfo. *Bless Me, Ultima.*
Frazier, Charles. *Cold Mountain.*
Flagg, Fannie. *Fried Green Tomatoes at the Whistle Stop Café.*
Glasgow, Ellen. *Barren Ground.*
Melville, Herman. *Billy Budd.*
Proulx, E. Annie. *The Shipping News.*
Rölvaag, O. E. *Giants in the Earth.*
Roth, Philip. *Goodbye, Columbus.*
Salinger, J. D. *The Catcher in the Rye.*
Saroyan, William. *The Human Comedy.*
Stegner, Wallace. *Angle of Repose.*
Stowe, Harriet Beecher. *Uncle Tom's Cabin.*

Corrupting Power

The corruption of the best is the worst.
—St. Thomas Aquinas, *Summa Theologica* (c.1270)

In literature, many characters misuse their power to fulfill their own needs and desires. Ahab waits until his crew sails before he announces the ship's pursuit of the white whale in *Moby-Dick*. Those who know that such a quest will doom them try to change his mind, but he, as captain, ignores their pleas. Parents make similar decisions who mistreat their children. Pecola's father abuses her sexually in *The Bluest Eye*. Mapes, the deputy sheriff in *The Ox-Bow Incident*, uses his brief authority to silently approve the lynching of three innocent men. Three novels, *The Chocolate War*, *Linden Hills*, and *All the King's Men*, most clearly reveal how power can corrupt those who have it and how they, in turn, use it to dominate others.

Definitions of "corrupt" and "power" will clarify the meaning of "corrupting power." As early as the fourteenth century, authors wrote of morally corrupt, or depraved, persons who functioned as corrupting influences on others. In 1425, Andrew of Wyntoun (*De Orygynale Cronykil of Scotland*) noted that bribery or favor caused perversion or destruction of integrity in the discharge of public duties. In 1563, Queen Elizabeth I made reference to corruption as an infection or taint of the blood causing a descendant to lose rights of rank, title, or land. "Infecting," "evil," "perverting," "despoiling," and "decomposing" all appear as definitions of "corrupting" in the *OED*. In essence, "corrupting" refers to the perverting of person or institution from an original state of purity.

To understand "corrupting power," one must also examine the meaning of "power." In 1297, Robert of Gloucester (*Metrical Chronicle*) noted that power revealed domination, control, and authority. Around 1325, "power" evolved into the "ability to do or effect something or anything, or to act upon a person or thing" (*OED*). Recently the terms "power-mad," "power-seekers," and "power brokers" who would "tread on anyone's face to get to the top" have become commonly used. Throughout history, therefore, people have used positions attained in the community to control the lives of others. In each of these novels, *The Chocolate War*, *Linden Hills*, and *All the King's Men*, persons with power corrupt those with whom they associate.

The Chocolate War by Robert Cormier

After jeopardizing a private Catholic high school's finances in *The Chocolate War* (1974) by "overextend[ing]" them, Brother Leon forces students to cover his mistakes. He, a supposedly trustworthy school administrator, usurps his responsibility and emotionally damages students and colleagues. Through omniscient point of view, Robert Cormier relates Jerry Renault's story as a new ninth-grade student suffering the football coach's verbal insults and the physical assaults of upperclassmen as he tries out for quarterback. Jerry's one friend, Roland Goubert, called "The Goober," catches his passes and marvels at Jerry's perseverance. Jerry wants desperately to play but can tell no one since Goubert is a new, not yet trustworthy friend, his mother has recently died, and his father continues to mourn. Although Jerry does not understand the phrase on the poster he has chosen to tape inside his locker, "Do I dare disturb the universe?" from T. S. Eliot's "The Love Song of J. Alfred Prufrock," he reflects it in his attitude.

Jerry must change, however, when Archie, the leader of "The Vigils," a secret school gang, confronts him. The same day, Brother Leon elicits Archie's aid in persuading students to sell extra boxes of chocolates for the school fund-raising drive. Archie knows that "Leon didn't mean Archie's help—he meant the help of The Vigils. Officially, The Vigils did not exist. . . . But it was there . . . because it served a purpose. The Vigils kept things under control." Archie, whose power comes through his ingenious methods of creating chaos without bloodshed, thinks "the world [contains] those who [are] victims and those who victimized." Archie decides to victimize Jerry by having him upset Brother Leon. Archie will not allow Jerry to sell chocolates for ten days. On the eleventh day, however, Jerry decides on his own not to sell chocolates. Surprised by Jerry's independence, Archie realizes he must punish Jerry.

Archie plans his attack carefully by having other students subtly disrupt Jerry's day with the worst insult being Emile Janza's accusation that Jerry is "queer." Archie then telephones Jerry and offers a way for him to both sell his chocolates and vindicate himself with Emile ("an animal [who] didn't play by the rules"). Archie organizes a raffle from which the money will purchase Jerry's chocolates, and Jerry can fight Janza as raffle entertainment. For Emile, Archie promises pictures rumored to expose Emile masturbating in the bathroom. Archie thinks, "I can con anybody. I am Archie." Jerry and Emile nearly kill each other in their clash, with Jerry leaving in an ambulance. As he boards, he warns Goubert to do exactly what they (Archie and Brother Leon) want because otherwise they will "murder" him.

Afterwards, Jerry knows he is lucky to be alive, and he knows Brother Leon barely saved him. In class, the seemingly "pale, ingratiating" Brother Leon was "smirking, sarcastic. His thin, high voice venomous . . . like a cobra." He once struck Bailey, an "A" student, on the cheek with a pointer, and another wondered, "Had it been an accident? Or another of Leon's little cruelties?" Leon allows Archie to victimize because "You [Archie], The Vigils—yes, I'm saying the name aloud—The Vigils must throw their full weight behind the sale." Brother Leon had watched Emile and Jerry in the dark, turning on the lights at the last moment before one of them suffered permanent physical damage. Obie, Archie's sidekick, "saw [Leon] on the hill over there—watching the fight, enjoying the whole thing." Brother Leon's corrupt and evil misuse of power in his community becomes very clear. And although Jerry retains his independence and does "dare to disturb the universe," he discerns the danger of his decision.

Linden Hills by Gloria Naylor

In *Linden Hills* (1985), Luther Nedeed also misuses his power. He controls both his community and his family. Gloria Naylor intertwines several narrative threads in the novel through omniscient point of view with the main action taking place during a bitterly cold week beginning December 19th. During that week, former school friends Lester Tilson and Willie Mason, both twenty, reunite and begin performing odd jobs for Linden Hills' wealthy inhabitants. From their positions as silent "hired hands," they learn about the other residents. By the end of the week, the two have discovered that Winston Alcott married to hide his long-standing homosexual love affair; that Laurel Dumont, separated from her husband, dove from her high board into a frozen pool after losing the right to remain in the Dumont home (deeded only to biological Dumonts); and that Reverend Hollis's infidelities drove away his wife.

Willie, resident of nearby lower-class Putney Wayne, exhibits a somewhat contradictory character—an eighth-grade school dropout who loves to write and read poetry. He has memorized 665 poems, including all of Baraka, Soynika, Hughes, and most of Coleridge and Whitman. He also has an intuitive understanding about the people who live inside Linden Hills, including Lester. After observing them, he realizes that they plan and carefully orchestrate everything from their love affairs to their choice of home decor; even Lester creates his disdainful attitude toward the others' successes.

Not as astute as Willie, Lester feels hostility toward his neighbors as did his grandmother before him, and he refuses to associate with them. A resident of the least desirable street at the top of the hills, First Crescent Drive (ironically, the least sinful circle in the *Inferno* of Dante's *The Divine Comedy*), Lester differs from the owner of the Linden Hills residents's deeds, Luther Nedeed, who lives at the bottom on Tupelo Drive, the most coveted area just below Eighth Crescent. When Xavier Donnell, a General Motors executive who lives closer to Nedeed, comes to court Lester's sister Roxanne, a college graduate, he disrespectfully blows the horn of his Porsche rather than coming to her door, infuriating Lester. However, as a Hills resident, Lester's neighbors readily accept him.

Naylor uses Willie and Lester as narrators but discloses further information through other characters. The reader discovers that Xavier hates the idiotic white secretary he escorts to a wedding and considers marrying Roxanne, although one of his colleagues disdains her social position. As Reverend Hollis dresses for his Christmas party, he remembers his youth, his disappearance from college on Sunday afternoons to attend church services, his current dependence on alcohol, and his unfaithfulness after graduating from Harvard Theological School. Through the eyes of Laurel Dumont's aunt, the reader learns of talented Laurel's success at Berkeley and as an IBM executive who stifled her love of diving and music to placate her Linden Hills husband. But, most important, Naylor divulges Willa Prescott Nedeed's recovery of her individuality while imprisoned in the basement of her own home.

The first Luther Nedeed (great-great-grandfather of the current one), a free black, was rumored to have sold his octoroon (one-eighth black) wife and six children for money to buy northern land in 1837. He chose land growing only linden trees from white farmers who "pocketed Nedeed's money and had a good laugh." Nedeed, however, saw the cemetery on his border and became a mortician. He and subsequent Luther Nedeeds continued the family business and began to lease unused land to persons of wealth and prestige. The Nedeeds retained control of their neighbors with leases and contained their wives while raising their own sons to be future Luther Nedeeds.

The current Luther Nedeed, Willa Prescott Nedeed's husband, is Linden Hills's most revered resident. Willie, amazed at Nedeed's power, surmises that Nedeed has succeeded in making all of the inhabitants become robots, trying constantly to acquire more respectability and greater wealth. Luther speaks at Winston Alcott's wedding and takes part in Reverend Hollis's church service. He even entices Willie and Lester to help him decorate his tree on Christmas Eve by promising to double their week's wages. At his home, they observe Nedeed's fanatical ritual for decorating his tree with real candles and begin to understand the depth of corrupting power inherited from his ancestors.

At Luther's, Lester and Willie also discover the source of the chilling scream they had heard from Lester's house on December 19th; the "aching throat of a woman who was crouching over the shrunken body of her son." During the week, Willie had begun to wonder if the invisible Luther Nedeed's wife existed. But on Christmas Eve, he sees her when she opens the door to the basement where Luther had locked her and her son after deciding that the light-skinned child could not be his.

Luther did not realize that his wife would discover documents containing secrets of the previous Nedeed wives in their basement while moping and mourning the death of her son. She finds letters that Luwana Packerville wrote and answered letters to herself while recording thoughts in appropriate biblical chapters as the first unhappy Nedeed wife. Another wife, Evelyn Creton Nedeed, made comments in a cookbook about the huge amounts of food she prepared, some with an aphrodisiac to entice her unaffectionate husband. Priscilla McGuire Nedeed, lovely in a youthful picture, eventually removed her head from another photograph, indicating her lost identity. The current

Nedeed wife, Willa Prescott Nedeed, reads these messages and refuses to succumb to her husband's plan. After Willie unwittingly helps Willa escape from
the basement by unlocking the door, she confronts Luther, and when they
scuffle, a candle ignites her veil. The devil Luther ("Lucifer") and his home on
the ninth level of Linden Hills, Tupelo Drive, burst into flames. Willie and
Lester jump the chain-link fence onto the frozen lake surrounding the lowest
of Dante's circles of Hell into their own purgatory.

All the King's Men by Robert Penn Warren

In *All the King's Men* (1946), Willie Stark, also a community leader, uses his
political power and its money for corruption. Robert Penn Warren's narrator,
Jack Burden, recalls his relationships with Willie Stark and the children of former Governor Stanton, Adam and Anne. Jack grew up in Burden's Landing
playing tennis, fishing, and enjoying the summers home from boarding
school. At twenty-one, Jack returned from college and realized that Anne,
then seventeen, "had sunk her harpoon [in him like] Queequeg sunk it." They
had expected to marry, but subsequent circumstances separated them. Instead
Jack married Lois, but he left her and abandoned his Ph.D. dissertation about
the letters of a deceased relative, Cass Mastern, that detailed his affair with a
friend's wife. Anne remained unmarried, and Adam became a renowned surgeon.

During the seventeen years between Jack's and Willie's first meeting in
1922 and Adam's and Willie's deaths in 1939, Willie rose from county
treasurer in Mason City to state governor. He turned from teetotaler to daily
drinker and from loyal husband to habitual philanderer. He punctuated his
long-standing affair with his pox-marked secretary and astute political advisor,
Sadie Burke, with one-night stands, until he met Anne Stanton. And after
Willie's wife retired to the country, Willie told Anne he would marry her. In
the months before his death, several events unravel Willie's political and personal control. A local man accuses Willie's star-quarterback son Tom of impregnating his daughter, and Willie pays to protect Tom's reputation. Soon
after, a hit in a football game turns Tom into a paraplegic. Willie declares too
late that he will no longer "buy" what he needs because, simultaneously, angry
Sadie Burke suggests that Willie's lieutenant governor, Tiny Duffy, tell Dr.
Adam Stanton, slated to be Willie's new hospital's administrator, about
Willie's affair with Anne. Adam, after long hours operating to save Tom's life,
appears at the capital and shoots Willie. Sugar-Boy, Willie's loyal Irish driver,
shoots Adam. Later, Tom dies, and discarded wife Lucy Stark arranges to raise
Tom's alleged child.

Throughout, Willie Stark exhibits his strength. As the governor, he makes
decisions based on securing his position. Robert Penn Warren, often accused
of fictionalizing the life of Louisiana's governor Huey Long in the character of
Willie, said in the introduction to the 1954 edition (Random) that "For better

or worse, Willie Stark was not Huey Long. Willie was only himself." Willie knows that all humans have secrets. He says, "Man is conceived in sin and born in corruption and . . . passeth . . . to the stench of the shroud. There is always something." He orders Jack to investigate Judge Irwin, a close family friend in Burden's Landing, after the Judge publicly supports Willie's opponent. Jack's research finds the one incident that damns the Judge, a respected man who had taught Jack to hunt and build models. Before telling Willie, Jack visits the Judge to confide what he knows. The Judge commits suicide later that afternoon, and Jack's mother, in anguish, tells Jack that his own father was not the "Scholarly Attorney" who abandoned them when Jack was six but was the Judge, her one love. During Willie's tenure as governor, he prefers to blackmail with his knowledge rather than "buy" with bribery. When Willie finally decides to "buy," he begins his own destruction.

Jack, political handyman and historical researcher, dispassionately relates the various episodes of Willie's life. Simultaneously he tries to assess what he has learned from each situation. But Jack has difficulty fitting the pieces of his life and Willie's into a coherent whole. Jack quit writing his dissertation because he could not understand Cass Mastern; he almost psychologically quits his own life because he cannot reconcile his identity as a failed student with no ambition, a loser at love, and a son of a misfit father and a self-absorbed mother. He tries to report rather than to judge and somehow fails at both. He voices ambivalence by noting that "the end of man is knowledge, but there is one thing he can't know. He can't know whether knowledge will save or kill him." Jack sees only the elderly imparting wisdom as they sit "in front of the harness shop . . . the place where Time gets tangled in its own feet and lies down like an old hound and gives up the struggle." He observes that "the old ones . . . emit a kind of metaphysical effluvium. . . . Time and motion cease to be."

After Anne tells Jack about her affair, Jack gets in his car "and kept on moving west. For West is where we all plan to go some day." When he returns from his drive to California, he has survived his "living death" in the West and is ready to accept reality. After the ensuing events, Jack and Anne can marry and create their own identities. Jack finally learns to face his self-deception from the corrupting power of Willie's political realm. Jack comments, "They say you are not you except in the terms of relation to other people. If there weren't any other people there wouldn't be any you because what you do, which is what you are, only has meaning in relation to other people." In essence, Jack Burden realizes that people are only who they are in terms of their relation to others. When a someone like Willie Stark refuses to be honest in his relationships and takes what serves him best, he defines the horror of corrupting power.

In all three novels, characters use their position of power to corrupt others. A student's surprise at Brother Leon's behavior in *The Chocolate War* wonders "were teachers as corrupt as the villains you read about in books or saw in movies and television?" In *Linden Hills*, the Luther Nedeeds have carefully destroyed the individuality in family and business acquaintances alike for their own benefit. Robert Penn Warren said that in *All the King's Men* he wanted to show a politician "whose personal motivation had been, in one sense, idealistic, who in many ways was to serve the cause of social betterment, but who was corrupted by power, even by power exercised against corruption." Willie's actions perfectly illustrate Warren's intent. Those who abuse their positions of authority in schools, in governments, or in communities can only experience corrupt relationships with others. They infect those around them with impurities that sometimes may be cleansed but most often function destructively. Only by refusing to succumb to the lure that one's word is infallible can a person in power keep from becoming corrupt and ruining the lives of those who have no choice but to acquiesce.

Additional Related Novels

Clark, Walter Van Tilburg. *The Ox-Bow Incident.*
Cormier, Robert. *I Am the Cheese.*
Heller, Joseph. *Catch-22.*
Malamud, Bernard. *The Natural.*
Melville, Herman. *Moby-Dick.*
Morrison, Toni. *The Bluest Eye.*
Twain, Mark. *A Connecticut Yankee in King Arthur's Court.*

Courage

> The courage of life is often a less dramatic spectacle than the courage of a final moment; but it is no less than a magnificent mixture of triumph and tragedy.
>
> —John F. Kennedy, *Profiles in Courage* (1955)

To do something of importance that might endanger one either physically or psychologically takes courage. People who show courage by doing something difficult for the first time or helping someone else in a time of stress earn admiration from those who hear of their actions. In *Barren Ground*, Dorinda's husband Nathan escapes from a train wreck but returns to a burning car to sacrifice his life by rescuing others. Ike McCaslin enters the forest unarmed to face the legendary bear that has eluded all its pursuers during years of hunting in *The Bear*. Robert Jordan and his comrades from *For Whom the Bell Tolls* infiltrate Fascist lines during the Spanish Civil War to defend democracy. Mildred Peacock exhibits enormous courage by leaving her husband and trying to raise her five children in *Mama*. Coalhouse Walker in *Ragtime* demands recompense from racist firemen after they laughingly destroy his automobile. The immigrants who settle Nebraska in *Giants in the Earth* bravely face seemingly unsurmountable obstacles. And during war, soldiers need courage to help each other survive as illustrated in *Shiloh* and *The Things They Carried*. In the novels, *The Last of the Mohicans*, *The Red Badge of Courage*, and *Uncle Tom's Cabin*, the protagonists find themselves in situations in which they must either face an enemy or flee in fear.

The term "courage" usually refers to a person's thoughts or intentions, revealing a particularly confident or proud spirit. Courage is "that quality of mind which shows itself in facing danger without fear or shrinking; bravery, boldness, valour" (*OED*). First-century author Tacitus said, "The gods looked with favour on superior courage." In 1275, John Barbour referred to Robert the Bruce as a "knycht off gret corage" ("knight of great courage"), and John Milton in *Paradise Lost* discusses the "courage never to submit or yield" (1667). Lord Charles Moran noted that "courage is a moral quality; it is not a chance gift of nature like an aptitude for games. It is a cold choice between two alternatives, the fixed resolve not to quit; an act of renunciation which must be made not once but many times by the power of the will" (*The Anatomy of Courage*, 1967). Finally, Alcoholics Anonymous acknowledges the power of courage in its prayer adapted from one of Reinhold Niebuhr's sermons: "God, give us grace to accept with serenity the things that cannot be changed, courage to change the things which should be changed and the wisdom to distinguish the one from the other" (1943). The protagonists in *The Last of the Mohicans*, *The Red Badge of Courage*, and *Uncle Tom's Cabin* eventually fulfull Niebuhr's concept.

The Last of the Mohicans by James Fenimore Cooper

In James Fenimore Cooper's *The Last of the Mohicans* (1826), characters reveal their courage through both helpful and hurtful actions. During the French and Indian War, the French at first thwarted the English attempt to annihilate them from the continent. They won the first battle decisively in 1754 by enticing support from nearby Native Americans. In 1756, under the Marquis de Montcalm, the French and the Native Americans with forces three times larger than those protecting Fort William Henry defeated Colonel George Monro [*sic*] in four days. Before the battle, Major Duncan Heyward attempts to find the fort with Cora and Alice, Munro's two daughters, and musician David Gamut. After the runner Magua agrees to guide them, they meet the frontiersman Hawk-eye and his two Mohawk friends, Chingachgook and his son Uncas (the "last of the Mohicans"). Hawk-eye realizes that Magua has misled them and planned an ambush, but when they try to seize Magua, he disappears. Hawk-eye takes command of the group, eventually delivering them to the fort. Cooper's use of omniscient point of view eases some of the suspense created when the party encounters difficulties along the route.

Magua, "Le Renard Subtil," exhibits a courage fueled by revenge, and he confidently welcomes danger. He wants to kidnap the women and Heyward because Colonel Munro once publicly beat him for being drunk. Throughout the journey toward the fort, Magua escapes and reappears with reinforcements to help him achieve his goal of hurting Munro by marrying Cora. Ironically, when Cora first meets him, she asks, "Should we distrust the man because his manners are not our manners, and that his skin is dark!" But later, after Magua demonstrates his maliciousness, Cora openly scorns him.

Heyward, Cora, and Alice must rely on Hawk-eye, Chingachgook, and Uncas to escape Magua's pursuit, even though they know nothing about them. The men's actions, however, soon gain their confidence. Uncas uses his bow and arrow to shoot a deer for dinner because a gunshot will indicate their location to Magua. Later, Heyward looks Uncas in the eye, and "the two young men exchanged looks of intelligence which caused Duncan to forget the character and condition of his wild associate." After Hurons steal their canoe, Heyward hears the Hurons exclaiming that "La Longue Carabine" (the man who shoots well) has killed some of them. The Hurons know and respect Hawk-eye's ability, although Hawk-eye calls himself a "man without a cross" (perhaps a religious reference to the freedom he has earned by leaving civilization for the primitivism of nature). Because Hawk-eye has formed no allegiance, he chooses to help only those worthy of his expertise. After the group reaches the fort, Munro surrenders to the French. Although Montcalm has guaranteed safe passage from the fort, Magua and the Hurons indiscriminately massacre the survivors. Hawk-eye finds hiding places for his charges before he rejects an opportunity to murder Magua. "Nothing but the color of his skin [Hawk-eye's] had saved the lives of Magua and the conjurer, who would have been the first victims sacrificed to his own security, had not the scout believed such an act, however congenial it might be to the nature of an Indian, utterly unworthy of one who boasted a descent from men that knew no cross of blood. Accordingly, he trusted to the withes and ligaments with which he had bound his captives, and pursued his way directly toward the center of the lodges." Hawk-eye's courage saves Alice and Heyward, but Cora refuses his offer to be a prisoner in her stead. At the novel's climax, Magua's apprentice murders Cora, and Magua kills Uncas. And as Hawk-eye has anticipated, Magua dies of his own hate, falling from the mountain into a precipice. Hawk-eye further exhibits his loyalty and courage by deciding to remain with the grieving Chingachgook as he laments his son's death and the end of his lineage.

The Red Badge of Courage by Stephen Crane

General William C. Westmoreland once commented that "war is fear cloaked in courage" (*McCall's*, 1966), and in *The Red Badge of Courage* (1895), Henry Fleming exhibits his fear before he finds his courage. Stephen Crane uses omniscient point of view to detail the attitudes of soldiers in the army and then the behavior of Henry himself. "[Henry] had, of course, dreamed of battles all his life—of vague and bloody conflicts that had thrilled him with their sweep and fire. In visions he had seen himself in many struggles. He had imagined peoples secure in the shadow of his eagle-eyed prowess. But awake he had regarded battles as crimson blotches on the pages of the past." Henry imagines that the battles of the Civil War will resemble those of the Greeks with "Homeric" marches and soldiers "returning with [their] shield[s] or on it" as Greek mothers expected from their sons. But when Henry volunteers in the Union Army, the battles become real rather than idealized. "It had suddenly appeared to him that perhaps in a battle he might run. He was forced to admit that as far as war was concerned he knew nothing of himself." Before his first battle, he dislikes the interminable marching and thinks of himself as a "mental outcast." And after, he runs. When he sees a squirrel scamper from him, he rationalizes his behavior by thinking that all creatures run from danger. Later Henry sees bloodied soldiers, and "regards the wounded soldiers in an envious way. He conceived persons with torn bodies to be peculiarly happy. He wished that he, too, had a wound, a red badge of courage." After another soldier inadvertently bloodies his head with the butt of a gun, Henry rejoins his regiment, and everyone thinks he has been wounded.

On his return, Henry feels relief that no one knows he deserted. When another battle begins the next day, Henry holds his position, repeatedly and methodically firing his rifle, without even seeing the enemy. Someone has to tell him when the battle has ended. "Yesterday, when he had imagined the universe to be against him, he had hated it, little gods and big gods; today he hated the army of the foe with the same great hatred." The lieutenant compliments him on his fierceness, and Henry recalls "he had been a barbarian, a beast. He had fought like a pagan who defends his religion." In the second half of the battle, Henry and the subdued Wilson take up the flag after the color-bearer falls. Even though they gain less ground than desired, they keep fighting, and by the third battle, Henry exhibits his courage as a matter of expected, normal behavior. "They speedily forgot many things. The past held no pictures of error and disappointment. They were very happy, and their hearts swelled with grateful affection for the colonel and the youthful lieutenant." They both feel invincible, "the swift wings of their desires would have shattered against the iron gates of the impossible." Henry "had rid himself of the red sickness of battle."

Crane symbolizes Henry's internal thoughts and emotions by his responses to nature throughout the story. At first, Henry talks with Jim and Wilson during seemingly endless waiting, and "the moon had been lighted and was hung in a treetop." After his first battle, he "felt a flash of astonishment at the blue, pure sky and the sun gleaming on the trees and fields. It was surprising that nature had gone tranquilly on with her golden process in the midst of so much devilment." He says that "nature had no ears." And he thinks of nature as "a woman with deep aversion to tragedy." In the forest after he has deserted, he sees a "chapel" under tree branches and discovers a corpse sitting against the trunk. He imagines that the "trees . . . sing hymn[s] of twilight," that the forest "brambles formed chains and tried to hold him back," and that "trees . . . stretched out their arms and forbade him to pass." When he returns to the battle site, he tries to comfort the bloodied and dazed Jim Conklin. But at Jim's death, Henry sees that "the red sun was pasted in the sky like a wafer." Henry's thoughts change the next day after he finds his courage. "The sun [is] now bright and gay in the blue, enameled sky." And almost in approval of his actions, "over the river a golden ray of sun came through the hosts of leaden rain clouds." In language of the New Testament gospel translations about the birth of Jesus, Crane indicates Henry's newfound confidence; "so it came to pass that as he trudged from the place of blood and wrath his soul changed. He came from hot plowshares to prospects of clover tranquilly, and it was as if hot plowshares were not. Scars faded as flowers." Henry matures when he bravely faces his duty and supports his peers.

Uncle Tom's Cabin by Harriet Beecher Stowe

In Uncle Tom's Cabin (1852), the protagonist is a deeply religious slave who courageously refuses to hurt others. Harriet Beecher Stowe began writing her novel after passage of the Fugitive Slave Law when many slaves were recaptured and returned to masters claiming to have owned them. The novel, serialized in the abolitionist weekly *National Era* from 5 June 1851 to 1 April 1852 and then published as a book, became one of the most controversial publications in America's history. As an international bestseller, it was translated into more than twenty-three languages. One must not underestimate Stowe's courage in defying furious slaveowners; even Abraham Lincoln acknowledged her contribution to the abolitionist movement. In the novel, Mr. Shelby's debts force him to sell Tom along with Eliza's ten-year-old son Harry. Other slaves hear the transaction enabling them to forewarn Eliza so that she can escape with Harry during the night. Tom, however, must travel south with the slave trader. On an Ohio River boat, Eva St. Clare falls overboard, and after Tom rescues her, she convinces her father to purchase him. Later, St. Clare promises Tom his freedom, but ruffians murder St. Claire before he completes the legal process. St. Clare's wife cares nothing for Tom and sells him to the evil Simon Legree. Legree decides that Tom will be an overseer responsible for beating slaves who do not work. Tom refuses, and Legree flogs him. Yet Tom refuses to kill Legree when Legree's mulatto mistress Cassy begs him to. After Cassy flees, Legree demands that Tom tell him where she has gone, but Tom refuses. Legree bludgeons him and just as George Shelby appears with money to buy Tom back, Tom dies. On the boat returning home, Shelby encounters Cassy, mother of Eliza, and George's sister. He informs them that their family is safe in Canada.

Stowe balances the characters, stereotyping neither slaves nor slaveowners. Although the term "Uncle Tom" now signifies an African American who agrees with whites too much, the original Uncle Tom obviously did not succumb to his masters' wishes. His goodness and his willingness to work exceeded boundaries of race, and he succored both black and white. Clearly, Tom is a model of the Christian Jesus (and of any other self-effacing religious figure found around the world), following his own beliefs in the best way he could. He refuses to succumb to Legree's demand that he beat the slaves. He tells Legree, "No! no! no! My soul an't yours, Mas'r! You haven't bought it,—ye can't buy it! It's been bought and paid for, by one that is able to keep it;—no matter, no matter, you can't harm me!" Slave traders were businessmen, and emotions did not encumber them. Haley, the slave trader who buys Tom from Shelby, says: "These critters an't like white folks, you know; they gets over things, only manage right. . . . It kinder makes my blood run cold to think on 't; and when they carried off the child, and locked her up, she [the mother] just went ravin' mad, and died in a week. Clear waste, sir, of a thousand dollars, just for want of management." Not all slaveowners were evil, and Mrs. Shelby's husband's decision to sell Tom and his unwillingness to tell her before he completes the transaction horrifies her. She says, "This is God's curse on slavery!—a bitter, bitter, most accursed thing!—a curse to the master and a curse to the slave! I was a fool to think I could make anything good out of such a deadly evil. It is a sin to hold a slave under laws like ours." And Augustine St. Clare expects to emancipate Tom but dies in an unfortunate and untimely manner.

Those slaves who try to escape their masters and those who help them are also extremely courageous. If they are caught, they will suffer more than before, yet they risk their lives for freedom. George, Eliza's husband, escapes after his master kills his dog and tells him to marry Mina. His master will not recognize his marriage to Eliza, even though a minister joined the two. Not until Eliza hears that Mr. Shelby has sold their son Harry will she attempt to leave their home and flee to Amherstberg, Canada. When they arrive in Canada, "these two had not one acre of ground,—not a roof that they could call their own,—they had spent their all, to the last dollar. They had nothing more than the birds of the air, or the flowers of the field,—yet they could not sleep for joy." The Quakers who offer them clothes and food also jeopardize themselves for breaking the Fugitive Slave Law. Discovering from Shelby that Eliza, her daughter, has reached Canada makes Cassy ecstatic. The additional coincidence, finding that George's sister, now a wealthy widow, is also aboard the riverboat, completes their happiness. Shelby returns to his own home, vowing, "I will do *what one man can* to drive out this curse of slavery from my land." After he frees his own slaves, he tells them, "Think of your freedom, every time you see Uncle Tom's Cabin; and let it be a memorial to put you all in mind to follow in his steps, and be as honest and faithful and Christian as he was."

Hawk-eye and Uncas in *The Last of the Mohicans*, Henry in *The Red Badge of Courage*, and Uncle Tom in *Uncle Tom's Cabin* all show their courage through helping others. When someone asked El Cordobés, the Spanish matador, how he learned to face the bulls, he responded: "Where is the university for courage? . . . The university for courage is to do what you believe in!" (*Or I'll Dress You in Mourning*, 1970). These men and other characters in these novels exhibit their beliefs in a variety of ways. One does not have to fight in a battle with guns and sabers to show courage. The bravery of humans surfaces daily as people support others and sacrifice themselves for their rights and their convictions.

Additional Related Novels

Doctorow, E. L. *Ragtime*.
Faulkner, William. *The Bear*.
Flagg, Fannie. *Fried Green Tomatoes at the Whistle Stop Café*.
Glasgow, Ellen. *Barren Ground*.
Hemingway, Ernest. *For Whom the Bell Tolls*.
Momaday, N. Scott. *House Made of Dawn*.
Mosley, Walter. *Devil in a Blue Dress*.
O'Brien, Tim. *The Things They Carried*.
Rölvaag, O. E. *Giants in the Earth*.
Welch, James. *Fools Crow*.

Cultural Conflict

By "culture" is meant the whole complex of learned behaviour, the traditions and techniques and the material possessions, the language and other symbolism, of some body of people.
—*British Journal of Sociology* (vol. 14, no. 21, 1963)

Abstracts of psychological studies on "cultural conflict" reveal that conflict among groups loosely defined as "cultures" knows no bounds. Residents of Hong Kong ignore and disdain immigrants from the surrounding rural areas. Hispanic parents and Caucasian teachers use different criteria for judging student success. Silas Lapham's family discovers that a small town background divides them from the cultural expectations of "old" society Bostonians in *The Rise of Silas Lapham*. June's mother wishes for June to have blonde hair and blue eyes like Shirley Temple instead of her Chinese features in *The Joy Luck Club*. In *Snow Falling on Cedars*, hostility toward the Japanese residents after World War II makes Kabuo Miyamoto the prime suspect in Carl Heine's 1953 murder. The cultural conflicts apparent in the three novels, *Goodbye, Columbus, Tar Baby*, and *How the Garcia Girls Lost Their Accents* are distinctive, but each involves persons whose attitudes conflict with persons they meet.

The phrase "cultural conflict" is a twentieth-century term. One of the first references comes from Margaret Mead in 1949 when she said, "Teacher, physician, nurse . . . each in turn represents some different form of culture conflict" (Fortes, *Social Structure*). In sociology, a cultural conflict arises as collective behavior and causes social disorganization and other malfunctions. "Cultural" refers to something obtained by breeding, and the breeding can occur in one's childhood home, in one's religious institution, or in the schools one attends. Bernard Bloch and George Leonard Trager assert that "the activities of a society—that is, of its members—constitute its culture" (*Outline of Linguistic Analysis*, 1942). And Stuart Piggott notes that "probably the word 'culture' should be employed to define the collective and tangible outcome (pot-making, house-planning, tomb-building) of the material and spiritual traditions of a group of people" (*The Neolithic Cultures of the British Isles*, 1954). When the desired outcomes differ, conflicts arise. Indeed, something as seemingly noncontroversial as one's choice of profession can cause conflict with someone in another discipline. The teacher processes information and distributes it differently from either the physician or the nurse. Society often stereotypes physicians as nonpatient centered, interested more in the process of medical treatment while nurses have a reputation as nurturers, focusing on the comfort of the patient in their care. In a cultural conflict, however, the minority position is usually disadvantaged to some extent. In *Goodbye, Columbus*, *Tar Baby*, and *How the Garcia Girls Lost Their Accents*, social disorganization does occur as the characters confront inconsistencies in behavior and feelings of isolation.

Goodbye, Columbus by Philip Roth

In Philip Roth's *Goodbye, Columbus* (1959), the protagonist Neil Klugman falls in love with Brenda Patimkin and finds himself in a cultural conflict with people of his own religion. Brenda is also Jewish, and Neil expects them to have a common basis for a relationship, but he discovers otherwise. Not only are they separated by religious practices but also by their attitudes toward society and education. Neil, a state college graduate and former soldier in the early 1950s, works in the local library. When he meets Brenda, he is visiting his cousin's suburban country club swimming pool. Neil gives a first-person account of his days off and vacation with Brenda and her family during the summer months.

Their social backgrounds and families are markedly different. Neil has lived in the lower-class Newark, New Jersey, home of his Aunt Gladys, Uncle Max, and cousin Susan since his parents moved to Arizona for relief from their asthma. In this house, they all eat at different times and rarely see each other. Neil says, "Life was a throwing off for poor Aunt Gladys, her greatest joys were taking out the garbage, emptying her pantry, and making threadbare bundles for what she still referred to as the Poor Jews in Palestine." An adult who has also served in the army, Neil determines his own choices. Brenda, however, lives with her Jewish family in an elegant upper-class Protestant community. Her wealthy father and socialite mother protect their three children, even spoiling their younger daughter Julie by allowing her to retake missed Ping-Pong shots and unfairly winning. Neil prefers the intelligence and curiosity of the young African-American boy who visits the library every day to gaze at the Gauguin book and dream of the lovely places depicted in the prints. Brenda's family knows her friends, helps make her decisions, and exerts an active control of her life.

Another important difference is their attitude toward education. Although Neil graduated from the Newark College of Rutgers University, Brenda's Radcliffe education appears more socially desirable. Yet Brenda's plastic surgery on her nose interests her more than learning. Neil, however, seems to have internalized his education rather than wearing knowledge like a façade. When he mentions Martin Buber (an important Jewish philosopher), Brenda's mother has never heard of him and only wonders if he is orthodox or conservative. Brenda's brother Ron starred in basketball at Ohio State, and he refers to his academic career once when he asks Neil to listen to his "Goodbye, Columbus" record, an overview of sports during Ron's senior year.

The most unexpected cultural conflict comes in the differences of their Judaic backgrounds. For many ethnic or religious groups, outsiders seem to think all the members are alike. Neil does not observe religious holidays, but his family has raised him in a Jewish immigrant neighborhood where people have retained their Jewish identity. Neil understands Yiddish and participates in the Workman's Circle, a Yiddish-socialist organization. Brenda's father has moved the family west (the symbolic direction for materialistic Americans) of the old Jewish neighborhoods into the suburbs. The family keeps a kosher home, but only Brenda's mother seems vaguely aware of Jewish rituals. Brenda's father knows Yiddish and expresses regret to Neil that his own children and wife do not. The parents have tried to raise the children with the social values of the neighborhood—wealthy Protestant. This assimilation and Brenda's reluctance to accept the reality of her relationship with Neil doom their future. Neil cannot understand her inability to make decisions without first acquiring her parents' approval. He knows that he has loved her, but he knows that she will never try to comprehend what is important to him. He says, "I simply looked at myself in the mirror the light made of the window. I was only that substance, I thought, those limbs, that face that I saw in front of me. I looked, but the outside of me gave up little information about the inside of me." And Brenda will not expend the effort to uncover the Neil "inside."

Tar Baby by Toni Morrison

Cultural conflict can also occur within races. In *Tar Baby* (1981), the orphaned Jadine returns for Christmas from Paris to the Caribbean home on the Isle de Chevaliers of her white patron Valerian Street where her Aunt Ondine and Uncle Sydney are servants. During her visit, the fugitive Son appears after having been shipwrecked off the coast, while Margaret, Valerian's wife, awaits the arrival of their son Michael. Among the cultural conflicts swirling through the house that Toni Morrison presents with omniscient point of view are black against black, white against white, and black against white.

The most subtle of the cultural conflicts occurs in Margaret and her relationships with her husband and son. Twenty years younger than Valerian, a wealthy candy manufacturer, she had married him after he saw her hugging a polar bear in Maine on a float when she was only seventeen. Known as "Principal Beauty" in her neighborhood, her red hair and creamy skin had overwhelmed him as it had many males before him. Her beauty threatened other women, even though she was poor and lived in a "tacky" trailer. After their marriage, Valerian finds Margaret watching soap operas on television with Ondine and discourages her socializing with the servants. Margaret is uneducated, and Valerian tries to teach her about music and flowers, two things he loves. While on the island, Margaret wants to return to the mainland to visit, but Valerian keeps making excuses to remain. Margaret seems never to have adjusted to Valerian's culture, but no one other than Ondine is aware of this chasm until the holidays. During a vitriolic argument on Christmas day after Michael has failed to arrive, Ondine reveals that Margaret had cut and burnt Michael during his childhood. Valerian himself had seen the child Michael hiding under a sink but did not notice either his fear or his neediness. Ondine accuses Margaret, "You cut him up. You cut your baby up. Made him bleed for you. For fun you did it. Made him scream, you, you freak. You crazy white freak. She did," Ondine addressed the others, still shouting. "She stuck pins in his behind. Burned him with cigarettes. Yes, she did, I saw her; I saw his little behind. She burned him!" After the accusation, "Every day she [Margaret] asked [Valerian to hit her], every day he answered, 'Tomorrow, perhaps tomorrow.' But he never did and she was hard-pressed to think of a way to ease their mutual sorrow." The conflict of their cultures destroys Margaret's ability to function sanely.

The most obvious cultural conflict would seem to be that between whites and blacks. But Morrison complicates the situation by having Jadine think of herself as a white woman wearing a black skin. Jadine explains, "I hate ear hoops," and she would like not to "have to straighten my hair . . . that sometimes I want to get out of my skin and be only the person inside—not American—not black—just me." Even though Ondine and Sydney are Valerian's servants, Valerian has allowed them to raise Jadine in his home, sent her to college, and supported opportunities for her to do as she has wanted. She has attended the Sorbonne and modeled for the cover of *Elle* magazine. She feels as comfortable at the Street dining room table as she does in New York and Paris. When Son arrives, he infuriates Jadine by calling her "white." Yet Jadine knows he tells the truth, and her sealskin coat, a present from her French boyfriend Ryk, symbolizes it.

The cultural conflict among blacks is unanticipated. Ondine and Sydney, delighted that Jadine has arrived for the holidays, think that she will defer to their desires. They tell each other "don't worry yourself. Remember, Jadine's here. Nothing can happen to us as long as she's here.'" But they soon realize that Jadine no longer exhibits some of the values they expect. Although furious with Son, Jadine discovers that Valerian has invited him to join them for dinner and enjoys Son's insights and his sage advice about Valerian's greenhouse flowers. After Jadine succumbs to her sexual attraction for Son, their ardent affair takes them to New York and then to Son's home in Eloe, Florida. In New York, Jadine encourages Son to attend school, but he is disinterested. In Eloe, Son wants Jadine to adopt the behavior expected of local black women. She refuses. What they discover is that strong physical attraction cannot overcome their cultural expectations, and the conflict ends the relationship.

How the Garcia Girls Lost Their Accents by Julia Alvarez

To explore the conflict between cultures in different countries, Julia Alvarez uses a backward chronology in *How the Garcia Girls Lost Their Accents*. The present tense and omniscient point of view in the novel's three sections weaving together fifteen stories reveal frustrations that each of the four Garcia sisters experiences after their family flees to the United States from the Dominican Republic during the Trujillo regime. As a minority, they face conflicts of language, of politics, and of family values. The frame of the novel introduces the girls after they become women and Americanized with Yolanda (Yo) visiting family members in the Dominican Republic after twenty-nine years of living in New York. Sofia (Fifi) then explores her estrangement from her father after her marriage to Otto, a German chemist. From 1970 to 1960, the sisters detail their experiences with sex and drugs and Yolanda's mental breakdown. And from 1960 to 1956, the girls address the alien New York culture.

The girls remember some of the events and people they have left behind, but the point of view allows readers to discover some things the girls do not know. The black Haitian maid, Chucha, sleeps in her coffin and casts spells while one of the male cousins, Mundín, wants to confirm that sister Sandi is a female by having her remove her clothes. None of the girls understands why they are coming to New York in 1956 with their parents since their father has often gone without them and brought back presents. They are unaware of the dangers their father has faced at home. The American Victor Hubbard helps their father Carlos (and them) escape Trujillo's regime by telling the police that the doctor has been granted a fellowship in the United States. The adult family members (Carlos is the youngest of thirty-five children, twenty-five legitimate and fifteen from his own mother, his father's second wife) think that Victor is a consul, but he is actually a Central Intelligence Agency (CIA) spy.

In the ten years after their arrival, they learn about the new culture. Yolanda sees snow for the first time; "Each flake was different, Sister Zoe had said, like a person, irreplaceable and beautiful." When her father dislikes and destroys her graduation speech, she angrily labels him "just another Chapita," or "Trujillo." What she does not know is how damning of him she has been. "She would have realized her father had lost brothers and friends to the dictator Trujillo. For the rest of his life, he would be haunted by blood in the streets and late night disappearances. Even after all these years, he cringed if a black Volkswagen passed him on the street. He feared anyone in uniform: the meter maid . . . a museum guard." But her father repents his rigidity and buys her a new typewriter. Carla, another sister, attends school in the next parish when she is twelve, and there the boys tease her and a man exposes himself to her from his car. Puberty and feeling like an outsider surprise her. The children have to cope with epithets such as "spic" and "greaseball" even while attending boarding school in Boston with wealthy New England girls. In the summers, the parents send the sisters to visit their family in the Dominican Republic. One summer, their mother's maid discovers a bag of marijuana behind the bookcase and identifies it as oregano. By the time Fifi begins to fall in love with a cousin in the islands, the girls know they cannot live there and force her to return to New York.

In the earliest part of the novel and the latest time frame, Alvarez focuses on Yolanda's and Fifi's relationships. After her divorce from John, another cultural divide because they "didn't speak the same language," the independent Yolanda returns to the islands, thinking she will be more relaxed. She discovers, however, that women alone in the countryside cannot function without fear. Previously unseen men emerge from the woods to help her change a flat tire, and even though she experiences no danger, she no longer feels safe. One of the main cultural conflicts the girls experience is their father's belief that he continues to control their behavior after their marriages. To appease him, the girls come home without their spouses each year to celebrate his birthday. But when Fifi's son is born, she names him Carlos, plans his baptism to coincide with her father's seventieth birthday, and invites her father to her house. He accepts, even though the two have been estranged because of her determination to marry a man her father did not know. At the party, her father says to the young Carlos and his father Otto, "You can be as great a man as your father.' This was the first compliment the father-in-law had ever paid any son-in-law in the family.'" But as the party progresses, "the older the evening got, the more withdrawn the father had become. Surrounded by his daughters and their husbands and fancy, intelligent, high-talking friends, he seemed to be realizing that he was just an old man sitting in their houses, eating up their roast lamb, impinging upon their lives." In this segment of the novel, the cultural conflict shifts to gender and age. Neither men and women nor old and young quite seem to understand each other's beliefs and values.

These three novels, *Goodbye, Columbus, Tar Baby,* and *How the Garcia Girls Lost Their Accents,* illustrate the various ways cultural conflict occurs. Religion, social status, money, race, country, and language are a few of the barriers that people must overcome if they are to understand each other. Neither Neil and Brenda nor Jadine and Son can reconcile their different value systems once the sexual attraction settles in their relationships. Yolanda in *How the Garcia Girls Lost Their Accents* remembers one of her college boyfriends who left her when she refused to sleep with him. Her reaction mirrors the response of anyone who experiences a cultural conflict with another. "I saw what a cold, lonely life awaited me in this country. I would never find someone who would understand my peculiar mix of Catholicism and agnosticism, Hispanic and American styles." Pausing to understand another's view takes an effort that many remain unwilling to expend.

Additional Related Novels

Cormier, Robert. *After the First Death.*
Craven, Margaret. *I Heard the Owl Call My Name.*

Guterson, David. *Snow Falling on Cedars.*
Kingston, Maxine Hong. *The Woman Warrior.*
Lewis, Sinclair. *Main Street.*
McCarthy, Cormac. *All the Pretty Horses.*
Silko, Leslie Marmon. *Ceremony.*
Tan, Amy. *The Joy Luck Club; The Kitchen God's Wife.*
Wharton, Edith. *The Age of Innocence.*

Death

Death is terrifying because it is so ordinary. It happens all the time.
—Susan Cheever, *Home before Dark* (1984)

As a human, one can only react to the deaths of other beings; therefore, one tends to categorize death in terms of one's response. The death of a younger person seems "tragic," but that of a much older person might be a "good" death. Other deaths can seem "untimely" or "painful" or "senseless." Because intense emotion often accompanies the death of someone close, many novels examine the reaction of a character to a death. In *The Accidental Tourist*, the parents mourn their son's murder. The novels *The Catcher in the Rye*, *Ordinary People*, and *A River Runs Through It* contemplate brothers recovering from the deaths of brothers. Fulfilling the wish of a deceased mother occupies the characters in *As I Lay Dying* and *The Joy Luck Club*. Friends die in *Fried Green Tomatoes at the Whistle Stop Café*, *Deliverance*, *The Old Man and the Sea*, and *Death Comes for the Archbishop*. In the novels, *A Separate Peace*, *The Human Comedy*, and *A Death in the Family*, the protagonists must deal with the death of someone who has shaped their concepts of living.

The denotation of death is "the act or fact of dying, the end of life, the final cessation of the vital functions of an individual" (*OED*). This meaning of "death" has remained unchanged throughout history, although persons of various cultures and religions have differed in their interpretations about what happens to the soul after the body dies. Stories of Egyptian pharaohs mummified and buried with all the comforts of their palaces to enhance their sojourn in the afterlife abound. Sir John Seeley reports that "the Greek did not believe death to be annihilation" (*Ecce homo*, 1865). Others recognize the impartiality of death. Publius Syrus noted that "as men, we are all equal in the presence of death" (100 B.C.E.). In *Richard II*, Shakespeare says that "nothing can we call our own but death / And that small model of the barren earth / Which serves as paste and cover to our bones" (1597). Although the Jacobean Philip Massinger refers to "grim death" in his plays, he also alleges that "death hath a thousand doors to let out life." John Milton's beginning of *Paradise Lost* recalls "man's first disobedience, and the fruit / Of that forbidden tree whose mortal taste / Brought death into the world, and all our woe" (1667). The twentieth-century existentialist view of Jean-Paul Sartre appears in his play *No*

Exit, "I think of death only with tranquillity, as an end. I refuse to let death hamper life. Death must enter life only to define it" (1947). And Jim Bishop offers that "death is as casual—and often as unexpected—as birth. It is as difficult to define grief as joy. Each is finite. Each will fade" (*Red Bank, New Jersey, Register,* 1973). In *A Separate Peace* and *A Death in the Family,* the deaths shock friends and family, and in *The Human Comedy,* a war casualty causes no less pain.

A Separate Peace by John Knowles

In John Knowles's *A Separate Peace* (1960), Gene and Phineas (Finny) become best friends at Devon Preparatory School during 1942, but two falls, one from a tree and one down marble steps, lead to Finny's death. Gene, the first-person narrator, tells the story after returning to the school in 1957. As he wanders around the grounds, he remembers his fear at sixteen and hopes to achieve "growth and harmony" from revisiting the experience. He first searches for a tree that "loomed in my memory as a huge lone spike dominating the riverbank, forbidding as an artillery piece, high as the beanstalk." But when he finally finds the tree, "it seemed to me standing there to resemble those men, the giants of your childhood, whom you encounter years later and find that they are not merely smaller in relation to your growth, but that they are absolutely smaller, shrunken by age." Gene's realization that he has exaggerated the past in his memory helps him to better understand his relationship to the school and to Finny during that turbulent time, both locally at the school and internationally with World War II.

Gene and Finny become best friends during the summer with Phineas's defiance of authority first attracting Gene's interest. Finny wears pink shirts while everything else seems gray. "Phineas didn't really dislike West Point in particular or authority in general, but just considered authority the necessary evil against which happiness was achieved by reaction." Sneaking to the beach for an overnight scares but intrigues Gene. But soon, Gene thinks that Finny has schemed to keep him from studying. When Gene confronts him, Finny answers that he thought Gene inherently intelligent. Phineas, unlike Gene, considers sports the "absolute good" and excels at them. He coerces Gene into racing, wins, and asks Gene not to spread the news. Finny also creates blitzball, a game in which the players imitate the war. However, Gene has an aversion to sports. "It was as though football players were really bent on crushing the life out of each other, as though boxers were in combat to the death, as though even a tennis ball might turn into a bullet. This didn't seem completely crazy imagination in 1942, when jumping out of trees stood for abandoning a torpedoed ship." Then when Phineas breaks his leg and says that Gene has to play sports in his stead, Gene recalls, "I lost part of myself to him then, and a soaring sense of freedom revealed that this must have been my purpose from the first: to become a part of Phineas." When he falls from the tree, Phineas is pretending to train Gene to enter the next Olympic Games.

During the summer, the tree becomes the major focus of Gene's experience. His description, "the tree was tremendous, an irate, steely black steeple beside the river," personifies it as a hostile god. The tree seems angry, but simultaneously it is a steeple, an architectural detail usually associated with churches. Then Finny decides that they need an initiation for the summer students. To accentuate this decision, Knowles stylistically emphasizes the role of the tree. Gene remembers, "We were still calmly, numbly reading Virgil and playing tag in the river farther downstream. Until Finny thought of the tree." The short clause about the tree and Finny follows a long sentence describing the games of young boys. For the ritual, each boy must jump from the tree, and each fears the consequences of his leap into the air. Their group calls itself "The Suicide Society of the Summer Session," and Gene hates to jump from the tree every night like Finny wants. On the night before exams, Gene moves on the tree limb, causing Finny to lose his balance. "Holding firmly to the trunk, I took a step toward him, and then my knees bent and I jounced the limb." Phineas falls from the tree and shatters his leg.

After other students return for the school year, they begin to question the event leading to Finny's fall. A class leader, Brinker, eventually stages a mock trial to determine if Gene deliberately shook the limb from which Finny fell. Leper, one of the students who joined the army but became mentally imbalanced, describes the scene in the tree: the rays of the sun were shooting past them, millions of rays shooting past them—like golden machine-gun fire. . . . The two of them looked as black as—as black as death standing up there with this fire burning all around them." Furious about the trial, Finny rushes out and falls down the marble steps. When Gene visits him in the infirmary the next day, the doctor informs Gene that bone marrow probably moved to Finny's heart and caused his death. Gene feels that Finny's funeral is his own, and since one does not cry at one's own funeral, he does not reveal his despair.

After Finny's death, Gene understands that he cannot support the patriotism that Brinker and his father profess because it emphasizes war rather than the peace that Finny espoused. "I could never agree with either of them. It would have been comfortable, but I could not believe it. Because it seemed clear that wars were not made by generations and their special stupidities, but that wars were made instead by something ignorant in the human heart." He sees his classmates in their relationships to each other and compares them to Finny and his attitudes. "All of them, all except Phineas, constructed at infinite cost to themselves these Maginot Lines against this enemy they thought they saw across the frontier, this enemy who never attacked that way—if he ever attacked at all; if he was indeed the enemy."

The Human Comedy by William Saroyan

Although the death in *The Human Comedy* (1943) occurs the same year of Finny's death in *A Separate Peace*, the circumstances are quite different. The Macauley family, including Mrs. Macauley, Homer (fourteen), Bess (seventeen), and Ulysses (four), receive notification that the oldest son and brother, Marcus, has died abroad fighting in World War II. Mr. Macauley has been dead for two years, but Mrs. Macauley says that he told her in a dream that Marcus would die. In the story of the Macauley family, William Saroyan employs autobiographical elements. His own father died when Saroyan was three, he lived in California, he suffered discrimination as an Armenian in a different culture, and he worked in a telegraph office. Saroyan's use of omniscient point of view in the thirty-eight short chapters of the book allows the reader to meet the family members, including Marcus before his death, and see the resemblance to Saroyan's life. However, the story focuses on Homer and his experiences.

Homer attends the Ithaca (Ithaca was also the home of the Greek Ulysses), California, high school where he experiences a microcosm of life. He admires the intelligent and beautiful Helen (Helen of Troy?) as she reads aloud in Miss Hicks's ancient history class. Wanting to be a track star like Mr. Spangler, his boss, Homer executes body building exercises before school each morning. However, the coach Mr. Byfield wants the wealthy white runner Hubert Ackley, III, to represent the school. When an Italian, Joe Terranova, defends Homer, Mr. Byfield calls him a "dirty little wop." Both attack Mr. Byfield, and Miss Hicks supports them. She asks Homer and Hubert to meet after school and informs them, "I am interested in what is truly beneath each kind of manners. Whether one of my children is rich or poor, Catholic or Protestant or Jew, white or black or yellow, brilliant or slow, genius or simple-minded, is no matter to me, if there is humanity in him—if he has a heart—if he loves truth and honor—if he respects his inferiors and loves his superiors." Thus adults outside the family also offer Homer advice.

After school, Homer delivers messages for the telegraph company (like the Greek Homer who informed through *The Iliad* and *The Odyssey*) and discovers the unspoken difficulties of the job. One of his duties is to alert Willie Grogan when asleep or drunk, but the other is to deliver telegrams, mostly to notify people that a husband or a son has died in battle. When Homer returns from delivering a message of death to a Mexican woman who could not read English, Grogan tells him, "I don't expect you to understand anything I'm telling you. But I know you will remember *this*—that nothing good ever ends. If it did, there would be no people in the world—no life at all, anywhere. And the world is full of people and full of wonderful life." (Grogan demonstrates his own goodness by being so overwhelmed when the message of Marcus's death arrives via telegraph that he has a heart attack and dies himself.) After Homer returns from conveying another message during a mother's birthday party, he cries. When he tells his mother that men do not cry, she reassures him. "Only good men weep. If a man has not wept at the world's pain he is less than the dirt he walks upon because dirt will nourish seed, root, stalk, leaf and flower, but the spirit of a man without pity is barren and will bring forth nothing." When a man demands money from Homer's boss Spangler, Spangler asks him how much he wants. The man replies, "I wanted to believe it, because I've been telling myself for years: 'Let me find one man uncorrupted, so that I may believe and live.' I wasn't sure the first time we met, but I'm sure now. I want nothing more from you. You've given me everything I want."

Homer's family has a strong, secure, and loving relationship under his mother's leadership. She encourages Homer's little brother Ulysses to accompany the slightly retarded Lionel to the neighborhood library where they look at picture books together. Marcus's girlfriend, Mary Arena, lives next door, and Mrs. Macauley also comforts her. She consoles Homer, "the loneliness you feel has come to you because you are no longer a child. But the whole world has always been full of that loneliness. The loneliness does not come from the War. The War did not make it. It was the loneliness that made the War. It was the despair in all things for no longer having in them the grace of God." "Seeing" her dead husband around the house seems to help Mrs. Macauley cope with their poverty and the hardship of having a son away at war. Marcus has told Tobey George, his friend in boot camp about the family and invites the orphaned Tobey to visit Ithaca after the war. When Tobey arrives on the same day that the family receives news of Marcus's death, Mrs. Macauley accepts him as a member of the family.

A Death in the Family by James Agee

Like Saroyan, James Agee uses autobiographical elements in *A Death in the Family* (1957). His father died in an automobile accident when he was a young boy, his mother was excessively religious, and his detested nickname was "Rufus," the name he gives his protagonist. In notes to the novel, Agee mentioned that the time in the days and months before a death become exalted in their importance after the event itself. In the novel, Rufus remembers vividly the moments with his father before he heard his father leave in the middle of the night on the trip from which he did not return alive. He also recalls summer evenings and activities of other fathers in the neighborhood during 1915, "Fathers of families, each in his space of lawn, his shirt fishlike pale in the unnatural light and his face nearly anonymous, hosing their lawns." The novel's omniscient point of view relates Rufus's mother Mary's memories as well. Agee posits that a person's reactions to hearing about a death and responding to it are archetypal, but those going through the experience are unaware of their actions as universal.

One of the important thematic threads underlying the novel is the sometimes strained relationship of Rufus's parents, Mary and Jay. Jay's rural background, refusal to join the Catholic Church, and relaxed manner have long bothered Mary. She thinks her family more accomplished and more sophisticated than his, and his disinterest in these advantages surprises her. Yet after Jay's death, Mary feels his presence, especially in the children's rooms, and is comforted. Hannah and Andrew, her siblings, also hear some kind of steps and think Jay might be near. Mary's father, however, attributes their reactions to shock. Even though Mary has disapproved of Jay's enjoyment of Charlie Chaplin's sexual innuendos and perhaps his beers with his peers in the local bar, she has loved him and appreciated his gentler qualities.

Rufus has spent most of the life he remembers trying to understand himself and gain his father's approval. As a child might, Rufus responds to his world in terms of imagery. He hears noises of the hoses in the neighborhood and the locusts, "the great order of noises, like the noises of the sea and of the blood her precocious grandchild, which you realize you are hearing only when you catch yourself listening." He does not know himself and feels "nothingness," in the dark, and then listens to his mother or father sing to him. He sees Chaplin use his cane to poke up women's dresses. And he says nothing to Victoria about her smell because his mother says that black people are sensitive about their smells. He is appreciative when his father takes him to the cinema and surprised when his father talks about his reading ability while in the bar after the movie. That his father does not flaunt Rufus's inability to protect himself from other boys in the neighborhood is a relief to Rufus. When they detour from their walk and view the lights over the city, Rufus thinks that his father might actually be enjoying his company rather than fulfilling a fatherly obligation.

After his father's death, Rufus lives in the same house, but everything has changed. His mother inadequately tries to explain what has happened to Rufus and his sister Catherine, four. Catherine thinks that an "accident" is what one has in one's pants; therefore, she does not understand how that could kill her father. On the first morning of their father's absence, Mary tries to discuss their grandfather's pending death with them since Jay left to see him after a frantic call from his brother. Rufus asks "why does God let us do bad things?" Mary answers "Because He wants us to make up our own minds." Rufus continues, "Why *doesn't* he want to? . . . It would be much easier for Him." Mary responds, "God wants us to *come* to Him, to *find* Him, the best we can." Catherine announces, "like hide-and-go-seek," but Rufus ascertains that they are not discussing a game. Ironically, they need to understand more clearly the next morning when the discussion concerns the death of their own father. Although something seems different because Aunt Hannah serves them their food, Rufus does not hear about his father until the boys outside tell him the newspaper story. Rufus dislikes the condescending priest who later comes and sits in his father's chair. The only sane person seems to be Uncle Andrew. He tells Rufus, after the funeral that Rufus is not allowed to attend, about the butterfly that landed on his father's casket, remaining until the sun came out as the pallbearers lowered the casket into the grave. Andrew imagines the butterfly as a symbol of Jay's spirit flying away in beauty. And Mr. Starr, the man designated to care for the children during the funeral, reassures them, "Your father was one of the finest men that ever lived."

In all three of these novels, the person who dies changes the lives of the protagonists. Gene in *A Separate Peace* has to accept himself and the possibility that his jealousy of Finny's free spirit led to Finny's death. After fifteen years, Gene concludes that "nothing endures, not a tree, not love, not even a death by violence." In *The Human Comedy*, the family's dynamics change at the death of Marcus, and, although Tobey arrives to take his place, the reader knows that Tobey has none of the collective memory and unspoken emotions that hold the family together. Simultaneously, Homer loses a trusted friend at his job with Mr. Grogan's death. And in *A Death in the Family*, Rufus and his mother do not want to believe that Jay is dead and do not want to either hear or experience the reality of Mary's father's comment: "You've got to bear it in mind that nobody that ever lived is specially privileged; the axe can fall at any moment, on any neck, without any warning or any regard for justice." And that is the horror of death—any moment, any time, any one—often with no warning and no reason.

Additional Related Novels

Bellow, Saul. *Seize the Day*.
Cather, Willa. *Death Comes for the Archbishop*.
Cormier, Robert. *After the First Death*.
Crane, Stephen. *The Red Badge of Courage*.
Fast, Howard. *April Morning*.
Faulkner, William. *As I Lay Dying*.
Flagg, Fannie. *Fried Green Tomatoes at the Whistle Stop Café*.
Frazier, Charles. *Cold Mountain*.
Gaines, Ernest J. *A Lesson Before Dying*.
Gibbons, Kaye. *Ellen Foster*.
Guest, Judith. *Ordinary People*.
Guterson, David. *Snow Falling on Cedars*.
Hemingway, Ernest. *A Farewell to Arms; The Old Man and the Sea*.
Maclean, Norman. *A River Runs Through It*.
McCullers, Carson. *A Member of the Wedding*.
Myers, Walter Dean. *Fallen Angels*.
Naylor, Gloria. *Mama Day; The Women of Brewster Place*.
O'Brien, Tim. *The Things They Carried*.
Olsen, Tillie. *Tell Me a Riddle*.
Salinger, J. D. *The Catcher in the Rye*.
Tan, Amy. *The Joy Luck Club*.
Turner, Nancy E. *These Is My Words*.
Tyler, Anne. *The Accidental Tourist*.
Welch, James. *The Death of Jim Loney*.

Disabled

The white, the Hispanic, the black, the Arab, the Jew, the woman, the Native American, the small farmer, the businessperson, the environmentalist, the peace activist, the young, the old, the lesbian, the gay and the disabled make up the American quilt.

—Jesse Jackson (1984)

One may be born disabled or become disabled either mentally or physically as a result of accident or disease. A disability often prohibits people from doing what they want and, if visible, may cause them to experience rejection and hostility from those around them. Novels sometimes deliberate these difficulties. After Lyman Ward's wife leaves him because he loses a leg and can no longer move freely in *Angle of Repose*, he decides to investigate the life of his grandmother. Roy Hobbs must delay playing baseball for many years in *The Natural* while recovering from a bullet wound. Jake Barnes's injury in World War I renders him sexually incapable in *The Sun Also Rises*. In *The Shipping News*, Wavey Prouse dedicates her life to her young son with Down's syndrome. And sometimes people have psychological disabilities that can damage them as much as a physical or mental problem such as Pecola in *The Bluest Eye*, who thinks people will love her if her eyes are blue. In the novels *Tender Is the Night, The Heart Is a Lonely Hunter*, and *Ethan Frome*, the characters have mental, physical, or imagined disabilities.

To have a disability is to be "unable or incapable, to be incapacitated either physically or mentally" (*OED*). A person may have a congenital injury or suffer injury after birth. Caxton mentioned in 1491, "I am all disabled of my members" (*Vitas Patrum*). In 1712, Thomas Hearne complained, "My writing [*sic*] hand hath been disabled by a sprain" (*Remarks and Collections*). In 1893, the *Weekly Notes* of the English House of Lords speaks of "a member being permanently disabled by an accident." At one time, Americans spoke of the "disabled" as "handicapped." Therefore, many references to someone "disabled" may use the term "handicapped" although the terms are not synonymous. To be "handicapped" implies that one is inadequate. "Disabled" simply means that one does not have the ability to do a particular thing, and all humans are disabled in some way. The novels, *Tender Is the Night, The Heart Is a Lonely Hunter*, and *Ethan Frome* illustrate different types and diverse levels of disability.

Tender Is the Night by F. Scott Fitzgerald

In *Tender Is the Night* (1934), the psychiatrist Dick Driver marries his wealthy schizophrenic patient Nicole, and, by the end of their marriage, Driver has become disabled and Nicole has regained her mental stability. F. Scott Fitzgerald structured the novel into five books, with the second presenting the Drivers' life together in a flashback beginning in 1917 when Dick is twenty-six. After attending Oxford as a Rhodes Scholar, Dick goes to Zurich, where he meets Nicole in a mental institution. Her mother had died when Nicole was eleven, and Nicole had come to the clinic at sixteen. Her father eventually confessed under duress that he had "accidentally" raped her, and her psychiatrist, Franz Gregorovius, demands that Nicole not see her father for five years. During Dick's two-year military service in France during World War I, Nicole writes him fifty letters in eight months. Franz then gives her case to Driver when he returns to Zurich. But the doctor-patient relationship dissolves when Dick and Nicole fall in love and decide to marry. Nicole's sister, Baby, disapproves, thinking Dick wants Nicole's money, but the two marry anyway and move to the hill village of Tarmes near the French Riviera. Throughout their marriage, friends congregate without discovering either Dick's or Nicole's disability. Between them, they pretend wellness by a willingness to do everything. "When, inevitably, their spirits flagged they shifted the blame to the weariness and fatigue of others."

Dick's relationship with Nicole mirrors his relationships with others because the attention on him keeps him vigorous. Dick attracts women; "he had the power of arousing a fascinated and uncritical love." He needs affection, and, in reflecting on his past, he remembers those who have succumbed to his charms "as a general might gaze upon a massacre he had ordered to satisfy an impersonal blood lust." When Rosemary Hoyt, a young movie star of seventeen, first meets him, "he looked at her and for a moment she lived in the bright blue worlds of his eyes, eagerly and confidently." She immediately falls in love with him, a relationship her mother encourages even though Dick is married. Dick professes love to Rosemary, but remains with Nicole. When Dick and Rosemary meet four years later in Paris, they consummate their affair, but, by then, Dick has become estranged from Nicole and more disabled. He admits to Rosemary "I guess I'm the Black Death. . . . I don't seem to bring people happiness any more."

Dick's personality changes dramatically as the novel progresses. Dick initially charms Rosemary with his sexuality, but the attraction eventually fades, and Franz watches Dick begin to drink more after they rejuvenate the Swiss clinic. By choosing alcohol as his drug, Dick resembles his friend Abe North, a superb but failed musician who was beaten to death in a Parisian speakeasy. Franz's wife notices that Driver "is no longer a serious man," and Franz gladly buys Driver's share of the clinic once Driver becomes professionally incapacitated. Dick does not expect Franz to agree to his departure so readily, "yet he was relieved. Not without desperation he had long felt the ethics of his profession dissolving into a lifeless mass." When he and Nicole visit Mary North and her new husband, an Indian, they unintentionally insult the family. Nicole admonishes Dick, "You used to want to create things—now you seem to want to smash them up." Later Dick extricates Mary North and a friend from an unpleasant situation and accuses them of being dull. Mary informs him, "But we're all there is! . . . If you don't like nice people, try the ones who aren't nice, and see how you like that! All people want is to have a good time and if you make them unhappy you cut yourself off from nourishment." Soon after, Nicole realizes that she no longer needs Dick. She asks for a divorce so that she can marry Tommy Barban, the Frenchman who has long loved her. Dick agrees, moves back to America, and sends postcards through the years, each from a smaller New York town than the last. Nicole overcomes her disability as she matures, but Dick's overtakes and undermines his ability to function personally or professionally.

The Heart Is a Lonely Hunter by Carson McCullers

In *The Heart Is a Lonely Hunter* (1940), each of the characters has a disability. Using omniscient point of view in the three parts of the novel, McCullers presents four people who idolize a fifth, unaware that he revers a sixth person whom they do not know. In the first part of the novel, McCullers introduces the characters, sets the book, and gives a sense of the plot. Even though McCullers says elsewhere that this work is a parable against fascism, each of these five characters unwittingly emphasizes the loneliness of human beings and their desires to interact with others. As they explore possible relationships, they reveal their need for love and their spiritual isolation. Many critics see the novel as representative of the southern Gothic novel because each person seems freakish to some extent as he or she reflects on the intolerance, the poverty, and the isolation in a small southern mill town where "[the] cotton mills were big and flourishing and most of the workers in the town were very poor . . . [with a] desperate look of hunger and loneliness." Because McCullers carefully forms each character, naming one as the protagonist slights the others. Although Mick seems to be the most delineated, Mr. Singer's crucial role gives her competition.

Of the five characters, some have more obvious disabilities than others, but all harbor lost dreams before the novel's end. Biff Brannon runs the New York Café with his wife Alice until Alice dies with an "infant-sized" tumor in her body. They have remained childless with Biff's impotence separating them. After Alice's death, Biff wants to establish relationships with others, but fears intimacy, preferring to dream of living in ancient Greece. Jake Blount, a newcomer in town, gets a job as a carnival show's carousel mechanic, and, while trying to unite the factory workers against their bosses, declares that "everybody is blind, dumb, and blunt-headed—stupid and mean." But the people fear his temper and refuse his leadership. Dr. Benedict Mady Copeland, an African American suffering tuberculosis of the lungs, reads Spinoza and remains isolated from both his family and his people because of his strong convictions. He has tried to guide them into excellence through hard work, and they have not listened. When police wrongly convict his grandson of assault, and prison guards' maltreatment cripples him, Copeland appeals to the white judge and is himself imprisoned. Copeland tells Blount, "I believed in the tongue instead of the fist. As an armor against oppression I taught patience and faith in the human soul. I know now how wrong I was. I have been a traitor to myself and to my people. All that is rot. Now is the time to act and to act quickly. Fight cunning with cunning and might with might." Mick Kelly, a girl of twelve living with her impoverished family, loves music and hides outside the homes in the town's wealthy section to listen to it float out their windows from radios. Her response while Beethoven's *Eroica* plays emphasizes her awe: "For a minute the opening balanced from one side to the other. Like a walk or march. Like God strutting in the night. . . . The music boiled inside her. . . . This was the worst hurt there could be. The whole world was this symphony, and there was not enough of her to listen." Mick dreams of becoming a composer until her family's economic desperation forces her to quit school and work in the local Woolworth's. Finally, John Singer, a deaf mute, fascinates and satisfies the others as he listens quietly to their dreams, neither scolding nor sanctioning them.

The characters relate to Singer, not to each other, while Singer has his own anguish. Singer adores another mute, a fat, disgusting Spiros Antonapoulos, who ignores him except when Singer brings him food or alcohol. After Antonapoulos's cousin commits him to an insane asylum in another town, Singer spends his vacation with him. Singer misses Antonapoulos and awakens uneasily when "the morning light struck suddenly beneath his opening eyelids like a scimitar." Singer begins to circulate around town after work in the jewelry store each day, moves to a room in Mick Kelly's house, and patronizes the New York Café where he writes notes for Biff saying what he wants at each meal. One night, Singer offers to take the too-drunk Blount home. Copeland also responds to Singer, recalling the smile on his white face and the peacefulness that seemed to encompass him. Mick often talks to Singer. "With her it was like there was two places—the inside room and the outside room. School and family and the things that happened every day were in the outside room. Mister Singer was in both rooms. Foreign countries and plans and music were in the inside room." Singer buys a radio at Christmas for the people to enjoy who visit him, and Mick is delighted. Since Singer cannot condemn in a language any of them understand, he becomes godlike to them, and they think he can help them. When Mick imagines God, whom she decides is dead, she sees "Mister Singer with a long, white sheet around him." One day near Christmas, all four visit him at one time, but they talk to each other only about the weather. They remain isolated, hiding their thoughts except when alone with him. Because the ironically named Singer cannot express his own heartache, they do not know why he commits suicide in August. They cannot know that, for his god, he selected a selfish slob, and after his own god's death, he has no reason to live.

Ethan Frome by Edith Wharton

In *Ethan Frome* (1911), Edith Wharton has united three characters who become physically disabled at different points in the story. A man overseeing the addition of electricity comes to Starkfield, Massachusetts, many years after Mattie Silver's arrival and stays with Mrs. Ned Hale. After meeting Ethan Frome, the man thinks, "he seemed a part of the mute melancholy landscape, an incarnation of its frozen woe, with all that was warm and sentient in him fast bound below the surface; but there was nothing unfriendly in his silence." After talking with Ethan, the man loans him a book on recent discoveries in biochemistry. Ethan remains interested in science although he had to leave technical college after one year when his father died. This man becomes the first-person narrator of Ethan's story after Mrs. Hale tells him about Ethan and Mattie, an inhabitant in Ethan's home, "one of those lonely New England farm-houses that make the landscape lonelier." But in telling the story of Ethan, Wharton shifts to limited omniscient point of view.

Not one of the characters in the novel has had a happy life. As a young man, Ethan married his cousin Zeena to have someone look after him. Zeena, eight years older, had nursed his mother during her illness, and after Ethan's mother died, Ethan asked Zeena to stay. Zeena soon developed a series of illnesses, her "sickliness," during the first year of their marriage when she comprehends that, unable to find a buyer, they will never leave the farm. Ethan has little money, and Zeena's spending for medicines worries him. The farm produces only a meager income and he has no prospects for improvement. Zeena's orphaned cousin Mattie comes to live with them because she has nowhere else to go. When Ethan falls in love with Mattie, he complicates his unhappiness. He becomes jealous when Mattie chats with the eligible Denis Eady, thinking that "he [Ethan] could show her things and tell her things, and taste the bliss of feeling that all he imparted left long reverberations and echoes he could wake at will."

By the end of the novel, the seemingly disabled character has overcome her problems, and the physically healthy have become disabled. Zeena continues to visit the doctor after Mattie's arrival, and one of her visits lasts overnight. Zeena's trip to the doctor delights Ethan because he will be alone with Mattie for the evening. "Ethan was suffocated with a sense of well-being." During dinner, Ethan and Mattie discuss taking a sleigh ride, but when Mattie breaks Zeena's prized pickle dish, they must focus on its repair. When Zeena returns the next day, she announces that "only the chosen had 'complications,'" and she has "complications" requiring her to hire help for one dollar a month. On discovering her broken pickle dish, she demands that Mattie immediately depart. Ethan realizes that "the one pleasure left her [Zeena] was to inflict pain on him." He feels that "there was no way out—none. He was a prisoner for life, and now his one ray of light was to be extinguished." Ironically, Zeena and Ethan both "inflict pain" on each other for the rest of their lives following the events that occur when Mattie prepares to leave. Against Zeena's instructions, Ethan takes Mattie to the train station. On the way, they stop for their delayed sleigh ride, and, on the second run, Ethan hits an elm tree. Mattie is paralyzed and Ethan maimed. For the next twenty years, Zeena, who could not look after herself before the accident, has the strength to care for both. The irony remains that indeed Ethan, Mattie, and Zeena are all "prisoner[s] for life," disabled in ways none of them could ever have imagined before the disaster.

Thus the characters in *Tender Is the Night*, *The Heart Is a Lonely Hunter*, and *Ethan Frome* have disabilities. Everyone has disabilities; some are visible and some are not. Mental imbalance, muteness, deafness, or paralyzation are conditions that people may find in themselves or others. Ethan in *Ethan Frome* gets to remain with Mattie, but at the cost of becoming physically disabled. In *The Heart Is a Lonely Hunter*, Copeland comments that "the most fatal thing a man can do is try to stand alone." And in the same novel, Biff offers hope to those facing adversity even if he is unsure of his own ability to grasp it. Briefly, "he saw a glimpse of human struggle and of valor. Of the endless fluid passage of humanity through endless time. And of those who labor and of those who—one word—love. His soul expanded. But for a moment only. For in him he felt a warning, a shaft of terror. Between the two worlds he was suspended." One must overcome the "terror," like Nicole in *Tender Is the Night*, to remove the fear of freedom that accompanies accepting or, if possible, overcoming a disability.

Additional Related Novels

Faulkner, William. *The Sound and the Fury.*
Hemingway, Ernest. *The Sun Also Rises.*
Kesey, Ken. *One Flew Over the Cuckoo's Nest.*
Malamud, Bernard. *The Natural.*
Morrison, Toni. *The Bluest Eye.*
Proulx, E. Annie. *The Shipping News.*
Stegner, Wallace. *Angle of Repose.*
Wilson, Harriet E. *Our Nig.*

Duty

I long to accomplish a great and noble task, but it is my chief duty to accomplish small tasks as if they were great and noble.
—Helen Keller (c. 1960)

When someone declares, "It's my *duty*," that person usually has an obligation impossible to neglect. He or she must complete a previously designated action before proceeding to another task. Parents do their duty when they feed and clothe children as does Quoyle in *The Shipping News*. A friend does a duty by supporting another in need like Danny Saunders and Reuven Malter in *The Chosen*. Soldiers like Paul Berlin in *Going after Cacciato* and Bull Meecham in *The Great Santini* do their duty by remaining at their posts. In the three novels, *Billy Budd*, *For Whom the Bell Tolls*, and *The Killer Angels*, each protagonist fulfills a patriotic duty.

An obligation imposed from a source outside the self is a duty. The *OED* defines "duty" as "the action and conduct due to a superior; homage, submission; due respect, reverence; an expression of submission, deference, or respect." As early as 1297, Richard of Gloucester noted that "[{Th}]e kyng. . . gret deuyte [duty] tolde of hem." A "duty" can also be a "moral or legal obligation; that which one ought or is bound to do." When Lord Nelson said that "England expects every man to do his duty" (1805), he embodied that concept. In 1859, Abraham Lincoln said, "Let us have faith that right makes might; and in that faith let us dare to do our duty as we understand it." Ulysses S. Grant added, "No personal considerations should stand in the way of performing a duty" (1875). When President Harry S. Truman relieved General Douglas MacArthur of his position in the United States Army in 1951, MacArthur announced, "I now close my military career and just fade away, an old soldier who tried to do his duty as God gave him the sight to see that duty." In *Billy Budd*, *For Whom the Bell Tolls*, and *The Killer Angels*, each protagonist experiences an externally imposed duty.

Billy Budd by Herman Melville

In *Billy Budd* (1924), Herman Melville examines the fate of a young man who willingly accepts his legal obligations. The omniscient point of view relates the story of Billy Budd, a foundling from Bristol, England, at twenty-one in 1797, who works on the ship, *Rights of Man*. British police come aboard and impress him for service on the seventy-four-gun H.M.S. *Bellipotent*. On that ship, he carefully performs his job, thinking that the master-at-arms (police-man), Claggart, likes him. But Claggart instructs his underlings, the corporals, to reprimand Budd for insignificant conduct breaches even though Billy so fears public flogging that he follows all commands. The old sailor Dansker informs Budd of Claggart's dislike, but has no explanation for it. One night, a sailor awakens Budd and instructs him to go to another area of the ship. When Budd goes, the sailor tries to involve Budd in a mutiny against Captain Vere. Budd refuses, but Claggart reports him, and after Captain Vere summons Budd, Claggart blames him for inciting a mutiny. Budd, a stutterer so angered by the false accusation that he cannot speak to defend himself, strikes Claggart. Claggart falls, hits his head, and dies. Captain Vere calls a court-martial that finds Budd guilty and sentences him to hang the following day.

Indications of Budd's virtue fill the novel. The captain of the *Rights of Man* wishes another of his men had been impressed instead of Budd because "I was worried to that degree my pipe had no comfort for me [about fights aboard ship]. But Billy came; and it was like a Catholic priest striking peace in an Irish shindy. Not that he preached to them or said or did anything in particular; but a virtue went out of him, sugaring the sour ones." All of the men on board ship except Claggart and Sneak admire Budd. Vere worries about Budd's surprise at Claggart's claim. He speaks kindly to Budd when "these words . . . prompted yet more violent efforts at utterance—efforts soon ending for the time in confirming the paralysis." Vere himself regrets that he must accuse Budd, but mutinies on other ships during the same year give him no leeway. "That the one condemned suffered less than he who mainly had effected the condemnation was apparently indicated by the former's exclamation in the scene soon perforce to be touched upon." Vere exclaims, "struck dead by an angel of God! Yet the angel must hang!" Then Vere's agitation over his deci-sion increases as Budd dies, when Budd utters "God bless Captain Vere!" After Budd's death, Vere suffers a fatal blow in a battle with the *Athée* (Atheist), and, as he dies, others hear him calling "Billy Budd! Billy Budd."

Critics have various interpretations of Budd's character and of the novel. One question focuses on whether Vere should have immediately executed Budd. He could have waited until the ship arrived in port but did not. Since Vere seems to be the fulcrum between Claggart and Budd, he might have been more moderate. One must also examine Budd's role. He has been compared to Adam, the innocent, pitted against Claggart, the serpent. Perhaps the most obvious symbolism connects Budd to Christ and Claggart to Judas Iscariot. On the *Rights of Man*, Budd was a peacemaker, a leader whom the other men respected. When he cannot speak after Claggart's charges, his face contorts in "an expression which was as a crucifixion to behold." As Budd dies, he utters "God bless Captain Vere!" recalling Jesus' words from the cross, and "at the same moment it chanced that the vapory fleece hanging low in the East was shot through with a soft glory as of the fleece of the Lamb of God seen in mystical vision, and simultaneously therewith, watched by the wedged mass of upturned faces, Billy ascended; and, ascending, took the full rose of the dawn." For years afterward, "to them [sailors] a chip of it [the spar from which Billy Budd hung] was as a piece of the Cross." Budd does his duty on a ship as an impressed sailor but suffers evil at the hands of a jealous man with the ultimate power over him.

For Whom the Bell Tolls by Ernest Hemingway

In *For Whom the Bell Tolls* (1940, the title taken from John Donne's "No Man Is an Island"), Ernest Hemingway introduces Robert Jordan through omniscient point of view. The formal language resembles a literal translation from the Spanish where characters use "thou" instead of "you" when speaking familiarly to each other. Jordan, an American professor of Spanish, comes to Spain during the Spanish Civil War to fight with the International Brigade against the fascists. When he accepts an assignment to eliminate a bridge, he has already blown up three trains in Estremadura. (Kashkin, the man first appointed to destroy the bridge, was mortally wounded from trying to blow up a train. He asked Jordan to shoot him ten days later.) Jordan joins other guerillas behind enemy lines while waiting to strike. Disloyalty by one of the group causes the death of another and eventually the death of Jordan himself.

The illiterate guerillas come from varied backgrounds and have their own agendas. Anselmo, sixty-eight, takes Jordan to the group's leader, Pablo. He tells Jordan, "I am against all killing of men. . . . with or without God, I think it is a sin to kill. To take the life of another is to me very grave. I will do it whenever necessary but I am not of the race of Pablo." While on guard duty, Anselmo does not see the enemy General Staff on the nearby road, and after Pablo ruins the initial plan to blow up the bridge by stealing the explosives, Anselmo dies when the secondary plan causes a shard of steel to penetrate his body. As soon as Jordan meets Pablo, he agrees with Anselmo's assessment and worries about Pablo's attitude. He observes, "The sadness is bad. That's the sadness they get before they quit or before they betray. That is the sadness that comes before the sell-out." Jordan accurately assesses Pablo's weakness, but Pablo's wife Pilar has strength to counteract it. Pilar tells Jordan her husband is a drunkard and that Pablo's men shot fascist guards in the head and tortured others before throwing them off a cliff. Pablo had to flee when the fascists regained the town three days later. Pilar laments her ugliness, but philosophizes, "For what are we born if not to aid one another? And to listen and say nothing is a cold enough aid." After taking Jordan to meet El Sordo, the guerilla leader of the region, she examines Jordan's hand but refuses to tell his fortune. She then offers Maria, a lovely young woman raped and tortured when imprisoned in Valladolid, to him. Jordan and Maria immediately fall in love.

Jordan seems to thrive on danger or the exotic. After Jordan accepts his perilous duty to destroy the bridge, he must trust those whom he does not know just as they must rely on him without knowledge of his past. Jordan thinks, "He was lucky that he had lived parts of ten years in Spain before the war. . . . They trusted you on understanding the language completely and speaking it idiomatically and having a knowledge of the different places. A Spaniard was only really loyal to his village in the end. First Spain of course, then his own tribe, then his province, then his village, his family and finally his trade." He enjoyed the company of Karkov, an intelligent Russian in Madrid, but he notes that, after talking to Karkov and his friends, they "corrupt[ed] very easily." In a way, Jordan commits suicide (as his father had) by choosing an alternate method to blow out the bridge. Although he has enjoyed fierce storms, the final one he experiences becomes his grave. "Sure, the snow. That had done it. The snow. Done it to others. Once you saw it again as it was to others, once you got rid of your own self, the always ridding of self that you had to do in war. Where there could be no self. Where yourself is only to be lost." After his horse falls on him and breaks his leg, he convinces Maria to evacuate by saying that only through her can he continue to live. His sacrifice allows the other guerillas to escape, and he completes his duty.

The Killer Angels by Michael Shaara

Michael Shaara's *The Killer Angels* (1974) also reveals the behavior of soldiers in a civil war. After introducing the main officers involved in the Battle of Gettysburg in 1863, Shaara focuses on their decisions during four days—Monday, June 29, Wednesday, July 1, Thursday, July 2, and Friday, July 3. Union officers include Joshua Lawrence Chamberlain (thirty-four), a Phi Beta Kappa professor of rhetoric at Bowdoin using his supposed 1862 sabbatical to Europe to become a soldier. He sings and speaks seven languages. John Buford (thirty-seven), the first leader to Gettysburg, "is a man who knows the value of ground." John Reynolds (forty-two), a West Point graduate and the best soldier in the Union Army, refuses command of the army, and George Gordon Meade (forty-seven), a vain and self-pitying man, takes over. Winfield Scott Hancock (thirty-nine) waits for his friend Lew Armistead (a Confederate) at the top of Cemetery Hill. For the Army of Northern Virginia, Robert E. Lee (fifty-seven) trusts his second in command, James Longstreet (forty-two), for honest answers and depends on other officers in varying degrees. Last in his West Point class, although anticipating Gettysburg, is George Pickett (thirty-eight), who wears his long hair perfumed. Wealthy Ambrose Powell Hill (thirty-seven) feels socially inferior and dislikes following orders. Lewis Armistead (forty-six), a widower and West Point graduate, is best friends with the Union's Hancock. Richard Brooke Garnett (forty-four) wants to regain his honor lost after Stonewall Jackson court-martialed him. Banjo-playing Jeb Stuart (thirty) failed his duty to inform Lee of the Union Army's movements before Gettysburg. New to a command is the indecisive, one-legged Richard Ewell (forty-six) who eventually allows Jubal Early (forty-six), a lawyer concerned about his reputation, to influence him. Longstreet despises Early, but Lee calls him "my bad old man."

The actions of these men control the battle's progression. When Lee hears from his spy Harrison on Monday, June 29, that nearly 100,000 Union soldiers waited only 200 miles away and that Major General George Meade had replaced "Fighting" Joe Hooker as commander, Lee decides to take advantage of the chaos surrounding a change in leadership by striking at Gettysburg. On July 1, the Confederates attack at dawn. Buford's calvary is dismounted, and after Reynolds arrives to help Buford with infantry reinforcements, Confederates kill Reynolds. However, the Army of Northern Virginia's advantage dissipates with unanticipated problems. Powell Hill becomes ill. Harry Heth misjudges the combined troops of Buford and Reynolds, thinking them to be only a "few militia men." Then Lee mistakenly sends Heth to support another group, allegedly attacking the Union soldiers. General Ewell follows Early's advice to ignore Lee's order to take the hill south of Gettysburg, and the Union subsequently gains control of Cemetery Hill. On July 2, Lee and Longstreet discuss tactics, and, ignoring Longstreet's advice, Lee decides to attack the Union soldiers in the hills. Then Longstreet must redirect 17,000 men (two divisions) because their march will expose them to the enemy. Longstreet's men attack the Union army because of Lee's command, and 8,000 men die before General Pickett arrives with 5,000 reinforcements. Then, on the final day, Lee mistakenly commands Longstreet to attack the middle of the Union line.

On the Union side, the leaders have more luck. Chamberlain's thoughtful treatment of the 120 mutinous men of the 20th Regiment of Infantry, Maine Volunteers, keeps them loyal. When given command of the men, he convinces them to remain after wondering, "How do you force a man to fight—for freedom? The idiocy of it jarred him." On July 2, Colonel Vincent orders Chamberlain not to withdraw from his new position at the left flank of the Union line, informing him that he must remain at the spot until the fighting ceases. His "ragtag" regiment holds the Union charge together as it anticipates the Rebels' advances. As Chamberlain observes the battle, he hears the shouts and screams of the officers to their men and reflects that "even above your own fear came the sensation of unspeakable beauty." He thinks of Aristotle's formula for tragedy—pity and fear. He then knows that "in the presence of real tragedy you feel neither pain nor joy nor hatred, only a sense of enormous space and time suspended, the great doors open to black eternity, the rising across the terrible field of that last enormous, unanswerable question." On July 3, Chamberlain's regiment protects the end of the Union line, and soon his exhausted men are moved to the center, thought to be the safest spot on the battlefield. But Lee attacks the middle of the line, and again Chamberlain's men rescue the

Union. During this Confederate defeat, 23,000 men for the Union and 28,000 for the Confederacy die.

The omniscient point of view suggests what these men might have been thinking during this awful week. Chamberlain listens to the Irishman Buster Kilrain announce his beliefs about the American attitude toward race. He thinks that only "peawits" evaluate other humans according to the group to which they belong. He recalls blacks for whom he has great respect and asserts that race remains unimportant. He expounds, "what matters is justice. 'Tis why I'm here. I'll be treated as I deserve, not as my father deserved." Chamberlain realizes as he observes the actions of the men on the battlefield that each decision the generals make, whether irresponsible or intelligent, affects the men's lives like a God. He thinks that "the General and God . . . have your future in their hands and they have all power and know all." However, Lee knows the elusiveness of this perceived power. As the commander of the generals, the supreme "God," Lee understands that he has no control over the results of his decisions although he has *all* the responsibility for the Confederate soldiers. Lee says to Longstreet, "to be a good soldier you must love the army. But to be a good officer you must be willing to order the death of the thing you love. . . . That is one reason why there are so very few good officers." Longstreet loves Lee, but at the same time, he objectively observes that "honor without intelligence is a disaster." He disapproves of some of those who have positions of leadership and concludes that the Confederates cannot win at Gettysburg. Lee assuages Longstreet's distress by downplaying the battle as merely one defeat in a string of battles to come. He questions, "If the war goes on—and it will, it will . . . does it matter after all who wins?'" The Frenchman Fremantle, who observes the battle, appropriately analyzes the conflict. "The North has those huge bloody cities and a thousand religions, and the only aristocracy is the aristocracy of wealth. The Northerner doesn't give a damn for tradition, or breeding, or the Old Country. He hates the Old Country. . . . Well, of course the South *is* the Old Country. They haven't left Europe. They've merely transplanted it. And *that's* what the war is about."

All these protagonists fulfill an externally imposed duty. Robert E. Lee said in his "Farewell to the Army of Northern Virginia" on 22 April 1865 that "you may take with you the satisfaction that proceeds from the consciousness of duty faithfully performed, and I earnestly pray that a merciful God will extend to you his blessing and protection." Billy Budd serves loyally on a ship he did not choose. Robert Jordan accepts a duty to destroy a bridge, hoping to stifle fascism in the Spanish Civil War. And the men who fought in the American Civil War accepted their duty rather than have the lives of those around them endangered. Budd and Jordan could repeat Lee's words when he resigned from the army, "I did only what my duty demanded," and be proud of their decisions.

Additional Related Novels

Cormier, Robert. *After the First Death.*
Faulkner, William. *As I Lay Dying.*
Hersey, John. *A Bell for Adano.*
O'Brien, Tim. *Going after Cacciato.*
Potok, Chaim. *The Chosen.*
Proulx, E. Annie. *The Shipping News.*

Emotional Abuse

Emotional abuse [is] "in-your-soul abuse" because the harm inflicted isn't outwardly apparent, like bruises or broken bones. The damage goes much deeper.

—RosaLinda Garcia Gusman (1999)

Those who want to control others employ a variety of methods, but one that has remained effective through the centuries is that of emotional abuse. Often victims of emotional abuse have difficulty establishing their identity because they see themselves through the eyes of another who has made them feel inadequate. Orleanna Price in *The Poisonwood Bible* tolerates her husband Nathan's attitude that only he can have the answers to life's problems and feels unqualified to dispute his decisions. In *Light in August*, Joe Christmas hears the orphanage janitor call him "nigger" and, although he does not understand the term, derives from the man's tone of voice that he must be inferior to the other children. The hospital staff in *One Flew Over the Cuckoo's Nest* berates the patients and makes them feel incapable of regaining mental health. When the protagonists in the three novels, *The Scarlet Letter*, *Invisible Man*, and *Ellen Foster*, hear other people say terrible and untruthful things about them, they have difficulty separating themselves from these accusations.

One of the most painful ways to hurt other people is to abuse them without causing physical harm. "To wrong with words; to speak injuriously of or to; to malign, revile" (*OED*) can be devastating for the victim. Such abuse causes emotional pain that often leaves permanent scars on that person's psychological health. One of Thomas Otway's characters in *The Orphan* asks, "What have I done? and why do you abuse me?" (1705). In *Arcadia*, Sir Philip Sidney asks, "Was it not enough for him to have deceived me, and through the deceit abused me, and after the abuse forsaken me?" (1580). Emotional abuse of the elderly "can involve namecalling, scolding or shouting or ignoring, intimidating or threatening" (The Sudbury Elder Abuse Committee, 1997). A 1990 study showed that "72 percent of victims reported that emotional abuse, especially ridicule, was harder to bear than physical abuse" (*Journal of Family Violence*). In *The Scarlet Letter*, *Invisible Man*, and *Ellen Foster*, another character abuses each protagonist, but all three eventually form a realistic concept of their capabilities.

The Scarlet Letter by Nathaniel Hawthorne

Hester Prynne in Nathaniel Hawthorne's *The Scarlet Letter* (1850) lives in the mid-seventeenth-century world of the Puritans, "a people among whom religion and law were almost identical." In the novel's introduction, a custom's house official in Salem, Massachusetts, writes about a scarlet letter "A" that he found hidden in old papers. He places the item on his chest, and it feels "as if the letter were not of red cloth, but red-hot iron." The documents identify its owner as Hester Prynne, a woman who became a voluntary nurse in her old age and gave advice in "matters of the heart." Hester's society condemned her to wear the letter because she had born a child out of wedlock to an unnamed father after two years of waiting for her husband to follow her to Boston. People in Boston begin to abuse her emotionally by calling her "corrupt" and "preordained to damnation." The novel's omniscient point of view allows several characters to fulfill the symbolism of their names. Chillingworth, Hester's husband, destroys while Dimmesdale, her lover, fails to "see the light" and confesses too late to save himself. Pearl, Hester's daughter, has a "great price" and is herself the embodiment of the scarlet letter.

Everyone Hester encounters blames and abuses long after Pearl's birth. Some condemn her for embroidering the "A" and think "it were well if we stripped Madame Hester's rich gown off her dainty shoulders." People declare that "this woman has brought shame upon us all, and ought to die," and children mock her. Even the minister Arthur Dimmesdale, revered by his congregation, implores her to reveal the father's name. The irony, of course, is that Dimmesdale *is* Pearl's father. Some call Hester a witch and believe that only "the child saved her from Satan's snare." Even preachers condemn her in their sermons. When Roger Chillingworth, her husband, arrives and discovers the situation, he forbids her to reveal his identity while he searches for her lover. Hester reluctantly obeys him, and Chillingworth condemns her, saying, "by thy first step awry, thou didst plant the germ of evil." After several years, when Hester tries to save the sickly Dimmesdale, she loosens her hair and discards her scarlet letter on the ground, but Pearl wants Hester to reattach the "A." Although Hester "had not known the weight until she felt the freedom," she agrees to Pearl's request instead of fleeing with Dimmesdale. After Dimmesdale and Chillingworth die, people begin to see her good qualities and begin to think of the "A" as meaning "able" or "angel."

Hester's real identity is very different from the one imposed upon her by those who taunt her in the street. She lives on the edge of town in an abandoned cottage, choosing to bear the shame of her "sin" for both herself and Dimmesdale so that his role in the community will not be compromised. She knows that "the young and pure would be taught to look at her . . . as the figure, the body, the reality of sin." The scarlet letter "had the effect of a spell, taking her out of the ordinary relations with humanity and enclosing her in a sphere by herself." Later, she reminds Chillingworth that she never pretended to love him and that he misled her into marriage. To financially support Pearl,

Hester embroiders fine cloth for the magistrates in town. She demonstrates her concern for the poor by making them clothes and giving them alms. Distressed about Dimmesdale's failing health, she queries Chillingworth as to why he has not "avenged thyself on me." Chillingworth knows that "when strangers looked curiously at the scarlet letter—and none ever failed to do so—they branded it afresh into Hester's soul." For Hester, "the spot never grew callous; it seemed, on the contrary, to grow more sensitive with daily torture." Hester leaves town with Pearl after Chillingworth and Dimmesdale die, but she later returns alone and becomes a volunteer nurse helping others who suffer with "matters of the heart."

Invisible Man by Ralph Ellison

In Ralph Ellison's *Invisible Man* (1952), the unnamed first-person narrator accepts the emotional abuse foisted upon him by those in power, both black and white, until he finally realizes that only he can create his identity. In a prologue, epilogue, and twenty-five chapters, this picaresque bildungsroman traces the narrator's journey from high school to Harlem. Ellison's dense style, reminiscent of William Faulkner, follows the progress of the narrator into a New York City manhole that he brightens with 1,369 electric lights tapped into Monopolated Light and Power. Ellison incorporates several twentieth-century literary movements in his basically naturalistic novel including the emotionalism of expressionism in the narrator's speeches for the Brotherhood and his comparison of unlike images in surrealism. A stripper's "hair was yellow like that of a circus kewpie-doll . . . the eyes hollow and smeared a cool blue, the colour of a baboon's butt." A white figure hanging from a lamppost during the Harlem race riot shocks him. At another point, the narrator compares his "eyes bulg[ing] and my tongue . . . [hanging] out" to "wagg[ing] like the door of an empty house in a high wind." An existentialist stance appears in the statement, "I am invisible, understand, simply because people refuse to see me." The constant memory of his grandfather's words before dying helps the narrator overcome his inertness in face of abuse of which he is initially unaware. His grandfather told him on his deathbed, "son, after I'm gone I want you to keep up the good fight. . . . our life is a war and I have been a traitor all my born days, a spy in the enemy's country ever since I give up my gun back in the Reconstruction. Live with your head in the lion's mouth. I want you to overcome 'em with yeses, undermine 'em with grins, agree 'em to death and destruction, let 'em swollen you till they vomit or bust wide open." The narrator often ponders this advice. Many years later, those words, and the words of the mad veteran on the bus to New York telling him that he could succeed without becoming a "complete fool" by calculating how to control those with power over him, help the narrator ignore emotional abuse and gain command of his identity.

The narrator does not understand the significance of many events until after the Brotherhood rehires him and his blindness to his situation disappears. While still in high school, he wins an essay contest for a college scholarship, but he has to box with another boy, walk on an electrified floor to pick up coins, and wait for a white stripper to finish her display before reading his acceptance speech at the benefactors' awards dinner. The indifferent white men seem too drunk to listen until he substitutes the word "equality" for "responsibility" after "social." In college, the president Dr. Bledsoe assigns him to drive the white trustee, Mr. Norton. The narrator unintentionally introduces Norton to Trueblood, a self-confessed child molester, before taking him to the Golden Day (a black bar and whorehouse). There he encounters a group of veterans from a nearby mental hospital including a black surgeon whom the Ku Klux Klan drove from the city for having the knowledge to save the life of another man. Dr. Bledsoe, a black man with a symbolic name (like Trueblood), calls the narrator "nigger" and expels him from college. Dr. Bledsoe informs the narrator that he will not lose his position by helping a mere student. Bledsoe understands that he can command his white trustees by limiting what they know and admits that "I'll have every Negro in the country hanging on tree limbs by morning if it means staying where I am." Dr. Bledsoe taunts him, "You're nobody, son. You don't exist—can't you see that?" With seven sealed letters from Dr. Bledsoe to deliver to prospective employers, the narrator leaves for New York. Not until distributing the last letter does he discover that Bledsoe has advised the men not to hire him. Against Bledsoe's recommendation, Mr. Emerson employs him at Liberty Paint making white ("white is right") paint. But the narrator fails when he contaminates the paint both literally and symbolically. After an accident, electric shock treatments deliberately administered at the hospital make him forget his identity. Back on the street, he meets Mary Rambo, the archetypal mother, who nurtures him until the Brotherhood recruits him.

The narrator keeps searching for himself, but abusive situations continue to sidetrack him. One day, he becomes enraged at the eviction of an elderly couple. When his speech mobilizes the crowd, Brother Jack follows him and suggests that he become the next Booker T. Washington by joining the Brotherhood as a spokesman. The narrator advocates peaceful relations with whites, unlike the black radical Ras the Exhorter, and discovers that others will follow him. Everyone who hears him speak, regardless of their trade or profession, wants something to improve their lives. But the adulation is unsatisfying, and he becomes aware of the blindness in others. "Well, I *was* and yet I was invisible, that was the fundamental contradiction. I was and yet I was unseen." One day he disguises himself with a zoot suiter's dark glasses to hide from Ras, and several people mistake him for someone they call "Rinehart." He hears that Rinehart is lover, gambler, policeman, or minister, depending on the person to whom he speaks. The narrator suddenly comprehends that one must wear a different disguise for each person. He begins to suspect that only people like Rinehart could be comfortable with themselves and their lives. "It was unbelievable, but perhaps only the unbelievable could be believed. Perhaps the truth was always a lie." The Brotherhood, however, continues to manipulate him until he revitalizes himself during the race riot and rejects the emotional abuses of his past. Not until he confronts Ras with his intense emotions—hatred and contempt not only for whites but also for blacks who associated with them—does the narrator know "who I was and where I was and knowing too that I had no longer to run for or from the Jacks and the Emersons and the Bledsoes and Nortons, but only from their confusion, impatience, and refusal to recognize the beautiful absurdity of their American identity and mine." When the narrator then stumbles into a manhole, he metaphorically finds himself, and suggests that "who knows but that, on the lower frequencies, I speak for you?" Then he completes the cyclical form of the novel with the statement, "The end was in the beginning."

Ellen Foster by Kaye Gibbons

In *Ellen Foster* (1987), Ellen's emotional abuse occurs over 300 years after Hester's in *The Scarlet Letter*. In the rural South during the 1970s, the orphaned Ellen thinks of herself as "old Ellen" even though she is only eleven. Kaye Gibbons begins the novel with the sentence, "When I was little I would think of ways to kill my daddy." Ellen uses a series of flashbacks to reconstruct her life with her mother and father, a "big wind-up toy of a man," before she came to live with the "Fosters" and a "new mama." Her wealthy mother had chosen to marry a man of whom the family disapproved, and the family emotionally abused the offspring of this union. When Ellen's mother returned from the hospital at forty after treatment for a heart condition, her father chastised her for not cooking supper. He complained about having to cook and clean while she was away as if she had been vacationing. Ellen, however, knows that her father did nothing. Ellen says that her mother "has not had a good heart" since she suffered from "romantic fever" as a child (these phrases metaphorically describe her mother's choice of husband). Soon Ellen's mother kills herself, but, at the funeral, the minister makes no mention of suicide, an omission that disturbs Ellen. Ellen remains with her father, but he deserts her for days at a time. Buying food for herself with money her uncle leaves in the mailbox for her father, Ellen becomes obsessed with clothing, money, and food. For entertainment, she has read *Canterbury Tales* and is reading the Brontës. (In her narration, however, she betrays her poor grammar.) At Christmas, she buys and wraps herself an inexpensive microscope. One night her father brings home African-American acquaintances who laugh at her carefully collected frozen dinners and suggest that she is old enough for her father to enjoy her sexually, another example of emotional abuse. Ellen locks herself in the closet. Although her situation is horrible, she still considers herself more fortunate than someone who is "colored." As a southerner, she embodies the prejudices of her time and, in turn, unwittingly inflicts emotional abuse on her black friend Starletta.

Ironically, the people who should welcome Ellen, her family, refuse her comfort. She says, "So many folks thinking and wanting you to be somebody else will confuse you if you are not very careful." Ellen runs away from her father to her Aunt Betsy's home but has to leave after one weekend. When her father dies at Christmas, she moves into her "mama's mama's" home. Her grandmother slaps her for grieving because she sees the father in Ellen and thus blames Ellen for everything. Her grandmother continues to emotionally abuse her by making her chop cotton. Then her grandmother dies, and, unhappy that she has to face a third death in her life, even if her grandmother abused her, Ellen places a hat on her grandmother's head and spreads flowers around her dead body before the mortician arrives. In her next home with her Aunt Nadine and spoiled cousin Dora, she finds out about the "Foster" woman at church whom Dora has said takes in "orphans to stray cats." Thinking that "fit[s] my description perfect," she decides to ask Mrs. Foster to let her move in.

When Ellen accepts help from nonfamily members, she realizes that her prejudices are unjustified. Starletta, a mute, has kind parents who welcome Ellen into their home and give her a winter coat even though they are poor with "little sticks all between the floorboards." When Ellen lives with her grandmother, Mavis befriends her in the fields and treats her kindly. Ellen loves living with her art teacher Julia and her husband because they plant a garden, read the comics aloud to each other on Sundays, and go to the movies. She is amazed when Julia tells her that she would like to rid the world of people like Ellen's father. Hearing that more men like her father, "a monster," ruin the lives of others disturbs her. She remarks, "My daddy was a mistake for a person." Ellen's "new mama" offers her safety, and Ellen wants to stay where it is warm and loving, and she can say, "I had me a egg sandwich." As Ellen reflects on the time before meeting her "new mama," she offers astute advice. "Now I know it is not the germs you cannot see . . . that will hurt you or turn you colored. What you had better worry about though is the people you knew and trusted they would be like you because you were all made in the same batch. You need to look over your shoulder at the one who is in charge of holding you up and see if that is a knife he has in his hand. And it might not be a colored hand. But it is a knife."

Perhaps the cry of all three of these protagonists—Hester, Ellen, and the narrator of *Invisible Man*—might be the narrator's insight. "You ache with the need to convince yourself that you do exist in the real world, that you're a part of all the sound and anguish, and you strike out with your fists, you curse and you swear to make them recognize you. And, alas, it's seldom successful." Only when people escape the pain from emotional abuse can they begin to create an identity that reveals their unique personalities.

Additional Related Novels

Dorris, Michael. *A Yellow Raft in Blue Water*.
Faulkner, William. *Light in August*.
Fitzgerald, F. Scott. *Tender Is the Night*.
Hurston, Zora Neale. *Their Eyes Were Watching God*.
Kesey, Ken. *One Flew Over the Cuckoo's Nest*.
Kingsolver, Barbara. *The Poisonwood Bible*.
Steinbeck, John. *Of Mice and Men*.
Wilson, Harriet E. *Our Nig*.

Family

We pass . . . through the love of our family . . . to love Mankind.
—J.H.B. de Saint-Pierre, *Studies of Nature*
(Henry Hunter, trans., 1796)

Families are as diverse as the individuals they contain. They may have one or two parents, stepparents, or grandparents. Sometimes families consist of only one parent and one child. Other families may incorporate children from several marriages trying to adjust to their surroundings. A few protagonists such as Billy Budd (*Billy Budd*) and Jadine (*Tar Baby*) are either orphaned or were abandoned as babies. Others exist as part of a family group, whether one other person or ten. In *Cold Sassy Tree*, Will Tweedy's family, including his new grandmother, influences his decisions. Only Macon Dead's aunt Pilate loves enough to help him find his family identity in *Song of Solomon*. The four sisters in *How the Garcia Girls Lost Their Accents* never escape their father's psychological control, even after marriage. The Chinese-American daughter in *The Woman Warrior* knows that her mother's seemingly extraneous stories are warnings about situations to avoid in life. In the three novels, *The Sound and the Fury*, *A Tree Grows in Brooklyn*, and *The Grapes of Wrath*, the family's interaction determines the protagonist's future.

Defining "family" in terms of humans seems obvious—a group of people related by blood. Through the nineteenth century, however, "family" also referred to servants and other members of a household. "His family were himself and his wife and daughters, two mayds, and a man" (reports of cases in the courts of Star chamber and High commission, 1631). The current usage refers to persons related by either blood or law. The Western concept of a family containing two opposite-sex parents, a boy, and a girl has often misled children about what a family should be. A family may include one parent and one child, several stepparents in addition to biological parents, and any number of half-siblings or stepsiblings. In these three novels examining family, *The Sound and the Fury*, *A Tree Grows in Brooklyn*, and *The Grapes of Wrath*, none of the protagonists have stepparents, but the parents' stability or lack of it irreversibly affects their children.

The Sound and the Fury by William Faulkner

William Faulkner's *The Sound and the Fury* (1929) presents a dysfunctional family through the eyes of its three sons and the woman who raised them and their sister. The stream-of-consciousness style allows each of the narrators to present a different aspect of the Compson family's life and, in the end, expose its disintegration. Descendants in an old southern family proud of its heritage, the Compson parents perpetuate an aristocratic attitude of privilege. But under the veneer, the reader finds a weak, self-absorbed mother, an alcoholic father, and their four children—a mongoloid son, a second son choosing death when he cannot retain the past, another son filled with greed, and a daughter who seeks acceptance through sexual encounters. The three sons as narrators respond to their situations, and their black maid, the decent and moral Dilsey, discloses her ways of holding the family together.

Three narrators, Benjy, Jason, and Dilsey, reveal the action in the novel. Benjy's section begins on 7 April 1928 as he hears golfers yell "Caddie!" on land that was once his favorite pasture before his father sold it to pay Quentin's Harvard tuition in 1909 and fund Caddy's wedding. Benjy's emotional response to the word reflects his feelings for Caddy, his sister and the one family member who has shown him love. Although thirty-three, Benjy only reacts to thoughts and feelings; he has no sense of past or present. Faulkner marks the time sequence of Benjy's thoughts with the different black men affiliated with him and Dilsey—Versh, T. P., Frony, and Luster. Benjy associates his grandmother's death with the young Caddy's muddy drawers showing after she climbs in a tree to peek into a window during the funeral. He also communicates Caddy's behavior while sitting in a swing with Charlie, one of her lovers. Jason's narrative takes place the previous day, 6 April 1928. Jason berates the dress and perceived attitudes of Miss Quentin, Caddy's seventeen-year-old daughter who lives with the family. Although Jason refuses for Caddy to visit, Caddy sends checks to support Quentin each month that Mrs. Compson refuses to cash. Jason intercepts the mail and gives his mother counterfeit checks that she then burns. Jason cashes the real ones and hides the money. Jason further reveals his selfishness and cruelty by burning free tickets for a traveling show in front of Luster, the fourteen year old who attends Benjy, because Luster does not have a nickel to pay for them. Dilsey's section, the final narrative, occurs on Easter Sunday, 8 April 1928. Unlike the other three, Faulkner tells Dilsey's story in limited omniscient point of view. Dilsey recalls buying a birthday cake for Benjy from her own money so that she would not have to listen to Jason's tirades against spending. On this day, Dilsey takes Benjy to church with her. When she hears that some members object to the "loony" white man, she responds, "Tell um de good Lawd don't keer whether he bright er not." Dilsey reveals that Miss Quentin "stole" her own money from Jason and ran away (a scene that Benjy observes in his narrative) and that Jason is frantically trying to find her. Unlike the others, Dilsey focuses on the present and creates the order that Benjy must have to survive his fragmented perception of life.

Quentin, on the other hand, focuses on the past. Faulkner places Quentin's section after Benjy's, but chronologically it occurs eighteen years prior. Quentin divulges his thoughts and actions on 2 June 1910, the day he commits suicide, thinking of himself as "i temporary." He has been unable to accept Caddy's lovers or her marriage in April 1910 to a man not the father of her unborn child. Quentin even told his father that he committed incest with her, but his father knows better.

In the South you are ashamed of being a virgin. Boys. Men. They lie about it. Because it means less to women, Father said. He said it was men invented virginity not women. Father said it's like death: only a state in which the others are left and I said, But to believe it doesn't matter and he said, That's what's so sad about anything: not only, virginity, and I said, Why couldn't it have been me and not her who is unvirgin and he said, That's why that's sad too; nothing is even worth the changing of it.

Time obsesses Quentin, and he wants to recapture his happiness while playing with Caddy as a child. Throughout the day, he references time in a variety of ways—"I suppose it takes at least one hour to lose time in"; "I passed a jeweler's window, but I looked away in time"; "I hope I haven't taken up your time"; "Father said clocks slay time. He said time is dead as long as it is being clicked off by little wheels—only when the clock stops does time come to life." Quentin's father gave him his Grandfather's watch, saying, "I give you the mausoleum of all hope and desire. . . . I give it to you not that you may remember time, but that you might forget it now and then for a moment and not spend all your breath trying to conquer it. Because no battle is ever won he said. They are not even fought. The field only reveals to man his own folly and despair, and the victory is an illusion of philosophers and fools." On the day Quentin commits suicide, he breaks the watch. Ironically, Quentin is the one hope for the family, at Harvard to pursue a different life, but he cannot sustain the present to create a future and symbolically kills the family along with himself.

A Tree Grows in Brooklyn by Betty Smith

A very different family appears in Betty Smith's *A Tree Grows in Brooklyn* (1943). The action starts in 1912 when Francie is eleven in the Williamsburg section of Brooklyn. Using omniscient point of view, Smith describes the Irish family of Francie, her brother Neely, ten, and her parents. Her mother Katie works as a janitress and her father, a member of the waiters' union, is a "free lance singing waiter." About her father the narrator says, "He was still gay and young and handsome. His wife had not turned bitter against him and his children did not know that they were supposed to be ashamed of him." Francie adores him. When Francie is six, the family moves to a tenement near a "tree which looked like a lot of opened green umbrellas. Some people called it the Tree of Heaven." Throughout this bildungsroman, Francie focuses on family and the value of education, influenced by her mother's belief: "It was education that made the difference. Education would pull them out of the grime and dirt." After learning to read, Francie reads a book a day beginning with the "As" and treats herself to any book in the alphabet on Saturdays. She eventually has a teacher who encourages her writing and instructs her, "in the future, when something comes up, you *tell* exactly how it happened but *write down for yourself the way you think it should have happened. Tell* the truth and *write* the story. Then you won't get mixed up."

Francie's extended family has a tremendous influence on her life. The narrator reveals the courtship and marriage of her parents and reveals that Francie was born with a caul, supposedly a charm. Additional information delineates the attributes of her aunts and uncles. Her mothers' sisters were "all slender, frail creatures with wondering eyes and soft fluttery voices" but "were made out of thin invisible steel." About Francie, the narrator reveals:

[She] was of all the Rommelys and all the Nolans. She had the violent weaknesses and passion for beauty of the shanty Nolans. She was a mosaic of her grandmother Rommely's mysticism, her tale-telling, her great belief in everything and her compassion for the weak ones. She had a lot of her grandfather Rommely's cruel will. She had some of her Aunt Evy's talent for mimicking, some of Ruthie Nolan's possessiveness. She had Aunt Sissy's love for life and her love for children. She had Johnny's sentimentality without his good looks. She had all of Katie's soft ways and only half of the invisible steel of Katie. She was made up of all these good and these bad things.

Her Aunt Sissy defends her by informing a teacher who ignores her students' physical needs that Francie has a medical problem and must relieve herself during class time.

After Francie's father's death in the fourth part of the novel, Francie must reassess her future. Following on her career as a "rag-picker" when she and her brother took items they had found to the junk dealer, she begins to work as a stemmer (covering wires for flowers) and then as a file clerk for the Model Press Clipping Bureau. She wants to go to high school, but her mother can only afford to send Neely, the male. Francie, therefore, starts night school. At sixteen, she passes exams and prepares to go to the University of Michigan. Throughout these last few years in Brooklyn, she learns about love, pledging herself to Ben whom she met in summer classes. Her mother marries a bar owner, and the family, without their biological father, seems poised to have a prosperous future. They resemble the tree Francie loved, "this tree in the yard—this tree that men chopped down. . . . This tree that they built a bonfire around, trying to burn up its stump—this tree lived? It lived! And nothing could destroy it."

The Grapes of Wrath by John Steinbeck

The Joad family in John Steinbeck's *The Grapes of Wrath* (1939) has every reason to disintegrate, but it remains, except for one son, united in its struggle to survive during the Depression. The family members find themselves imitating their crops before they begin their journey. "As the sharp sun struck day after day, the leaves of the young corn became less stiff and erect; they bent in a curve at first, and then, as the central ribs of strength grew weak, each leaf tilted downward." The family, like its neighbors, "huddled in their houses . . . tied handkerchiefs over their noses when they went out, and wore goggles to protect their eyes." After losing its Oklahoma land, the Joad family becomes "a people in flight, refugees from dust and shrinking land, from the thunder of tractors and shrinking ownership," traveling to California in search of work and, more important, food. Others call them "Okies," a derogatory term meaning "tramps."

On the journey, each member of the family either functions as part of the unit or disappears. Al, the sixteen year old, interested only in girls and engines, transforms an old Hudson into a truck to carry the twelve family members to California. Initially, Ma, Pa, the pregnant Rose of Sharon, her husband Connie, Grampa, Gramma, Noah (the oldest), Al, Tom (returned from four years in prison for self-defense), Ruthie (the youngest), Jim Casy (a minister Tom met on his way home who believes "there ain't no sin and there ain't no virtue. There's just stuff people do"), and Uncle John, leave the farm. Grampa dies the first night away from home, Gramma dies soon after, and Noah, supposedly retarded, decides to follow a river. Connie disappears one night without telling anyone, including his wife, his plans. Jim Casy stays until he worries about taking their food. He reappears heading a group of striking migrant workers making two and one-half cents a day where the Joads work as "scabs" for five cents. The day Jim and Tom reunite, owners slay Jim, and Tom kills them. Ma helps Tom hide until Ruthie boasts that her brother has killed two others and will kill again if anyone bothers her. Tom then has to leave the family. However, Tom decides to carry on Casy's work elsewhere by continuing to organize the strikers. Al falls in love with Annie, and Ma and Pa acknowledge that her family needs his aid. And while the Joads fight flood waters in a trailer camp, Rose of Sharon (Rosasharn) delivers a dead child.

The Joad family, unlike the families in *The Sound and the Fury* and *A Tree Grows in Brooklyn*, become members of a larger family, a group of people who need each other to survive. They begin to function on a macrocosmic level and some of their actions take on religious symbolism. They set Rose of Sharon's stillborn child adrift on a river like Moses. The family discovers that good for one is better for all, and their decisions seem to come from books containing law—Leviticus, Numbers, Deuteronomy. "As the worlds moved westward, rules became laws, although no one told the families. It is unlawful to foul near the camp; it is unlawful in any way to foul the drinking water; it is unlawful to eat good rich food near one who is hungry, unless he is asked to share." As the novel progresses, Steinbeck's language assumes a biblical tone—"And it came about that owners no longer worked on their farms." To protect their businesses, owners kill the fruit and rot the meat so that people will not steal it or if the prices are low, even when people are starving. Then the Christ figure, Jim Casy, suffers for Tom's crime, and he forgives those who murder him. Like Jesus and the parable of the loaves and fishes, "a man with food fed a hungry man, and thus insured himself against hunger." Then the farm owners lose their ability to intimidate the people. "How can you frighten a man whose hunger is not only in his own cramped stomach but in the wretched bellies of his children? You can't scare him—he has known a fear beyond every other." The starving people eventually refuse to accept this maltreatment. "And in the eyes of the hungry there is a growing wrath. In the souls of the people the grapes of wrath are filling and growing heavy, growing heavy for the vintage." The final acknowledgment of a family of all humans occurs at the end of the novel. When the family escapes to higher ground during the flood and finds shelter in a barn, a son and his dying father need food. To save the father, Rose of Sharon nurses him with the milk that her stillborn child will never drink.

People use the term "family" daily without realizing that each use redefines the term. In the case of *The Sound and the Fury*, the nuclear family consists of six humans who cannot function as a unit. The members of the Neely family in *A Tree Grows in Brooklyn* love and support each other, changing their goals as necessary. In *The Grapes of Wrath*, the Joad family extends itself, first to Jim Casy, and then to the other migrants needing food and shelter. Agreeing with Jim Casy, the Joads become a family that "has one big soul and ever'body's a part of it." Their family, unlike the Compsons or the Neelys, encompasses the human family, unlimited by size or race.

Additional Related Novels

Agee, James. *A Death in the Family.*
Alexie, Sherman. *Reservation Blues.*
Alvarez, Julia. *How the Garcia Girls Lost Their Accents; In the Time of the Butterflies.*
Buck, Pearl S. *The Good Earth.*
Burns, Olive Ann. *Cold Sassy Tree.*
Conroy, Pat. *The Great Santini.*
Doctorow, E. L. *Ragtime.*
Erdrich, Louise. *Love Medicine.*
Fast, Howard. *April Morning.*
Faulkner, William. *Absalom, Absalom! As I Lay Dying.*
Flagg, Fannie. *Fried Green Tomatoes at the Whistle Stop Café.*
Gibbons, Kaye. *Ellen Foster.*
Guest, Judith. *Ordinary People.*
Hawthorne, Nathaniel. *The House of the Seven Gables.*
Kingsolver, Barbara. *The Poisonwood Bible.*
Kingston, Maxine Hong. *The Woman Warrior.*
Maclean, Norman. *A River Runs Through It.*

McMillan, Terry. *Mama.*
Morrison, Toni. *Song of Solomon; Tar Baby.*
Naylor, Gloria. *Linden Hills; Mama Day.*
Ng, Fae Myenne. *Bone.*
Olsen, Tillie. *Tell Me a Riddle.*
Potok, Chaim. *The Chosen.*
Rowson, Susanna. *Charlotte Temple.*
Saroyan, William. *The Human Comedy.*
Sinclair, Upton. *The Jungle.*
Stegner, Wallace. *Angle of Repose.*
Steinbeck, John. *The Pearl.*
Tan, Amy. *The Kitchen God's Wife.*
Tyler, Anne. *Dinner at the Homesick Restaurant.*

Fathers and Sons

> For thousands of years, father and son have stretched wistful hands across the canyon of time, each eager to help the other to his side, but neither quite able to desert the loyalties of his contemporaries. The relationship is always changing and hence always fragile; nothing endures except the sense of difference.
>
> —Alan Valentine (1963)

A stereotypical image of a father-son relationship might be a father throwing balls for his son's batting practice. The actual relationship can be strikingly different. In *Absalom, Absalom!*, Thomas Sutpen will not acknowledge one son and exposes the son he does recognize to illegal cock fights. General Marchand betrays his son Ben in *After the First Death* by asking him to negotiate with terrorists. And Beck Tull deserts his sons in *Dinner at the Homesick Restaurant*. The novels, *Seize the Day, The Great Santini*, and *A River Runs Through It*, present relationships between fathers and sons of different ages and degrees.

The *OED* defines "father" as "one by whom a child is or has been begotten, a male parent, the nearest male ancestor." A son, in the *OED*, refers to a "male child or person in relation to either or to both of his parents," or "one who inherits the spirit, or displays the character, of some person." In Western society, "father" also refers to a spiritual teacher or a mentor who has exhibited a paternal kindness. In some instances, the term can become derogatory if one associates severe paternalism with the person called "father." Ironically, only when one uses the connotation of "father" or "son" does one sense the possibility of an emotional or psychological bond. In the three novels, *Seize the Day, The Great Santini*, and *A River Runs Through It*, each of the sons is the biological child of his father, and, in each case, a son leaves the expectations of his father unfulfilled.

Seize the Day by Saul Bellow

Seize the Day (1956) presents the protagonist, Tommy Wilhelm, during one day of his life. Saul Bellow renders Tommy's story in six sections, the first three examining Tommy's past and his breakfast with his father and the other three covering his relationship with Dr. Tamkin, his surrogate father. In his early forties, Tommy has no job and lives in New York's Gloriana Hotel, where his father, Dr. Adler, a retired professor and internist whom everyone respects, also lives. Tommy has lied to people throughout his life. He claims to have graduated from Penn State but actually left in sophomore year when the swindler Maurice Venice screen-tested him and suggested he go to Hollywood. Tommy changed his name to "Wilhelm," rejecting his Jewish heritage but failed as an actor. He has given his last money to Dr. Tamkin to invest in lard and rye on margin and has nothing left to pay either his rent or his estranged wife. Tommy meets his father at breakfast and requests money, but his father refuses him. Later, Tommy's investment fails. At the end of the day, while mourning at a funeral for someone he does not know, he finally experiences a catharsis.

When Tommy pauses to reflect, he understands his poor choices, but he seems powerless to change. When he recalls his meeting with Venice, "he was about to make his first great mistake. Like, he sometimes thought, I was going to pick up a weapon and strike myself a blow with it." He rationalizes that "the making of mistakes expressed the very purpose of his life and the essence of his being here. Maybe he was supposed to make them and suffer from them on this earth." Other blunders he has made include the rejection of his father and his choice of the fraudulent Dr. Tamkin as a substitute. Leaving his wife Margaret (who will not divorce him) in anticipation of marriage to Olive is another mistake. Tommy does not think others understand him, noting "you had to talk with yourself in the daytime and reason with yourself at night. Who else was there to talk to in a city like New York?" But Wilhelm does have insight about his pretenses. He thinks, "and even Wilky might not be himself. Might the name of his true soul be the one by which his old grandfather had called him—Velvel? The name of a soul, however, must be only that—soul. . . . Where does the true soul get its strength? Why does it have to love truth?"

In his choice of surrogate father, the psychologist Dr. Tamkin, Wilhelm exposes his ultimate lack of wisdom. The superficial Tamkin advises his patients through platitudes, and Tommy believes him. Tamkin's adage that "only the present is real—the here-and-now. Seize the day," guides Tommy's decisions. Tamkin also says, "If thou canst not love, what art thou?" and "A man is only as good as what he loves." Wilhelm, however, cannot identify his love, and his denial of truth foils his search for his "true soul." After Tamkin invests and loses Tommy's money, Tommy realizes that Tamkin has forfeited nothing. However, Dr. Tamkin does impart one valuable insight by recognizing that when some people suffer, they become fearful that if they stop suffering, "they'll have nothing."

Tommy's actions and attitudes throughout his life have undermined his relationship with his biological father. Tommy rejects his father's achievements. "No one seemed satisfied, and Wilhelm was especially horrified by the cynicism of successful people. Cynicism was bread and meat to everyone." Tommy bemoans their relationship while also revealing a glimmer of understanding.

"Dad never was a pal to me when I was young, he reflected. He was at the office or the hospital, or lecturing. He expected me to look out for myself and never gave me much thought. Now he looks down on me. And maybe in some respects he's right." Like other relationships in which "the fathers were no fathers and the sons no sons," they have failed to communicate. Not until the end of the day when Tommy wanders into a funeral parlor with mourners does he show any possibility of facing the reality of his life. The unknown dead man stirs an emotion in Tommy, and his tears become sobs as he looks at "another human creature." Both his real and his surrogate father have abandoned him, and only from facing death does he find the possibility of connecting with truth and his own soul.

The Great Santini by Pat Conroy

Pat Conroy allegedly includes autobiographical elements in *The Great Santini* (1976). His own military family moved often, and when his father had overseas duty, the others returned to Atlanta to stay with Conroy's grandmother. Using omniscient point of view, Conroy creates the story of the Meecham family after Bull, a marine fighter pilot, returns from duty in Barcelona and takes the family from Atlanta to his next assignment in Beaufort, South Carolina. As "middle-class migrants," the Meecham family has moved often, its members unable to establish roots in any community. They gain, according to the narrator, "a vision of America where nothing was permanent and everything possible." Ben (seventeen), his sister Mary Anne (sixteen), and the twins Matt and Karen (thirteen) must compose themselves for reuniting with their father. Ben clarifies that their father's absence gave the family a chance to relax. "For a year, there was a looseness, a freedom from tension, a time when martial law was suspended." The bildungsroman focuses on Ben during this tour of duty beginning in 1962 when he must adjust to a new school and readjust to his father's well-meaning but misconceived tyrannies.

Bull Meecham believes in tradition, loyalty, and the institution over the individual. On the road with his family, Bull will not stop for anyone needing to use the toilet unless he has to go himself. At home, Bull expects Ben to keep his marine uniform ribboned and his shoes polished. Mr. Dacus, Ben's high school principal, tries to reassure Ben about his father's belief in the infallibility of a rule, an attitude that allows him to be a perfect Marine. Ben's father "believes in the institution over the individual even when the individual is his own child.'" In addition to his children, Bull also has altercations with his wife. Grits early become an institutional symbol of their differences. When Lillian first served grits to Bull, he would not eat them. As their marriage lengthened, Lillian's preparation of grits and Bull's refusal of them "had become a resolute ceremony fraught with competition and even with something deeper, something almost mythological that separated them." In Beaufort, Bull appears regularly at Hobie's Grill at 7:15 A.M. because he knows the residents will be discussing the local news and he will learn what Beaufort's citizens expect from their neighbors. And later, in deference to the common good rather than to himself, Bull guides his burning jet over water to keep from crashing in a populated area.

As the oldest son, Ben has become a buffer between his mother and his father's temper and has adjusted to his father's concept of family. His father expects everyone to fulfill specific duties like the Marines. "A family without ritual and order was a rootless tribe subject to boredom and anarchy, lowered heads, pouting mouths, and sorrowing memories of friends left behind." Thus neither the children nor the mother could express feelings of regret for past homes and friends. His parents seem to love each other, but in the relationship, his mother continues to make the sacrifices that his father demands. When the family arrives at its new home, Mrs. Meecham tells Ben, "You've got to watch movers very closely, son. They are brutes like your father. They are destroyers of beautiful things." Soon Ben surveys the neighborhood and meets the new maid's son Toomer who grows and sells flowers while raising bees for honey. When Toomer takes Ben to see a turtle lay its eggs, Ben notices that only when he sings does Toomer not stutter. Then he meets the Jewish Sammy Wetzberger and protects him from Red Pettus, a knife-wielding thug. Later, Red Pettus comes to Toomer's house, and after he mistakenly shoots him, Toomer's dogs attack and kill Red. But the events Ben remembers best occur between him and his father.

Bull expects to win every contest against his children. Soon after they settle in Beaufort, Bull challenges Ben to a basketball game, and the family cheers for Ben. Ben wins, but confides to his mother "Do you know I wake up every day with the possibility of him hitting me? I mean if he gets mad, he goes for me. . . . I'm his primary target. He hones in on me when he's angry.'" Basketball to Ben is special. "This sport in all its absurdity did a special thing for Ben Meecham: it made him happy. The court was a testing ground of purpose. There was a reason. There were goals, rewards, and instant punishments for failure. It was life reduced to a set of rules, an existential life, a life clarified by the eyes of fathers." Ben also wins when Bull hits Lillian, and Ben knocks him over; "a new dimension entered the combat: a father's awareness of a growing son, the son as challenger, the son as threat, the son as successor, the son as man." Lillian thinks that Bull "brags and struts . . . because he's covering up . . . his fear." This flaw may be what allows Ben to endure his father's unbending authority.

Even though Bull acknowledges Ben's approaching adulthood, he retains control over Ben's decisions. He awakens Ben at four o'clock in the morning on his eighteenth birthday to give him his prized first flight jacket. Then Bull takes Ben to the marine base, makes him drink coffee and puff a cigarette. After school, Bull takes Ben to the club and makes him drink a double martini. But Bull's statement at that time indicates his deep love for his son. Bull announces to his comrades, "He has just ordered his first drink and before he begins drinking it, I would like to wish him a long life, a wife as fine as his mother, and a son as fine as he has been. To my son." But Bull also chastises Ben for helping an opponent stand up after being knocked down in a basketball game. And Bull strikes Ben after finding Ben in jail before discovering that Ben's arrest is a mistake. In the end, Ben knows intellectually that Bull wanted the best for him but could not give him what he needed most—affection.

A River Runs Through It by Norman Maclean

Like Conroy in *The Great Santini*, Norman Maclean also uses autobiographical elements in *A River Runs Through It* (1976) including the names of his family members. Maclean's father was a Presbyterian minister who home-schooled his two sons in the morning and allowed them to wander in the nearby woods and fields during the afternoon. The protagonist in the novel, Norman Maclean, recalls his experiences fishing with his father and younger brother Paul on Montana's Big Blackfoot River while growing up. The first-person narrator, now in his thirties, acknowledges that his family made little distinction "between religion and fly fishing." He remembers beginning his story while waiting to go fishing with his brother but admits that "at the time I did not know that stories of life are often more like rivers than books." Paul's later comments affirm Norman; "'all there is to thinking,' he said, 'is seeing something noticeable which makes you see something you weren't noticing which makes you see something that isn't even visible.' "

Norman and Paul have grown up without overtly competing, but Norman indicates that he thinks Paul was superior in some ways. He remembers that Paul had discovered *The Compleat Angler* first and reminisces that Paul always wanted to compete and always believed that he would win. During the summers of World War I, Norman worked in logging camps, but Paul devoted himself to two things, "to fish and not to work." As an adult, Norman attends college and teaches while Paul becomes a reporter who gambles in "big stud poker games" and keeps company with a half-breed Indian woman named Mo-nah-se-tah who likes to have men fight over her. Police call Norman one night when Paul is losing at poker, trying to protect him because he covers the police beat. Norman notes, "We are probably those referred to as 'our brothers' keepers,' possessed of one of the oldest and possibly one of the most futile and certainly one of the most haunting of instincts." Norman can only offer his brother respite from his "demons" by fishing with him as their father taught them because, even though Norman tries, he cannot save Paul.

The lessons of the father stay with the sons. Norman says, "My father was very sure about certain matters pertaining to the universe. To him, all good things—trout as well as eternal salvation—come by grace and grace comes by art and art does not come easy." The sons work at fishing, and Norman and his father watch Paul; "when we saw him catch his fast fish, we never saw the fish but only the artistry of the fisherman." Norman remembers, "Although

[Paul] and I had acquired freedoms as we grew up, we never violated our early religious training of always being on time for church, work, and fishing." For Paul to be late means that something is wrong. After Paul dies, Norman and his father have difficulty understanding why. Norman wants to know, "Tell me, why is it that people who want help do better without it—at least, no worse. Actually, that's what it is, no worse. They take all the help they can get, and are just the same as they always have been." His father responds, "Help . . . is giving part of your self to somebody who comes to accept it willingly and needs it badly." What both Mr. Maclean and Norman can admit is they could not give something that the receiver would not take. Norman's reflections about his father and his brother guide him in his comprehension of life. "Eventually, all things merge into one, and a river runs through it. The river was cut by the world's great flood and runs over rocks from the basement of time. On some of the rocks are timeless raindrops. Under the rocks are the words, and some of the words are theirs. I am haunted by waters." Neither the stern but loving guidance of a father nor the concern of a brother could lighten the darkness in Paul's soul. He remained unable to transfer the art and the beauty of fly fishing to the other parts of his life.

At the end of *Seize the Day*, Tommy has tried to connect with his own father and his chosen surrogate father and failed; he realizes that "he had hidden himself in the center of a crowd" and he "sobs and cries toward the consummation of his heart's ultimate need." He has to admit to himself that he has made poor choices by alienating his caring father, and the reader has feeble hope that he can change. Ben has also lost his father in *The Great Santini*, but neither had power to stop the separation. Ben knows that his father cared in the only way that he could—as a Catholic Marine fighter pilot who believed in country, God, and duty while commanding that his family duplicate his beliefs. In *A River Runs Through It*, the father cares and expresses his love by teaching his sons how to fly fish, something he equates with religion. One son reflects and survives; the other does not. A father often does the best he can for his son, but sometimes the gift is inappropriate, and, if it is, sometimes a son will not accept it.

Additional Related Novels

Agee, James. *A Death in the Family*.
Cormier, Robert. *After the First Death*; *The Chocolate War*.
Faulkner, William. *Absalom, Absalom!*
Guest, Judith. *Ordinary People*.
Potok, Chaim. *The Chosen*.
Tyler, Anne. *Dinner at the Homesick Restaurant*.

Friendship

Friendship! Mysterious cement of the soul! Sweetener of life! and solder of society!

—Robert Blair, "The Grave" (1743)

Often people feel more comfortable conveying their innermost feelings to friends rather than to blood relatives because people may choose friends but not family. In *The Color Purple*, although Shug is Celie's husband's mistress, she helps Celie find confidence by appreciating her talents. Although very different, Spud and Lymie develop an intense friendship in high school that continues to college in *The Folded Leaf*. Four women in *Waiting to Exhale* unite against the injustices they find throughout society by verbally and physically supporting each other's needs. The narrator of *My Ántonia*, Jim Burden, recalls his friendship with Ántonia before he moved away and its resurgence on a visit twenty years later. In the three novels, *Sula, The Bean Trees*, and *The Chosen*, the protagonists create a strong relationship with another character.

In the *OED*, "one joined to another in mutual benevolence and intimacy" defines friendship. A notation clarifies that this description does not ordinarily apply to lovers or relatives. In *Beowulf* appears the comment, "Heorot innan w?s freondum afylled" [Heorot was now filled with friends] (1018). Tottel states in his *Miscellany* that "A faythfull frende [faithful friend] is thing most worth" (1557), and Thomas Hobbes notes in his *Rhetoric of Leviathan* that "A friend is he that loves, and he that is beloved" (1651). In 1960, the American Medical Association President Louis Orr noted, "Science will never be able to reduce the value of a sunset to arithmetic. Nor can it reduce friendship or statesmanship to a formula." In *Sula, The Bean Trees*, and *The Chosen*, the friendships are each unique, demanding diverse responses from the protagonists.

Sula by Toni Morrison

Sula, the protagonist of Toni Morrison's novel *Sula* (1973), contrasts to her friend Nel in almost every way. The story begins in 1921 when the two girls are twelve in Bottom, Ohio, and ends in 1965 after Sula's death. Nel follows the expectations of her society by marrying and having children while Sula leaves the community for college and stays away for ten years. Because Sula will not accept Bottom's mores, the townspeople interpret her actions as supernatural and proof of her evil nature. One of these signs is her affair with Nel's husband Jude, an action that Nel cannot forgive. Ironically, Sula's presence in town moves mothers to watch their children and their husbands more carefully. When she dies, the town rejoices at her death, but the women return to their neglectful ways. As Sula lies on her deathbed talking to Nel, she recalls their friendship as "the days when we were two throats and one eye and we had no price."

Nel Wright's perception of life completely contradicts Sula's. She arrives in Bottom with her mother Helene after the death of her grandmother, a Creole prostitute. Nel's mother acts "white" and expects Nel to do likewise. As she matures, Nel disciplines herself and controls her emotions. She assumes that she is morally responsible and correct in her decisions, denying any part in the death of Chicken Little when she and Sula were young teenagers. Sula and Nel lured the boy to play with them, and when they swung Chicken Little toward the river on a tree limb, his hand slipped and he fell into the water. When his head hit the rocky bottom, he drowned. Nel claims that she was only a by-stander and blames Sula for his death.

Sula's home and her perspectives are very different from Nel's. Sula grows up in the home of her grandmother, Eva Peace, a boarding house built with in-surance money in which Eva and Sula's mother Hannah (Pearl) entertain men and protect stray children. Sula's grandfather had left her grandmother, her mother, and her uncle Ralph (Plum) with no money and three beets for food. Eva had protected her children by lying in bed with them under the covers. She then left them at a neighbor's house and disappeared, returning eighteen months later minus her leg. (People gossiped that Eva had let a train run over it so that she could collect insurance money.) Hannah and Sula moved in with Eva after Sula's father Rekus died. There Sula witnessed Hannah's lovemaking with the men in town, helping them keep their high opinions of themselves by never making demands. When Plum returns from the war and will not leave his room, Eva sets his room on fire. Then Hannah catches fire and burns while Sula watches. After Eva herself jumped from the second floor window with her one leg attempting to save Hannah, she accuses Sula of killing Hannah by not trying to put out the flames. Thus two deaths are attributed to Sula. With this unconventional heritage, Sula has to live by her own standards.

During the early years of their friendship, Nel says that "talking with Sula had always been a conversation with herself." But when Sula puts Eva in a nurs-ing home after her return, the town and Nel think she is evil. Following Sula's seduction of Nel's husband, he disappears. Sula and Nel do not see each other for three years, but when Nel hears that Sula is sick, she finds her in Eva's room in their old house. Sula needs medicine but has no money; she appeals to Nel to purchase it for her. When Nel asks Sula why she slept with Jude, Sula says simply that he filled an empty space in her brain. Nel tells Sula that she never did anything bad to her and was always good, but Sula surprises Nel by suggesting that maybe she herself was the good one, and that Nel had their positions backward. After Sula dies, Nel visits Eva, and Eva accuses her of Chicken Little's death. Nel realizes as she rushes away from the Old Folks' home that the pain of the past three years was her missing Sula when "all that time, all that time, I thought I was missing Jude." Nel has allowed her conventions and concerns about community approval to separate her from her friend, the one person she needed. She laments "O Lord, Sula . . . girl, girl, girlgirlgirl."

The Bean Trees by Barbara Kingsolver

In *The Bean Trees* (1988), Barbara Kingsolver introduces Missy (Miss Marietta) Greer who departs Pittman County, Kentucky, in the 1980s after graduation from high school and working in a hospital. The area still seemed like the 1950s during the 1970s, and she had grown up in poverty after her father deserted her and her mother. She says she decided in high school that "if I couldn't dress elegant, I'd dress memorable," and one of her dates said she "dressed like an eye test." Missy's mother Alice has remained strong, teaching Missy that "the only difference between [a scarecrow] that stands up good and one that blows over is what kind of a stick they're stuck up there on." Alice remarries, and Missy leaves, knowing only that she is going west (toward her American dream) to a new life. She changes her name to Taylor after her old 1955 Volkswagen runs out of gas in Taylorsville. Taylor stops at a restaurant in Oklahoma's Cherokee Nation and finds an abandoned child in one of the empty booths. She picks up the child and later recalls "the way that child held on. From the first moment . . . it attached itself to me by its little hands like roots sucking on dry dirt. I think it would have been easier to separate me from my hair." Taylor takes the child with her, and her first-person narrative alternating with the limited omniscient viewpoint of Lou Ann Ruiz, the young mother whom Taylor meets in Tucson, Arizona (where she decides to stop), reveals a biological mother and an accidental mother both concerned about a child. But also important in the novel are the other characters who help them and each other in evolving bonds of love and friendship.

Taylor's relationship with Mattie changes many of Taylor's attitudes. She meets Mattie, the manager of Jesus Is Lord Used Tires, the day she arrives in town and needs a tire. Later Mattie hires Taylor when she needs a job. When Mattie appears on television one night, Taylor discovers that Mattie has created a sanctuary for illegal immigrants on her second floor and passes them to safe places in the United States. Immigration officials have identified Mattie, but she refuses to betray those whom she has befriended in their need. Taylor has never heard of political problems in Central America, and when the illegal aliens Estevan and Esperanza tell her that the Guatemalan government took their daughter Ismeme after they refused to name members of their teachers' union, she enters a new awareness of human problems. The two had to flee without Ismene in order to save all three. Taylor thinks, "There was no way on earth I could explain what I felt, that my whole life had been running along on dumb luck and I hadn't even noticed." The additional knowledge that the two cannot obtain political asylum without proof of escaping for their lives further disturbs Taylor, and she willingly becomes an accomplice in Mattie's work. She contemplates, "I didn't want to believe the world could be so unjust. But of course it was right there in front of my nose." Later, when the social worker tells Taylor that she has no legal documents proving that she is Turtle's guardian, Estevan and Esperanza, Mayans resembling Cherokees, help her. They go with Taylor to Oklahoma, pretending that, as Turtle's parents, they need to give her to Taylor.

When Lou Ann and Taylor meet, they realize that they have the same values. Lou Ann also comes from Kentucky, and after Taylor answers Lou Ann's advertisement for someone to share her house, Lou Ann says "'It's been so long. . . . You talk just like me.'" Lou Ann's husband Angel, a former rodeo rider who lost a leg below the knee, left before Dwayne Ray was born. The two women combine their resources to create a whole family. Lou Ann agonizes over Dwayne Ray, and Taylor consoles her, "The flip side of worrying too much is just not caring. . . . If anything, Lou Ann, you're just too good of a mother." Taylor is also apprehensive. "I wondered how many other things were lurking around waiting to take a child's life when you weren't paying attention. I was useless. I was crazy to think I was doing this child a favor by whisking her away from the Cherokee Nation. Now she would probably end up mummified in Arizona."

Taylor also wants to be able to communicate more readily with Turtle, but "whoever she was talking to in her dream, she told them a lot more than she'd ever told me. I would have paid good money to be in that dream." Then someone tries to molest Turtle in the park. Turtle becomes catatonic, and Taylor takes her to a pediatrician who confirms Turtle's sexual abuse and reveals that Turtle is actually three rather than eighteen months, her growth stopped by the trauma. When the social worker tells Taylor she has no rights to Turtle, Lou Ann empathizes, and after Taylor "legally" becomes Turtle's guardian, Lou Ann assures her that no one knows how to be a decent mother. Turtle begins growing again, and her first word, "bean," honors Mattie's purple bean plant. The wonder of nature and the interdependence of friendship appears in references to two plants. An ugly plant, a ceres, bursts with stunning blooms only one day a year, after dark. The blind Edna smells it and tells the others so that they can enjoy its fleeting beauty. And in a scientific article, Taylor reads about another ugly plant. "The wisteria vines on their own would just barely get by, is how I explained it to Turtle, but put them together with rhibozia and they make miracles"—just like friends.

The Chosen by Chaim Potok

Using the first-person point of view of Reuven Malter in *The Chosen* (1967), Chaim Potok unfolds the friendship of two young Jews from the Williamsburg section of New York City. When Reuven is fifteen in 1944, his yeshiva baseball team plays another from a Russian Hasidic yeshiva. "To the rabbis . . . baseball was an evil waste of time . . . but to the students . . . an inter-league baseball victory . . . was an unquestioned mark of one's Americanism, and to be counted a loyal American had become increasingly important to us during these last years of the war." Reuven, however, feels hostile during the game; "What annoyed him was their fanatic sense of righteousness, their absolute certainty that they and they alone had God's ear, and every other Jew was wrong, totally wrong, a sinner, a hypocrite, an *apikoros*, and doomed, therefore, to burn in hell." During the game, one of the opposing players, Danny Saunders, hits Reuven in the eye, and a piece of his glasses sticks in his pupil. Next to Reuven in the hospital is Tony Savo, a former boxer with eye problems and a young boy blinded in a car accident that killed his mother. Thus immediately the symbolism of blindness and vision enters the novel, a motif of contrasts that Potok subtly develops throughout the story. While Reuven is in the hospital, Danny comes to apologize. Furious, Reuven asks him to leave, and the next day Danny returns and says, "I don't understand why I wanted to kill you." Their friendship begins, develops, and continues through the end of the novel when they graduate from college.

The boys both have unusual relationships with their own fathers and, after they become friends, with each other's father. Soon after Danny befriends Reuven, Reuven's father David realizes that Danny is the boy to whom he has been suggesting books to read in the library. Reuven discovers from Danny that Danny must succeed his father as the *tzaddik* and that Reb Saunders quizzes his son about the Talmud by giving him wrong answers to see if he notices. This practice makes Reuven uncomfortable, especially when Danny's father quizzes him. Reuven notices that one of the *gematriya* (numerical value of a Hebrew word since Hebrew letters are also numbers) that Reb Saunders uses is wrong and haltingly corrects him. Reuven's identification of the mistake pleases Reb Saunders, but Reuven thinks, "What a ridiculous way to gain admiration and friendship!" When Reuven discovers that a Cossack shot Danny's father, his wife, and his son and daughter, and a Russian peasant saved only him, he has more tolerance; he realizes that "Danny's soul had been born" in Poland as well. Danny's father never speaks to Danny except when discussing the Talmud; he raises him in silence. Finally as Danny finishes college, Reb Saunders adjusts to Danny's unhappiness with his future and communicates to him through Reuven that he will approve of his becoming a psychologist, a *tzaddik* for the world.

Reuven and his father, a writer, have an open relationship based on trust and respect. Reuven annoys his father when he rejects Danny's first apology, and David Malter admonishes Reuven's rudeness. His father warns him about his attitudes toward Danny's father and comments, "Treat the son as you would the father, because one day the son will be the father." David Malter supports the Zionist movement in Palestine, and Reb Saunders abhors it. Both David and Reuven lament Reb Saunders' decisions. "If he were not a tzaddik he could make a great contribution to the world. But he lives only in his own world." They both understand that "that is the way the world is. If a person has a contribution to make, he must make it in public. If learning is not made public, it is a waste." And they think that the isolationism of Reb Saunders and his congregation can only be detrimental. When Reuven's father has a heart attack, Reuven spends July with Danny's family, and David expects Reuven to show tolerance for whatever he observes there. He also wants Reuven to know the value of life. He advises him, "A man must fill his life with meaning, meaning is not automatically given to life. It is hard work to fill one's life with meaning. That I do not think you understand yet. A life filled with meaning is worthy of rest. I want to be worthy of rest when I am no longer here." When Danny's father refuses to allow Danny to speak to Reuven during the Zionist fight for Israel, David tells Reuven, "Honest differences of opinion should never be permitted to destroy a friendship."

Like Sula and Nel in *Sula*, Danny and Reuven resemble two halves of a single personality, born two days apart in the same year and complementing each other in many ways. Committed to learning, both admire those with greater knowledge. They both want to improve themselves morally and spiritually. Danny tells Rueven that he must become a rabbi, an inherited position in his family for six generations, but that he wants to be a psychologist. Reuven, a gifted mathematician, wants to be a rabbi. Danny understands nothing about symbolic logic, and Reuven knows no Freud. They both, however, study Talmud, knowing that "virtuosity in Talmud . . . was the automatic guarantee of a reputation for brilliance." Both graduate summa cum laude from high school and attend the same college, although at that time, Reb Saunders has decreed that Danny can no longer speak to Reuven. When the state of Israel becomes official, Reb Saunders revokes his decree, and the two reunite.

Each of these novels illustrates the importance of friendship. *The Bean Trees* elucidates the necessity of a true friend, and Estevan conveys it specifically by feeding Turtle with a chopstick longer than her arm. He states that people cannot feed themselves with a long spoon, but if they feed each other, all will be full. In *The Chosen*, David Malter recalls a Greek philosopher's comment that "two people who are true friends are like two bodies with one soul." The novels *Sula* and *The Chosen* each present friends who together are more effective in understanding themselves and dealing with others than they are alone. But in all three novels, the protagonists prove what Erasmus said in his 1539 *Proverbs* "A frende is more necessary than either fyer or water."

Additional Related Novels

Capote, Truman. *Breakfast at Tiffany's.*
Cather, Willa. *Death Comes for the Archbishop; My Ántonia.*
Craven, Margaret. *I Heard the Owl Call My Name.*

Flagg, Fannie. *Fried Green Tomatoes at the Whistle Stop Café*.
Gaines, Ernest J. *A Lesson Before Dying*.
Hemingway, Ernest. *The Old Man and the Sea; The Sun Also Rises*.
Kerouac, Jack. *On the Road*.
Knowles, John. *A Separate Peace*.
Maxwell, William. *The Folded Leaf*.
McMillan, Terry. *Waiting to Exhale*.
Melville, Herman. *Moby-Dick*.
Morrison, Toni. *Song of Solomon*.
O'Brien, Tim. *The Things They Carried*.
Steinbeck, John. *Of Mice and Men*.
Twain, Mark. *The Adventures of Huckleberry Finn*.
Walker, Alice. *The Color Purple*.
Warren, Robert Penn. *All the King's Men*.

Greed

From top to bottom of the ladder, greed is aroused without knowing
where to find ultimate foothold. Nothing can calm it, since its goal is far
beyond all it can attain.

—Emile Durkheim, *Suicide* (1897)

Few humans have admitted that having less would be better than more.
Usually greed leads people to devise methods of accumulating what they perceive as necessary to obtain their desire. Wang Lung's sons in *The Good Earth*
decide that they can do more with cash than land. Gatsby begins selling stolen
securities to obtain the wealth for wooing Daisy Buchanan in *The Great Gatsby*.
In *House of Mirth*, Lily Bart must marry a wealthy man to keep a place in society. Morris Townsend in *Washington Square* decides that Catherine Sloper's
property makes her a desirable mate. In the novels *The Great Train Robbery*,
The House of the Seven Gables, and *The Pearl*, an underlying greed motivates either a protagonist or an antagonist.

Greed, according to the *OED* is an eagerness "for gain, an inordinate or in-
satiate longing for wealth, or an avaricious or covetous desire." In the sixth
century B.C.E, Zoroaster stated: "Form no covetous desire, so that the demon
of greediness may not deceive thee, and the treasure of the world may not be
tasteless to thee." Mahatma Gandhi believed that "there is sufficiency in the
world for man's need but not for man's greed" in the twentieth century. And
in 1964, Edmund Davies reported the sentencing of twelve men convicted in a
twentieth-century train robbery for taking more than $30 million (£20 mil-
lion) from Britain's Royal Mail, "Let us clear any romantic notion of
daredeviltry from our minds. It is nothing less than a sordid crime of violence
inspired by vast greed" (*Time*). Protagonists in *The Great Train Robbery*, *The
House of the Seven Gables*, and *The Pearl* have to deal with greed in some way,
either their own or that of others.

The Great Train Robbery by Michael Crichton

Michael Crichton uses the train robbery of 1855 in Britain as the basis for
his novel, *The Great Train Robbery* (1975). The actual robbery became "The
Crime of the Century" and "The Most Sensational Exploit of the Modern
Era" in newspaper headlines of the time. During the Crimean War, British au-

thorities transported the army payroll of gold bullion in Chubb safes out of England by train and ship and then by train through France on the way to the Crimea. Although they were certain that their methods were impenetrable, thieves proved them wrong and stole £12 million. In the novel, Edward Pierce, allegedly a Cambridge man whose residence on fashionable Curzon Street makes him acceptable to society, masterminds the crime. However, few know his background or that he has a collection of aliases. He hires accomplices—Robert Agar, a "screwsman" (keymaker and safe-breaker), and Burgess—but authorities help his plan almost as much. The unwitting accessories who trust Pierce include Henry Fowler, general manager of the banking firm of Huddleston and Bradford in Westminster, who dines with Pierce at his house, and the senior partner of the firm, Edgar Trent, who introduces Pierce to his unmarried daughter.

Pierce's careful planning of the robbery reveals his thorough attention to all details and introduces the reader to men ready to join his endeavor. In the criminal hierarchy, Pierce is at the top, and he knows people with many specialities who can help him. Agar gives Pierce additional certification by identifying him as a cracksman in towns outside London. In preparation, Pierce times portions of the robbery process with a stopwatch, learns the weaknesses of people who can thwart his design, and schemes for an escape if he is sent to prison. Pierce needs a "snakesman" (tiny man who can negotiate small spaces), a "dipper" (thief), a "bone skipper" (someone who sleeps in strange places), and an "eel-skinner" (unlawful metalworker) who can evade the "crushers" (police) to complete the heist. For his snakesman, he chooses Clean Willy. Although Clean Willy is incarcerated in Newgate prison, he escapes when Pierce sends him a message. Pierce sees young Teddy Burke take a purse from a woman in a "pull," and hires him as a dipper. The bone skipper helps steal a policeman's uniform, and Taggert, a "resurrection trade" expert (someone who digs up corpses and sells them to medical schools), locates a leopard for Pierce. Also helping Pierce is his mistress, Miss Miriam. She poses as a Lady Charlotte Simms, becomes a "virgin" conquest for Fowler, and discovers from him that the Chubb locks have not changed. Crichton details the process in five parts, the first dealing with the preparation, the second with finding the holders of the safe's four keys, the third detailing the delays and difficulties in the execution of the robbery, the fourth the event itself, and the fifth part or aftermath when Pierce is arrested and tried. Pierce, however, would have never been caught had one of his underworld contacts not announced his identity.

A "code of honor" exists in the underworld, and those who break it suffer. Pierce's unofficial background checks of his helpers reveal to him that all but one would focus on their assignments. Clean Willy Williams, the snakesman, however, is a "nose" for the police. After Clean Willy completes his job, Pierce's cohort Barlow kills him and leaves him on the street where children take the dead man's clothes. Pierce discovers that Chokee Bill, another "nose," will sell him guns. Pierce uses Chokee Bill to mislead the police into thinking that he plans to steal the payroll from men in Greenwich who are building the transatlantic cable, and Chokee Bill dutifully reports to the second head of the Scotland Yard. When no one bothers the men in Greenwich, Chokee Bill's effect as a spy deteriorates. Later, police arrest Alice Nelson for thievery, and as Agar's mistress wanting leniency, she informs them about Pierce. Already in prison for forgery, Agar denies any knowledge of the situation until police threaten to send him to Australia. He discloses Pierce's address, and police arrest Pierce on November 13.

The crime itself captures the public's intense interest. "The *Times* complained that this fascination with a criminal was 'unseemly, even decadent,' and went so far as to suggest that the behavior of the public reflected 'some fatal flaw' in the character of the English mind." No one outside the police community knows of the capture until four months later when a *Times* reporter uncovers the news. After two more months, the Cawnpore uprising occurs in India, and the British public forgets Pierce. "In short order, the master criminal ceased to be fascinating to anyone." When Pierce goes to trial, he asserts that he has killed no one whereas Lord Cardigan killed 500 men at the Charge of the Light Brigade. The prosecutor asks Pierce, "Did you never feel, at any time, some sense of impropriety, some recognition of misconduct, some comprehension of unlawful behaving, some moral misgivings, in the performance of these various criminal acts?" Pierce responds, "I do not comprehend the question." Pierce does not understand his amorality but admits his greed; he planned the crime because he "wanted the money." On Pierce's way to prison (Old Bailey), Miriam, dressed as a "scabrous old whore," passes him the handcuff key via mouth when she kisses him. He escapes and disappears with the money, never to be seen again. Pierce's greed severs him from his past.

The House of the Seven Gables by Nathaniel Hawthorne

In *The House of the Seven Gables* (1851), Nathaniel Hawthorne used his own family's history as a basis, but he incorporates Romanticism through symbolism and the supernatural. Hawthorne expounds at the beginning of the novel that he has used a point of view that defines the story "under the Romantic" tradition. He calls it a "Legend," in which he connects the past with a present already "flitting away from us." One of Hawthorne's ancestors had ordered that a Quaker woman be whipped in the streets. In the novel, Colonel Pyncheon orders that the magician Matthew Maule be killed on the scaffold and eagerly takes ownership of Maule's land. Pyncheon also claims Native-American land, but after he dies in his new house on Maule's land, none of his heirs can find the deed. When the next heir, the bachelor Jaffrey Pyncheon, is discovered dead in the house, Judge Pyncheon creates a murder case against his rival heir Clifford so that the Pyncheon inheritance will be his alone. Ironically, "the Judge, beyond all question, was a man of eminent respectability. The church acknowledged it; the state acknowledged it. It was denied by nobody." But a daguerreotypist living in the Pyncheon house thirty years later when Clifford returns from serving his prison sentence takes Judge Pyncheon's picture, and comments, "Here we have the man, sly, subtle, hard, imperious, and withal, cold as ice." The Judge, like Colonel Pyncheon before him, focuses on satisfying his greed.

The destitute Phoebe comes to live with Miss Hepzibah, Clifford's sister, and helps the elderly pair just as Clifford returns from years in prison following his unjustified conviction for Jaffrey Pyncheon's murder. Miss Hepzibah imagines that Phoebe resembles a previous resident of the house, Alice, "who had been exceedingly beautiful and accomplished in her lifetime, a hundred years ago . . . [but] had met with some great and mysterious calamity, and had grown thin and white, and gradually faded out of the world." Phoebe helps Miss Hepzibah make money in her tiny store, and Uncle Venner, a neighbor, notes "I never knew a human creature do her work so much like one of God's angels, as this child Phoebe does!" They think that "there was a spiritual quality in Phoebe's activity." The tired chickens in the yard find new energy when she feeds them, and Clifford loves being on the terrace with her. "She was not an actual fact for him, but the interpretation of all that he had lacked on earth, brought warmly home to his conception; so that this mere symbol or lifelike picture had almost the comfort of reality." After she feels relaxed with the daguerreotypist Holgrave, she chastises him for his reticence to aid Clifford and Phoebe. But Holgrave has reasons for refusing "either to help or hinder"; he wants to observe.

At his death, Matthew entangles the Maule family with the Pyncheons. "'God,' said the dying man [Matthew], pointing his finger with a ghastly look at the undismayed countenance of his enemy [Pyncheon], 'God will give him blood to drink!'" In response, Pyncheon hires Matthew's son Thomas to be the head architect for his new house. Matthew's magical qualities "had fallen upon his children. They were half-believed to inherit mysterious attributes; the family eye was said to possess strange power. Among other good-for-nothing properties and privileges, one was especially assigned them, of exercising an influence over people's dreams." Maule supposedly took control of Alice Pyncheon's spirit 100 years before and mistakenly killed her. The current Maule in the Pyncheon household, Holgrave, finds that he has a similar power over the young Phoebe who arrives from the country after he becomes a tenant. But like his ancestor, he means no harm; "He had never violated the innermost man, but had carried his conscience along with him."

The Judge's unexpected death of apoplexy while he has neighbors spying on Clifford to find another reason to incarcerate him allows the family to desert the dark, dismal house. Hepzibah describes the house. "It lets in the wind and rain—and the snow, too, in the garret and upper chambers, in winter-time—but it never lets in the sunshine." Hepzibah says that Phoebe is also an "inmate" of the old house. Clifford says to Phoebe, "The house, in my view, is expressive of that odious and abominable Past, with all its bad influences, against which I have just been declaiming. I dwell in it for awhile, that I may know the better how to hate it." When Clifford and Hepzibah leave while the Judge waits to question Clifford on the whereabouts of the will, Clifford briefly feels youthful again. On their return, they discover the Judge dead, the useless deed of Indian lands, and Clifford as Jaffrey's original heir. They depart for their new life in a country home, and Holgrave, in love with Phoebe, reveals to her that he is a Maule with Matthew's powers. They rid themselves of the family's curse, having paid the price of loneliness and imprisonment while neither the colonel nor the judge enjoyed fulfillment of their greed.

The Pearl by John Steinbeck

John Steinbeck's *The Pearl* (1947), unlike *The Great Train Robbery* or *The House of the Seven Gables*, has no basis in reality. As an allegory, it reveals how wealth can ruin people's lives when greedy people try to appropriate it. The omniscient point of view allows the reader to know how different people respond to the news of Kino's finding the "Pearl of the World." Before he finds the pearl, the poor Kino and his wife Juana are happy with their baby Coyotito. "Sometimes it rose to an aching chord that caught the throat, saying this is safety, this is warmth, this is the *Whole*." He loves the beauty around him, happy with the dawn's appearance; "a wash, a glow, a lightness, and then an explosion of fire as the sun arose out of the Gulf." Although poor, he is fully content. "[Kino's] people had once been great makers of songs so that everything they saw or thought or did or heard became a song. That was very long ago. . . . In Kino's head there was a song now, clear and soft, and if he had been able to speak of it, he would have called it the Song of the Family."

But on the same day that he admires the dawn and enjoys his family, his life changes. A scorpion stings Coyotito. They rush to the doctor but have only seed pearls for payment. The doctor, therefore, tells the servant to inform them that he is traveling. Kino and Juana take the child with them on their boat, "The one thing of value [Kino] owned in the world," their "property and source of food" that once belonged to Kino's father and grandfather. Worrying about his son, "in [Kino's] mind a new song had come, the Song of Evil, the music of the enemy, of any foe of the family, a savage, secret, dangerous melody, and underneath, the Song of the Family cried plaintively." Yet on this trip, they find a beautiful pearl, and, simultaneously, Coyotito begins recovering from the bite. Lured into thinking their troubles have ended, Kino imagines using the proceeds from the pearl to marry in the church and for his son to go to school. Both Kino and Juana "knew that time would now date from Kino's pearl, and that they would discuss this moment for many years to come."

How other people react to their good fortune, discovering "The Pearl of the World," surprises Kino and Juana. The news travels rapidly, almost before they return to shore. The priest needs certain repairs on the church and wonders if he married Kino and Juana or baptized their baby. After the priest visits them, Kino hears another "evil song" permeate the air. The shopkeepers anticipate the things he will buy. The beggars expect him to be generous like other poor men suddenly rich. The doctor quickly appears, claims Kino as a client, and treats the child to keep the scorpion poison from returning. Instead, the doctor's powder makes the child sicker, and he has to prescribe an antidote to his first medicine. When Kino goes to the pearl buyers to sell his treasure, they offer him a price much too low. He refuses to sell, noting that "there is a great deal to be seen in the tilt of the hat on a man." Someone begins digging outside his house, and Kino starts to fear everyone except his brother Juan Tomás who understands the problem. Juan Tomás says, "We do know that we are cheated from birth to the overcharge on our coffins. But we survive. You have defied not the pearl buyers, but the whole structure, the whole way of life, and I am afraid for you." He warns Kino that his friends will protect him, "only so long as they are not in danger or discomfort from it." When someone commits the ultimate sin, breaking Kino's boat, the canoe of his grandfather, and follows it with burning his house, Kino and Juana escape with Coyotito.

Kino himself transforms during the story, and his changes are transmitted through Coyotito. Coyotito's poison seems to symbolize the evil that will accompany the pearl. The additional poison administered by the doctor to Coyotito almost kills him as well. After someone attacks Kino outside their house, Juana wants to destroy the pearl, but Kino hits her when she tries to throw it into the ocean. His belief that "I am a man" makes him "half insane and half God." After they leave their village with Juana refusing to abandon Kino, trackers follow them. Kino tries to protect Coyotito, but the trackers hear him cry and a shot at Kino blows off the top of Coyotito's head. Then Kino becomes a murderer by shooting the two trackers. He and Juana return to their village, and Kino himself throws the pearl back into the ocean. He has experienced the evil that can accompany greed, and it destroys everything he has except his wife. Fortunately, he can salvage that part of his life by returning the pearl to its source.

In *The Pearl*, Kino sees himself as "a soldier sent by God to guard some part of the castle of the Universe . . . but . . . one must remain faithful to his post and must not go running about, else the castle is in danger from the assaults of hell." In all the novels, *The Great Train Robbery*, *The House of the Seven Gables*, and *The Pearl*, those who do not carefully guard "some part of the castle," either the evil of others or the evil within themselves, may irreparably suffer from the effects of greed. Having a focus in life other than money allows one to enjoy the beauty of the dawn or the pleasure in smiling faces.

Additional Related Novels

Bellow, Saul. *Seize the Day.*
Buck, Pearl S. *The Good Earth.*

Erdrich, Louise. *Love Medicine.*
Fitzgerald, F. Scott. *The Great Gatsby; Tender Is the Night.*
Frazier, Charles. *Cold Mountain.*
James, Henry. *Washington Square.*
Johnson, Charles. *Middle Passage.*
Malamud, Bernard. *The Natural.*
Morrison, Toni. *Song of Solomon.*
Mosley, Walter. *Devil in a Blue Dress.*
Naylor, Gloria. *Linden Hills.*
Wharton, Edith. *House of Mirth.*

Grotesques

It is no accident that the grotesque mode in art and literature tends to be prevalent in societies and eras marked by strife, radical changes or disorientation.

—Philip Thomson, *The Grotesque* (1972)

The strange situations in which characters find themselves or the incongruity of their actions can cause others to label them "grotesques." They may be eccentric, make bizarre choices in clothing, or simply seem absurd. Jay Gatsby in *The Great Gatsby* has a background incompatible with the lavish surroundings he assembles to attract Daisy. Mick, Biff, Dr. Copeland, and Blount in *The Heart Is a Lonely Hunter* are grotesques who circle another grotesque, John Singer, fearful of exposing their feelings to themselves or to others. Quentin and Jason become grotesques in *The Sound and the Fury* through their inability to adjust to the reality and responsibilities of adulthood, with Quentin exhibiting the ultimate fear of life by committing suicide. In *Memoirs of a Geisha*, Chiyo functions in a world of grotesques as she learns the skills for survival expected in her profession. Characters in *The Day of the Locust*, *Winesburg, Ohio*, and *Grendel* cause others to fear a life that might include similar conditions. However, each protagonist finds that art—whether prose, poetry, or painting—offers an escape.

Philip Thomson defines the grotesque as "the unresolved clash of incompatibles and the "ambivalently abnormal." To him, the grotesque indicates disharmony, whether "conflict, clash, mixture of the heterogeneous, or conflation of disparates"(*The Grotesque*, 1972). Joyce Carol Oates posits that "the grotesque always possesses a blunt physicality. . . . One might define it, in fact, as the very antithesis of 'nice.'" She summarizes by noting that "the grotesque is the estranged world." Humans who feel separated from others inhabit this world and seem unable to normalize themselves in ways acceptable to the public in general. They are, in essence, the misfits of society. Oates adds that "suddenness and surprise are essential elements of the grotesque," and that "the grotesque instills fear of life rather than death." The *OED* reveals that "grotesque" has meant "distortion" since the early seventeenth century, specifically clown or buffoon behavior. A writer in *Gentlemen's Magazine* commented, "A woman with her head peeping out of a sack, could hardly . . . make a more Grotesque figure" (1747). And Voltaire noted that "some men of true genius seem only to make sure of fame by straining themselves into grotesques" (Trans. Morley, 1871). In three novels, *The Day of the Locust*, *Winesburg, Ohio*, and *Grendel*, each of the protagonists and many of the other characters inhabit the world of the grotesque, clashing with the cultures in which they find themselves.

The Day of the Locust by Nathanael West

In *The Day of the Locust* (1939), Nathanael West's omniscient point of view exposes some of Hollywood's grotesques, people who have come to the city with expectations. The narrator pities the arrivals, refusing to condemn them and their need of "beauty and romance, no matter how tasteless." Yet the narrator also realizes their misguided search, knowing that "few things are sadder than the truly monstrous." When Yale graduate Tod arrives (symbolically bearing the German word for "death" as his name), planning to learn set and costume design, he discovers some of the distortions. He attends a party at the home of a successful screenwriter, Claude Estee, and becomes baffled at a rubber horse upside down in the swimming pool that one female guest thinks is hilarious. At a brothel frequented by filmmakers, he observes the madam, Audrey Jennings, and her meticulous behavior. She admits only men with wealth and power whom she has previously interviewed. The superficiality of façades and of interiors surprises Tod equally. He notices that even home decoration has pretense when he sees "a Governor Winthrop dresser painted to look like unpainted pine" sitting in one of the character's homes. The unwritten rules for living that Tod finds in Hollywood fit no other place.

Tod desires to become an artist and expects his new job to advance his career, but the people he meets sidetrack him. His initial project is to create a scene depicting the burning of Los Angeles. Tod knows little about people living there "except that they had come to California to die." Later, he changes his assessment of the inhabitants. " He . . . wondered if he weren't exaggerating the importance of people who come to California. Maybe they weren't really desperate enough to set a single city on fire, let alone the whole country. Maybe they were only the pick of America's madmen and not all typical of the rest of the land." But in the end, he realizes, "they turned arrogant and pugnacious. . . . They were savage and bitter, especially the middle-aged and the old, and had been made so by boredom and disappointment." A dwarf, Abe Kusich, helps Tod find an apartment in the same complex as Faye Greener and her father Harry. His own emotions propel him into obsessive behavior when he becomes attracted to seventeen-year-old Faye. She rejects him, saying "he had . . . neither money nor looks, and she could only love a handsome man and would only let a wealthy man love her." After Tod spots one of Faye's friends at the brothel, he imagines paying for Faye's company. But as he spends more time near Faye, her "self-sufficiency made him squirm and the desire to break its smooth surface with a blow, or at least a sudden obscene gesture, became irresistible." When he admonishes her for empty aspirations, Faye tells him that "any dream was better than no dream and that beggars couldn't be choosers."

Faye circulates in a world of Hollywood grotesques. At seventeen, she relentlessly pursues an acting career, interested only in herself. Her father, once a vaudevillian performer, sells silver polish and performs on the doorsteps of his prospective clients. Through Faye, Tod meets Earle Shoop, a handsome "two-dimensional" cowboy from Arizona who stands in front of a saddlery all day and rolls a cigarette twice every hour. He also meets the Mexican Miguel, who raises fighting cocks and infuriates Earle by dancing with Faye at an impromptu party. Tod begins to admire Estee, the screenwriter, because unlike the others, "he was master of an involved comic rhetoric that permitted him to express his moral indignation and still keep his reputation for worldliness and wit."

Although Homer Simpson, forty, comes from Iowa to Hollywood to recover from pneumonia, he has a collection of other problems. His hands have a life of their own, and constantly aware of their errant movement, he tries to control them. Before Faye's father Harry has a heart attack on his doorstep, "between the sun, the lizard and the house, he [Homer] was fairly well occupied. But whether he was happy or not is hard to say. . . . He had memories to disturb him and a plant hasn't, but after the first night his memories were quiet." Homer focuses on Faye during the ensuing turmoil. After Harry dies, Faye moves into Homer's spare room. He begins buying her audition clothes, with a "servility . . . like that of a cringing, clumsy dog, who is always anticipating a blow, welcoming it even, and, in a way that makes overwhelming the desire to strike him." Homer's generosity begins to entrap Faye, and, to free herself, she brings Miguel into the house and sleeps with him. Tod suggests that Homer evict her, but she disappears first. Soon after, Homer becomes berserk in a Hollywood crowd at a movie premiere, killing a boy intent on humiliating him, because for "those without hope, like Homer, whose anguish is basic and permanent, no good comes from crying." While Tod observes the ensuing chaos and escapes with minor injuries, his short sojourn in Hollywood has almost turned him into one of the grotesques that he associates with the city. However, as one still able to accept reality, Tod has the possibility of escape.

Winesburg, Ohio by Sherwood Anderson

Although Sherwood Anderson wrote *Winesburg, Ohio* (1919) after he had moved to Chicago, he based some of the attributes of his characters on people he had known in Clyde, Ohio. To Anderson, the grotesque "was nothing more than a metaphor of the national condition of man, of his being at cross-purposes with himself" (Ciancio, "The Grotesque in American Fiction," 1964). Anderson subtitled *Winesburg, Ohio*, the "Book of Grotesques." In the loosely structured novel, he includes twenty-three vignettes with eighteen-year-old George Willard as the unifying source. Anderson introduces his story with a writer who rises from bed one night to record his thoughts. "In the beginning when the world was young there were a great many thoughts but no such thing as truth. Man made the truths himself and each truth was a composite of a great many vague thoughts. All about in the world were the truths and they were beautiful." He surmises that "it was the truths [virginity, passion, wealth, poverty, carelessness, etc.] that made the people the grotesques."

Some of the women in town need to confess their secrets, and they choose George Willard, a reporter on the local paper, as their surrogate priest. Against her own father's wishes, George's deceased mother Elizabeth married his father Tom hoping that the relationship would fulfill her; it did not. Tom Willard's political aspirations, ineffectualness, and attitude of superiority irritate Elizabeth, and, at her death, she despises him. Alice Hindman had an affair with a man nine years younger who had left for the city, promising to return for her. She rejected all other suitors in expectation, but he never reappeared. Louise Bentley seduced John Hardy so she would have a friend, but after they marry and have a son, she remains unhappy. Belle Carpenter loves Ed Hanby, a bartender beneath her social level whom she must reject. Kate Swift, George's teacher, tries to explain to him the value of experience for writers and almost seduces him to prove her point.

George also learns much about life from the men who disclose their pasts to him in casual conversation. Wing Biddlebaum, like Homer Simpson in *The Day of the Locust*, has trouble controlling his inexplicably moving hands, but he implores George to dream. Dr. Reefy married happily late in life, but his wife died the following year. Dr. Parcival, a former reporter and a physician who now prefers to have no patients, has been in Winesburg for only five years, and suggests that George practice "hatred and contempt so that you will be a superior being." Jesse Bentley's grandson David disappears at fifteen after thinking he has killed his grandfather with a slingshot and a rock (most likely an Old Testament reference to David descending from the lineage of Jesse). Joe Welling wins the admiration of the skeptical brother and father of the woman he loves when he details all of his intriguing ideas. Wash Williams, the ugliest man in town, discovered that his wife entertained lovers while he worked. The paltry preacher Curtis Hartman becomes obsessed by Kate Swift when he sees her smoking and reading in bed from his church study window. After he beholds her naked, he rushes to tell George that she is an "instrument of God bearing the message of truth." The artist Enoch Robinson leaves his family and converses with the two dozen shadow people he creates in his room. And Ed Handby finally wins Belle Carpenter with his persistance.

After hearing from the grotesques in Winesburg, George has to ponder his future. "He was depressed by the thought that he was not a part of the life in his own town, but the depression did not cut deeply as he did not think of himself as at fault." When he receives an invitation from Louise Trunnion, he visits her one night at her farm. He prefers Helen White, whom he sees when she returns from college for a day at the local fair, and drops his pursuit of Louise.

The narrator interjects, "In the mind of each was the same thought. I have come to this lovely place and here is this other. . . . Man or boy, woman or girl, they had for a moment taken hold of the thing that makes the mature life of men and women in the modern world possible." But neither George nor Helen attempts a lasting relationship. Thus, to escape becoming one of the grotesques, George leaves Winesburg; however, the town becomes his "background on which to paint the dreams of his manhood."

Grendel by John Gardner

Unlike *The Day of the Locust* or *Winesburg, Ohio*, the protagonist in *Grendel* (1971) is the grotesque. John Gardner examines the Beowulf saga from the first-person point of view of the monster. Because Grendel has human feelings and emotions, he quickly gains the reader's sympathy. This "ridiculous hairy creature" wants to be loved and accepted. Instead, estranged from the world because of his disparateness from it, he exhibits all attributes of a grotesque. The only creature who cares about him is his mother, and she possibly loves him because of her need to feel "son-ness." She, a "horrible, humpbacked, carp-toothed creature," adores him unconditionally, her "eyes on fire with useless, mindless love." Grendel begins his story in the twelfth year of an "idiotic war" and includes in it the "tiresome memories of a shadow-shooter, earth-rim-roamer, walker of the world's weird wall." The novel's twelve chapters each represent a sign in the zodiac beginning and ending in the spring with the number "twelve" symbolically representing the rhythm of the cosmos. The "only friend and comfort" that Grendel has is his shadow, and not until he discovers an exit from his cave does he see humans for the first time. His surprised response is to eat them.

But humans intrigue him, and while observing the inhabitants of Hrothgar's hall, Grendel becomes aware of political reality. He watches Hrothgar's power increase after his six closest neighbors begin paying him tributes for his protection. Then Hrothgar decides to build a giant meadhall overlooking the sea to underscore his benevolence as professed in the Shaper's songs. Grendel likes Hrothgar and does not want to accost him, but when Grendel defends himself from Hrothgar's attacks, the Shaper defiles his name, calling him "Ruiner of Meadhalls, Wrecker of Kings." However, Grendel shows restraint when he refrains from killing Wealtheow, the beautiful young sister of the Helmings king, Hygmod. Grendel understands an old peasant's words to Hrothulf, the young orphan living with his uncle, Hrothgar. The peasant says, "The incitement to violence depends upon total transvaluation of the ordinary values. By a single stroke, the most criminal acts must be converted to heroic and meritorious deeds. If the Revolution comes to grief, it will be because you and those you lead have become alarmed at your own brutality."

As a grotesque perceived as brutal, Grendel has no followers, but he can mold reputations. When Unferth, who thinks himself a hero, realizes that Grendel can talk, he decides that being killed by Grendel will make him a legend. Grendel refuses, instead placing the wounded Unferth on the meadhall steps before killing the nearby guards. Grendel observes as Hrothgar fulfills the old peasant's dictum that "A kingdom pretend[s to] save the values of the community—regulate compromise—improve the quality of the commonwealth! In other words, protect the power of the people in power and keep the others down." The peasant's insight about Hrothgar's rule exposes corrupt governing. "Public force is the life and soul of every state: not merely army and police but prisons, judges, tax collectors, every conceivable trick of coercive repression. The state is an organization of violence, a monopoly in what it is pleased to call *legitimate* violence." Grendel also senses the hostilities that fester in humans. He learns that for the Danes, "honor is very big . . . they'd rather be eaten alive than bailed out by strangers [the Geats]."

With his dismal life, isolated as a grotesque, Grendel finds beauty in one thing—the poetry of the Shaper. Grendel realizes that the Shaper conceives his stories and creates men's reputations through his songs rather than vice versa. Grendel hears the Shaper promise to tell the deeds of Hrothgar's glory. Grendel first hears the Shaper's noble song while he is still an adolescent, but soon he realizes the Shaper's invaluable role for Hrothgar's society. The Shaper has declared that of the world's first two races, only the blessed survive. The Shaper's identification of Grendel as one of the cursed race so affects him that he goes to Hrothgar's hall to ask forgiveness because "my heart was light with Hrothgar's goodness, and leaden with grief at my own bloodthirsty ways." Grendel comes to Hrothgar as a friend, but Hrothgar's people still attack him.

Grendel thinks about the meaning of existence throughout his life. He observes the cyclical sense of ideas, noting that "theology does not thrive in the world of action and reaction, change: it grows on calm, like the scum in a stagnant pool. And it flourishes, it prospers, on decline." He consults the dragon about humans who responds that "they'd map out roads through Hell with their crackpot theories!" Grendel hopes for insight, but the dragon has "eyes not firey but cold as the memory of family deaths." The dragon acknowledges knowing both the past and the future, but he will not admit to causing either. He advises Grendel to seek gold but becomes angry when Grendel touches *his* gold. After their consultation, Grendel begins hating the human songs of hope because the dragon has shown him only emptiness. When Grendel senses that the son of Ecgtheow is nearing, he becomes excited. He thinks, "all order . . . is theoretical, unreal—a harmless, sensible, smiling mask men slide between the two great, dark realities, the self and the world—two snakepits." He goes to Hrothgar's hall after Ecgtheow arrives, and kills one man. Ecgtheow, who silently awaits him, tears out his arm, and kills Grendel in turn. As Grendel dies, he concedes that he has had an accident. However, he leaves the legacy that only creations of art (poetry) can combat loneliness and the grotesque.

In *The Day of the Locust, Winesburg, Ohio,* and *Grendel,* the protagonist is either an artist or one who understands art's value. The artists, one a painter and one a writer, are the two characters who escape from becoming "ambivalently abnormal." Grendel comprehends that art can rescue beauty, although it cannot extricate him from the reality of his condition. Grotesques remain estranged because they have not incorporated the dragon's wisdom in *Grendel* that "connectedness is the essence of everything" and that "importance is derived from the immanence of infinitude in the finite."

Additional Related Novels

Faulkner, William. *The Sound and the Fury.*
Fitzgerald, F. Scott. *The Great Gatsby.*
Golden, Arthur. *Memoirs of a Geisha.*
Johnson, Charles. *Middle Passage.*
Kesey, Ken. *One Flew Over the Cuckoo's Nest.*
McCullers, Carson. *The Heart Is a Lonely Hunter.*
Saroyan, William. *The Human Comedy.*

Healers

Thy function was to heal and to restore,
To soothe and cleanse, not madden and pollute!
—William Wordsworth, "The River Duddon" (1820)

Physicians use scientific methods to identify ailments and prescribe remedies, some successful and some not. Healers not formally trained in school may use folk medicines or their mysterious "second sense" to diagnose and cure a patient. Often, the mode of instruction matters less than the compassionate care of another human being. In *The Women of Brewster Place*, Mattie Michael soothes those around her with words of comfort and practical wisdom. In *Tender Is the Night*, psychiatrist Dick Driver helps Nicole recover from childhood traumas but remains unaware that he needs healing himself. When a Los Angeles hospital fails to improve Tayo's health in *Ceremony*, the medicine man Betonie prescribes a procedure for him that restores the equilibrium between Tayo and the earth. In the three novels, *One Flew Over the Cuckoo's Nest*, *Mama Day*, and *Bless Me, Ultima*, each protagonist interacts with a healer but receives very different treatments.

For at least 2,000 years, the term "heal" has meant to "make whole or sound in bodily condition; to free from disease or ailment, restore to health or soundness; to cure" (*OED*). How the healing occurs or who achieves it does not appear in the definition. In the gospel of Matthew, one learns "Heo weren iheled from alle untrumnesse" [He was healed from all illness] and assumes Jesus was the healer (trans. c1000). In Tennyson's *Morte d'Arthur*, Arthur announces, "I will heal me of my grievous wound" (1842). The speaker in "When Philoctetes in the Lemnian Isle" wishes for any source of relief, "and trust[s] that spiritual Creatures round us move, / Griefs to allay which Reason cannot heal" (William Wordsworth, 1827). Humans, therefore, search widely for a remedy to illness. In *One Flew Over the Cuckoo's Nest*, a trained healer tries to "madden and pollute" the protagonist while the untrained healers in *Mama Day* and *Bless Me, Ultima* are prescient and use knowledge passed through cultural and family traditions "to soothe and cleanse."

One Flew Over the Cuckoo's Nest by Ken Kesey

In *One Flew Over the Cuckoo's Nest* (1962), Ken Kesey illustrates what can happen when a designated healer prefers control to empowerment. The narrator, half-Indian Umpqua tribe member and fellow inmate "Chief" Bromden, recalls Randle Patrick McMurphy's term in a mental hospital. He admits that remembering his encounter with McMurphy and watching the Big Nurse, Ratched, mistreat him will anger him again. "I been silent so long now it's gonna roar out of me like floodwaters." Bromden has pretended to be a deaf mute because he has neither spoken nor seemed able to hear anyone. Therefore, the doctors and Ratched have carelessly discussed confidential information in front of him. Bromden's observations have made him an expert about various treatments and their results. He divides the patients into two categories—the Acutes whom doctors expect to heal and the Chronics who will spend the remainder of their lives in the institution. The Acutes "snicker in their fists," he remarks, and some of them become Chronics after returning from the "Shock Shop." He separates the Chronics into more specific divisions. He identifies himself as an "Acute Walker" with others as "Wheelers" and "Vegetables." Of them all he says, "Most of us are machines with flaws inside that can't be repaired, flaws born in, or flaws beat in over so many years."

As an inmate in the hospital ward since World War II, Bromden has no hope of leaving. The new patient McMurphy quickly realizes that Bromden *can* hear because he jumps when McMurphy broadcasts that the African-American orderlies are coming. When McMurphy pressures him about his past, Bromden divulges that, as son of a full Chief, he had attended college for a year. He remembers serving in the war and parallels it to his life in the tribe. He confides to McMurphy, "I was hurt by seeing things in the Army, in the war. . . . by seeing what happened to Papa and the tribe. I thought I'd got over seeing those things and fretting over them." Those things from his childhood included visitors ignoring him and talking "around" him while discussing their purchase of tribal land. Unlike others in the tribe, Bromden's father disapproved of the sale, wondering, "What can you pay for the way a man lives?" When McMurphy first sees the six-foot, seven-inch-tall Bromden, Ratched has had him wrapped in a straightjacket for his violent reaction toward shaving before breakfast. Chief hates the bathroom's "faces all round you trapped screaming behind the mirrors." Bromden calls Nurse Ratched the "Combine," comparing her to the powerful farm machine that devours wheat and asks, "What chance you got against one of their machines?" McMurphy decides that the Chief only needs to feel "big" again and he will be able to leave the hospital.

Nurse Ratched controls the patients and other staff, including the doctors. She dominates the patients by enumerating their fears and insecurities. She wants their "cures" to comply to her standards rather than to what might be best for them. Bromden describes her approach: "The ward is a factory for the Combine. It's the fixing up mistakes made in the neighborhoods and in the schools and in the churches. . . . something that came in all twisted different is now a functioning, adjusted component, a credit to the whole outfit and a marvel to behold." When McMurphy rebels under Ratched's dictatorship, Ratched determines to destroy him. She accuses him of her own deeds; "sometimes a manipulator's own ends are simply the actual *disruption* of the ward for the sake of disruption." Later, she again describes herself when angry about McMurphy. "Playing with human lives—gambling with human lives—as if you thought yourself to be a *God!*" To subdue McMurphy, who chose the hospital over a cell in which to serve a short prison term, Ratched reminds the other staffers, "Mr. McMurphy is committed. The length of time he spends in this hospital is entirely up to us."

After he notices that Bromden lacks confidence, McMurphy understands that laughter may help other inmates identify and overcome their individual fears. Surprised at Ratched's disinterest in curing mental illness on the ward, McMurphy assumes the role of healer. That McMurphy went to high school with one of the doctors disturbs Miss Ratched because she cannot tolerate others conversing without her. McMurphy defines group therapy as a "pecking party" with the Nurse "drawing the first blood" and other patients nastily joining. He calls Ratched a "bitch and a buzzard and a ballcutter," adding that she "grinds our noses in our mistakes." He invents ways to make the men laugh by singing, throwing butter at the clock while they await dismissal from breakfast, and cheering a blank screen during the World Series when Ratched will not allow them to turn on the television. Then he ignores her. He "knows that there's no better way in the world to aggravate somebody who's trying to make it hard for you than by acting like you're not bothered." McMurphy takes the men fishing, and outside the hospital, the college graduate Harding notices how the public fears them. He comments, "Never before did I realize that mental illness could have the aspect of power, *power*. Think of it: perhaps the more insane a man is, the more powerful he could become. Hitler an example. Fair makes the old brain reel, doesn't it? Food for thought there." When George, another inmate, safely brings the boat into dock during a sudden storm, he admits that he captained a PT boat during the war. Even in danger, however, the men's laughter helps them heal.

McMurphy cannot tolerate Ratched's attitudes toward him or the other men. Bromden compares McMurphy's discovery that McMurphy cannot leave the hospital without Ratched's approval to his father's lack of choice in signing the deed to sell the tribal land. After Ratched catches Billy with a prostitute and says that Billy's mother would be disappointed in him, Billy commits suicide. Furious, McMurphy tears Ratched's uniform and exposes her breasts. Although she sends him to the "shock shop," the men comprehend that she is a woman rather than a machine and find her less threatening. When McMurphy returns to the ward, he has been lobotomized. Although mentally defeated, McMurphy has still won, and, to honor his sacrifice, the Chief smothers McMurphy during the night and then safely escapes using a predetermined route. Ratched, the hypocritical healer, loses the patients whose health was never as important as her control over them.

Mama Day by Gloria Naylor

Unlike Ratched in *One Flew Over the Cuckoo's Nest*, Miranda Mama Day in Gloria Naylor's *Mama Day* (1988) uses her healing abilities to empower those who need help. Mama Day resembles Prospero in Shakespeare's *The Tempest* (rather than his daughter Miranda) on Willow Springs (an island halfway between Georgia and South Carolina but not on any map) using her knowledge of herbs and nature to begin relationships, encourage conception, ease childbirth, cure ills, and thwart harm, especially from developers vying for the island. Naylor shifts the point of view, using first person with Ophelia (called "Cocoa," but named for her great-grandmother who drowned herself like Ophelia in *Hamlet*), and George, Cocoa's husband. Naylor shifts to limited omniscient point of view with present tense for Mama Day, Cocoa's great aunt.

On a visit to the island after moving to New York, Cocoa becomes aware of her family's long heritage. Sapphira Wade, born in 1799, married her master Bascombe Wade and had seven sons and seven grandsons. A nurse and midwife as well as a conjure woman, the townspeople accused her of seducing her husband and killing him after he deeded his land to his seven sons. When Miranda climbs into the attic after a hurricane, she finds the family ledger proving that Bascombe freed Sapphira because he loved her. Miranda, granddaughter of Sapphira's seventh grandson, also has a "double consciousness" of understanding and knew beforehand that her younger sister Peace would drown in a well. Cocoa's mother was Miranda and Abigail's sister Grace. Miranda steadily prepares Cocoa for her role in the family's legacy, and, when she is ready, Miranda watches her from a distance and observes, "It's a face that's been given the meaning of peace. A face ready to go in search of answers, so at last there ain't no need for words." Cocoa herself realizes that "my bond with them was such that even if hate and rage were to tear us totally apart, they knew I was always theirs."

Important to both her family and the community, everyone agrees, "Mama Day say no, everybody say no." She understands their natures as well as the natural world. When Miranda observes the snakes and chickens behaving strangely, she warns about a bad storm coming. Afterward, George declares, "The winds coming around the corners of that house was God" (like the hurricane in *Their Eyes Were Watching God*). Bernice wants to get pregnant, and when Mama Day offers her pumpkin seeds, Abigail says, "Bernice gonna know they're nothing but pumpkin seeds." Miranda responds, "The mind is a funny thing, Abigail—and a powerful thing at that. Bernice is gonna believe they are what I tell her they are—magic seeds. And the only magic is that what she believes they are, they're gonna become." Two others in town also claim healing powers—Dr. Buzzard and Ruth. Dr. Buzzard uses elixirs, and the vindictive

Ruth employs voodoo. But Miranda knows that "ain't no hoodoo anywhere as powerful as hate" because "the mind is everything."

Mama Day's knowledge of nature also helps Cocoa survive. Cocoa meets George at a job interview just before her yearly visit to Willow Springs for Abigail's birthday. Miranda mails Cocoa's "thank you" note after slipping yellow powder (probably lavender) into the envelope. George sends Cocoa yellow roses in New York and takes her to dinner. Cocoa marries him in New Orleans when his beloved New England Patriots play in the Super Bowl, and he announces to Miranda by telephone, "She has all I have." The second time Miranda overtly helps Cocoa is when jealous Ruby's voodoo almost kills her. At a party for George and Cocoa in Willow Springs, Ruby's boyfriend Junior Lee flirts with Cocoa. Ruby invites Cocoa to visit and generously plaits her hair. After returning to Mama Day's house, Cocoa becomes ill, and Miranda ascertains that Ruby has incorporated poisonous nightshade into the braids. Furious, Miranda scatters a silvery powder around Ruby's house that attracts lightning. In the next storm, the house explodes when the lightning strikes it. To revive Cocoa from the poison, Miranda needs George. But George does not listen carefully to her directions. When he enters the chicken coop as Miranda directed, the disturbed chicken assaults him, and George's weak heart fails. Cocoa survives, but she mistakenly admits to Miranda that she wants to commit suicide. For the third time, Miranda saves her. She remembers, "I had never seen Mama Day so furious—never. . . . There was actually hatred in her eyes. There ain't no pain—no pain—that you could be having worse than what that boy went through for your life. And you would throw it back in his face, heifer?"

Fourteen years after George's death, on her annual August trip when Miranda is nearing the end of her century-long life, Cocoa visits George's grave and chats with him. He tells her, "I didn't feel anything after my heart burst. As my bleeding hand slid gently down your arm, there was total peace." And she admits to him, "I thought my world had come to an end. And I wasn't really wrong—one of my worlds had. But being so young, I didn't understand that every hour we keep living is building material for a new world, of some sort. I wasn't ready to believe that a further existence would be worth anything without you." Cocoa has a son named George who asks about his namesake. She tells George that, "after washing my face and making myself a cup of mint tea, I called my son inside. I put him on my lap and told him that he was named after a man who looked just like love."

Bless Me, Ultima by Rudolfo Anaya

In *Bless Me, Ultima* (1972), the first-person narrator Antonio Maréz dates his maturity from the arrival of Ultima "the summer I was seven . . ." to live with his family in Guadalupe. In this partial bildungsroman, Antonio says, "My soul grew under her careful guidance." Ultima, a *curandera* (healer), teaches Antonio to recognize much about himself and those around him.

Throughout the novel, Rudolfo Anaya combines mythology, folklore, and mainstream Catholicism with the subconscious to create a sense of life's complexities. Following his father one night after Lupito, crazed by the war, kills the town sheriff, Chávez's brother, Antonio sees the townsmen ignoring Narciso's pleas for reason and murdering Lupito. Frightened, Antonio rushes home but there he realizes that Ultima's owl has protected him. Later, Antonio witnesses a second murder when Tenorio shoots Narciso outside Rosie's, the local brothel. Antonio also has many dreams through which he tries to filter the world of reality. One of Antonio's friends, Florence, rejects the god of the church who killed his mother and father and left him a young orphan. After Florence drowns, Antonio refuses to attend his funeral because of his unbelief. Another of Antonio's friends, Cico, tells him about a god, a golden carp, swimming in the water surrounding the town but while carefully hiding from the jealous priest. But Antonio then wonders, "Why had the new god, the golden carp, chosen also to punish people? The old God did it already. Drowning or burning, the punishment was all the same. The soul was lost, unsafe, unsure, suffering—why couldn't there be a god who would never punish his people, a god who would be forgiving all of the time?" He then wonders if "perhaps the best god would be like a woman because only women really knew how to forgive." Later, Antonio wonders why his family summons Ultima when his uncle is ill because "in my mind I could not understand how the power of God could fail." During his first confession, he expects God to answer his questions about the two deaths he has witnessed, but God remains silent.

Through all his doubts, the actions of the "owl-eyed" Ultima guide him. Soon after her arrival, Antonio dreams that she had delivered him at his birth and that his father's laughing, loud brothers and his mother's quiet farmer brothers had come to visit. Ultima tries to cure everyone's ills, including Tenerio's curse on Antonio's uncle. Ultima challenges Tenerio because she says "The smallest bit of good can stand against all the powers of evil in the world and it will emerge triumphant." But Tenorio blames Ultima for killing his daughters and, in retaliation, kills her owl. When Antonio finds her, Ultima tells him that the owl was part of her and she is dying. "Her hand touched my forehead and her last words were, 'I bless you in the name of all that is good and strong and beautiful, Antonio. Always have the strength to live. Love life, and if despair enters your heart, look for me in the evening when the wind is gentle and the owls sing in the hills, I shall be with you—.' "

Three different healers appear in these novels. Nurse Ratched abuses her gift by focusing on and emphasizing the fears of those around her. Mama Day heals anyone who needs her. Ultima entrusts Antonio with the knowledge of beauty and complexity in nature necessary to heal himself from present and future scars of reality. When Ultima came, she gave Antonio the ability to "see," and he retains her gift. "When she came the beauty of the llano [plain] unfolded before my eyes, and the gurgling waters of the river sang to the hum of the turning earth. . . . Time stood still, and it shared with me all that has been, and all that was to come."

Additional Related Novels

Bellow, Saul. *Henderson, the Rain King.*
Fitzgerald, F. Scott. *Tender Is the Night.*
Flagg, Fannie. *Fried Green Tomatoes at the Whistle Stop Café.*
Naylor, Gloria. *The Women of Brewster Place.*
Silko, Leslie Marmon. *Ceremony.*

Immigrant Life

Our country was built on immigrants—our strength truly is our diversity.
—Norm Coleman (1996)

Other than Native Americans, people who live in the United States are either immigrants or descendants of immigrants from places all over the world who have developed the country and continued to change it. Maggie's family in *Maggie: A Girl of the Streets* immigrated to Boston from Ireland. Political refugees from South American countries have found hope in the Southwest, including Estevan and Esperanza from Guatemala in *The Bean Trees*. Of the Jewish refugees who escaped Russia, David Levinsky arrives in New York destitute but eventually becomes wealthy in *The Rise of David Levinsky*. Kabuo Miyamoto suffers after World War II in *Snow Falling on Cedars* because his family is Japanese. In the novels, *My Ántonia*; *The Jungle*; and *Brown Girl, Brownstones*, the immigrant protagonists struggle for financial and emotional survival.

An immigrant "migrates into a country as a settler" (*OED*). Henry Cockeram defined the verb "immigrate" in *The English Dictionarie, or an Interpreter of Hard English Words* as "to goe dwell in some place" (1623). In 1809, Edward Kendall said, "Immigrant is perhaps the only new word, of which the circumstances of the United States has in any degree demanded the addition to the English language" (*Travels through the Northern Parts of the United States*). In 2000, Doris Meissner commented that "the fear of not measuring up is universal in the immigrant experience" (*Washington Post*). The protagonists in *My Ántonia*; *The Jungle*; and *Brown Girl, Brownstones* have difficulty adjusting to or "measuring up" in their new environments because others have misinformed or maltreated them.

My Ántonia by Willa Cather

When the Shimerdas arrive at their destination in Willa Cather's *My Ántonia* (1918), their English is limited to Ántonia's three words, "Black Hawk, Nebraska." The Shimerdas share similar adversities with other immigrants. They spend too much money for a house, and the former owner will not leave. Russian brothers blamed and exiled for accidental deaths watch their money dwindle before one dies of tuberculosis and the other auctions their farm to repay Wick Cutter, the moneylender. After the narrator Jim teaches English to Ántonia, she admits to him that her mother expected to become wealthy in America. Instead, their difficult life defeats her father. He stops playing his beloved violin, ignores the sunflowers making "a golden ribbon across the prairie," and finally commits suicide during a blizzard.

Early in the novel, Jim establishes himself as a reliable narrator. He loves his grandparents' isolated Nebraska farm where he feels "that the world was left behind, that we had got over the edge of it, and were outside man's jurisdiction." Jim admires his grandfather's reticence. "Because he talked so little, his words had a peculiar force; they were not worn dull from constant use." Jim remembers, "I was entirely happy. Perhaps we feel like that when we die and become a part of something entire, whether it is sun and air, or goodness and knowledge. At any rate, that is happiness; to be dissolved into something complete and great." He becomes friends with the older Ántonia (having arrived in Black Hawk on the same train with her when coming to live with his grandparents after being orphaned) after his grandfather takes him to visit the family. When Jim's grandparents move into town, Jim suggests that Ántonia work there as a "hired" girl. He then watches her pleasing personality attract local males at the weekly Saturday night dances until he leaves for Harvard. Later, on a visit to Prague, he sends Ántonia a postcard. After he returns twenty years later and renews their friendship, he writes her story from the perspective of an adult but incorporating much of the emotion of a maturing adolescent who loved her from afar. He realizes that "whatever we had missed, we possessed together the precious, the incommunicable past." Jim's story of Ántonia emphasizes her strong character.

In town, Ántonia must adjust to a variety of standards. She works for the Harlings, next-door neighbors to Jim and his grandparents, and makes friends with other hired girls including Lena and Tiny. Their poor language skills prohibit them from teaching like pioneers from the East, but their families need additional income, and their hard work helps their families prosper. During the summer, the Vannis come to town with a tent, teach dancing, and sponsor nighttime socials. Young men arrive to dance with "the hired girls," and because the country girls are wholesome and lovely, they "were considered a menace to the social order. Their beauty shone out too boldly against a conventional background." One of the men kisses Ántonia after bringing her home, and she slaps him. Her employer, Mr. Harling, tells her she must give up dancing or leave. She goes to work for Cutter, but he harasses her sexually, a fact confirmed when Jim agrees to sleep in Ántonia's bed while Mrs. Cutter (whose face was "the very color and shape of anger") is away and Cutter enters the room. Afterward, Ántonia returns to the Harling family, and Larry Donovan wants to marry her.

Ántonia and the other hired girls survive much adversity. Donovan summons Ántonia to the city to marry him after he has lost his job, but he does not tell her. She supports him financially, but after her money is gone and she is pregnant, he disappears. Another hired girl, Lena, makes money in the Klondike, and when Jim sees her in 1908, "she was satisfied with her success, but not elated. She was like someone in whom the faculty of becoming interested is worn out." When Jim returns to Black Hawk, he discovers that Ántonia has married a Bohemian named Cuzak. And, although they are poor, they and their very large family of ten children, a son-in-law, and a granddaughter are very happy. When Jim arrives, the family already knows about him. Ántonia, filled with vitality and unencumbered with wealth, "was a rich mine of life, like the founders of early races." Thus the narrator can contentedly tell Ántonia's story, that of an immigrant who worked hard, overcame disappointment, and created positive forces around her.

The Jungle by Upton Sinclair

In *The Jungle* (1906), the Lithuanian immigrant, Jurgis Rudkus, comes to Chicago expecting to improve his life. A series of difficulties thwarts his progress until he finally finds solace in the Socialist Party. Upton Sinclair himself was a socialist, attracted to its tenets around the turn of the century after he had difficulty supporting his family. Sinclair then began investigating the corruption in the meat-packing industry, a business that started to thrive after mechanization during the late nineteenth century. As Sinclair revealed the horrible practices of these Chicago monopolies, he became what Theodore Roosevelt called a "muckraker" (a term from John Bunyan's *Pilgrim's Progress*). Although *The Jungle* is fiction, its omniscient point of view created a reality at its publication that led to a reformation in the industry.

When Jurgis arrives in Chicago with his family and his fiancée, he is a strong man who has no difficulty getting a job in a meat-packing plant. The family earns enough money to buy a home, but after they sign papers they cannot read, they discover that they are renting. Their neighbor, Grandmother Majauszkiene, tells them that the sellers will evict them if the family misses a month's rent, then paint and resell the house as they have done to all the homes of immigrants in arrears. Additional costs arise when the family needs furniture and discovers they owe interest and must purchase insurance. To afford these new charges, Jurgis's unwell father Antanas has to "buy" a job in the "pickle room" by paying an agent one-third of his salary; there the wet floor makes him sicker. Jurgis's young brother Stanislavas has to go to work to pay the interest on their loan.

During their second year in Chicago, Jurgis and Ona, fifteen, decide to marry. People in Lithuania always had a *Veseliza* to celebrate with the entire community. Ona wants to forego the traditional wedding because of its expense, but a sister, Elzbieta, disagrees. The people come and enjoy the celebration. Tamoszius Kuszleika, who taught himself to play the violin, says "it is the music which makes it what it is; it is the music which changes the place from the rear room of a saloon in back of the yards to a fairy place, a wonderland, a little corner of the high mansions of the sky." But many of the men attending do not honor the tradition of the *acziavimas* where they give the bride money for dancing with her. Instead they eat and leave, and at the end of the evening, the family is in debt by the huge sum of $100.

After the wedding, the financial difficulties continue. Antanas dies, and they nearly go bankrupt paying for his funeral. Fortunately, Marija, another sister, brings home food from parties she attends with Tamoszius. But when her canning factory unexpectedly shuts down, she no longer has a regular income. After Jurgis discovers that his company docks him an entire hour when he is only a minute late, he knows that he must learn English to join a union and protect himself. He slowly acquires knowledge about the contents of the items at the meat-packing factory and the diseases the men contract from their work. He hears of one man who went undiscovered after falling into a steam vat until his body, except for his bones, had become Durham's Pure Leaf Lard. Ona's peers do not like her because she works hard. While she is pregnant with her second child, her boss Connor threatens to fire her unless she becomes his prostitute.

Other reversals slowly subjugate Jurgis. He falls into a trap and misses two months of work with an injured foot. Then he loses his job and has difficulty finding another. "In the beginning he had been fresh and strong, and he had gotten a job the first day; but now he was second-hand, a damaged article, so to speak, and they did not want him. They had got the best out of him—they had worn him out, with their speeding up and their carelessness, and now they had thrown him away!" Arrested after trying to kill Ona's boss, Jurgis has no money for bail and stays incarcerated over Christmas. "These midnight hours were fateful ones to Jurgis; in them was the beginning of his rebellion, of his outlawry and his unbelief." While he is in jail for thirty days, the family loses the house. Just after he returns, Ona dies following the delivery of a stillborn child. Blacklisted, Jurgis cannot get a job until a settlement worker intervenes. Then his son Antanas accidentally drowns. Jurgis leaves Chicago, becomes a tramp, a migrant worker, and a beggar. When he returns and discovers that Ona's boss has political ambitions, he embraces socialist principles. As the novel ends, Jurgis is exposing the vile stockyard practices to other socialists advocating change.

Brown Girl, Brownstones by Paule Marshall

In *Brown Girl, Brownstones* (1981), Selina's parents have come from Barbados in the West Indies to New York City. Paule Marshall tells Selina's story in four parts using omniscient point of view. During this bildungsroman beginning in 1939, Selina learns from her family and friends how to understand and accept herself, a process preparing her to leave home in the early 1950s. Marshall uses a precise vocabulary in contrast to the Barbadian English dialect, including such words as "fulgent," "tumenescent," and "fecund," as Selina listens to the adults who board in the brownstone—her father, Deighton Boyce; her mother Silla ("the mother"); her sister Ina; Miss Mary and her daughter, Maritze; and Miss Suggie. Selina loves the house and feels herself "something vulgar in a holy place," even with its used furniture. The family is especially proud of the unique sun parlor where Selina's father pursues his interest of the moment from studying accounting to playing the trumpet.

Selina's friends and her mother's acquaintances instruct her in a variety of ways. At home, the boarders keep Selina connected to her culture. Miss Suggie prepares "cuckoo," a mixture of okra and yellow corn meal. Her mother's friend Florrie believes in *obeah*, ties a piece of coal around her waist, and carries finny and goat foot for luck. Miss Mary's daughter Maritze is the posthumous daughter of her master, and Miss Mary lives in the past, remembering only him and his funeral before the family abandoned her. Outside the house, Selina's older friend Beryl Challenor intrigues her. She wants to know all about her and wonders "what would Beryl be like inside? Like a small well-lighted room with the furniture neatly arranged around it." Beryl's parents work hard, and Beryl's father Percy berates Selina's father for not yet purchasing a house. When they are alone, Beryl informs Selina about the female body, but the "cult of blood and breasts" disgusts her. When Selina turns fifteen, one of the new girls in her lunch group shocks her by discussing her sexual experiences.

Selina's attitude soon changes. When her friend Miss Thompson encourages her to attend the Association parties, Selina asks why. "To understand, that's why. So when you start talking so big and smart against people, you'll be talking from understanding." Selina eventually meets twenty-nine-year-old Clive Springer at an Association meeting, and, after he walks her home, she makes love to him. But Clive's mother controls his life, and Selina discovers that "love was the greater burden than hate." After excelling in a modern dance group at City College, she experiences racism when a white girl friend's mother unintentionally insults her. Selina thinks, "her dark face must be confused in their minds . . . with the night, symbol of their ancient fears, which seethed with sin and harbored violence, which spawned the beast in its fen; with the heart of darkness within them and all its horror and fascination." She knows that "along with the fierce struggle of her humanity she must also battle illusions."

Selina adores her father, although he is ineffectual. Throughout her childhood, she sees him dress carefully on Saturdays and, frightened of his wife, leave home to visit his concubine. He disables his arm at work, and, in his numerous shifts of interest, she sees him more willing to fail than to succeed. In the hospital, however, he starts following Father Peace of *The New Light*. She watches him act like a satisfied child when allowed to sit next to the hallowed man in church. Distressed, Selina becomes Antigone to her father's blinded Oedipus at Colonus as she leads him home. Deighton no longer wants her to call him "father," and he moves into a small room behind Father Peace's restaurant. Selina's mother, angry at his escape from her control, reports him to the police as an illegal alien, and police deport him. Before he arrives in Barbados, he either falls or jumps overboard the ship. Furious, Selina blames her mother for his death and calls her "Hitler."

Throughout her youth, Selina clashes with her mother. Not until the week before she decides to leave home does she understand their conflict. As a child, Selina sensed her mother's arrival from work; "Silla Boyce brought the theme of winter into the park with her dark dress amid the summer green and the bright-figured housedresses of the women lounging on the benches there." Selina has heard Silla tell her friends, "how there don seem to be no plan a-tall, a-tall to this life. How things just happen and don happen for no good reason. I tell you, it's like God is sleeping." Silla's main objective is to purchase a house, and anything, such as Deighton's refusal to make money, annoys her. Silla cannot accept her husband's deficiencies, and although the "nebula of lights sprinkled like iridescent dust on the night sky held the meaning of Saturday night—its abandonment and gaiety, love in dark rooms," she ignores love. She calls Deighton "beautiful-ugly." Selina knows her father wants to return to Barbados, but Silla refuses, telling her about "Third Class," working dawn to dusk picking grass in a cane field when only ten. She adds that Bimshire, Barbados, is "people having to work for next skin to nothing. The white people treating we like slaves still and we taking it. The rum shop and the church join together to keep we pacify and in ignorance. That's Barbados. It's a terrible thing to know that you gon be poor all yuh life, no matter how hard you work. You does stop trying after a time. People does see you so and call you lazy. But it ain laziness. It just that you does give up. You does kind of die inside."

Silla decides to sell Deighton's land in Barbados by forging his signature to give power of attorney to his sister. When the check arrives, Deighton cashes it and spends it on clothes for everyone, infuriating Silla because he thwarts her plan to purchase a house. After Silla evicts the tenants and denounces Selina's dancing, Selina discards one of the two silver arm bangles that she, like every Barbadian-American girl, has worn since birth. The other, symbolizing her heritage, she retains. She leaves behind a mother focusing on material gain but simultaneously understands that her mother needs a success, something she has never been allowed.

In *My Ántonia*, *The Jungle*, and *Brown Girl, Brownstones*, the protagonists have to learn to adjust to their new surroundings. Unable to speak the language, the Shimerdas and the Rudkus family cannot rely on others to help them, and they make many mistakes. Jurgis loses everything. Ántonia, however, masters a discouraging situation and communicates the loveliness of life to others. As the first generation, Selina suffers from her parents' distresses, but she escapes the shackles. To come to a new place takes enormous courage, and the diversity of immigrants such as these protagonists has created America's great depth and power.

Additional Related Novels

Alvarez, Julia. *How the Garcia Girls Lost Their Accents.*
Cahan, Abraham. *The Rise of David Levinsky.*
Cather, Willa. *O Pioneers!*
Crane, Stephen. *Maggie: A Girl of the Streets.*
Doctorow, E. L. *Ragtime.*
Guterson, David. *Snow Falling on Cedars.*
Kingsolver, Barbara. *The Bean Trees; Pigs in Heaven.*
Lewis, Sinclair. *Main Street.*
Ng, Fae Myenne. *Bone.*
Rölvaag. O. E. *Giants in the Earth.*
Tan, Amy. *The Joy Luck Club; The Kitchen God's Wife.*

Imprisonment

Stone walls do not a prison make,
Nor Iron bars a cage.
> —Richard Lovelace, "To Althea from Prison" (1642)

One assumes that if someone is imprisoned that he or she is incarcerated inside locked iron bars. In many cases, this physical condition exists; however, being imprisoned may also mean that one is invisibly bound by attitudes or events. In *The Heart Is a Lonely Hunter*, the small Southern mill town where the characters live refuses to let them change and grow. Carol Kennicott moves to Gopher Prairie, Minnesota, with her new husband and soon feels bound by the superficiality and insincerity of the town's socialites in *Main Street*. Throughout her marriage, Eva has suffered her husband's insensitivity as he smothered the things and ideas that she cherished in *Tell Me a Riddle*. The horrible conditions of actual imprisonment on the slave vessel *Republic* in *Middle Passage* horrify the black narrator, initially a carefree stowaway. In each of the novels, *The Fixer*, *The Confessions of Nat Turner*, and *A Lesson Before Dying*, a character languishes in jail, waiting for justice; however, other characters in these novels suffer from invisible imprisonment as well.

According to the *OED*, the denotation of "imprisonment" is "to put into prison, to confine in a prison or other place of confinement; to detain in custody, to keep in close confinement; to incarcerate." Nowhere does the definition give the impression that being incarcerated implies guilt. Thomas Hobbes notes simply in *The Leviathian*: "Imprisonment is when a man is by publique Authority deprived of liberty" (1651). In the nineteenth century, Sarah Austin refers to detainment because of religion: "They imprison men and women, and make inquisition into their faith" *(Ranke's History of the Reformation in Germany*, 1845). Martin Luther King Jr. explains another reason for confinement. "An individual who breaks a law that conscience tells him is unjust, and who willingly accepts the penalty of imprisonment in order to arouse the conscience of the community over its injustice, is in reality expressing the highest respect for the law *(Why We Can't Wait*, 1964). In the three novels, *The Fixer*, *The Confessions of Nat Turner*, and *A Lesson Before Dying*, the characters incarcerated as members of racial or cultural minorities "arouse the conscience" over the prejudice of their condition, even the one legally guilty of a crime.

The Fixer by Bernard Malamud

Bernard Malamud based *The Fixer* (1966) on the true story of an office manager in a Kiev brick factory, Mendel Beiliss, whom authorities arrested in 1911 for murdering a twelve-year-old Christian boy in order to use his blood in religious rituals. Imprisoned for two years, Beiliss was finally brought to trial and acquitted. *The Fixer*'s protagonist, Yakov Bok, is also a Kiev brick factory manager who is arrested for a similar crime and waits more than two years for trial. In the novel, however, Bok's story stops as he walks to the courtroom, leaving the reader unsure of his physical fate but certain of the psychological one. Malamud uses limited omniscient point of view and rhetorical questions to project Bok's thoughts and actions as he relates his life in two parts. First he describes his departure from his village ("I have little but I have plans") and his journey to Kiev, his experiences, and his arrest. When Bok arrives in Kiev, he can find no work in the Jewish sector ("he was a fixer and had to keep his hands busy") so he illegally moves into the Lukianovsky District and takes an assumed name, Yakov Ivanovitch Dologushev (the name of a pighandler in his village). When members of the Black Hundreds flashing their Imperial double-headed eagle symbol with the motto "Save Russia from the Jews" run through the area distributing leaflets accusing Jews of the death of a Russian boy, Zhenia Golov, Bok becomes fearful. He wonders, "What choice has a man who doesn't know what his choices are?" After his unsubstantiated arrest, Bok lands in prison.

From his birth forward, Bok has been misfortunate. His mother perished when he was ten days old, and his father perished in a pogrom when he was only one. While in school, he barely survived a pogrom himself. As a poor boy, he had little education, although on his own he had read Spinoza and taught himself some Hebrew and Russian. He married a peddlar's daughter, Raisl, a worthless and faithless woman who eventually left him for a *goy*. After Bok begins working in Kiev, he discovers that Prosliko, the brickyard foreman, steals, and Prosliko begins lying about Bok to others. After police arrest Bok for the death of Zhenia, Zhenia's mother Marfa Golov slanders Bok although she has never met him. A priest then associates Bok with tales of Jews using gentile blood for their rituals. Two prisoners beat him for the slaying, and his feet get infected from the nails in his shoes. Soon his food is poisoned, and guards begin searching his body three, and then six, times a day.

Not only does Bok have dismal luck, but he also suffers for trying to help others in need. After arriving in Kiev, he rescues the drunken Nikolai Maximovitch Lebedev, a man wearing a Black Hundred badge on his chest, from the ice. Lebedev subsequently hires him as a manager in his brickyard, never asking for his identity papers. During a snowstorm, Bok uprights an elderly Hasid and keeps him in his room until the storm ends, an action that substantiates the claim of murder against him, according to the police. While he is in prison, Raisl visits and asks him to claim her illegitimate son as his own so that he will not be ostracized. Bok agrees. When police arrest Bok, he admits that he is a Jew. His name, "Bok," means goat in German and Yiddish, and Bok continues to be a scapegoat for all those who would hide their own failures.

While in prison, Bok learns about himself. The Investigating Magistrate for Important Cases, B. A. Bibikov, discusses Spinoza with him and realizes that Bok is not guilty. But Grubeshov, his boss, says Bok must be the criminal because he is the only Jew in the district. "We suspected a Jew at once because a Russian couldn't possibly commit that kind of crime." After Bibikov tells Bok that he thinks Marfa is guilty but cannot quite prove it, Bok goes outside his cell after a drunken guard leaves the door open and sees Bibikov hanging from a belt, having commited suicide. Never having had a concern for being Jewish, Bok discovers that his whole life has centered around the one fact that he *is* Jewish. Wondering about the intense hatred of people whom he does not know, he asks, "How can anyone love Christ and keep an innocent man suffering in prison?" Later Grubeshov accuses Yakov of killing Bibikov. Finally Julius Ostrovsky comes to see Bok and gives him news that his father-in-law has died and that Marfa and her lover have already spent the insurance money that Zhenia's father left to him. He reminds Bok of the lengthy Dreyfus case in France and adds that "in a sick country every step to health is an insult to those who live in sickness." The basic lesson that Bok learns throughout the entire ordeal is that to be a Jew is to be political, something he had never before understood. He had had to review and reorder his thinking during his prison years because "where do you go if you had been nowhere?" His early observation of his trade applies to him as well—"I fix what's broken—except in the heart."

The Confessions of Nat Turner by William Styron

Like *The Fixer*, *The Confessions of Nat Turner* (1967) is also based on a true story. Nat Turner led a revolt against slave owners in Tidewater Virginia on 21 August 1831, just after his thirtieth birthday. In this fictional account, William Styron uses actual transcripts from Turner's confession and adds fictional emotions and motives to Turner's actions in a first-person account of four separate sections. Turner, called the "great bandit," hid in a cave where Benjamin Phipps captured him without resistance on Sunday, 30 October 1831. Born the property of Benjamin Turner, Nat went to live with Benjamin's brother Samuel when he was eight or nine. Samuel promised him freedom at twenty-five, but poor finances led Samuel to lend Nat to Reverend Eppes who in turn sold him to the Putnam family. When Mrs. Putnam married Joseph Travis, Nat became his de facto property. At twenty-one, he was sold to Thomas Moore and belonged to Moore when he led the rebellion.

Nat had a vision in 1826, five years before the insurrection, and thought that God confirmed his destiny as a leader for freedom. During these years, Nat worked for the Whitehead family for two months repairing their furniture and saw a gunroom behind glass where his accomplices later took guns to kill approximately fifty-five people. Nat Turner himself killed only one, a young woman of eighteen, Miss Margaret Whitehead. For this novel, some critics have maligned Stryon's use of historical record for a fictional account. Yet the indictment against slavery and its psychological imprisonment caused by tyranny, condescension, and misunderstanding cannot be underestimated.

One type of imprisonment embodied in the slaves that Nat Turner knew was the hate fostered of tyrants. Not until Samuel sends Nat to Eppes does he experience the physical pain normal for many other slaves. When Nat escapes from Eppes' attempt to sodomize him, Eppes retaliates by forcing him to work excessively hard. Nat knows that he must be patient: "I do not know how I would have survived . . . without the ability to fall into mediation upon spiritual matters." Will, one of the most vicious killers during the rebellion, has been victimized repeatedly by his owner. After beating Will and another slave named Sam, Nathaniel Francis makes the two fight as entertainment for the uneducated, crude whites in town. Will strikes out at Francis in uncontrollable anger and almost kills him. When the rebellion begins and Nat tries unsuccessfully to kill Travis, Will accuses him of being incapable of leading the slaves, and Nat has to regain control. He knows that Will is more dangerous than helpful, but Nat cannot control Will's rampage of killing as retribution for inhumane treatment throughout his life.

Other slaves feel demeaned not only physically but psychologically. Their masters treat them like objects and deny that they have any feelings. A smart slave wanted to be almost invisible. "A Negro's most cherished possession is the drab, neutral cloak of anonymity he can manage to gather around himself, allowing him to merge faceless and nameless." At the Putnam house, Nat meets other slaves including Hark, but Judge Cobb does not believe Nat at his trial who says that Hark was miserable because his wife and son had been sold. Yet the only way that the slaves can feel human is through their relationships with each other. As news of a possible rebellion spreads, the slaves meet at church, and "we gazed at each other from vast distances, yet close, awesomely close, as if sharing for the briefest instant some rare secret—unknown to other men—of all time, all mortality and sin and grief."

Nat's actual imprisonment is ironically a direct result of intelligence and knowledge. His owner Samuel, who detests the institution of slavery, discovers that Nat has stolen a book, *The Life and Death of the Badman*, because he likes the words. Samuel then breaks the law by teaching Nat to read and write. Samuel's brother Benjamin mocks him, saying "a darky, gentlemen, is basically as unteachable as a chicken." Nat admits in his discussions with his lawyer Gray, "I began as surely an experiment as a lesson in pig-breeding or the broadcasting of a new type of manure." When Judge Cobb demands that he spell "C-A-T" at his trial, Nat asks not to be mocked for his ability. While Nat is still a child, Miss Nell gives him a Bible, and Nat comments, "I must have been (though all unaware) the only black boy in Virginia who possessed a book."

Nat measures his problems with his position as a slave from his learning. "Samuel Turner . . . could not have realized, in his innocence and decency, in his awesome goodness and softness of heart, what sorrow he was guilty of creating by feeding me that half-loaf of learning." Nat becomes an asset to Samuel and his other owners because, as a master carpenter, others want to hire him. Because of his intelligence and his knowledge of the Bible, he is able to conduct thoughtful conversations with Miss Margaret Whitehead. Sexually attracted to her while she pities him, he has to deny his masculinity—a black slave considered inferior in all aspects to any white, regardless of intelligence or education. This painful knowledge leads him to start preaching to other slaves and inciting them against their suppressors. During the rebellion, killing Margaret is the only way he can regain a sense of his humanity. While in prison, he loses interest in praying until he feels remorseful for her murder. Because of the unconscionable treatment by whites of thinking and feeling humans, Nat breaks an unjust law with an unjust but justifiable action.

A Lesson Before Dying by Ernest J. Gaines

Ernest J. Gaines's novel *A Lesson Before Dying* (1993) also examines a black man's humanity. Over 100 years after the setting in *The Confessions of Nat Turner*, slavery has ended in Louisiana by 1948, but maltreatment of blacks in the community continues. Blacks must act subservient to white leaders if they need something they cannot obtain otherwise. When Jefferson is twenty-one, he accepts a ride with two black males who have been drinking. They stop at Alcee Gropé's store to ask for liquor on credit, but Gropé refuses. They protest, and he pulls out a gun. They also shoot, and all three of them die. Jefferson watches, unable to act, and, when the authorities find him, they accuse him of being involved. His lawyer tries to defend him by saying that Jefferson is only an unthinking "hog," so he could have premeditated neither the murder nor the robbery. Jefferson is convicted. "Twelve white men say a black man must die, and another white man sets the date and time without consulting one black person. Justice?" Grant Wiggins' aunt, Aunt Lou, and Miss Emma, Jefferson's godmother, attend the trial, and, distressed at the lawyer's words, the women want Jefferson to understand that he is not a hog. Grant Wiggins, the man the women choose to communicate with Jefferson, tells the story in first-person point of view except for the diary that Jefferson keeps during the last days of his life.

Grant, a teacher in the local elementary school at the church, wants to refuse the women's request to visit Jefferson. He laments his problem to his lover, Vivian, a woman not yet divorced with three children. While waiting for her after school in a local bar, he listens to the men talk about Jackie Robinson and remembers their distress after a German beat Joe Louis. He begins to understand that the old men talk about their glorious dead and their heroes just as the Irish did in a James Joyce story he once read, "Ivy Day in the Committee

Room." He asks Vivian, "What do I say to him? Do I know what a man is? Do I know how a man is supposed to die?" He finally agrees but must obtain permission from the sheriff, Henri Pichot. Although a college-educated man, Grant has to wait for nearly three hours before the sheriff will talk with him. Yet Grant knows that not only whites but also some blacks treat blacks with disdain. Vivian's family refused to visit her, accepting neither her dark-skinned husband, a graduate of Xavier University in New Orleans, nor her three children. Their actions illustrate the insidious imprisonment of race.

Grant's communication with Jefferson slowly develops over a series of visits. Jefferson at first only says that he is a hog. When Grant brings food from Miss Emma, Jefferson refuses to eat much of it, and the other prisoners share the leftovers. Grant tells Jefferson that he must act like a man for all of the blacks before him and after (like a Jackie Robinson or a Joe Louis to be revered in future conversations). Jefferson changes after the date of the execution is set, on a Friday between noon and three, two weeks after Easter. (The connection with Easter and its symbolic sacrifice identifies Jefferson as a scapegoat for the white community.) When Grant asks Jefferson what he wants, he admits that he has never had anything much but never enough ice cream. When Grant takes Jefferson a radio and pecans and peanuts from the children in his school, Jefferson tells him to thank the children, and Grant is delighted and relieved to relay the message. Jefferson also begins writing on the notepad that Grant brings and asks Paul, the guard he trusts, to give it to Grant after his death. While the journal reveals Jefferson's lack of education, it also reveals his thoughtfulness about his situation.

Although the novel focuses on Jefferson's impending execution, it also discloses Grant's growth through his interaction with Jefferson. Grant tells Jefferson, "A hero is someone who does something for other people. He does something that other men don't and can't do. He is different from other men. He is above other men. No matter who those other men are, the hero, no matter who he is, is above them." Although Grant describes Jefferson, he is also outlining the path he himself has begun by agreeing to visit Jefferson. Grant's initial reluctance to come to the prison was because he did not know what he believed (his aunt has chastised him for refusing to attend church, and the minister has told him that he is lost) and was bereft of ability to help someone in greater need. Grant has felt unable to communicate with his students and has been anticipating a move to another town. But Jefferson's responsiveness has renewed his spirit. When Paul brings Grant the journal immediately after the execution and recounts that "he was the strongest man in that crowded room. . . . Straight he walked," Grant reports it to his students, who have been on their knees since noon, and cries. Grant realizes that "only when the mind is free has the body a chance to be free." Grant's lost and found soul becomes as important as Jefferson's ability to rise to heroism.

Imprisonment detains or confines a human. In *The Fixer*, being Jewish imprisons Yakov Bok, while being black confines Nat Turner in *The Confessions of*

Nat Turner and Jefferson in *A Lesson Before Dying*. But psychological imprisonment, not being able to break from the bonds of convention or tradition, can be almost as damaging. And many other protagonists must overcome these difficulties if they will free themselves to achieve their aspirations.

Additional Related Novels

Alvarez, Julia, *In the Time of the Butterflies.*
Johnson, Charles. *Middle Passage.*
Lewis, Sinclair. *Main Street.*
Malamud, Bernard. *The Assistant.*
McCarthy, Cormac. *All the Pretty Horses.*
McCullers, Carson. *The Heart Is a Lonely Hunter.*
Oates, Joyce Carol. *Foxfire.*
Olsen, Tillie. *Tell Me a Riddle.*

Independent Women

Nothing can be more absurd than the practice that prevails in our country of men and women not following the same pursuits with all their strengths and with one mind, for thus, the state instead of being whole is reduced to half.

—Plato, *The Laws* (ca. 400 B.C.E.)

For a woman to assert her independence threatens the autonomy that many men cherish. She also disturbs other women who have not examined their beliefs and prefer to acquiesce to the wishes of fathers or husbands. When Edna Pontellier decides to separate from her husband in *The Awakening*, her friend Adèle Ratignolle admonishes her not to forget her children. Sula, in *Sula*, leaves town and faces hostility when she returns for refusing to accept the status quo. Legs Sadovsky in *Foxfire* shocks her peers with her decisions and disappears from town on her own terms. Janie in *Their Eyes Were Watching God* has to leave one husband and wait for another to die before finding her identity. The women in *Sister Carrie*, *The Autobiography of Miss Jane Pittman*, and *The Women of Brewster Place* gain their independence in a variety of ways, earning both disapproval and respect from others.

The phrase, "to be one's own man (or woman)" is "to be master of oneself; to be independent; to have the full control or use of one's faculties" (*OED*). This concept is not new. Around 1374, Chaucer's character Criseyde says "I am myn owene woman wel at ese" *(Troilus and Criseyde)*. Although Criseyde seems to control her position, women both before and after her in history have not been so fortunate. In her important treatise, "A Vindication of the Rights of Woman," Mary Wollstonecraft, like Plato two millennia before, questioned "Is not that government then very defective, and very unmindful of the happiness of one half of its members, that does not provide for honest, independent women, by encouraging them to fill respectable stations?" (1792). Desmond Bagley's character in *Snow Tiger* must still announce 200 years later, "There'll be no strings. I'm my own woman, I am" (1975). Thus women are not yet fully recognized for their abilities in Western society. Women achieve independence by having confidence in themselves. Women in *Sister Carrie*, *The Autobiography of Miss Jane Pittman*, and *The Women of Brewster Place* assert themselves and, therefore, find independence.

Sister Carrie by Theodore Dreiser

In *Sister Carrie* (1900), Theodore Dreiser creates the realism of the lower middle classes who must work to eat. He details their daily lives along with the precise amount Carrie earns for each occupation from her job in the Chicago shoe factory through her increasingly important positions as a New York chorus girl. The omniscient point of view reveals the changes that the protagonist, Caroline Meeber (Sister Carrie), undergoes after leaving her Wisconsin home to join her sister's family in Chicago during 1899 as well as those of Charles Drouet and G. W. Hurstwood, her two lovers. A narrator who comments throughout the novel's forty-seven chapters seems reliable; however, the reader must question an omniscient narrator in the assessments of Carrie's emotional responses. The narrator describes Carrie as unfulfilled after first asserting her independence by leaving home and going to Chicago. "With her sister she was much alone, a lone figure in a tossing, thoughtless sea." And independence does not bring her happiness. Carrie thinks after meeting Drouet, "Now am I lifted into that which is best," and when she joins Hurstwood, she thinks, "Now am I happy." But in interpreting her feelings after removing both from her life, the narrator implies that Carrie's relationships are her only happiness.

On the train to Chicago, the well-dressed "masher" Drouet spots Carrie and begins their relationship with a conversation. Not until after she has been sick and lost her job does she see him again. Drouet takes her to dinner at an agreeable restaurant, hears of her reduced circumstances, and offers her money for clothes. She accepts, and the narrator interjects, "The best proof that there was something open and commendable about the man was the fact that Carrie took the money." When Drouet suggests paying for her room, she agrees, eager to escape the "discordantly papered" walls, "the hall laid with a thin rag carpet," and the "poor, hurriedly patched together quality" furniture in her sister's home. Carrie, however, soon realizes that she is "more clever" than Drouet, but she remains because "fine clothes to her were a vast persuasion; they spoke tenderly and Jesuitically for themselves. When she came within earshot of their pleading, desire in her bent a willing ear." Drouet encourages Carrie to take the female lead in his Elk Lodge's play *Under the Gaslight* using his name for her, Carrie Madenda. After initial nervousness, she performs well, and Drouet considers marrying her. Unfortunately, Carrie has lost interest in him, illustrating one of the lines in the play, "Her beauty, her wit, her accomplishments, she may sell to you; but her love is the treasure without money and without price."

Carrie's relationship with Hurstwood begins when Drouet invites Hurstwood, manager of Fitzgerald and Moy's saloon, to visit him and his "wife." Hurstwood realizes that the two are unmarried, but Carrie does not know that Hurstwood has two children, Jessica, seventeen, and George, twenty, and a wife Julia, although they have "no love lost between them . . . she had her ideas and he had his." Hurstwood reveals his insensitivity when he refuses to give a dime to a homeless man outside the theater. While Drouet travels on business, Hurstwood takes Carrie driving and writes her letters. Surprised when Carrie says she will not stay with him unless they are married, Hurstwood has no idea how he will manage. His and his wife Julia's property is titled in her name, and he loses everything when she expels him from the house. At the saloon, he steals money from the open safe and, rushing to Carrie, pretends that Drouet is sick and they must go to him. Instead, he takes her to Montreal where they "marry" under the name "Wheeler." Dreiser's use of dramatic irony allows the reader to know that they are not legally married, but Carrie has no idea. After Hurstwood returns most of the money to his company, they move to New York. The newspaper headlines announce the crime, but Carrie does not read them. The narrator has observed of her that "books were beyond her interest—knowledge a sealed book." After two years in New York, Carrie decides that she wants to try acting again—another attempt at becoming independent. While Hurstwood remains unemployed, Carrie rises in her career. She leaves him, and soon Hurstwood becomes a Bowery beggar, dying on the night Jessica and her wealthy husband and his wife Julia arrive in New York on their way to Rome.

Carrie discovers that she can support herself through her acting. As soon as she obtains stage experience in a low-paying job, she rises to more lucrative positions. She goes from $12 to $30 to $150 a week. A man wanting publicity for his hotel invites her to live there for nearly nothing. When Drouet appears at her theater, he informs her of Hurstwood's actions, and for the first time, she becomes aware of the deception and her unlawful "marriage." Later she encounters Ames, the man who went to the theater with her and the Vances when Hurstwood was unavailable. Ames values her role in the theater and explains that she is obligated to use her talent. Such responsibility removes some of the glamour of her situation, especially when the attractive and philosophically intellectual Ames no longer finds her appealing. Thus "she now found herself alone." Carrie has her independence, but she says nothing to indicate that being unencumbered by any man makes her "unhappy." The narrator comments that "through a fog of longing and conflicting desires she was beginning to see. Oh, ye legions of hope and pity—of sorrow and pain! She was rocking, and beginning to see." Whatever she "sees" remains vague, although the narrator wants the reader to think she sees a long, lonely life.

The Autobiography of Miss Jane Pittman by Ernest J. Gaines

Unlike Carrie, Jane Pittman in *The Autobiography of Miss Jane Pittman* (1971), has nowhere to go when she leaves the only home she has known. An orphaned slave known as Ticey, she hauls water first for the "Secesh" army and then for the Yankees before she escapes from the plantation. A Yankee soldier named Brown calls her Jane (for his own daughter in Ohio) and suggests that she visit him. Jane first asserts her independence when she corrects her mistress for calling her Ticey, saying that her name is Jane Brown. Jane suffers the penalty—a beating. Ernest J. Gaines uses the frame of an editor taping Jane's story as she narrates it at the age of 108. Her first-person point of view gives a chronological history, in four parts (War Years, Reconstruction, The Plantation, The Quarters of the South), from before the Civil War into the second half of the twentieth century. Jane foreshadows her response to a situation to give the sense of telling a story after it has happened.

During her century-long life, Jane admires a few people and describes their feats. The man who treats her, a slave child, humanely, is her first hero. When she escapes the plantation, she plans to find Mr. Brown, but on the ferry crossing the river into Louisiana, she realizes that she will probably never reach Ohio or find Mr. Brown so she seeks work instead. Her next hero is Huey P. Long. He came in 1928, "after the high water" (Jane measures time by a flood in 1927) and gave everyone free books. She thinks, "nothing better could 'a happened to the poor black or the poor white man no matter what they say." His choices helped African Americans. "When he [Long] said nigger he said, 'Here a book, nigger. Go read your name.' When the other ones said nigger they said, 'Here a sack, nigger. Go pick that cotton.'" Jane decides that rich people wanted to kill Long because he helped the poor. She thinks they suggested that Long's guards shoot him and that the doctors in the hospital then neglected to save him. She observes the rich and their attitude to "let the poor work, let the poor fight in your wars, then let them die. But you're not suppose to help the poor." Other heroes include Jackie Robinson and Joe Lewis. She believes that God gave people Louis during the Depression "to lift colored people's heart." A local hero is Jimmy, a young boy who reads to her and lies about Jackie's home runs to cheer her. Jane and her friends expect Jimmy to be a preacher, but when he "gets religion" in 1951, he says that he does not want to preach but to satisfy that tiger "gnawing and gnawing" in his chest. Jimmy becomes involved in Civil Rights and marches with Martin Luther King Jr. But a year before the desegregation bill passes, someone assassinates Jimmy. In describing her heroes, however, Jane does not mention her own courageous actions.

As the Civil War ends, Jane begins her parenting and reveals her prescience. Because of beatings suffered as a child, Jane is unable to bear children. She encourages a group including Big Laura and her child Ned to escape from the plantation as soon as the war ends, but Confederate veterans kill everyone except Jane and Ned. Thus Jane becomes Ned's surrogate mother. She works on Bone's plantation and sends Ned to school, although she will not herself attend. She hears about secret groups—Ku Klux Klan, White Brotherhood, and the Camellias o'Luzana in Alexandria, Louisiana—and tries to protect Ned and others from them. After Ned joins a group concerned about working conditions, Jane sends him to New Orleans to evade white-sheeted Ku Klux Klan members searching for him. When Jane meets Joe Pittman, a horse trainer, she joins him and becomes mother to his two daughters. After Jane dreams that a black horse will kill Joe, she goes to Madame Eloise Gautier, a mulatto "hoo-doo" woman claiming to rival Marie Laveau in New Orleans. Madame tells her, "man must always search somewhere to prove himself. He don't know everything is already inside him." After Jane lets the black horse in her dream escape from a real corral, Joe rides after it, and it kills him. When Ned returns with his wife Vivian and three children in 1899, Jane helps raise his children and dreams that he dies in the bayou. Instead, Albert Cluveau, a hired killer, shoots him while he is returning from Bayonne with a load of wood to build a school on land he has purchased.

Even though she experiences prejudice throughout her life, Jane refuses to let it defeat her. When Jane works for Robert Samson's cane and cotton plantation, she sees his half-black son Timmy blamed for injuries to his white son Tee Bob. Samson banishes Timmy from the plantation when Tee Bob breaks an arm, and Tee Bob, not knowing Timmy's relationship to him, wants his playmate to return. But Samson accepts only his white son. After Albert Cluveau, the man with whom Jane fishes, murders Ned, she helps Ned's wife build the school. She says that the land "will never be sold. It is for the children of this parish and this State. Black and white, we don't care. We want them to know a black man died many many years ago for them. . . . He shed his precious blood for them." Jane recalls the teachers they hire—the first one who only knows the basics; Miss Lilly, a mulatto teacher, who wants the children to dress and brush their teeth; Joe Hardy, who tries to seduce the daughters, and finally Mary Agnes LeFabre, a girl whose Creole neighbors blame her for her family's wrongs. Tee Bob falls in love with her. Not understanding why she cannot marry him, he commits suicide rather than marry his father's choice for his bride. On the morning that Jimmy dies, Jane leaves the Samson's plantation to march for civil rights, even though Samson threatens not to let anyone return who marches. She continues to assert her independence and integrity throughout her life, regardless of the consequences.

The Women of Brewster Place by Gloria Naylor

Other strong African-American women, propelled to independence by their circumstances, appear in Gloria Naylor's *The Women of Brewster Place* (1982). Naylor introduces her novel, a collection of seven integrated stories, with Langston Hughes's poem, "A Raisin in the Sun," asking what happens when a person must "defer" dreams of the future. In the case of the seven women in this novel, "deferring" forces them to become independent, some successfully, and some not. The women—Mattie Michael, Etta Mae Johnson, Kiswana (Melanie) Browne, Lucielia Louise Turner, Cora Lee, and "the two," Theresa and Lorraine—meet when they move to Brewster Place in Detroit, personified as "*the bastard child of several clandestine meetings between the alderman of the sixth district and the managing director of Unico Realty Company.*" These women are survivors, and the narrator knows that wherever they live after

Brewster Place is condemned and deserted, that "*the colored daughters of Brewster, spread over the canvas of time, still wake up with their dreams misted on the edge of a yawn. They get up and pin those dreams to wet laundry hung out to dry, they're mixed with a pinch of salt and thrown into pots of soup, and they're diapered around babies. They ebb and flow, ebb and flow, but never disappear. So Brewster Place still waits to die.*"

The woman who comforts the others, Mattie Michael, has endured enough heartache to appreciate the anguish of her friends. Beaten by her own father for refusing to reveal the identity of her unborn child's father, Mattie left her home in Rock Vale, Tennessee, before Basil's birth, seeking refuge in North Carolina with her friend, Etta Mae, who had left Rock Vale in 1937, refusing to be subservient to whites. After thirty years of Mattie's pampering, Basil jumps the bail that she posts on her house after his arrest for manslaughter. Left with nothing, she moves to Brewster Place. She offers solace to her friend Etta Mae and her surrogate daughter Ciel when her child electrocutes herself. She rocks Ciel "into a blue vastness just underneath the sun and above time." Ciel's reaction is to regurgitate the residue of bereavement and physically clean the pain from her body. Mattie remains available to all who need her and refuses to judge the others' choices, including the newly arrived lesbians, Lorraine and Therese. She accepts the two, although she does not understand the relationship. And she supports Lorraine, rejected by her father, when Lorraine, deranged after a gang rape, kills the first man she sees, her friend Ben.

Young Kiswana Browne hails from wealthy Linden Hills but asserts her independence from her family by living on Brewster Place and refusing to get a telephone. From her sixth-floor apartment window, Kiswana sees her mother arrive and asks her boyfriend Abshu to leave before her mother knocks on the door. But when confronting her mother, Kiswana learns something about herself and her heritage that allows her to become an effective protester. Her mother admonishes Kiswana for changing her name from Melanie to one found in an African dictionary. Then she instructs Kiswana on her own past by noting that the woman for whom Melanie (Kiswana) was named was her great-grandmother, a full-bloodied Iroquois married to a "free black from a long line of journeymen who had lived in Connecticut since the establishment of the colonies." She was "a woman who bore nine children and educated them all, who held off six white men with a shotgun when they tried to drag one of her sons to jail for 'not knowing his place.' " Melanie's grandfather was a Bajan who arrived in America on a merchant mariner. These people, according to Mrs. Browne, "never scraped or begged or apologized for what they were. They lived asking only one thing of this world—to be allowed to be." She adds, "I learned through the blood of these people that black isn't beautiful and it isn't ugly—black is! It's not kinky hair and it's not straight hair—it just is." After Kiswana notices that her mother has painted her toenails red, she realizes that her mother and father have a life without her. She suddenly understands and appreciates that she resembles her mother in many ways and then successfully organizes rent protests. She also encourages another Brewster Place resident, Cora Lee, to take her children to a Shakespeare play in the park, and her thoughtfulness begins to change Cora Lee's life as well.

Thus the women in *Sister Carrie, The Autobiography of Miss Jane Pittman,* and *The Women of Brewster Place* have asserted their independence, not necessarily because they wanted it at first, but because they had to survive. They do not reject men; they simply have learned to live without them after disappointment or death. They have become successful in a variety of ways—as actress, as surrogate mother and real mother, as friend, as healer, as lover, as protester—and they have found contentment with themselves and their choices.

Additional Related Novels

Capote, Truman. *Breakfast at Tiffany's.*
Cather, Willa. *My Ántonia.*
Chopin, Kate. *The Awakening.*
Flagg, Fannie. *Fried Green Tomatoes at the Whistle Stop Café.*
Gibbons, Kaye. *Ellen Foster.*
Kingsolver, Barbara. *The Bean Trees; Pigs in Heaven.*
McMillan, Terry. *Mama; Waiting to Exhale.*
Morrison, Toni. *Sula.*
Oates, Joyce Carol. *Foxfire.*
Proulx, E. Annie. *The Shipping News.*
Smith, Betty. *A Tree Grows in Brooklyn.*
Turner, Nancy E. *These Is My Words.*
Wharton, Edith. *The Age of Innocence.*

Injustice

It is more disgraceful to do injustice than to suffer it.
—Plato, *Gorgias* (ca. 385 B.C.E.)

People who suffer injustice have no power to overcome those who profit from their unequal status. Such injustice occurs not only in governments but also in families and in businesses. Nat Turner faces injustice his entire life, even after he defends his rights by raising an insurrection in *The Confessions of Nat Turner*. In *The Fixer*, Yakov Bok spends years in prison, blamed for a crime he did not commit. The men congregated at Mathu's house in *A Gathering of Old Men* have long been victims of landowners. In the three novels, *A Connecticut Yankee in King Arthur's Court*, *Middle Passage*, and *In the Time of the Butterflies*, the injustices that characters experience affect everyone's lives.

In the *OED*, "injustice" is the "opposite of justice; unjust action; wrong; want of equity, unfairness." A word closely associated, "unjust," adds the synonyms of "faithless" and "dishonest," words clearly applicable to someone who treats others with injustice. Throughout history, people have assailed injustice. Plato hated it. Voltaire fought injustice constantly in his scathing satires claiming, "Men use thought only as authority for their injustice, and employ speech only to conceal their thoughts" (*Le Chapon et la Poularde*, 1763). Soon after, William Pitt responded to the American Revolution, "The Americans have been wronged. They have been driven to madness by injustice" (1792). R. G. Ingersoll declared, "There is but one blasphemy and that is injustice" (1880). Henry David Thoreau believed that "if . . . the machine of government . . . is of such a nature that it requires you to be the agent of injustice to another, then, I say, break the law" (1849). In these novels, *A Connecticut Yankee in King Arthur's Court*, *Middle Passage*, and *In the Time of the Butterflies*, injustice charades as justice, and innocent people suffer the dishonesty and unfairness of people with power over them.

A Connecticut Yankee in King Arthur's Court by Mark Twain

In Mark Twain's *A Connecticut Yankee in King Arthur's Court* (1889), Hank Morgan, a nineteenth-century arms factory superintendent from Hartford, Connecticut, is knocked on the head and awakens in the sixth century of

King Arthur's court. Hank's experiences reveal the society's slavish devotion to ritual, extolling the injustice of unequal power and devoid of any reason. In Camelot, everyone stares at Hank's oddness, and he thinks he is in an insane asylum when he spots "an airy slim boy in shrimp-colored tights." The boy informs Hank that he is a page, and Hank responds, "You ain't more than a paragraph." The page, whom Hank names Clarence, announces that he was born in 513 and that the current date is 19 June 528. Hank conveniently remembers that an eclipse occurred on June 21 of that year, and he foretells it, hoping to stay his impending execution. He interjects, "One thing at a time, is my motto—and just play that thing for all it is worth, even if it's only two pair and a jack." After the eclipse and his resulting freedom, Hank expresses dismay at the lack of intelligence and backward living. The people treat him like an elephant: "I was admired, also feared . . . as an animal is admired and feared. The animal is not reverenced, neither was I; I was not even respected."

Hank observes the people deferring to those with power in the society. He soon assesses that everyone lives and works only "to grovel before king and Church and noble." Hank concludes that the Roman Catholic Church, although merely 200 or 300 years old, "had converted a nation of men to a nation of worms." The Church preaches "divine right of kings" to the common peasant along with the beatitudes, and the people believe the propaganda. But Hank begins to gain power himself when a blacksmith calls him "The Boss," and others follow. He watches the nobles and their tournaments ("human bullfights") and the married ladies who wanted to flaunt their illicit affairs. But he remains shocked at the disregard for life. "*Any*body could kill *some*body, except the commoner and the slave. . . . If they killed, it was murder, and the law wouldn't stand murder." He hears of one woman's complaint about the Church taking her fattest pig for a tithe, "thou beast without bowels of mercy, why leave me my child, yet rob me of the wherewithal to feed it?"

Hank decides to upgrade the living conditions in Arthur's kingdom. Since his changes seem fantastic in the sixth century, they place him in competition with Merlin, the local magician. No one challenges Hank's assertions after the eclipse occurs, and his popularity infuriates Merlin. When Hank identifies a need, he tries to fill it. "There was no gas, there were no candles . . . no books, pens, paper, or ink. . . . But perhaps worst of all was, that there wasn't any sugar, coffee, tea, or tobacco." Hank starts Sunday schools and regular schools, improves the mines, founds a West Point and a naval academy, creates a telegraph and a telephone, and starts a newspaper with Clarence as the editor. After three years, "slavery was dead and gone; all men were equal before the law; taxation had been equalized." The king asks him to go "holy grailing" and save women. Eventually Hank dons heavy, bug-filled armor and rides off with Alisande (Sandy). When six knights rush at him, he blows smoke out of the helmet to scare them. One of his destinations is the castle of Morgan le Fay where he declares, "To my relief she was presently interrupted by the call to prayers. I will say this much for nobility: that, tyrannical, murderous, rapacious and morally rotten as they were, they were deeply and enthusiastically religious." He joins a pilgrim's procession and unplugs the Holy Fountain in the Valley of Holiness where Merlin has staked his reputation on magically restarting the water flow.

After being in Camelot for a number of years, Hank begins to believe some of his own power, and this attitude causes his fortunes to vacillate. At Morgan le Fay's, Hank frees forty-seven prisoners, and one of them says that "men were about all alike, and one man as good as another, barring clothes. He said he believed if you were to strip the nation naked and send a stranger through the crowd, he couldn't tell the king from a quack doctor." Hank creates a regiment whose members must renounce the Royal Grant for prominence, which helps him get rid of the grant. He is pleased to have established a newspaper until he sees the printing and layout mistakes. When he and the king travel through the countryside, Lord Grip captures them and sells them as slaves when they cannot produce identity papers. Hank says of the king as a slave, "It only shows that there is nothing diviner about a king than there is about a tramp, after all. He is just a cheap and hollow artificiality when you don't know he is a king," and, conversely, the king becomes unhappy when someone pays only seven dollars instead of twenty-five for him. Hank secretly telephones Clarence about their predicament, and knights riding bicycles come to their rescue. Having to fight Sir Sagramor begins Hank's demise in Camelot. He tries to lasso and pull him out of the saddle, but Merlin steals the rope. Instead, Hank has to shoot Sagramor and the defending knights. After Arthur dies, Merlin disguises himself as a woman, waits on the wounded Hank, and sentences him to thirteen centuries of sleep. Thus Hank loses his position in Camelot after establishing control and then creating his own injustices to retain his power.

Middle Passage by Charles Johnson

Charles Johnson's *Middle Passage* (1990) begins on 14 April 1830 when Rutherford Calhoun, freed slave of twenty-three from Illinois, stows aboard the *Republic* to escape his creditors and marriage to the intelligent Isadora, a northern free black relocated to Louisiana. In a first-person narrative, Calhoun shares the resulting horror of returning to New Orleans from the barracoon (slave factory) at Bangalang on the Guinea coast with captured men destined to become slaves in the American South. While in New Orleans, however, Calhoun wants excitement and adventure. On board, after a crew member discovers Calhoun, he becomes the cook's assistant. Then he meets the Captain, Ebenezer Falcon, a dwarf who like "all refugees from responsibility and, like social misfits ever pushing westward to escape citified life, took to the sea as the last frontier that welcomed miscreants, dreamers, and fools." Falcon buggers the cabin boy Tom and upsets the first mate, Cringle. Falcon tells Calhoun that they ate a Negro boy on one voyage, but Calhoun's intelligence surprises Falcon, and Falcon asks Calhoun to keep the ship's log. Here Calhoun discovers that Philippe Zeringue (Papa), the Creole who ordered him to marry Isadora, is one of the ship's owners. He realizes that the civic spirit Papa has showered on fellow blacks ends when it threatens Papa's wealth.

On the return voyage, Calhoun observes the crew's callow treatment of the cargo, forty members of the Allmuseri tribe. While he watches them and their overseer, a slave Ngonyama who studies everything, his hair begins to go white. "Compared to other African tribes, the Allmuseri were the most popular servants. They brought twice the price of a Bantu or Kru. . . . Eating no meat, they were easy to feed. Disliking property, they were simple to clothe. Able to heal themselves, they required no medication. They seldom fought. They could not steal. They fell *sick*, it was said, if they wronged anyone." Calhoun begins sharing his food with eight-year-old Baleka and her mother. When Baleka's mother falls overboard in a storm, Calhoun becomes her surrogate father. Simultaneously, he hears that Ngonyama has planned a mutiny and informs Falcon. When the Africans overcome the crew and fire the cannon on 12 June, only fifteen Allmuseri and four crewmen survive. After the mutiny, Falcon kills himself.

A part of Calhoun's past that he cannot reconcile is the disappearance of his father when he was a young boy. His father left the plantation where Calhoun was a slave, promising to return, but did not. Calhoun has assumed that his father abandoned him and his brother. When his brother Jackson, eight years older, refused to take their master's inheritance, Calhoun was furious at the decision because he had no money. Not until he experiences the injustice of the slave quarters aboard ship and the terror of the mutiny, can he begin to understand his brother's wisdom. The most profitable part of the cargo, a creature that Falcon refuses to introduce, helps Calhoun gain valuable knowledge. When Tommy returns from looking at him in the hole, he goes crazy, and Cringle begins protecting Tommy from Falcon. Finally Falcon discloses to Calhoun that the creature is a god. He says, "For example, a god can't know its own nature. For itself, it can't be an object of knowledge. D'you see the logic here? The Allmuseri god is everything, so the very knowing situation we mortals rely on—a separation between knower and known—never rises in its experience." When Calhoun must feed the god, a shape-shifter, it presents itself to Calhoun as Calhoun's father, Riley Calhoun, the fugitive. The god reveals to Calhoun that Riley died at twenty-eight as soon as he left the farm, unable to defend himself in a different world. When Calhoun comprehends that the god's name is "Rutherford," he becomes irrational for three days, and the rest of his hair turns white.

After the mutiny, Rutherford reassesses his priorities. While waiting for rescue, the dying Cringle asks for Squibb, another crewman, to kill him so that his body can nourish the crew. Soon the ship sinks, and a "floating gin palace" sailing between New Orleans and the West Indies rescues Calhoun, Squibb, and three children. Calhoun thinks that "by surviving, I sometimes felt I'd stolen life from Cringle, or was living on time belonging to Ngonyama and the other mates; I felt like a thief to the bitter end. . . . I considered how easy it would be, and perhaps just, to join my drowned shipmates by hanging myself." When Calhoun finally exits his cabin, he discovers that Papa Zeringue is on board with Isadora, planning to marry her. But Isadora has been stalling Papa by making booties for abandoned dogs and unraveling them like Penelope in *The Odyssey*. When Calhoun accuses Papa, Papa's bodyguard Santos reveals that his own father was an Allmuseri. Shocked that Papa has been dealing in slaves, Santos deserts him. When Isadora sees the changes in Rutherford, especially his concern for the child Baleka, she agrees to marry him. Thus a man controlled by money treats those unjustly who would thwart him, even members of his own minority race.

In the Time of the Butterflies by Julia Alvarez

In the Time of the Butterflies (1994) presents the story of the four Mirabel sisters living under Rafael Leonidas Trujillo's regime in the Dominican Republic during the 1930s. Trujillo had three of the Mirabel women murdered in an ambush as they returned from visiting their husbands in prison. Julia Alvarez creates a fictional account through the eyes of Dedé, the fourth Mirabel, who survived to keep the story of her sisters alive and tells it to a writer in 1994. The novel, in three parts, with both an epilogue and a postscript, covers the years 1938–1946, 1948–1959, and 1953–1958. Each focuses on one sister from her first-person point of view. The sisters faced injustices related to their politics and their sex throughout their lives.

Dedé recalls the story of each of her sisters after she has become a divorced prize-winning life insurance salesperson and victim of breast cancer, one breast removed. After her sisters' deaths, she wants to commit suicide, but her then-husband Jaimito tells her, "This is *your* martyrdom, Dedé, to be alive without them." The oldest sister (born in 1924), Patria Mercedes Mirabel, was quite religious and planned to take orders until she met Pedrito González from the next town at sixteen. She marries him, but when her third child is born dead, she loses her faith. Minerva Mirabel (born in 1926) wants to be a lawyer, and she coerces Trujillo to let her attend school against her father's wishes. The youngest (born in 1935), Mate (Maria Teresa) says about her schooling as a young student in her diary, "We are having Rest & Silence before lights-out. We must keep quiet and not visit with each other, but think only of our immortal souls. I am so tired of mine."

The injustices of the Trujillo regime affect the entire family. When Minerva goes away to school in 1938, she changes. She recalls "that's how I got free. I . . . realized that I'd just left a small cage to go into a bigger one, the size of our whole country." Minerva discovers that Trujillo had murdered her friend Sinita's uncles and then Sinita's brother just as Trujillo had arranged for all his superiors to be murdered for a variety of complicities before declaring himself president. The dwarf who sold lottery tickets stabbed Sinita's brother on his way home from church. Lina Lovatón, another student, attracts Trujillo's attention, and he starts visiting her. Then he gives her a birthday party and moves her to a house where he can see her often, even though he is married to someone else. On one visit, four students present a play in which they camouflage a protest for freedom, but they anger Trujillo when Sinita shoots a real arrow at him. When Trujillo becomes interested in Minerva at a Discover Day Ball, she slaps him in the face while they are dancing. Near the end of his regime, the Church finally declares against him, but not until thirty-one years after he established power is Trujillo assassinated and free elections held.

As adults, the sisters discover surprises about themselves and their family. Their mother has hidden her illiteracy while raising them. Minerva uncovers her father's other family, a mistress and four daughters, when she is twenty-three. Although furious at first, she understands that that family has suffered its own injustices. She invites them to his funeral, and she and Patria use part of their inheritance to educate the half-sisters. After Minerva marries and has a child, she finishes her law degree, but Trujillo betrays her by not allowing her to obtain a license to practice. Always angry at the Mirabel sisters for insulting him, Trujillo seems to have devoted time to finding the best way to destroy them and their underground work as the Mariposas (butterflies).

The underground network first includes the three sisters and their husbands, but eventually Dedé disobeys her husband and aligns with the others. Minerva and her husband Manolo lead the way, and Mate willingly joins. Then when Patria's husband and son are arrested, her home becomes a meeting place for their group calling itself "The Fourteenth of June." While in prison, news of an assassination attempt against Trujillo encourages Mate and Minerva. Finally, they are released and placed under house arrest, allowed only to visit their husbands. On one trip with their favorite driver Rufino, they face a road blockage. After they stop, someone kills them and pushes their vehicle over the side of a cliff. When news reports call them "The Butterflies," Dedé laments that "people romanticized other people's terror!" She chooses to tell their stories so that someone will know the truth.

Through his satire, Twain produces a scathing commentary on the injustice of the nineteenth century—the inequality of humans and the meaningless conventions they accept as standards in society. Calhoun notices that the Allmuseri in *Middle Passage* think, "What came *out* of us, not what went in, made us clean or unclean." Thus humans who treat others unjustly should suffer the consequences of their own inhumanity. In *In the Time of the Butterflies*, the terrible injustice of a political dictatorship becomes apparent as well as the silent suffering expected of women in a machismo society. An examination of these three novels exposes the insidious and subtle forms that injustice can take in human lives.

Additional Related Novels

Clark, Walter Van Tilburg. *The Ox-Bow Incident.*

Doctorow, E. L. *Ragtime*.
Gaines, Ernest J. *The Autobiography of Miss Jane Pittman*; *A Gathering of Old Men*; *A Lesson Before Dying*.
Guterson, David. *Snow Falling on Cedars*.
Kingsolver, Barbara. *The Poisonwood Bible*.
Lee, Harper. *To Kill a Mockingbird*.
Malamud, Bernard. *The Fixer*.
McCarthy, Cormac. *All the Pretty Horses*.
Oates, Joyce Carol. *Foxfire*.
Sinclair, Upton. *The Jungle*.
Styron, William. *The Confessions of Nat Turner*.

Journeys

> The journey is the reward.
>
> —Taoist saying

One who takes a journey moves from one place to another. Usually the journey is physical, but often characters take metaphoric journeys. In *The Adventures of Huckleberry Finn*, Huck rafts down the Mississippi River and observes the horrors of "civilization." Taylor drives from Arizona to Oklahoma on her way to legally claim Turtle as her adopted daughter in *The Bean Trees*. Five people cross a Peruvian rope bridge between Lima and Cuzco, and after they die when it breaks, a priest examines their lives to find their common bond in *The Bridge of San Luis Rey*. In *The Lilies of the Field*, Homer Smith tarries from his western travel to build a chapel for a group of German nuns. In three novels, *On the Road*, *The Crying of Lot 49*, and *Cold Mountain*, the protagonists take journeys that move them both physically and psychologically from their starting points.

In the *OED*, a journey is "a 'spell' or continued course of going or traveling." A journey has a beginning and an end "in place or time," making it "a distinct whole." It is "a march, ride, drive, or combination of these or other modes of progression to a certain more or less distant place, or extending over a certain distance of space or time." The term usually refers to travel on land rather than by sea, and an adjective or phrase such as "long, short, quick" or "to New York" usually qualifies it. Throughout history, movement from one place to another has been termed a "journey." In the fifth century B.C.E., Confucius claimed, "a journey of a thousand miles begins with a single step." In the twentieth century, Ursula K. LeGuin professed, "It is good to have an end to journey toward, but it is the journey that matters in the end." And Alex Noble noted that "success is not a place at which one arrives but rather . . . the spirit with which one undertakes and continues the journey" (1979). In *On the Road*, the protagonist has no destination; in *The Crying of Lot 49*, the journey changes focus; and in *Cold Mountain*, others interrupt the protagonist's desired straight path.

On the Road by Jack Kerouac

Considered by some to be a critique of the Beat generation of the late 1940s and early 1950s, Jack Kerouac's *On the Road* (1957) presents Sal Paradise, a young man whose character is loosely based on Kerouac's own experiences, as he tries to escape from himself and others by aimlessly crisscrossing the United States. Paradise meets Dean Moriarty after he has left his wife, overcome a serious illness, and moved in with his aunt in Paterson, New Jersey. In a first-person narration, Paradise itemizes, with digressions, their journeys and his own. He emphasizes the value of moving rapidly, drinking alcohol continually, and enjoying sex frequently. He moves through time and space, seeming to have a destination, but, once he reaches a place, he leaves unsatisfied with what he has found. He visits Denver, San Francisco, Los Angeles, Washington, D.C., New Orleans, Tucson, New York, and places in between. When he ceases his journey, he still has not found the father for whom he and Dean seem to be searching.

Sal meets and uses or abuses several people during these two years, often saying in response to anything, "It's not my fault." In Denver on his first trip, he stays with friends who dislike Dean and his friend, poet Carlo Marx (a minor character based on Allen Ginsburg). Sal says of them, "They were like the man with the dungeon stone and the gloom, rising from the underground, the sordid hipsters of America, a new beat generation that I was slowly joining." Sal arrives in San Francisco two weeks later than he had told his prep school friend Remi Boncoeur to expect him. After working a little and drinking a lot while living with Remi and his girlfriend, Sal resumes his journey. On the bus, he meets Terry, a Mexican girl, as immature and childlike as he is. Although he says he knows himself, his actions belie him. He muses, "You start your life a sweet child . . . Then . . . you know you are wretched and miserable and poor and blind and naked." Yet Paradise continues his wanderings, while admitting weakness that he seems not to believe. "This is the night, what it does to you. I had nothing to offer anybody except my own confusion." Not only has he nothing to offer but he also has no understanding of what he observes. He misses the nuances of poverty, unhappiness, and need in those he meets, seeing them only in his terms of what he would have them be.

Sal seems to depend on Dean, although Dean offers no stability. Dean and Sal join for a trip, separate, rejoin, and separate—each time both entertaining and irritating each other. Sal leaves his brother's home in Testament, Virginia, after Christmas when Dean unexpectedly appears, and the two travel across country. Sal says, "With frantic Dean I was rushing through the world without a chance to see it." But Sal never asks to stop. Back in New York, they frequent clubs where black musicians play, a risky occupation for white men in 1949. During this time, Dean marries a third wife. When Sal's publisher pays him for his book, Sal has money to keep moving. Later Dean rejoins Sal, and they reach Mexico. While Sal suffers from dysentery, Dean again leaves him. Finally Sal returns to New York where, after meeting Laura, he decides to stay. Denying both commitment and responsibility, he has learned little about himself. He remembers his journeys one evening at dusk and says, "I think of Dean Moriarty, I even think of Old Dean Moriarty the father we never found, I think of

Dean Moriarty." Sal seems to realize that his journey was a search for someone to look after him, a father, but he remains unfulfilled after thousands of miles have taken him nowhere and has no understanding of either himself or others.

The Crying of Lot 49 by Thomas Pynchon

In *The Crying of Lot 49* (1966), the protagonist, Oedipa Maas learns that deceased California real estate mogul and her former lover, Pierce Inverarity, has made her the executrix of his estate. After consulting with her husband and their lawyer, Oedipa agrees to take the job. She leaves her home in fictional Kinneret-Among-The Pines, California, and travels south to San Narciso near Los Angeles, a town that from an elevated height looks like an electronic circuit with a "hieroglyphic sense of concealed meaning, of an intent to communicate." Here, instead of answers to her questions about executing estates, she finds new questions without answers. Thomas Pynchon's puns and wordplay create humorous complexities underlying the main plot that quickly shifts from Oedipa as executrix to Oedipa trying to understand the concept of history and the role of entropy in her life as she exposes an underground mail system allowing people to communicate outside the U.S. postal system monopoly.

On her physical journey, Oedipa travels to unexpected destinations and meets unique characters. Oedipa (her first name reminiscent of Greek myth and her last the word for "mesh" in Afrikaans) leaves her husband Wendell "Mucho" Maas (Spanish language pun), a former used car salesman and current disk jockey who believes that used cars had more redeeming value for the buyer than the music he plays on the radio, for San Narciso. At her motel, she meets Miles, leader of the Paranoids (a rock band) and Pierce's lawyer Metzger (once a child star named Baby Igor) who tells her that all lawyers have to be actors. During their examination of Pierce's estate, Oedipa discovers that Pierce owns holdings in the Galatronics Division of Yoyodyne (an aerospace contractor), Vesperhaven House (a rest home), Zapf's Used Books, Fangoso Lagoons (a housing development), a theater playing *The Courier's Tragedy*, and a stamp collection containing counterfeit stamps relating to the Trystero in the W.A.S.T.E. system.

The first indication that she must investigate new questions occurs in The Scope, a bar close to Yoyodyne. There Mike Fallopian discusses his book on the history of private mail carriers with Oedipa and Metzger, they observe a "mail call," and Oedipa finds the acronym WASTE next to a muted horn symbol etched on the bathroom wall. On a visit to Fangoso Lagoons with the Paranoids, they meet Manny di Presso, lawyer to black-market dealer Tony Jaguar who wants his payment for human bones delivered to Pierce and deposited in the Lagoons to attract skin divers. Having just seen *The Courier's Tragedy*, the Paranoids think that di Presso's story resembles the play in which a despot deposited human bones in a lake. Oedipa's journey involves the stockholders' meeting at Yoyodyne and an encounter with Stanley Koteks doodling the Trystero symbol of a muted horn; continues to Berkeley where she stops at the Greek Way (a gay bar); meets John Nefastis (experimenter with thermodynamic and communication entropy), a Mexican anarchist, and a derelict sailor; and follows a mail carrier back to John Nefastis. Then she visits Fangoso Lagoons, the Vesperhaven House and Mr. Thoth, and home, before returning to San Narciso to contact Emory Bortz and consult with Genghis Cohen about the stamp collection.

Oedipa's mental journey develops as answers elude her at each stop. Identifying the muted horn symbol becomes her focus as soon as she begins her duties as executrix. Thus, her intellectual search defines her journey. After the Paranoids mention *The Courier's Tragedy*, she attends a performance of the five-act play by Richard Wharfinger suggesting incest between Duke Angelo and his sister Francesca and his attempt to marry her to Pasquale, the Faggian usurper, who happens to be Francesca's son with the Duke of Faggio (elements of Oedipus). The complicated play reveals that Angelo murdered the Lost Guard of Faggio and threw its members into the lake. The bones are retrieved, made into charcoal, and then ground into ink that Angelo uses to write a letter confessing his guilt. The mysterious Trystero attempts to infiltrate the actual Thurn and Taxis mail system and overtake the lucrative courier business. Curious, Oedipa questions Driblette, the director who plays Gennaro, a quiet man who becomes ruler after Angelo dies. Driblette admits, "I'm the projector at the planetarium, all the closed little universe visible in the circle of that stage is coming out of my mouth, eyes, sometimes other orifices also." Genghis Cohen, the philatelist, later tells Oedipa that the horn is the coat of arms of Thurn and Taxis and that the mute on the horn would symbolize the Trystero's intent to silence their house.

Oedipa has additional unsettling experiences during her trip to Berkeley. She wants to talk to the published play's editor, Emory Bordz, but he has moved to San Narciso, so she visits the last inventor to receive an individual patent from Yoyodyne, John Nefastis. He tells her that "entropy is a figure of speech, then . . . a metaphor. It connects the world of thermodynamics to the world of information flow. The Machine uses both. The Demon makes the metaphor not only verbally graceful, but also objectively true." She fails to activate his machine, a Maxwell Demon box, as one of the "sensitives" and rushes out when Nefastis proposes sex and watching cartoons instead. During her continued search for the identity of the Trysteros, she consults the aged Mr. Thoth (Egyptian god of magic and knowledge) and discovers that his father, a Pony Express rider, had a ring inscribed with the muted horn. At the Greek Way, a man wearing the symbol on his coat declares his allegiance to Inamorati Anonymous, a group believing that love is the worst addiction.

Finally, Oedipa meets a sailor who asks her to mail his year-old letter to his wife and tells her where the W.A.S.T.E. mailbox sits. She waits for the letter carrier and follows him, only to find herself completing a circle as she comes back to the home of John Nefastis. Totally confused, she attempts suicide by driving on the freeway with her vehicle lights extinguished. Her failure and the deaths or desertions of men who might know answers means that she must continue her journey alone. Metzger runs away with a Paranoid's girlfriend; "Mucho begins taking LSD"; Driblette commits suicide; and Dr. Hilarus, her psychiatrist who goes berserk, tells her to cherish her fantasy. Expecting to have the solution to the Tristero at the auction of Pierce's unusual stamp collection, lot 49, she waits at the novel's indeterminate ending for the auctioneer to "cry" it. Oedipa's journey goes in circles and whether she reaches "the central truth itself" remains unknown.

Cold Mountain by Charles Frazier

Charles Frazier sets *Cold Mountain* (1998) during the time of the Civil War; however, he focuses on the characters and their personal needs rather than the scope of the conflict itself. His own great-great uncle, W. P. Inman, deserted from the Confederate Army after being wounded. Frazier's character, Inman, does the same. Frazier structures the novel with alternating chapters from the point of view of Inman and Ada, the woman he loves back home. Although the war separates them, each journeys toward the other, one remaining stationary with the other walking 300 miles. The people with whom they interact, some exemplary and some evil, instruct them about the ways of others.

Before Inman leaves Cold Mountain, he falls in love with Ada, and he anticipates the time he will see her again during his battles, his recovery from a neck wound at Petersburg reading Bertram's *Travels* as a way to pass the time, and his journey home. Detesting the war, Inman recalls Swimmer, the Cherokee whose "spells portrayed the spirit as a frail thing, constantly under attack and in need of strength, always threatening to die inside you." Inman worries about his soul and knows he must desert instead of returning to battle. After dressing and disappearing from the hospital, Inman begins his journey home. But he knows that what he seeks may not be waiting for him. He told Ada on the day he left for war, "that's not a thing any of us are granted. To go back. Wipe away what later doesn't suit us and make it the way we wish it. You just go on." While he walks, he remembers first seeing Ada on the day he heard her father preach the best sermon he had ever witnessed. While trying to reach her, Inman staves off three attackers at the Cape Fear River; ties up Veasey, a preacher trying to murder a woman he impregnated; meets helpful gypsies; encounters Odell who searches for the octoroon slave he loves after leaving his fortune to his wife; and helps Junior dislodge a bull from a stream before Junior reports him to the Home Guard as a deserter for a five-dollar bounty. Inman escapes death when guards hit Veasey instead of him, and a slave gives him food and a place to hide. Then a woman who raises goats furnishes him with medicine before he saves a young mother from three Federals who take her hog. When he reaches Cold Mountain, he finds Ada in the woods, and, for Inman, his journey ends.

Ada's physical journey ended before Inman left. She and her father had moved from Charleston, South Carolina, six years before when he took a church in Cold Mountain. Her father had married her mother, Claire Dechutes, after falling in love before she married an old Frenchman, and waiting twenty years for her to be widowed. She died at Ada's birth two years later. After Ada's father's death, Ada let the farm lapse, not being capable of or interested in preserving it. When an embargo on Charleston prevents her from obtaining her father's money, she must act. A neighbor sends Ruby to her, and Ruby teaches her how to survive. When Ruby's shiftless father Stobrod had deserted her, she had learned enough from nature to stay alive. When Ruby's father reappears at Ada's house, Ruby agrees to feed him, and, in appreciation, he joyfully plays the fiddle. "To Ada, though, it seemed akin to miracle that Stobrod, of all people, should offer himself up as proof positive that no matter what a waste one has made of one's life, it is ever possible to find some path to redemption, however partial." But the Home Guard finds Strobrod and tries to kill him. When Ada and Ruby go into the woods to bury him, they discover him still living, although barely. While they try to resuscitate him, Inman appears. Ada's journey has inadvertently led her to Inman, and she sleeps with him. The next day, however, the Home Guard returns for Inman, and after Inman kills all but a young boy, the young boy retaliates and kills him. In the epilogue set nine years later, Ruby and the Georgian boy who helped them, their children, and Ada and Inman's child live together at her home, Black Cove. Ada's and Inman's journeys toward each other from opposite places culminate in the child of their brief union.

In none of these novels, *On the Road*, *The Crying of Lot 49*, and *Cold Mountain*, does the character complete the journey as anticipated. Sal flounders, Oedipa waits expectantly, Inman dies, and Ada raises her extended family. The unplanned path of the journey itself provides the protagonists with their experiences of doubt and confusion and hope of reaching a desired destination. After the emotional and physical upheavals, all of them might issue the same advice of one woman to Inman in *Cold Mountain*, "Our minds aren't made to hold on to the particulars of pain the way we do bliss. It's a gift God gives us, a sign of His care for us."

Additional Related Novels

Barrett, William E. *The Lilies of the Field.*
Bellow, Saul. *Henderson, the Rain King.*
Dickey, James. *Deliverance.*
Johnson, Charles. *Middle Passage.*
Kingsolver, Barbara. *The Bean Trees.*
Maxwell, William. *The Folded Leaf.*
McCarthy, Cormac. *All the Pretty Horses.*

Melville, Herman. *Moby-Dick.*
Steinbeck, John. *The Grapes of Wrath.*
Twain, Mark. *The Adventures of Huckleberry Finn.*
Wilder, Thornton. *The Bridge of San Luis Rey.*

Knowableness of God

God is the most Knowable and most Lovely Thing in the world; excess of
Knowableness following the Greatness of his Essence.
                    —Nathaniel Ingelo, *Bentivolio and Urania* (1660)

One of the basic questions about life concerns the existence of God. Some ada-
mantly support it; others vehemently deny it. Although no tangible proof exists for either viewpoint, almost everyone has a strong opinion. Holden
Caulfield in *The Catcher in the Rye* wants to know about God. Nat Turner severs his relationship with God in *The Confessions of Nat Turner* after his imprisonment. When Rutherford Calhoun comes face-to-face with the god of the
Allmuseri tribe in *Middle Passage*, his hair turns white. Atticus Finch in *To Kill
a Mockingbird* declares that he cannot attend church unless he defends the innocent Tom Robinson in a case Atticus knows he will lose. In *Bless Me, Ultima*,
the lines between God and Ultima blur as Antonio experiences Ultima's love
and kindness. The novels, *The Poisonwood Bible*, *Go Tell It on the Mountain*,
and *Cold Sassy Tree*, each contain a protagonist grappling with the abstractness
of God.

   That which is "knowable," according to the *OED*, is something "capable of
being apprehended, understood, or ascertained." God, "in the specific Christian and monotheistic sense," is the "one object of supreme adoration; the
Creator and Ruler of the Universe." Eustace R. Conder notes, "For by this
name God we understand an Infinite Mind, everywhere present, the source
and foundation of all other existence, possessed of all possible power, wisdom,
and excellence" (*The Basis of Faith*, 1877). Because individuals apprehend in
diverse ways, whether someone can "know" God seems improbable. Religious
philosophers differ in their explanations of knowing God—oral tradition, intuition, or reason are a few. Adolf Hitler asked after accusations against him,
"Who says I am not under the special protection of God?" And Albert Einstein
mused, "I want to know all God's thoughts . . . all the rest are just details."
Cervantes refuses to question in *Don Quixote*; he asserts, "God knows the
truth, and let it rest there" (1605). In *The Poisonwood Bible*, one man convinced that he knows God's will endangers his family. In *Go Tell It on the Mountain*, the protagonist has a conversion experience after which he anticipates
finding answers about suffering. And in *Cold Sassy Tree*, one of the characters

has a close relationship with the being he calls God, although it bears no resemblance to the expectations of his neighbors.

The Poisonwood Bible by Barbara Kingsolver

In 1959, the missionary Nathan Price takes his family from Bethlehem, Georgia, to Kilanga in the Belgium Congo in *The Poisonwood Bible* (1998). In the novel's seven books, Barbara Kingsolver presents the points of view of the mother, Orleanna Price, and the four daughters—Rachel, fifteen; the twins Leah and Adah, fourteen; and Ruth May, five. During their stay, the Congo wins independence from Belgium; the first elected prime minister, Lumumba, is murdered; and the Central Intelligence Agency of the United States supports a coup stripping autonomy from the people. Price refuses to remove his family from danger, convinced that his presence is necessary to save the natives from hell. His single vision destroys his future and kills one of his children.

Voices of the daughters include Ruth Mae and Rachel along with their mother, Orleanna. Blonde and blue-eyed Rachel regrets missing her sixteenth birthday party in Georgia. Later, she remains in Africa, seemingly unaware of any spiritual possibilities through her three marriages, the first to the shifty expatriate Axelroot, to the third from which she inherited the hotel and business. Ruth May makes friends with the villagers but contracts a disease. After nursing her and combating army ants, hookworm, incessant rain, drought, and hunger, Orleanna grieves over Ruth May's death from the bite of a deadly green mamba snake, barely surviving the pain. Of Ruth May, Orleanna says, "the substance of grief is . . . as real as rope or the absence of air, and like both those things it can kill." Orleanna has had to dog paddle through this sargasso on which she "had washed up . . . on the riptide of my husband's confidence and the undertow of my children's needs." After Orleanna and her three daughters leave Nathan, Orleanna discloses, "Hell hath no fury like a Baptist preacher. I married a man who could never love me. . . . I remained his wife because it was one thing I was able to do each day." Her cherished memory of the African experience is the beautiful rarely seen okapi that she glimpsed fleeting through the brush one day.

The twins, Leah and Adah, perceive life differently. Leah thinks that gaining her father's approval and following his guidance will save her soul from chaos. She believes "that the Lord would see my goodness and fill me with light." When initially leaving Georgia, the family carried excess baggage, and Leah says, "My father, of course, was bringing the Word of God—which fortunately weighs nothing at all." When she wonders why Nathan keeps his family in the Congo while other expatriates leave daily, she begins to question his other choices. He shatters her secure world with "only faith in My father and love for the Lord" though his inability to perceive real danger. Leah falls in love with Anatole, a native who helps the family, and she decides that he will marry her, although she knows that her being white will jeopardize both his future and his life in the Congo.

Adah, a victim of hemiplegia, limps and refuses to talk but writes in palindromes. She notes, "It is true I do not speak as well as I can think. But that is true of most people." She loves poetry, especially that of the physician William Carlos Williams and Emily Dickinson. When she returns to Atlanta with her mother, leaving Leah and Rachel in Africa, she presents herself to the medical school dean at Emory University and tells him that although poor, she must attend. He disagrees until she creates a formula just looking at his books and reverses his name into a French word. In the school, however, she finds a god that she wants to know. She immerses herself in the sciences—organic chemistry, invertebrate zoology, and genetics. They become the foundation of her worship. She remarks, "I recite the Periodic Table of Elements like a prayer; I take my examinations as Holy Communion." At the end of her first semester, she responds to her success as a "sacrament." Adah retrains her body to overcome her disability, a long practiced habit instead of a deformity, but simultaneously loses her ability to see words and their reverse. Even though she looks normal to others and stands straight, she views herself as "Adah inside. A crooked little person trying to tell the truth." She cannot deny her past physical imperfections because they helped form her present shortcomings and "successes." She sees her mother, reasonably content, and remembers her father's unshaken faith in his God, and realizes that each family member had lived with "a misunderstanding, and if ever I tried to pull it out and fix it now I would fall down flat. Misunderstanding is my cornerstone."

Seen through the eyes of his wife and daughters, Nathan thinks he knows God and God's design for humans, perceives himself as a direct conduit to God through the official source of the Bible, and expects all around him to revere his elevated position as God's chosen speaker. Price's egoistical and irrational decisions surprise and dismay the reader. The people of Kilanga, recently exposed to elections, logically interrupt Nathan's church service to vote on whether to accept Jesus as savior in Kilanga; much to Nathan's horror, Jesus loses. Nathan seems unable to accurately hear a just God, and his translations to Kikongo, a language built on intonation as well as words, illustrates this fault. When he says "Tata Jesus is bangala," his incorrect accent makes "bangala" translate as "poisonwood tree" instead of "precious and dear." When he ignores local advice and touches a poisonwood tree, he almost dies as his body swells and burns. When snake venom kills Ruth May, Price seems more concerned that she died unbaptized than that she suffered. As one who has shadowed her father and wanted his unconditional approval, Leah finally faces the reality of him. "If I had a prayer left in me, it was that this red-faced man shaking with rage would never lay a hand on me again." Neither in Georgia nor in Kilanga did Nathan allow his wife to grow flowers, and after she and the girls leave him, Oleanna reveals a love for and an ability to grow beautiful flowers. Adah describes her as "an entire botanical garden waiting to happen." About Nathan, Orleanna finally reflects that men with his intractability always face defeat. Whether a leader of a country or the patriarch in a family, "They stand still, and their stake moves underneath them." Adah has the insight, "we are the balance of our damage and our transgressions. He was my father. . . . I am born of a man who believed he could tell nothing but the truth, while he set down for all time the Poisonwood Bible." In the Price family, Nathan remains the one with no knowableness of a loving God.

Go Tell It on the Mountain by James Baldwin

In *Go Tell It on the Mountain* (1953), the protagonist, John Grimes, searches for answers from God about the difficulties of his family. James Baldwin tells his story in three parts—"The Seventh Day," "Prayers of the Saints," and "The Threshing Floor"—with differing points of view. Baldwin examines the emotions of several characters through psychological realism. All have to function in the same community, and when they confront themselves, they comprehend the complexities of their relationships with each other and with society and its institutions. Almost all the characters have names from the Bible. John lives in Harlem with his parents, Elizabeth and Gabriel, and three siblings, Roy, Sarah, and Ruth. Once a famous minister in the South, Gabriel now works and helps maintain the church, preaching only occasionally. On John's fourteenth birthday in March 1935, his mother gives him money to spend as he wishes, and he chooses to go to a movie on Sixth Avenue. When he returns, Roy has instigated a fight, and whites have slashed his eye. Gabriel blames Elizabeth and John for not protecting Roy since Gabriel's alleged love for God does not extend to all his family.

John feels discomfort about his conflicting emotions for family and friends. He "cherishes" his intelligence (he loves the lions guarding the New York City Library on 42nd Street), and holds it over his father. He compares cleaning the rug on Saturdays to the myth of Sisyphus and remembers the principal calling him a "very bright boy" at six. But he also "cherishes" his hatred and guiltily wants his father dead. He especially enjoys the company of Elisha, the seventeen-year-old nephew of the minister who helps the youth at church. When the minister admonishes Elisha for walking with Ella Mae, trying to keep him from sinning "a sin beyond all forgiveness," John realizes that he has sinned with his hands in the school bathroom while thinking about the older boys. People at church think John will be a leader, but he is "not much interested in his people and still less in leading them anywhere." Until his conversion, after he and Elisha have cleaned the church, he has no interest in succumbing to religion. His decision to be "saved" seems based on his need for answers from God about his confusions.

Others in John's family have serious emotional issues to resolve, and through their prayers at the Tarry service, John becomes aware of adult problems that only change can solve. His mother's text for life is "Everything works together for good for them that love the Lord.'" Her own mother died when Elizabeth was nine, disappointed that Elizabeth was too dark, and, although her father loved her, her aunt took her to Maryland, away from her father's "house." In New York at eighteen, she met Richard who worked in the same hotel, and since he studied at night to learn as much as white men knew, they went to museums on Saturdays. As his concubine, a word "tart like lemon rind," she becomes pregnant. Before she can tell him, he is unjustly accused of robbery while awaiting a subway train at two o'clock on a Sunday morning and standing next to the culprits when the police make their arrest. They take four instead of the guilty three. He is beaten and freed but commits suicide anyway.

After John's birth, Elizabeth creates a new life when she meets Gabriel's sister Florence at work. Florence had left for New York after her mother had sent Gabriel to school and her current employer had proposed an affair. She married Frank who left for another woman after ten years. When Gabriel comes North, Florence tells Elizabeth, "Folks . . . can change their ways much as they want to. But I don't care how many times you change your ways, what's in you is in you, and it's got to come out." Then when Gabriel misrepresents his former life, Florence saves letters from his wife Deborah who knew about Gabriel's illegitimate son Royal with Esther who died in childbirth. Esther met Gabriel while he was preaching, and he, forgetting, the "knowableness" of God, began an affair with her. Then he stole money from Deborah so that Esther could go North to have their child. The barren Deborah admitted that she would have raised Royal as her own, but Gabriel worried more for reputation than responsibility and allowed Esther's grandparents to raise Royal. Gabriel has never disclosed his past to Elizabeth and has pretended sacrifice by accepting John as his own. When Gabriel tells Florence that he "is a poor man trying to serve the Lord. *That's* my life," she responds, "then I guarantee *you* . . . that they going to do their best to keep it from being *their* life. *You* mark my words.'" But she decides not to show the letter to Elizabeth. Discovering that Gabriel is not his real father relieves John, and he feels more attuned to the possibilities of a relationship with God in which he will discover why God let all of these things happen to his family.

Cold Sassy Tree by Olive Ann Burns

Of the characters in these three novels, the one who seems to understand his God best is Rucker Blakeslee, the narrator's grandfather in *Cold Sassy Tree* (1984). Will Tweedy's first- person point of view story at the age of twenty-two flashes back to his grandfather eight years before. Three weeks after Will's grandmother, Miss Mattie Lou, dies in June 1906, his grandfather marries his milliner, Miss Love. As the local storeowner, Mr. Blakeslee does what he wants when he desires to do it. The family, astonished not only with the decision but also with the rapidity with which it is executed, slowly adjusts to the new relative. But Miss Love informs Will that their union is a business arrangement. She, once jilted, wanted a house, a piano, and a family, and Rucker wanted someone at home.

During his fourteenth year, Will's experiences vary. While on a train trestle with his dog, he falls between the tracks as a train rumbles above. He remembers his "fancy praying. . . . 'God save me! Please God save me!' And then it was 'Thank you Lord, thank you God, thank you, sir.'" He becomes infatuated with Miss Love and tells friends stories about his Aunt Loma who "like Grandpa and me . . . preferred three-legged chickens to the usual kind." Aunt Loma's husband Camp remains incommunicative, but after Camp commits suicide, Will's grandfather has him buried properly. When his grandfather contracts pneumonia after being robbed and beaten, Miss Love announces to Will that she is pregnant and wants to tell Blakeslee. Unfortunately the opportunity never arises before he dies. The year ends when Will shaves for the first time on his fifteenth birthday, April 30.

Will knows secrets about his grandfather. When Mr. Blakeslee marries so soon, people accuse him of not having loved his wife. But Will saw his grandfather cut every rose in his large garden so that he could bury his wife on a bed of roses. But most important is Rucker's attitude toward God. The townspeople disapprove of him because he refuses to attend church. He, meanwhile, wonders about their sincerity. Miss Love responds, "Rucker, you can't write Holy Scripture. It's already been written." He asserts in turn, "Well, I shore can question what it means. . . . And hit fine'ly come to me in the night, what Jesus must a-meant by *ast*." He tells her that God preordains nothing. "God ain't said you won't git nothin' good less'n you pray for it. But I'm shore thankful for you, Love." Mr. Blakeslee's attitude toward prayer reveals his own need to talk with God. "Ain't the best prayin' jest bein' with God and talkin' a while, like. He's a good friend." Rucker understands his relationship to God, prayer, and faith. "Faith don't mean the Lord is go'n make lions lay down with lambs just cause you ast him to, or make fire not burn. . . . When Jesus said ast and you'll git it, He was givin' a gar'ntee a-spiritual healin,' not body healin.' . . . Jesus meant us to ast God to help us stand the pain, not beg Him to take the pain away." When he leaves money at his death for the town to have a party and tell stories about him, Rucker exhibits his generosity and forgiveness of those who have maligned him.

Many humans maintain that they know God while many only aspire to know God. Since individuals have their own concept of God's identity, knowing God must be a discrete endeavor. However, a person's treatment of others gives a reliable indication of the qualities he or she perceives in a personal god. Adah's God in *The Poisonwood Bible*, somewhat like Blakeslee's in *Cold Sassy Tree*, does not make decisions affecting individuals. She concludes, "The death of something living is the price of our own survival, and we pay it again and again." The knowableness may be the acceptance of what *is*, without trying to either judge or define.

Additional Related Novels

Alexie, Sherman. *Reservation Blues.*
Johnson, Charles. *Middle Passage.*
Salinger, J. D. *The Catcher in the Rye.*
Styron, William. *The Confessions of Nat Turner.*
Vonnegut, Kurt. *Slaughterhouse-Five.*

Loneliness

Loneliness is an unhappy compound of having lost one's point of reference, of suffering the fate of individual and collective discontinuity and of living through or dying from a crisis of identity to the point of alienation of one's self.

—Dr. Ludwig Binswanger, *National Observer* (1972)

A crowded department store, two or three people walking together on a sidewalk, an empty room—all can evoke moments of loneliness for those who feel that they are observers rather than participants. Being lonely is a state of mind rather than a physical condition. Although she has a stream of guests, Holly Golightly in *Breakfast at Tiffany's* travels alone. Loneliness might be the underlying motivation for Ona's suicide in *Bone*. Cut off from friends by his ugliness and his behavior, Grendel in *Grendel* always feels isolated. In *Tell Me a Riddle*, *The Assistant*, and *A Member of the Wedding*, the protagonists think that no one understands their needs and that they are, therefore, alone.

"Loneliness" in the *OED* means "want of society or company; the condition of being alone or solitary." Two additional definitions use the word "dejected" as a description of a lonely person. The term appears early in literary history. In Sir Philip Sidney's *Arcadia*, "that huge and sportfull assemblie grewe to him a tedious lonelinesse, esteeming no body founde, since Daiphantus was lost" (1586). John Milton noted that "it is not good for man to be alone. . . . Loneliness is the first thing which God's eye nam'd not good (*Tetrachordon*, 1645). Twentieth-century spokespersons include Mother Teresa and Kurt Vonnegut. Mother Teresa taught that "when Christ said: 'I was hungry and you fed me,' he didn't mean only the hunger for bread and for food; he also meant the hunger to be loved. Jesus himself experienced this loneliness." And Vonnegut comments, "What should young people do with their lives today? Many things, obviously. But the most daring thing is to create stable communities in which the terrible disease of loneliness can be cured." The three protagonists of the novels, *Tell Me a Riddle*, *The Assistant*, and *A Member of the Wedding*, have a disease of loneliness that they contract through three different processes.

Tell Me a Riddle by Tillie Olsen

Although critics consider Tillie Olsen's work, *Tell Me a Riddle* (1962), a long short story rather than a novel, its themes communicate much about perceptions of mothers and wives in a family and the loneliness that can separate them. The omniscient point of view reveals Eva's thoughts about her husband and her children and their inability to know her. At sixty-nine, Eva has been married to David for forty-seven years and born him seven children. She appreciates music, flowers, and reading, and when reflecting on her life, lovingly remembers the woman who taught her to read when she was a child in Russia. "To her, life was holy, knowledge was holy, and she taught me to read. They hung her." Eva's experiences in a Russian prison and after escaping lead her to accept much that she might not otherwise have tolerated, but instead she thinks, "All that happens, one must try to understand." After feeling ill, Eva goes to a doctor who declares that she is healthy, but old. Then Eva's physician son-in-law examines her, finds gall bladder cancer, and operates immediately. The cancer has spread throughout her body, but her family's attitude does not change when hearing her diagnosis of less than a year to live except to send her the flowers that she loves.

Having always to be available for her children and friends, Eva associates her loss of privacy with their presence. The oldest daughter Clara has resented the other six children and the work she had to do for them, thinking, *"Pay me back, Mother, pay me back for all you took from me. Those others you crowded into your heart. The hands I needed to be for you, the heaviness, the responsibility."* When her daughter Vivi was a child, Eva's heavy Russian accent shamed her. But as an adult, Vivi wants to discuss being Jewish, even though Eva has denied her Jewish heritage after suffering persecution fifty-six years before—*"hunger; secret meetings; human rights; spies; betrayals; prison; escape."* Vivi's daughter understands her grandmother better than her mother because she finds Eva hiding in a closet and tells her that she also has a closet she calls her secret space. When another granddaughter tells her about the feast night in Oaxaca with candles and "picnics on the graves of those they loved," Eva responds, "Yes, Jeannie, the living must comfort themselves." Jeannie stays to help Eva while Eva is dying, and David interprets Jeannie's contented expression as signifying a love affair. However, Jeannie has "the pure overwhelming joy from being with her grandmother; the peace, the serenity that breathed." And when Eva dies, Jeannie comforts her grandfather, telling him that Eva had said she would return "to when she first heard music, a little girl on the road of the village where she was born. She promised me."

But the loneliness that Eva feels stems mostly from her relationship with her husband David. She defines their relationship. "How deep back the stubborn, gnarled roots of the quarrel reached, no one could say." David has never listened to or considered her desires. He has sarcastically called her "Mrs. Enlightened," "Mrs. Unpleasant," and "Mrs. Cultured" and chastised her when he found her reading after returning from his lodge meetings at night because he elevated his own physical needs over her delight in a book. After the children leave home, he wants to move to his lodge's Haven so he will have no responsibilities; she does not want to go. She recalls his demeanor around others, "clown, grimacer, floormat, yesman, entertainer, whatever they want of you." She wants more control over her choices. "Enough. Now they had no children. Let *him* wrack his head for how they would live. She would not exchange her solitude for anything. *Never again to be forced to move to the rhythms of others.*" But he coerces her to accompany him on a cross-country trip to California while she is ill. Still ignoring her needs, he feels an affront when she curses him, "old-country curses from their childhood: Grow, oh shall you grow like an onion, with your head in the ground. Like the hide of a drum shall you be, beaten in life, beaten in death. Oh shall you be like a chandelier, to hang, and to burn." Her medical bills upset him because in them he sees his retirement fund dwindling. He thinks, "*prop me up, children, think of me, too. Shuffled, chained with her, bitter woman. No Haven, and the little money going. . . . How happy she looks, poor creature.*" Thus Eva's loneliness continues until her death in a place where she does not want to be. David made her come to California, and there she dies—always alone in the midst of self-interested family members.

The Assistant by Bernard Malamud

In Bernard Malamud's *The Assistant* (1957), the Italian Frank Alpine searches for something in which he can believe. The omniscient point of view exposes not only Alpine's foibles but also those of Morris; his wife Ida; and Helen, his daughter of twenty-three. Frank seems unable to relate to people and finds himself lonely for appropriate companionship. In an attempt to change his life, he implores the Jew Morris Bober to employ him in his grocery store, but Bober's wife does not want a Gentile so close to Helen. When Morris discovers that Frank has been sleeping in the cellar while drinking the milk and eating the rolls that he puts on the doorstep each morning, he decides to hire him.

Morris cannot be a successful businessman because he feels too much empathy for his customers. He allows them credit when he knows they will never be able to pay him for the food they take. He says that to be a Jew "means to do what is right, to be honest, to be good." Located on the fringe of the Jewish ghetto, Morris attracts few Jewish customers and even fewer Gentiles. He seems to hate being a storeowner, commenting that "in a store you were entombed," but when his wife wanted to sell the business, he would not do so. He enjoys his afternoon nap upstairs because "sleep was his one true refreshment." He is completely honest with everyone—"the harder he worked—his toil was a form of time devouring time—the less he seemed to have." One night, robbers appear, and disgusted to find only thirteen dollars in the cash register, beat him up. Later Frank admits to him that he and Ward Minogue robbed Morris "because he was a Jew." They had intended to rob a liquor store across the street, but the owner, Karp, turned off the lights too soon, and they targeted Morris instead. After Frank works for Morris, gains customers, and receives a raise, Morris suspects that Frank has been stealing from him. Morris then catches Frank and fires him. Throughout, Morris feels anguish because he wishes Karp's thriving business across the street would be destroyed, and three days after Karp offers to buy the store and house, Morris dies from overexertion while shoveling snow. In his despair as well as his honesty, Morris also feels the disease of loneliness. Helen thinks of him, "He could, with a little more courage, have been more than he was."

Frank wants to change himself, but he remains a thief until Morris dies. He steals food and money from Morris and sexual satisfaction from Helen. When he peeks at her in the bathroom window, he "felt a moving joy." Additionally, he defies Ida by summoning Helen to the telephone just to hear her voice. By working with Morris, however, he is able to observe Morris's selflessness. Morris gives Frank the impression that Jews "were born prisoners" and that "they live . . . to suffer." When he rescues Helen from Ward Minogue in the park, he realizes that "he was really a man of stern morality." However, he rapes Helen himself after which she insults him as an "uncircumcized dog." Following Morris's death, Frank has himself circumcised, professes to Judaism, tries to rebuild the business by adding carryout hot food and then changing the store to a restaurant. He also sends Helen to college as Morris's son Ephraim might have done had he lived. Although some critics see Frank's change as a redemption, one must also think that in his loneliness, he will repeat the cycle that Morris began—remaining a prisoner and suffering while never having the courage for more.

A Member of the Wedding by Carson McCullers

In *A Member of the Wedding* (1946), Carson McCullers presents Frances Jasmine Addams, a twelve-year-old girl who worries about her freakish appearance after growing four inches in one year. Frankie's mother died at Frankie's birth, and her father decided the previous year that Frankie was too big to sleep in his bed any more. The only people who will talk to her in this hot August during World War II are the maid Berenice Sadie Brown and John Henry West, her six-year-old cousin. The limited omniscient point of view in three parts focuses on Frankie's loneliness, her disappointment in the doll that her brother Jarvis has sent her while serving in the military, her surprise that her cat has disappeared, and her distress at being excluded from clubs for older girls in the neighborhood. "She was afraid of these things that made her suddenly wonder who she was, and what she was going to be in the world, and why she was standing at that minute, seeing a light, or listening, or staring up into the sky: alone." To emphasize Frankie's discomfort, McCullers uses music as symbol like she does in *The Heart Is a Lonely Hunter*. A trumpeter stops playing, leaving the chords unresolved, and a piano being tuned becomes a disconcerting noise. Against this background, Frankie tries desperately to find some way to become part of something larger than herself. She says to Berenice, "But while we're talking right now, this minute is passing. And it will never come again. Never in all the world. When it is gone it is gone. No power on earth could bring it back again. It is gone. Have you ever thought about that?"

In this gothic novel, Frankie knows several grotesque characters and faces extreme events. The African-American Berenice has a blue glass eye to replace the eye stabbed by one of her four husbands. A stable force for Frankie, Berenice advises her about life as she reviews her attempts to replace her first husband who died after nine years of marriage. The others, failures, were only parts of him. She laments, "Sometimes I almost wish I had never knew Ludie at all. It spoils you too much. It leaves you too lonesome afterward." Berenice tells her about a man who fell in love with another man and changed himself into a girl. Persons with other oddities that Frankie encounters during the summer include the freaks from the Fair—the fat lady, the eight-foot-tall giant, and the midget—and Big Mama in Sugartown who tells her fortune. Additionally, Berenice's relative Honey Brown looks Cuban and smokes reefers. She thinks that all of them "had looked at her in a secret way and tried to connect their eyes with hers as though to say: We know you."

During the summer, three deaths of people she knows affect her. The black boy Lon Baker was slashed with a razor blade in the alley, "throat cut open like a crazy shivering mouth that spoke ghost words." Then her Uncle Charles became sick so that "only his eyes had moved, and they were like blue jelly." Finally John Henry contracts meningitis, and, before he dies, "his eyeballs were walled up in a corner, stuck and, blind." He becomes ill during "the time of golden weather and Shasta daisies and the butterflies," and Frankie reports, "He died on a Tuesday after the Fair was gone, a golden morning of the most butterflies, the clearest sky."

Frankie has her own deficiencies as an adolescent. Since the older girls exclude her from their conversations, she searches for a connection with someone outside her family circle. She meets a soldier and agrees to a rendezvous in his Blue Moon Hotel room. When he makes a pass at her, she bites his tongue and hits him with a water pitcher, worrying later that she has killed him. Not able to handle an adult situation, she continues to feel rejected. "All other people had a we to claim, all others except her. When Berenice said we, she meant Honey and Big Mama, her lodge, or her church. The we of her father was the store. All members of clubs have a we to belong to and talk about. The soldiers in the army can say we, and even the criminals on chain-gangs. But the old Frankie had no we to claim."

Frankie (who has renamed herself F. Jasmine) decides to join her brother and his bride on their honeymoon the following week, thinking "*They are the we of me,*" but fails. She purchases an orange dress in a department store bargain basement to wear in the wedding, and Berenice politely compliments her choice rather than scolding her for its garish appearance. On the Sunday morning of the wedding, she, her father, Berenice, and John Henry take the bus to Winter Hill for the ceremony. The wedding leads to more disappointment. Unable to wear her dress when the bride wears a suit and thwarted when she declares her intention to accompany Jarvis and Janice, Frankie runs away. Unfortunately, she does not know how to hop a freight train and returns to the Blue Moon, where a policeman finds her and telephones her father. After this distressing day, she finds a new friend, Mary Littlejohn, and she and her father move into another house with her Aunt Pet and Uncle Ustace while Berenice plans a fifth marriage. For the first time, Frankie answers to her given name, "Francis," and feels less lonely.

Eva in *Tell Me a Riddle* never has a chance to overcome her loneliness, and she sees how empty life can be for other women as well when she meets a former Denver neighbor on a California beach. The widow, Ellen May, lives alone with her pictures and plastic flowers. Eva notes from their conversation that "thirty years are compressed into a dozen sentences; and the present, not even three. All is told: the children scattered; the husband dead; she lives in a room two blocks up." Frank in *The Assistant* may find a friendship with Helen, but his newly established pattern for his life indicates that he will remain isolated and lonely like Morris. He realizes only after reading Dostoyevsky's *Crime and Punishment* and *Anna Karenina* "how quick some people's lives went to pot when they couldn't make up their minds what to do when they had to do it; and he was troubled by the thought of how easy it was for a man to wreck his life in a single wrong act." Frank wants redemption for his bad decisions and to stop himself from repeating his mistakes. Of these protagonists, only Frankie in *A Member of the Wedding* has the possibility of recovering from the disease of loneliness and finding an authentic "we" to join.

Additional Related Novels

Agee, James. *A Death in the Family.*
Alexie, Sherman. *Reservation Blues.*
Anderson, Sherwood. *Winesburg, Ohio.*
Bellow, Saul. *Seize the Day.*
Cahan, Abraham. *The Rise of David Levinsky.*
Capote, Truman. *Breakfast at Tiffany's.*
Cormier, Robert. *I Am the Cheese.*
Crane, Stephen. *Maggie: A Girl of the Streets.*
Gardner, John. *Grendel.*
Gibbons, Kaye. *Ellen Foster.*
Glasgow, Ellen. *Barren Ground.*
Guterson, David. *Snow Falling on Cedars.*
Lewis, Sinclair. *Main Street.*
McCullers, Carson. *The Heart Is a Lonely Hunter.*
McMillan, Terry. *Mama.*
Momaday, N. Scott. *House Made of Dawn.*
Morrison, Toni. *Song of Solomon; Tar Baby.*

Ng, Fae Myenne. *Bone.*
Proulx, E. Annie. *The Shipping News.*
Rölvaag, O. E. *Giants in the Earth.*
Salinger, J. D. *The Catcher in the Rye.*
Smith, Betty. *A Tree Grows in Brooklyn.*
Steinbeck, John. *Of Mice and Men.*
Welch, James. *The Death of Jim Loney.*
West, Nathanael. *The Day of the Locust.*
Wharton, Edith. *Ethan Frome.*
Wilder, Thornton. *The Bridge of San Luis Rey.*
Wilson, Harriet E. *Our Nig.*

Loss

Sorrows cannot all be explained away . . . in a life truly lived, grief and loss accumulate like possessions.

—Stefan Kanfer, *Time* (1984)

One may lose a job or a friendship or a loved one in death. Every loss changes the lives of those whom it affects. After the loss of his friend Snowden, Yossarian knows that he must remove himself from the battlefront in *Catch-22*. Jack Burden's inability to act results from losing Anne's love and having Willie Stark betray him in *All the King's Men*. The loss of a job starts Easy's new career as a detective in *Devil in a Blue Dress*. In *April Morning, A Farewell to Arms*, and *The Things They Carried*, those participating in the wars depicted have to learn unexpected ways to survive the losses they regularly experience.

"Loss" in the *OED* refers to "being deprived by death, separation, or estrangement, of (a friend, relative, servant, or the like)." In 42 B.C.E., Publius Syrus philosophizes that "the loss which is unknown is no loss at all." In the fifteenth century, Leonardo Da Vinci wrote in his unpublished notebooks, "He who possesses most must be most afraid of loss." In *Antony and Cleopatra*, Shakespeare speaks of the irony of loss for combatants, "Who does i' the wars more than his captain can / Becomes his captain's captain; and ambition, / The soldier's virtue, rather makes choice of loss, / Than gain which darkens him." Loss changes the lives of the protagonists of these three novels, *April Morning, A Farewell to Arms*, and *The Things They Carried*.

April Morning by Howard Fast

Adam Cooper, the protagonist in Howard Fast's *April Morning* (1961), chafes under his father's admonishments, seeks the admiration of his girlfriend, and enjoys his grandmother's doting attention. As the first-person narrator, Adam, fifteen, describes his family's home, food, and position in the community of Lexington, Massachusetts. The eight chapters name the times of day beginning in the afternoon of 18 April 1775 and ending in the late evening of the following day. His family eats donkers (meat leftovers cooked with bread, apples, raisins, and spices) and sets an extra place at the table for unexpected visitors. The names Adam, Moses (for Adam's father), and Solomon all seem to symbolize the roles of the characters they signify. Moses carries the laws of the family and teaches Adam, the son who loses his innocence; and Solomon uses his wisdom to help Adam cope with his changed circumstances. Since Adam does not pause to analyze his actions, the reader observes him as he matures from a boy into a man during thirty hours. In this contracted bildingsroman, Adam loses his father and his childhood along with his safety.

With his father's death, Adam has to take responsibility for the family—his younger brother Levi, his mother, and his grandmother, but before his father dies, he and others ready Adam for the task. From his father, Adam has learned the values of his community and to question them. His father hates the Church of England and fat George, the "antichrist." When wanting to understand religion, Adam wonders why Isaiah Peterkin can be mean and also a deacon in the church. He observes that Peterkin "can get away with anything, just so long as he says the right words about religion." He has further questions after hearing a Committeeman in Boston say "the highest good was to doubt." Adam's relatives and their friends practice tolerance since his great-grandfather Isaac had two families, one in Boston and one in Philadelphia with an unbaptized half-Shawnee Indian woman. Adam's girlfriend's father Joseph (cousin to Adam) has remained a blacksmith rather than join his brothers' new Connecticut ironworks in Boston that their slave ship shares financed.

Because his father has punished him for pranks and berated him, Adam has been unaware of his father's love until overhearing a conversation among his grandmother, mother, and father, and talking to others at the battle's end. When Adam sees his father die, one of the first to fall in the British attack, he runs away and vomits. Then Adam encounters Solomon Chandler, and in comforting Adam, Chandler recounts Adam's father's high regard for his son. Adam's cousin Simmons tells Adam later, "We took up arms for our home place, and he died for it. That's an old, old way, Adam, older than you or me, remember. There are worse ways for a man to die." Rather than chastize Adam for leaving the battle, the kind and wise Solomon Chandler guides him through his grief by taking him to meet other Committeemen and listen to Chandler's advice about fighting the British since he fought them in the French and Indian War. Adam soon begins to sense the end of his childhood and smokes for the first time, a symbol of manhood in prerevolutionary America. When he returns home on the next day, he observes the preparations for his father's funeral, surprised with the attention to food. He soon comprehends that "food is close to the meaning of life. There are tributes enough to the dead; the food is a tribute to the living, who are in the need of it at the time." He takes candles to the church so that his resting father can still have light through the night. Adam also realizes that his grandmother has become an old woman, with the loss of the last of her five sons, and that he is no longer a child.

Adam and his family also lose their safety. On the afternoon before the British attack, Adam and Ruth, his girlfriend, have walked around the community superficially discussing their future. During the night when Adam and Levi hear hoofbeats, their father knows that the rider coming up Menotomy Road from Cambridge has an express for the Committee and that the British have started crossing the Charles River to Concord. Adam's father respects the Committee as a "tribunal dedicated to unity, justice, and the rights of man." When the call to battle comes, Moses muses, "It sometimes seems to me that we live inside invisible shells, but just as much shells as the fat Maine lobsters inhabit; and only at a time like this do the shells melt away and the real people emerge." The men muster at four o'clock in the morning, and when Adam signs the muster book, his father says nothing. During the battle, Adam falls asleep behind a tree, and people think him dead. But Adam joins the battle after his father's death. He helps the Revolutionaries make the British soldiers, youngsters from London fighting for pay rather than for their land, retreat. Adam understands that the beginning of the war signals the end of his comfortable life, and he must decide soon if he will answer the muster called for Boston. Thus Adam's unexpected loss of parent and childhood forces him to reconsider his future.

A Farewell to Arms by **Ernest Hemingway**

Frederic Henry, the first-person narrator of Ernest Hemingway's *A Farewell to Arms* (1929) also suffers losses related to war. He exposes the ultimate wastes and uninformed decisions that often control the progress of a war in the five "books" of the novel. Hemingway focuses on the war itself in books one and three and on the relationship between Henry and Catherine in the three remaining books. During World War I, the American Henry serves as an ambulance driver in Italy where his surgeon friend Rinaldi introduces him to Catherine Barkley, a nurse from Great Britain. At first a game, their relationship changes after trench mortar shells shred Henry's knee, and he eventually deserts the army to be with her. They and everyone else lose during this devastating war.

The people in the countryside where the soldiers are bivouacked suffer greatly. One of Henry's companions says about the war, "There is nothing as bad as war. . . . When people realize how bad it is they cannot do anything to stop it because they go crazy. . . . There are people who are afraid of their officers. It is with them the war is made." The people cope with chaos. Laws and rules disappear when news arrives that the Germans are coming, with those in the rear guard of the military during the ensuing retreat sniping at anyone of suspicion. After Henry's subordinates disobey him, he has to shoot an engineer sergeant who openly defies his command. Another officer then kills the man. When the guards notice that Henry is a foreigner, they aim at him, even though he has been serving their cause. To escape their irrational behavior, Henry has to desert his position.

During the war, Catherine loses everything. Before she meets Henry, Catherine's fiancé whom she had known since childhood and to whom she had been engaged for eight years died on the Somme. After she falls in love with Henry, she loses her freedom, wanting to be with him all the time. She then loses her decorum and offends some of her friends by having an affair with him. She even visits him in the hospital and stays with him in his room while the others are sleeping. Her penultimate loss is the death of their son, born with his umbilical cord wrapped around his neck. And then she dies herself from the complications of bearing the child.

Henry also loses during this war. After he loses the use of his leg and has to go to the hospital, he reunites with Catherine and falls in love with her. He becomes separated from his friends while spending time with Catherine. He wants to marry when she discloses the pregnancy, but she fears that her superiors might transfer her back to England without him. When Henry's subordinates die during the retreat, he loses his post by jumping into a river and swimming away. Someone identifies him as a deserter, and he and Catherine must then escape to Switzerland. After Catherine and his child die, Henry has to restructure his life. Ironically, Henry comments that war "did not have anything to do with me." But on reflection, war had *all* to do with him. It changed his life.

The Things They Carried by Tim O'Brien

Tim O'Brien has declared in interviews that the Vietnam War made him a writer. The dilemma of deserting to Canada or facing induction during that war led O'Brien to assess his values. The narrator of *The Things They Carried* (1990), also named Tim O'Brien, remembers the painful summer of 1968 when he had to decide his future. Faced with going to Vietnam to fight in a war he did not understand or to seek safety in a foreign country, possibly to be exiled forever from his home and family, created an immeasurable dilemma. After driving close to the Canadian border, the narrator meets elderly Elroy Berdahl, who takes him on a boat across a river into Canada. The narrator remembers their trip and understands that the old man acted as an intermediary, a welcome stranger, who helped him make a choice with which he could live. The narrator decides that he will go to Vietnam where he might kill others, or die himself "because I was embarrassed not to." Dismayed about deciding his future based on what others might think of him, he cries. After the war's end, O'Brien, the writer, began recording his Vietnam experiences, using a version of faction (fiction extrapolated from fact) to create his stories and finally comprehending that the war developed the writer inside him. Nearly thirty years later, he perceives himself as "Tim trying to save Timmy's life with a story." *The Things They Carried* depends on O'Brien's memory and his creativity along with the real horrors of a war that had little meaning to many who fought in it. Although the narrator of the novel (or closely related short stories, depending on the reader's definition) is Tim O'Brien, a forty-year-old man visiting Vietnam with his ten-year-old daughter, the author does not allow his seemingly factual frame to be literal. The reader, however, has little idea as to the moments of fantasy, fact, or fiction as the storyteller weaves it into truth. After recalling his childhood friend, nine-year-old Linda, whose cap covered her bald head following treatment for a brain tumor, the narrator (and writer) defines his craft as a way to enter the soul of someone who has touched his own life and, if necessary, make that person, long dead, live again. "It's not the surface that matters, it's the identity that lives inside." And as he thinks and writes about Linda, she can remind him "once you're alive . . . you can't ever be dead."

The men whom O'Brien remembers from the war carried items of importance to them personally during and between battles. The platoon leader, First Lieutenant Jimmy Cross, carries "a compass, maps, code books, binoculars . . . a .45–caliber pistol . . . a strobe light and the responsibility for the lives of his men." He also carries letters from a college girl, Martha, until he berates himself for fantasizing about her instead of saving Ted Lavender, killed by a mine while rejoining the platoon after urinating in the bushes. No longer does Ted have to carry tranquilizers and drugs to alleviate his fear. Henry Dobbins wraps his girlfriend's pantyhose around his neck like a muffler and carries the loaded M-60 machine gun that weighs twenty-three pounds unloaded. Dave Jensen carries dental floss, night-sight vitamins with carotene, soap stolen in Australia, and a rabbit's foot. Lee Strunk carries a slingshot and tanning lotion. (Jensen breaks Strunk's nose for stealing his jackknife, and then breaks his own nose so that Strunk will not knife him in the back. They become friends and make a pack to kill the other if he loses a limb.) The platoon medic, Rat Kiley, carries the emergency medical kit, comic books, M&M candies, and brandy. The Native American Kiowa carries the New Testament, moccasins, and a feathered hatchet. Norman Bowker carries a diary and the thumb of a dead Viet Cong boy. The horrible Azar straps a mine to a puppy and enjoys watching it disintegrate in air, justifying his behavior by announcing "I'm just a boy." The narrator admits that he cannot describe the war because of its contradictions. He knows that the gestalt of war incorporates every aspect of its environment and the people within it. The war encompasses the "sunlight . . . the special way that dawn spreads out on a river" that might lead to death but must be crossed. The war includes "love and memory . . . sorrow . . . sisters who never write back and people who never listen." The losses during and as a result of the war affect all the men. One thing they lose is civility. "You can tell a true war story if it embarrasses you. If you don't care for obscenity, you don't care for the truth; if you don't care for the truth, watch how you vote. Send guys to war, they come home talking dirty."

Many of them lose their girlfriends. Mark Fossie's girl, seventeen-year-old Mary Anne Bell, visits, joins the Green Berets, and "crosses to the other side."

Henry Dobbins' girlfriend severs their relationship, although he continues wearing her pantyhose muffler to keep warm. Rat shoots himself in the foot. Kiowa dies from suffocation in a hole filled with excrement. After the war, Cross discovers that Martha is a lesbian. Norman Bowker commits suicide on July 4 because no one, including his father, will listen to him talk about his war experiences. The narrator almost loses his life, being shot twice, and his ambitions and his hopes in the mud of Vietnam. He says, "There were times in my life when I couldn't feel much, not sadness or pity or passion, and somehow I blamed this place for what I had become, and I blamed it for taking away the person I had once been." When he returns with his daughter twenty years later, he symbolically "buries the hatchet" at the spot where he thinks Kiowa died. He allows the war to become part of his past so that he can proceed with his future, although he has the awareness that "you're never more alive than when you're almost dead. You recognize what's valuable."

War means loss—loss of life, of the past, of a perceived future. In *April Morning*, not only does the Cooper family's life change overnight but also the life of the country changes when war begins. Frederic Henry, in *A Farewell to Arms*, faces a different life after the war with both physical and psychological wounds resulting from the mortar to his knee and the death of both his beloved and his newborn son. *The Things They Carried*, like the other two novels, refuses to glorify war. The narrator notes the contradictions of the experience. "War is hell, but that's not the half of it, because war is also mystery and terror and adventure and courage and discovery and holiness and pity and despair and longing and love. War is nasty; war is fun. War is thrilling; war is drudgery. War makes you a man; war makes you dead." But like Adam Cooper and Frederic Henry, he clearly mourns the losses, each one for its uniqueness to his life. He adds, "In a true war story, if there's a moral at all, it's like the thread that makes the cloth. You can't tease it out. You can't extract the meaning without unraveling the deeper meaning. And in the end, really, there's nothing much to say about a true war story, except maybe 'Oh.' "

Additional Related Novels

Faulkner, William. *The Bear.*
Flagg, Fannie. *Fried Green Tomatoes at the Whistle Stop Café*
Frazier, Charles. *Cold Mountain.*
Glasgow, Ellen. *Barren Ground.*
Heller, Joseph. *Catch-22.*
McCullers, Carson. *The Heart Is a Lonely Hunter.*
Oates, Joyce Carol. *Foxfire.*
Olsen, Tillie. *Tell Me a Riddle.*
Salinger, J. D. *The Catcher in the Rye.*
Stegner, Wallace. *Angle of Repose.*
Styron, William. *The Confessions of Nat Turner.*
Wideman, John Edgar. *The Hiding Place.*

Love

Love and compassion are necessities, not luxuries. Without them humanity cannot survive.

—Dalai Lama (ca. 1980)

The mention of "love" brings myriad examples to mind, including sweethearts
and parents. Although often misused, the term refers to a relationship, and every protagonist experiences some version of it. Catherine and Frederic's love
in *A Farewell to Arms* leads to Frederic's desertion from the military. Neil
thinks that he loves Brenda in *Goodbye, Columbus* until he becomes aware of
her selfishness. Hester's love for her daughter Pearl overshadows her desire for
happiness in *The Scarlet Letter*. In the three novels, *The Lilies of the Field*, *The
Bridge of San Luis Rey*, and *Beloved*, someone intensely cares for another person.

"Love," in the *OED*, is "that disposition or state of feeling with regard to a
person which (arising from recognition of attractive qualities, from instincts of
natural relationship, or from sympathy) manifests itself in solicitude for the
welfare of the object, and usually also in delight in his or her presence and desire for his or her approval." It is " warm affection" and "attachment." The
term has been part of the language throughout human existence. Sophocles
avowed, "One word frees us of all the weight and pain of life. That word is
love." In 1526, *The Pilgrimage of Perfection* mentions "fraternall charite or
brotherly loue [love]." Albert Einstein wrote in a letter, "more and More I
come to value charity and love of one's fellow being above everything else. . . .
All our lauded technological progress—our very civilization—is like the axe in
the hand of the pathological criminal" (1917). Henry Drummond analyzes,
"you will find as You look back upon your life that the moments when you have
really lived are the moments when you have done things in a spirit of love" (*The
Greatest Thing in the World*, 1987). Each protagonist in these novels, *The Lilies
of the Field*, *The Bridge of San Luis Rey*, and *Beloved*, becomes involved in circumstances in which their love makes them legendary figures.

The Lilies of the Field by William E. Barrett

Homer Smith in *The Lilies of the Field* (1962) becomes a legend at
twenty-four after helping German nuns in the American southwest construct a

chapel. William E. Barrett allows Homer to tell his story in first person except for the last chapter when another narrator reveals the anecdotes of those who knew him before he disappeared. A South Carolinian, Smith leaves military service in Seattle. On his journey home, he spots women working near a "dilapidated farmhouse." He stops and discovers that they are German Catholic nuns who speak little English. When Mother Maria Marthe and Sisters Gertrud, Albertine, Elisabeth, and Agnes offer him food, he quickly realizes they are oblivious to his "sensitivity born of race and skin color that set a man apart." They accept him as a human in need and call him "Schmidt." Homer takes them to town for Sunday mass while he, a Baptist, waits in a café. The proprietor tells him that the exiled East Germans live on money one of the sisters in their Order inherited at the death of her heartless brother, Gus Ritter. He refused to spend money, and his son and wife perished in the fire that burned their house.

Homer helps the sisters in several ways. They ask him to teach them English along with their English phonograph record; he agrees but warns that he speaks with a South Carolina accent, a distinction they do not understand. The local priest tells Homer that Maria Marthe had prayed for someone to help her build a chapel, and he, Homer, had come. Although Mother Maria Marthe's thinking that Homer belongs to her because she prayed for him "stirred a racial antagonism," he decides to clear a foundation for the chapel. Since she plans to bring poor Spanish boys from the city to work and study on the land, "he did not want this woman justified in thinking ill of him." He has no concept of the process of building a chapel, but the problem intrigues him. "He was all alone, one man, with a hole in the ground and a church to be built, and no one to tell him how." When he takes Mother Maria Marthe to North Fork where she asks the owner of Livingston Construction to give her brick, the man refuses when he sees an African American with her. He agrees, however, to give Smith a job for two days a week. Homer purchases food for the sisters who only eat bread, eggs, and a bite of cheese. But discouraged after amassing only 500 bricks, Homer leaves. A new job and his freedom do not satisfy Smith because he eyes a discarded bathtub and pays for two unused colored windows for the church before returning to the nuns.

The nuns, therefore, give him a sense of purpose with their unconditional love and acceptance. They want him to play his guitar for them and then they want him to play while they sing so Sister Albertine teaches him a Latin chant. He knows their strong sense of charity because Mother Maria Marthe had responded to his initial request to be paid for his work with the New Testament verses Matthew 6:28 and 29. "And why take ye thought for raiment? Consider the lilies of the field, how they grow; they toil not, neither do they spin." A man he meets in the local café defines the situation. "Faith. It is a word for what is unreasonable. If a man believes in an unreasonable thing, that is faith." After Homer's return, someone brings bricks who says, "I am happy to bring these bricks for the chapel. I have had in my heart a doubt of you and I am sorry." Homer becomes proprietary about building the chapel for the sisters himself, but he finally allows Juan Archuleta help him set the window. Juan then invites him to to play his guitar and dine on a delicious bean dinner. Homer admires his work when he finishes. "His church stood strong with the blue sky behind it, a church with angles that would be stiff and harsh in wood, soft in adobe." The following day, he leaves without saying goodbye even though he would like to tell Sister Albertine that he enjoyed her singing and her pictures. But his abrupt arrival, building of the chapel, and expeditious exit help publicize the project. Money arrives, and after the women add more buildings and begin their school, Albertine paints a picture of Homer Smith—a labor of love—for the back of the church, dedicating it to Saint Benedict the Moor.

The Bridge of San Luis Rey by Thornton Wilder

In Thornton Wilder's *The Bridge of San Luis Rey* (1927), Brother Juniper explores the lives of five characters united in death. On 20 July 1714, the bridge between Lima and Cuzco in Peru that the Incas wove from osier in the 1600s broke while five people were crossing. The event distresses everyone who hears about it, and Brother Juniper, who witnessed it, wonders about the strong response from people who had suffered tidal waves, earthquakes, diseases, and old age. He spends six years asking questions about the five and writes a huge book recording their responses. He concludes that the five shared a common experience of allowing themselves to be consumed in life by a selfish love, with each of them realizing the mistake just before the fatal accident occurred. Wilder divides the novel into five parts, using a combination of first person and omniscient point of view, reserving the middle three sections to relate the stories of the characters—the Marquesa de Montemayor, Pepita, Esteban, Uncle Pío, and Jaime. The first and last parts report the reasons for Brother Juniper's investigation and the results, including his own death at the stake for trying to justify God's ways to humans.

All the victims thought those they loved would fulfill their own needs. The unattractive Doña María, the Marquesa de Montemayor, had wanted to remain single, but her parents made her marry a ruined nobleman at twenty-six. He left her with their daughter, Clara, on whom she doted. Clara escaped by marrying a Spaniard and moving to Spain. Doña María tries to learn interesting things ("All her existence lay in the burning center of her mind") so that her letters will stimulate her daughter, but Clara hardly reads them. The son-in-law, however, preserves them all, and Brother Juniper uses them in his research. In one letter, Doña María describes a visit from the Perichole (a young actress) who comes the day after a performance that Doña María attended to apologize for something she said about Doña María during her performance. Doña María had not even heard the insult because she had been mentally composing her next letter to her daughter, but her maid Pepita had and had made her leave the theater. Clara does not see her mother's qualities, such as her dispute "against the obstinacy of her time in her desire to attach a little dignity to women." Nor is Clara aware that Doña María supports a hospital, a convent, and an orphanage and worries who will succeed her. When Doña María hears of Clara's pregnancy, she wonders about ways to ease it.

Esteban mourns the death of his twin Manuel. As boys, "because they had no family, because they were twins, and because they were brought up by women, they were silent." They had their own language for each other which they would not disclose to others, even the Archbishop of Lima, a man who studied languages. The boys are copiers and write letters for the illiterate. When Manuel works for the Perichole, he falls in love with her. Esteban discovers Manuel's secret and becomes miserable, so Manuel decides to stop seeing her. But Manuel soon scrapes his leg, and the subsequent infection kills him three days later. Esteban remains despondent when Manuel yells in his delirium about his love for the Perichole. The educated harlequin, Pio, who speaks the language of Caldéron and loves his independence, discovers Camila Perichole (Micaela Villegas) when she is twelve and nurtures her into a fine actress by continually criticizing her performances. After she meets the Viceroy and bears him three children, she decides that performing on the stage is inappropriate for her status and retires at thirty. She refuses to see Pio, and he "regarded love as a sort of cruel malady through which the elect are required to pass in their late youth and from which they emerge, pale and wrung, but ready for the business of living." Eventually, Pio sees her, discovers that smallpox has scarred her face, and offers to educate her son, Don Jaime. She agrees.

Each character experiences an epiphany before falling from the bridge. After finding and reading an unmailed letter that Pepita wrote to her adored Madre, Doña María realizes that she has misused Pepita and that "she loved her daughter not for her daughter's sake, but for her own." In her last letter, Doña María expresses her desire to begin anew. Pepita longs to return to the convent but does not send the letter because she "wasn't brave'" Doña María, however, encourages her. The Madre coerces Captain Alvarado, a man still mourning over the loss of his daughter, to suggest to Esteban, twenty-two, that he go to sea with him. Esteban says he cannot leave Peru, but Alvarado counters. "We do what we can. We push on, Esteban, as best we can. It isn't for long, you know. Time keeps going by. You'll be surprised at the way time passes." Pio's offer to support Don Jaime expresses his shift from abusing Camile to selflessly loving her. Although the reader has no knowledge of Don Jaime's emotions, one can surmise that his willingness to leave home with Pio indicates a respect for his mother's wishes. Afterward, Camille visits the Abbess and finds solace from her loneliness. When Clara arrives, the Abbess informs her of her mother's achievements. Brother Juniper's report integrates the importance of love to both the living and the dead. "There is a land of the living and a land of the dead and the bridge is love, the only survival, the only meaning."

Beloved by Toni Morrison

Sethe makes the ultimate sacrifice of love for her child in Toni Morrison's *Beloved* (1987). The revelation of her deed occurs slowly, through multiple narrators (some speaking dialect), segments employing stream of consciousness, poetry, and supernatural forces, making its discovery as difficult as any secret. Not until the second of the three parts in the novel does the reader discover that Sethe has killed her baby Beloved so that Beloved will not have to become a slave in 1855. After Sethe's master, Mr. Garner, died, in 1853, his wife asked her cruel brother-in-law, "Schoolteacher," to help her. He reversed all of Garner's decisions, and one of the male slaves, Paul D, "believed schoolteacher broke into children what Garner had raised into men." Paul D, Sethe's husband Halle, Paul A, and Sixo decide to escape, but, before they can leave, the schoolteacher's two nephews suck milk from the pregnant Sethe's breasts, driving Halle (hidden in the barn and watching) insane. Sethe sends her three children, Howard (five), Buglar (four), and Beloved (nine months), to Baby Suggs, her mother-in-law whose freedom Halle had purchased by renting himself out on Saturdays. On the appointed day, only Sethe escapes. On the way, she encounters a white girl, Amy Denver, who helps her deliver her baby. Sethe and Denver arrive in Cincinnati and join Baby Suggs and the other three children. To reveal the central event of Sethe's life, Morrison shifts to present tense, "This day they are outside." On that day, Schoolteacher and slave catchers arrive while everyone is celebrating in the yard. Sethe spots them and attempts to kill her children, only succeeding with the unnamed baby crawling on the ground. The child receives the name Beloved when a gravestone chiseler agrees to carve that one word without charge during his ten minutes of free time. Beloved haunts the family at 124 Bluestone Road (the first words of the book reveal that "124 was spiteful"), and Sethe's act of love affects everyone for nearly twenty years.

Sethe suffers unceasingly for her action. She wants Beloved to understand that "the best thing she was, was her children. Whites might dirty *her* all right, but not her best thing, her beautiful, magical best thing—the part of her that was clean." In her agony, she never notices color except "blood red" and "pink gravestone chips" and discovers that "the future was a matter of keeping the past at bay." She wants safety for her children, but with Beloved haunting the house, she cannot find it at 124. Paul D arrives eighteen years later, having found his way north. He purges the house of its ghost, and Sethe tries to take Baby Suggs's advice to "lay it all down." But a nineteen year old waits for them after they return from a fair, saying her name is "Beloved." She spells the name as if she were reading it. Beloved again consumes Sethe, and Paul D leaves after Stamp Paid, a friend, tells him that Sethe murdered her baby. Sethe "sat in the chair licking her lips like a chastised child while Beloved ate up her life, took it, swelled up with it, grew taller on it. And the older woman yielded it up without a murmur." Sethe interacts only with Beloved and eventually loses her job. Beloved claws her neck so that "rubies of blood" opened, and Sethe rushes to "wipe the jewels away." After Denver seeks help from the Bodwins, Sethe thinks the white man is "Schoolteacher" and tries to attack him with an ice pick. At that point Beloved disappears, some thinking that she "poofs." So intense are Sethe's responses, her "rememories," that she says to Denver who thinks she is praying, "I was talking about time. It's so hard for me to believe in it."

Beloved's haunting and Sethe's obsession with her affect everyone she knows. Her sons Howard and Buglar run away before they are thirteen after Howard notices two tiny handprints in the cake and Buglar sees a mirror shatter. Baby Suggs, their grandmother, becomes "suspended between the nastiness of life and the meanness of the dead, she couldn't get interested in leaving life or living it" after Sethe kills Beloved. On the day she dies, she says, "There is no bad luck in the world but whitefolks." She still believes, however, that "freeing yourself was one thing; claiming ownership of that freed self was another." Denver remains with Sethe and, needing love, silently suffers. Sethe thinks that nothing bad can happen to Denver since the rats did not bite her when Sethe was in jail. Denver remembers how she and her brothers huddled on the steps telling "Die-witch! stories" so she could kill her mother if she needed to after they left. Although later afraid of the harm that Beloved might do to Sethe, Denver "felt helpless to thwart it, so unrestricted was her need to love another." When Denver asks a former teacher how to obtain food, she suggests the church, and Denver becomes acquainted with some of the neighbors. After Paul D comes, he experiences the unexplained movement of items in the house. He has to leave when the adult Beloved arrives because she tries to seduce him. He then wonders how much a black man has to take in life, and Stamp Paid responds, "All he can." Denver contacts Paul D after Beloved "poofs," and he tries to convince Sethe that the best part of herself is herself, not her children.

Selfless love, therefore, connects in surprising ways. Homer Smith in *The Lilies of the Field* "become[s] a legendary figure . . . perhaps, of greater stature in simple reality than he ever will be in the oft-repeated, and expanded, tales which commemorate his deeds." Paul D, remembering the words of his fellow slave Sixo about the woman he loved, begins to help Sethe heal in *Beloved*. "The pieces I am, she gather them and give them back to me in all the right order." And in *The Bridge of San Luis Rey*, all the characters have to understand their motivations for love before they can wholly love another. In the words of Brother Juniper, "But soon we shall die and all memory of those five will have left the earth, and we ourselves shall be loved for a while and forgotten. But the love will have been enough; all those impulses of love return to the love that made them."

Additional Related Novels

Chopin, Kate. *The Awakening*.
Flagg, Fannie. *Fried Green Tomatoes at the Whistle Stop Café*.

Frazier, Charles. *Cold Mountain.*
Glasgow, Ellen. *Barren Ground.*
Golden, Arthur. *Memoirs of a Geisha.*
Guterson, David. *Snow Falling on Cedars.*
Hawthorne, Nathaniel. *The Scarlet Letter.*
Hemingway, Ernest. *A Farewell to Arms; For Whom the Bell Tolls.*
Howells, William Dean. *The Rise of Silas Lapham.*
Hurston, Zora Neale. *Their Eyes Were Watching God.*
McMillan, Terry. *Waiting to Exhale.*
Mosley, Walter. *Devil in a Blue Dress.*
Naylor, Gloria. *Mama Day; The Women of Brewster Place.*
Roth, Philip. *Goodbye Columbus.*
Saroyan, William. *The Human Comedy.*
Stegner, Wallace. *Angle of Repose.*
Stowe, Harriet Beecher. *Uncle Tom's Cabin.*
Walker, Alice. *The Color Purple.*
Warren, Robert Penn. *All the King's Men.*
Wharton, Edith. *Ethan Frome.*

Male Behavior

Men weren't really the enemy—they were fellow victims suffering from an outmoded masculine mystique that made them feel unnecessarily inadequate when there were no bears to kill.
                    —Betty Friedan, *Christian Science Monitor* (1974)

Those who accuse others of stereotyping when associating specific character traits with men rather than women must reconsider because recent research reveals that, indeed, certain characteristics appear more often in males (and others in females). In the 1990s, Carolyn Desjardins interviewed seventy-four college presidents and discovered that moral orientation (the act of making decisions) differed between males and females. Males often examine situations for what seems equitable rather than what will maintain personal connections. Males more often fear oppression and intimacy, wanting autonomy rather than interdependence. Deborah Tannen's research shows that males bond through their activities while females prefer conversation (*You Just Don't Understand*, 1990). Obviously, these traits are more gender related than gender specific since females can exhibit male attributes at a particular time; however, these masculine expectations appear in the behavior of males in many novels. The men in *Deliverance*, *The Sun Also Rises*, and *Shiloh* all relate to each other through their activities rather than their talk whether work, war, or fishing.

The *OED* notes that "men" pertains to more than one male human being, usually adults of that species. Until the twentieth century, "men" referred to all humans without regard to gender, but a concern about sexist language has halted this practice in the United States. References to the activities and interests of males occur throughout literature. Samuel Taylor Coleridge wrote in "The Life of Sir William Hamilton," "man's heart must be in his head. Woman's head must be in her heart" (1832). Sir Alfred Tennyson notes, "Woman is not undevelopt man, But diverse" (*The Princess*, 1847). In confirming the universality of men's ways, Mary Kingsley reports with conviction in *Travel in West Africa*, "As for the men, well of course they would marry any lady of any tribe, if she had a pretty face . . . that's just man's way" (1897). John Braine asserts: "Every day one was tested, the men were separated from the boys" (*Life at the Top*, 1962). The men in *Deliverance*, *The Sun Also Rises*, and *Shiloh* reveal their maleness through their choices.

Deliverance by James Dickey

In James Dickey's *Deliverance* (1970), four men decide to canoe down the fictional Cahulawassee River in North Georgia before flooding transforms it into a lake. In five chapters—one about planning the trip, three on the trip, and one afterward—Ed Gentry serves as the first-person narrator. Lewis Medlock, an independently wealthy married man with three children, coerces Ed, Drew Ballinger, and Bobby Trippe to go with him to the hills where the "authentic" people live. Graphics consultant Ed owns a business, devoted family man and guitarist Drew is a corporate executive, and Bobby is a salesman. Before Lewis's invitation, Ed's work has become so commercially slick that it bores him, and he feels slightly emasculated by the "inconsequence of whatever I would do, of anything I would pick up or think about or turn to see." He questions how someone can survive such an empty life and decides that "by doing something that is at hand to be done was the best answer I could give." He also concludes that by not telling anyone about his helplessness, his "time-terrified human feeling," even his wife, that he might escape it. Lewis declares that he and Ed should take their bows and twenty-nine-inch aluminum arrows. An accomplished sportsman, Lewis's command of archery, fly casting, and weight lifting defines him to himself. He maintains his mastery by constantly repeating these skills. He says, "I'll tell you. Sliding is living antifriction. Or, no, sliding is living *by* antifriction. It is finding a modest thing you can do, and then greasing that thing. On both sides. It is grooving with comfort."

As the men begin their journey, an activity independent of family and responsibility, they begin to discover each other. In the town of Oree near the river's entrance, a resident warns them that being caught by rain in the gorge can destroy them. The warning becomes less sinister while they listen to Drew playing a guitar duet with Lonnie, a young albino working at the local gas station. On the first morning, after their campfire euphoria of the previous night, they awaken with fog surrounding them. An owl hunts from the top of Ed's tent, and Ed tries to kill a deer but misses with both his arrows. Later, Ed and Bobby canoe downstream ahead of Lewis and Drew and stop for them to catch up. Two men appear with guns. They tie Ed to a tree with his belt, and one sodomizes the sobbing Bobby. Just as the other orders Ed to perform fellatio, an arrow kills him, and his partner escapes in the woods. Drew thinks they should report the incident to police, but the other three want to bury the man. Although disagreeing, they realize that they must act together. Ed thinks, "Without the creek to go back down, could I find the river? Probably not, and I bound myself with my brain and heart to the others; with them was the only way I would ever get out." After the other man shoots Drew from atop the nearby cliff, they know he will kill each one of them when they enter the gorge. The gorge thus becomes a symbolic hell harboring a variety of evils. Lewis breaks his leg, and, to survive, Ed knows that only he can scale the cliff during the night to kill the man. He reaches the top, climbs to a hideout on a tree limb, and in the morning light, kills the man with his bow and arrow. The report from the man's gun before he dies dislodges Ed from the tree, however, and he falls, injuring himself on the point of another arrow. When Ed rejoins Bobby and Lewis, they find Drew in the water and tie a rock to him so that he will sink to the riverbed. "I undid his life belt and let him fall away under me. On his knees beside Lewis in the canoe, Bobby heaved the stone overboard. One of Drew's feet flew up and touched my calf, and we were free and in hell." At their journey's end, they mislead the searchers by saying that Drew fell out of the canoe at a different place so that no one will find him. As Ed and Lewis create the episodes of the story, "For me they were happening as I talked; it was hard to realize that they had not taken place in the actual world . . . they became part of a world, the believed world, the world of recorded events, of history." Ed's and Lewis's necessary familiarity reveals more about each of them than they want to know.

Dickey emphasizes the universal implications of this male activity. Of the men, Drew seems the most content with his life, and he cannot survive the imbalance of the wilderness where men act like vicious animals. The rapists Stovall and Benson function not according to what is right for others but what is right for themselves, thinking that the ultimate masculine symbol, a gun, provides unlimited protection against the uninitiated. Bobby, the least prepared for the journey, complains about the physical effort, and when raped like a woman, seems effeminate. Lewis imagines himself immortal, but he becomes helpless when wounded. Ed has to save them, and, for some critics, his growth makes the novel into a bildingsroman, even though he is an adult. Another critic sees him as fulfilling the archetypal protagonist's role based on Joseph Campbell's monomyth through his initiation, separation, and return to his society as a different man. All of them fall into the water and, by surviving this baptism, can face new challenges like Odysseus, Aeneas, characters in Dante's Circle of Hell, Ishmael, and Ahab before them. As Ed recalls the experience through the years, "The river and everything I remembered about it became a possession to me, a personal, private possession. . . . It pleases me in some curious way that the river does not exist, and that I have it. In me it still is, and will be until I die, green, rocky, deep, fast, slow, and beautiful beyond reality. I had a friend there who in a way had died for me, and my enemy was there."

The Sun Also Rises by **Ernest Hemingway**

In Ernest Hemingway's *The Sun Also Rises* (1926), men also return to the water for bonding when Jake Barnes and Bill Gorton go trout fishing before attending the annual festival in Pamplona. Jake, the expatriate narrator from Kansas City, is a newspaper correspondent in Paris whom Bill, an alcoholic American war veteran, visits. Also in Paris are Lady Brett Ashley and Robert Cohn. Former middle-weight boxing champion at Princeton, Cohn, another expatriate, is a writer pleased with the reception of his latest novel, especially the attention American women gave him when he visited the States after its publication. When Cohn wants Jake to go to South America with him, Jake advises, "You can't get away from yourself by moving from one place to another. There's nothing to that." Cohn falls in love with Brett, and she agrees to accompany him to San Sebastian, even though she is engaged to Michael Campbell. Members of the group journey separately to Pamplona and, after the festival, leave separately. Disillusioned by the war, they dine, become inebriated, think about sex, and fulfill Jake's belief that moving from place to place accomplishes nothing.

Jake's love for Brett leads him to focus on her actions. Brett's first husband died of dysentery during the war, and her abusive second husband gave her a title. She has become engaged to Mike, another alcoholic war veteran, even though he has no money. Jake wants to marry her, but he is impotent, having been emasculated during World War I. Brett enjoys sex and, although emotionally close to Jake, refuses to commit. The two seem to reverse roles, with Jake becoming the feminine persona, interdependent by wanting Brett to live with him even without sexual fulfillment, and Brett's promiscuity and desire for autonomy as masculine. Additionally, Hemingway has given her an androgynous name, appropriate for persons of either sex. She seems disinterested in concealing her affair with Cohn after she and Mike are engaged and that she had a brief sexual liaison with Count Mippipopolous in Paris just before traveling with Cohn. She also misses an appointment with Jake and makes no apology. When she lusts for the handsome nineteen-year-old matador Pedro Romero, Jake arranges a rendezvous. Then Pedro gives Brett the ear of the bull he kills the next day; the previous day that same bull had gored a man to death. Later, when she leaves Pedro in Madrid, irritated that he wants her to grow her hair longer to become more feminine and realizing, in turn, that she will destroy his career, she summons Jake for help. And like every other time she has needed Jake, he responds.

The men in the story expect their independence without particular regard for others (Jake as narrator omits details that would make them sensitive). Before Pamplona, Jake and Bill take an annual trout fishing trip to the Irati River in the mountains where they enjoy nature and wine. In Pamplona, Brett disappoints Cohn with her disinterest after they have spent two weeks together, and Mike makes openly hostile comments about Cohn's behavior. Jake, whom the Pamplona innkeeper Montoya considers an *aficionado* (lover of the beauty of the bull fight), angers Montoya by introducing Pedro to Brett since such a relationship could ruin Pedro's talent. And then Cohn beats Romero almost senseless after discovering his affair with Brett. The characters in this novel, supposedly of the "Lost Generation," have no purpose to their lives. They limit themselves to drinking, eating, wandering from place to place, and defending their imagined rights. They help others only by tipping them for better rooms and tables. Connected by American citizenship and having survived the war, they face lives of futility unless they can find a meaningful way to occupy their time.

Shiloh by Shelby Foote

In *Shiloh* (1952), war functions as a setting for male bonding. Shelby Foote has chosen a real battle during the American Civil War that began on 6 April 1862 in western Tennessee and lasted two days. Foote has noted in interviews that the northerners called the spot Pittsburgh Landing and the South called it Shiloh, although none of the men who fought there knew (or cared) by what name this momentous event involving over 100,000 men would be remembered. The North under Ulysses S. Grant had 40,000, and the South under Albert Sidney Johnston had 40,000. Then the northern general Buell brought 20,000 reinforcements. During the two days, 24,000 people died. Before Shiloh, the Confederacy's advantage over the Union had been increasing. General Johnston expected to crush Grant and his sleeping troops, camped between two creeks with their backs to a river, with his pre-dawn attack, but the men quickly responded and fought valiantly while waiting for Buell's arrival with his troops. This fictional account of the two days, in seven chapters, includes a series of first-person monologues from five soldiers and a squad from Indiana. The first and last chapters contain the thoughts of Johnston's aide at the beginning and at the end of the battle. None of the narrators has a sense of the complete battle, and their stories emphasize disorganization and the terrible killing. With this battle, Grant gained an advantage in position over Robert E. Lee's Army of Northern Virginia, and the Confederacy lost Johnston, their best officer in the West.

Attitudes of the participants before the battle show little understanding of its possible devastation. New Orleans-born and educated nineteen-year-old Lieutenant Palmer Metcalfe, aide-de-camp for Johnston's staff, describes the march of Johnston's men through the April rain from Mississippi to Tennessee. Because they arrive one day late, Beauregard, who emulates Napoleon and his battle plans, prefers not to attack the Union soldiers since they can no longer be surprised, but the other generals, including Johnston, disagree. Metcalfe anticipates the battle because he helped to create the plan. On the Union side, thirty-two-year-old Captain Walter Fountain, Adjutant of the 53rd Ohio, complains to his sweetheart Martha in a letter about guard duty and wants her to send a cake. He describes Grant to her and says that a man named John Rawlins is Grant's "conscience." Fountain expects nothing to happen because Shiloh means "place of peace," and when his general, Appler, says that Confederates have arrived nearby, the others ridicule him for this preposterous report. A third soldier, the enlisted Private Luther Dade, rifleman of the 6th Mississippi, seems happy. He declares, "The best thing about the army: no cows." Although he has never experienced a battle, he blithely and uncomprehendingly shares the information that veterans call the enemy the "elephant."

During the battle, men experience an intense rapport, while after, they suffer its loss. Dade remembers, "My heart was hammering at my throat—it seemed like every breath would burst my lungs." He watches Confederates grab food from the Union officers' table and a man who has been shot continue to run. After someone bayonets his arm, he looks for a doctor and discovers Johnston dead. "I thought: Luther, you got no business mixed up in all this ruckus." And of the 425 men in his group, only 100 remain after an hour. Private Otto Flickner, a cannoneer in the 1st Minnesota Battery, watches a shell kill Fountain while writing his letter to Martha. Flickner epitomizes the stereotypical male response to the fray when he says, "What can you do when a man talks like that? saying right out in front of God and everybody that he's scared." A more understanding response comes from Sergeant Buterbaugh, who says of men who ran away after Appler yelled for them to retreat and save themselves, "They weren't necessarily cowards; they were just demoralized from losing confidence." Flickner joins other soldiers on the bluff to watch Buell and his men arrive but fears that some will think he lacks courage, so he returns to battle.

The hero of the battle becomes Nathan Bedford Forrest on the Confederate side. He leads his men into battle, even when they are losing, and refuses to surrender. Sergeant Jefferson Polly, a scout in Forrest's Calvary, reports that 6,000 deserters hide under the bluff. Then a squad of twelve Union men from the 23rd Indiana wonders why two of their group have died. They think they may have died in vain, and one of their leaders asserts that the rebels "wanted the same things we wanted, the right kind of life, the right kind of government—all that—but theyd been misled by bad men." At the end of the battle, after Johnston dies, Palmer Metcalfe finds himself unattached. He wears riding boots, but with his horse dead, he can barely walk. Additionally, he realizes that the losing battle plan had not worked at Waterloo for Napoleon either. He remembers Sherman's words when visiting Metcalfe's father that the North had the machinery, but the South had men like Forrest who would go into battle and sacrifice themselves for what they believed. Metcalfe decides that he will join Forrest even after his father's words that the South is "sick from an old malady . . . incurable romanticism and misplaced chivalry, too much Walter Scott and Dumas read too seriously. We were in love with the past, he said; in love with death." War proceeds from the minds of men (rarely from women), and excessive pride and unwarranted confidence can lead to their defeat.

Men who expect equity, freedom, and independence to be their right often ridicule or malign those who seem cowardly, physically weak, or effeminate. Jake escapes abuse because his impotence results from a war wound. But in Ed's memories of his experiences on the Cahulawassee River and his resulting activities, he does not mention Bobby. After the canoe trip, Ed no longer feels emasculated by the mediocre expectations of his clients; he has a secret that only one other man can share. At Shiloh, Flickner disdains the deserter. Thus men have different standards than women for their relationships—they want to act, to *do* things rather than talk about them.

Additional Related Novels

Baldwin, James. *Go Tell It on the Mountain.*
Conroy, Pat. *The Great Santini.*
Johnson, Charles. *Middle Passage.*
Kesey, Ken. *One Flew Over the Cuckoo's Nest.*
Knowles, John. *A Separate Peace.*
Malamud, Bernard. *The Assistant.*
McCarthy, Cormac. *All the Pretty Horses.*
Steinbeck, John. *The Pearl; Of Mice and Men.*
Twain, Mark. *The Adventures of Huckleberry Finn.*

Masquerading

And after all, what is a lie? 'Tis but
   The truth in masquerade; and I defy
Historians, heroes, lawyers, priests, to put
   A fact without some leaven of a lie.

                —Lord Byron, *Don Juan* (1818)

When people discern that something desired can only be attained if they hide their true identity or circumstances, they assume a persona or mask to prevent others from knowing the reality. In *The Kitchen God's Wife*, Winnie hides her past life in China from her daughter Pearl because of the pain it causes her. Edward Pierce in *The Great Train Robbery* creates identities for himself that will deter others from connecting him with a criminal career. Paul Delmonte's family assumes a new identity in order to survive after his journalist father uncovers Mafia crimes in *I Am the Cheese*. In the novels, *House of Mirth*, *Breakfast at Tiffany's*, and *Passing*, the protagonists want a better life for themselves, and the only way they see to achieve it is to masquerade, hiding the reality of their situations.

The idea of using a mask to mesh or hide appears in literature as early as the thirteenth century. One definition in the *OED*, "to be bewildered, lose one's way," appears in St. Brendan's *A Medieval Legend of the Sea*, "Hi wende alond as maskede [v.r. masid] men, hi nuste whar hi were [He went along as masked men, he knew not where he was]" (c. 1290). Chaucer describes his character in *Troilus and Criseyde* as "He was so narwe [narrowly] y-masked and y-knet [knit], / That it undon on any manere syde, / That nil not been, for ought that may betyde" (c. 1374). In Tottel's *Miscellany*, one finds "thus in the net of my conceit I masked styll [style] among the sort Of such as fed vpon [upon] the bayt [bait], That Cupide laide for his disport" (1557). In another definition, that of "pretending," Ben Jonson says, "I tell thee, I will have no more masquing" (*Love Restored*, 1616). George Walter Thornbury commented in *True as Steel* that "no one ever confesses that he has committed an injury; he calls it retaliation, or justice, or conceals it by some masking name" (1863). And in Carl Sandburg's, "They All Want to Play Hamlet," the speaker declares: "Yet they all want to play Hamlet because it is sad like all / actors are sad and to stand by an open grave with a joker's / skull in the hand and then to say over slow and say over / slow wise, keen, beautiful words masking a heart that's / breaking, breaking" (1922). In these three novels, *House of Mirth*, *Breakfast at Tiffany's*, and *Passing*, the protagonists try to contain "a heart that's breaking" by masquerading.

House of Mirth by Edith Wharton

Lily Bart, the protagonist in Edith Wharton's *House of Mirth* (1905), illustrates what can happen to a woman who knows that to be acceptable in the society she desires, she must pretend to be wealthier than she is. Wharton uses an omniscient point of view that focuses on Lily. Orphaned daughter of a once-wealthy man who lost his money and a woman who told her she could succeed only by marrying a monied male, Lily lives with her aunt, Mrs. Peniston. To attract this elusive wealthy man, the lovely Lily needs the accoutrements of the class to which she aspires because "a woman is asked out as much for her clothes as for herself." After a country weekend during which Lily bumbles her chance to marry the affluent Percy Gryce, she becomes indebted to a man with dishonorable intentions. Her refusal to acquiesce to his demands leads to her downfall.

Although Lily tells her friend Lawrence Selden that she wants to escape from society's "great gilt cage," she does not have the will. "How alluring the world outside the cage appeared to Lily, as she heard its door clang on her. In reality, as she knew, the door never clanged: it stood always open; but most of the captives were like flies in a bottle, and having once flown in, could never regain their freedom." Selden loves Lily, but she knows that he cannot keep her in the "gilt cage" for which she professes dislike but refuses to leave. Some critics posit that Bart's environment and heredity inherent in Wharton's statement, "she was so evidently the victim of the civilization which had produced her that the links of her bracelet seemed like manacles chaining her to her fate," place the novel in the naturalistic school. The Bible verse from which the title comes, "The heart of the wise is in the house of mourning; but the heart of fools is in the house of mirth" (Ecclesiastes 7:3), indicates that Lily has the power of choice, but, in refusing to exercise it, she disapproves of her own actions. "She wanted to get away from herself, and conversation was the only means of escape that she knew." She carefully prepares for a conversation with Gryce on a train to the country weekend by first quizzing Selden about Gryce's interests. At the party, after gambling away almost all of her money at bridge, she pretends to have been coerced to play against her will. She also hides her smoking habit from Gryce. When Selden unexpectedly arrives at the party, Lily ignores Gryce to be with Selden, a choice that ironically begins to extricate her from "the gilt cage." Later Lily buys letters that Bertha Dorset wrote to Selden after marriage to George, to blackmail her but realizes in time that she cares too much for Selden. After Lily invests money with Gus Treanor, she thinks she has earned interest, but later Treanor accuses her of knowing that the returns were a personal loan from him and that she owes him sexual favors. Lily's final hope for appropriate wealth disappears when her aunt leaves her estate to another relative rather than Lily. Although Selden loves Lily, he knows that "when [society] becomes the thing worked for, it distorts all the relations of life." Lily summarizes her entire life with the insight from her final days, "I can hardly be said to have an independent existence."

Lily masquerades as a woman of means in order to be acceptable in upper-class society, but, to continue her charade, she becomes indebted to her aunt and eventually to Treanor. However, Lily compromises her position several times. First, she decides to accompany Selden from Grand Central Station to his apartment for tea while she waits for the next train to Bellomont. When she leaves his apartment building for bachelors, she encounters Simon Rosedale, the Jewish social climber "who made it his business to know everything about every one." On the train she sits with Gryce, discusses Americana with him, and fully expects him to propose at Bellomont; however, she abandons him for Selden, and Gryce meets another woman. Lily joins Rosedale and Treanor for the opera, and Treanor propositions her since his wife is out of town. Then Selden sees her leaving Treanor's house at night. Lily's cousin informs Mrs. Peniston that Lily has gambling debts, and Mrs. Peniston refuses to pay them. Her former friends ignoring her, Lily joins those on a lower rung of society, the Gorners, for a trip to Alaska. Bertha Dorset continues to malign Lily, and finally Lily has to work, first as a secretary for the newly rich, socially undesirable Mrs. Hatch and then as a milliner, although she cannot sew. Out of the "gilt cage," she can find no shelter without seeming to compromise herself.

Lily masquerades because she thinks she must. Her choices show that she was not as deceitful as she might seem. She could not make herself settle for the wealthy but enormously boring Gryce. She burns Bertha's letters rather than using them for blackmail. Toward the end of her travails, Nettie Struther, a woman Lily had sent to a sanatorium with money borrowed from Gus Treanor, rescues Lily and takes her home for coffee. And when she receives her small check of $10,000 from Mrs. Peniston's estate, she writes Treanor a check for the same amount. After she has settled her accounts, she accidentally overdoses on chloral, a sleeping medicine. When the honorable Selden discovers her the next morning, he realizes that he loves Lily, an emotion he could not have felt for someone totally untrue to either herself or others. By allowing society to mislead her, Lily becomes the fool and sacrifices happiness for both herself and Selden.

Breakfast at Tiffany's by Truman Capote

In Truman Capote's *Breakfast at Tiffany's* (1958), the protagonist, Holly Golightly, masquerades as a carefree woman with few attachments. Living in New York City in 1942, Holly meets the narrator when, locked out of her building, she buzzes his apartment in their East 70s brownstone late one night. She calls the narrator "Fred" after her brother fighting in the war on the European front. When Fred meets her, nineteen-year-old Holly smokes Picayunes, eats cottage cheese and Melba toast, plays a guitar, and houses a red cat that she refuses to name because she does not own it. On Thursdays, she delivers Sally Tomato's weather report to Mr. O'Shaughnessy in prison. This Holly lives in the present, unencumbered by the past or any relatives except her absent brother.

The narrator knows nothing about Holly except what he personally observes. He mentions that someone once treated him to dinner at an expensive and famous restaurant; he saw Holly there, but she seemed bored. At Christmas, he accompanies her to Woolworth's where she persuades him to steal masks. Then she gives him a $350 birdcage, telling him not to put anything in it. When he asks Holly about her private life, she rubs her nose and does not answer. Holly invites the narrator-author to a party in her apartment where he meets the wealthy Rusty Trawler. For the many men present, including military officers, "baby-faced" Trawler acts as if he is the host. Holly makes a cruel remark about one of her guests, the model Mag Wildwood, when she leaves the room. The others ignore Mag when she reenters. The narrator then discovers that Holly has invited Mag to move in with her. Later, Holly announces to him that Brazilian José Ybarra-Jaegar wants to marry her immediately, but Trawler and Mag elope next. On the day that the newspapers announce Rusty and Mag's marriage, Holly receives a telegram notifying her of her brother Fred's death in the war. Anguished at the loss and that he never received the peanut butter she sent, Holly stops calling the narrator "Fred."

Holly's masquerading hides her unhappiness with her former life. Her cards from Tiffany's are engraved with her name and her chosen address, "Traveling." She admits that on days when she feels depressed (has the "mean reds") only the happy atmosphere at Tiffany's can revive her. When a stranger appears, he introduces himself to the narrator and discloses that he, a widower, married the orphaned Lulamae Barnes when she was barely fourteen in 1938 because his children needed a mother. Holly admits to the marriage but refuses to return to Texas because she plans to marry José and move to Brazil. Police thwart her plans, however, when they arrest her for passing information from Sally Tomato to the former priest in Sing Sing in the form of weather reports. Even though she received $100 a week, she admits to nothing illegal.

Somewhat lost after José returns to Brazil without her, Holly decides to follow him when she leaves jail. The narrator accompanies her to the airport, and, on the way, she throws the cat out of the taxi. As soon as it disappears, she realizes that the cat *does* belong to her and asks the narrator to find it later. Holly says she will send her permanent address to the narrator, but he never hears from her again. One night, Joe Bell, the owner of a bar on Lexington where Holly used to make telephone calls, contacts the narrator to tell him that a photographer living nearby had come into the bar and shown him a picture taken in Africa of a sculpture that looked like Holly. And although the narrator can never be sure if Holly has been to Africa, he understands that wherever she is, she is masquerading as a woman unburdened with cares. Only he knows the lonely Holly behind the mask.

Passing by Nella Larsen

The masquerading depicted in Nella Larsen's *Passing* (1929) involves the pretense of one of the characters, Clare Kendry, to be white rather than black. As the child of a black father and a white mother, Larsen herself experienced the hostility toward multiracial children. In the United States, children with any percentage of African ancestry have been considered "black" instead of "white," and by law before 1954, forbidden to patronize any segregated place. Irene Redfield, a wealthy New York matron who knew Clare when they were children, tells their three-part story in limited omniscient point of view. When Irene receives a letter written on elegant Italian paper from Clare, she ignores it. She remembers their last meeting in Chicago two years before in the Drayton Hotel at tea where Irene had gone after almost fainting on the street. Irene had wondered if the woman sitting next to her realized that she was black and then Clare introduced herself. Thus two of the women in the segregated room happened to be trespassers who knew each other before Clare's white aunts had taken her away after the death of her father when Clare was fifteen.

Although compromised when she meets Clare, Irene has chosen to live as a black woman, marrying a black physician, a man darker than she, and raising her two sons in racially divided New York. Irene has refused to move to Brazil with her husband Brian, although he thinks that raising their children in Brazil will protect them from the hostilities and humilities of racist America. Irene does not seem to comprehend the additional problems facing blacks with dark skin. When she visited Clare in Chicago, Clare's white husband John Bellew had come home and met Irene. During the conversation, he had chastised Clare because she seemed to be getting darker, like a "nig." Bellew declared, "You can get as black as you please as far as I'm concerned, since I know you're no nigger. I draw the line at that. No niggers in my family. Never have been and never will be." Irene asks him if he has known any to dislike, and he responds, "Nothing like that at all. I don't dislike them, I hate them. And so does Nig, for all she's trying to turn into one." The encounter shocks Irene, especially since she must masquerade to protect herself from Bellew's wrath. That Clare has exposed her to such rancor also makes her angry. After Irene and Clare renew their acquaintance in New York, Irene realizes that she too has worn a mask by not admitting to an unhappy marriage.

Only through Irene's eyes does the reader see Clare. "Catlike" Clare has a "having way," and in Chicago she refuses to visit Irene because someone might see her in a black neighborhood. Irene thinks that Clare had "no allegiance beyond her own immediate desire. She was selfish, and cold, and hard." Simultaneously, Clare can have "warmth and passion, verging sometimes almost on theatrical heroics." Clare confesses to Irene that she ran away from her disapproving aunts to marry the wealthy Bellew and never told him her heritage. Clare admits, however, her huge fear that her daughter Margery would be dark so she refused to have another child. When Clare appears at Irene's New York door, even after Irene has ignored Clare's letter, Irene graciously invites her inside. Clare decides she will go to the Negro Welfare League dance that Irene is coordinating since a lot of white people go. Her husband is out of town and her daughter attends a Swiss school. After the dance, Clare comes to Irene's tea, invited not by Irene but by her husband Brian, and Irene realizes that Clare is having an affair with her husband.

The allure of "passing" or masquerading as someone else both attracts and repels. Irene later says to her husband, "We disapprove of [passing] and at the same time condone it. It excites our contempt and yet we rather admire it. We shy away from it with an odd kind of revulsion, but we protect it." Irene wonders what "this hazardous business of 'passing,'" might be like, "this breaking away from all that was familiar and friendly to take one's chance in another environment, not entirely strange, perhaps, but certainly not entirely friendly." Clare admits to Irene in New York that she has been unhappy while isolated from her past. And Irene realizes that Clare's dilemma, caused solely by her race, can never be resolved. "Whatever steps [Clare] took, or if she took none at all, something would be crushed. A person or the race. Clare, herself, or the race." And, "Irene Redfield wished, for the first time in her life, that she had not been born a Negro. For the first time she suffered and rebelled because she was unable to disregard the burden of race." Irene knows that she can destroy Clare and Brian by revealing Clare's identity to Bellew, but she does not. When Bellew, supposedly in Philadelphia, finds Clare at a party, Clare falls out a window. No one knows if she committed suicide or if Irene pushed her. Whatever the answer, Clare's agony over her birth can no longer concern her.

People who cannot cope with the reality of their lives may try to masquerade as someone whom they perceive would be more desirable to others. In *House of Mirth*, Lily Bart hides behind the façade of society. Holly Golightly in *Breakfast at Tiffany's* changes her name and travels far from her origins. And in *Passing*, Clare Kendry denies her heritage to masquerade as white. All three protagonists allow people outside themselves to define their identities, and their lives fail because they are always existentially inauthentic "beings."

Additional Related Novels

Cormier, Robert. *I Am the Cheese.*
Crichton, Michael. *The Great Train Robbery.*
Fitzgerald, F. Scott. *The Great Gatsby; Tender Is the Night.*
Tan, Amy. *The Joy Luck Club; The Kitchen God's Wife.*
West, Nathanael. *The Day of the Locust.*

Mothers and Daughters

Oft wont is the son to be like the father, while the daughter lightly follows her mother's path.

—Rabelais, *Pantagruel* (1545)

The mother-daughter relationship changes from symbiotic to separate; sometimes they become enemies and, sometimes, the closest of friends. In *Beloved*, Sethe murders her daughter to save her from slavery and welcomes Beloved's supernatural presence for the next twenty years. Selina cannot understand her mother's hostility toward her father or her determination to buy a house until Selina reaches adulthood in *Brown Girl, Brownstones*. Disappointed when her destitute mother chooses to spend money on her brother's high schooling instead of hers, Francie Nolan in *A Tree Grows in Brooklyn* gets a job and saves money for her own education. In the three novels, *Annie John, Mama*, and *Pigs in Heaven*, the daughters become independent by very different means.

A mother is usually a female parent "who has given birth to a child" (*OED*). When a female offers protection to someone not born to her, that person may lovingly call her "mother." A female child can be either a daughter by birth or a "term of affectionate address to a woman or girl by an older person or one in a superior relation" (*OED*). Throughout recorded history, these terms have referred to a female. A speaker at Trinity College, Oxford, addressed himself "to sunes and to dohtres [daughters]" (ca. 1200). In her autobiography, Countess Warwick noted that, "My lady Claytone . . . grew to make so much of me as if she had been an own mother to me" (1671). Rudyard Kipling recognizes the difference between the two: "Daughter am I in my mother's house, But mistress in my own" (*Our Lady of the Snows*, 1897). More recently, Celia Fremlin speaks in *Possession* of the "closeness of the mother-daughter relationship" (1969). She also mentions "an ordinary, typical mother-daughter misunderstanding" in *By Horror Haunted* (1974). In *Annie John, Mama*, and *Pigs in Heaven*, the daughters, in different developmental stages because of their ages, illustrate some of the changes that often occur in the bond between mother and daughter.

Annie John by Jamaica Kincaid

To explore the changes in Annie John, the protagonist of *Annie John* (1986), Jamaica Kincaid divides her life into eight segments represented in eight chapters. Annie begins telling her story in first person when she is ten and completes it at seventeen. Annie's mother had left her father's house at sixteen after a quarrel and had come to Antigua where she had married a man thirty-five years older with children from other liaisons. Annie's father's parents had left him with his grandmother and gone to South America, and, when he was eighteen, his grandmother had died in bed next to him. When he tells Annie the story, they weep together. Annie John remembers her relationship to her mother as a young child and describes the changes that occur because of her own behavior or that of her mother. Since they live in the Caribbean, a set of complex rules for women on their island underlies Annie's mother's attitudes and those of her grandmother who retains her strong African spiritual and healing beliefs.

During the novel, a bildungsroman, Annie begins to experience the world around her. Death surprises, and she reacts by refusing to speak to the beautiful Sonia after she hears that Sonia's mother had died. "I was afraid of the dead, as was everyone I knew. We were afraid of the dead because we never could tell when they might show up again." A neighbor, Miss Charlotte, dies, and then a hunchbacked girl she had known in school. Annie attends her funeral and comments, "When I looked at this girl, it was as if the View-Master wasn't working properly." When Annie lists the items her mother saved in a trunk from Annie's infancy, Kincaid uses the parallel structure of "There was" to emphasize their equal standing as well as their developmental distance from Annie at the time she catalogues them, including her second birthday earrings and gold from British Guiana.

Annie's especially strong, symbiotic relationship with her mother has to dissolve for Annie to gain any separate identity or independence. When young, Annie thinks her mother is beautiful, and she loves to kiss her and smell her. "Beautiful long neck, and long plaited hair. . . . Her nose was the shape of a flower on the brink of opening." Annie's mother very early begins teaching her about her responsibilities as a Caribbean woman. She takes Annie shopping on school holidays where she instructs her about buying different items. At home, she demonstrates the correct way to wash clothes on the circle of stones in their yard. Annie first seems aware of her mother's participation in events outside the family when she hears that her mother has helped prepare Naida, a young girl, for burial. Then the smell of the cleansing bay rum on her mother's body makes her "feel ill" for a long time, and she does not want her mother to touch her. She admits that, "until then, I had not known that children died."

When she is twelve, Annie's attitudes begin to change as her body changes. "I could see that I had grown taller, most of my clothes no longer fit. . . . My legs had become spindle-like, the hair on my head even more unruly than usual, small tufts of hair had appeared under my arms and when I perspired the smell was strange, as if I had turned into a strange animal." Annie becomes angry when her mother makes her wear a dress from different material after they have been wearing matching dresses all of Annie's life. Annie begins misbehaving, "I was such a good liar that, almost as if to prove all too true my mother's saying 'Where there's a liar, there's a thief,' I began to steal." Her mother requires her to take lessons on manners, and Annie makes "farting-like noises each time I had to practice a curtsy, it made the other girls laugh so." She goes to a new school, meets Gwen who has heard that Annie is smart, and makes friends with her the first day. To spite her mother, Annie then befriends the Red Girl who neither cleans nor attends Sunday school. They play marbles, something her mother has asked her not to do, and Annie collects treasures from the Red Girl and hides them under the house. Annie lies about playing marbles, but admits, "I couldn't imagine my life without her. Worse than that, if my mother died I would have to die, too, and even less than I could imagine my mother dead could I imagine myself dead." Then Annie starts to menstruate and grow breasts. Since she attends a girls' school, she demonstrates her new condition for the other girls who also want to be adult. But Annie wishes that one of them had been first instead of her. One day when she arrives home unexpectedly, she sees her mother rubbing her father's back, "a white circle of bone," and the intimacy offends her, making her think she no longer loves her mother.

Annie's impending adulthood separates her further from her mother. Her mother's inability to discuss sex with Annie curtails their closeness, cemented when her mother lashes out at her, calling her "slut," for talking to the boy Mineu whom she had known for years. At fifteen, Annie feels "unhappiness . . . deep inside me . . . and it took the shape of a small black ball, all wrapped up in cobwebs." She feels that "everything I used to care about had turned sour." She has a nervous breakdown, and while she suffers, she thinks it rains for three months. During that time, she briefly regresses to comfortable dependency, when her grandmother, Ma Chess, "would lie next to me, curled up like a bigger comma, into which I fit." Annie's mother leaves her alone one day, and Annie washes photographs so that they are ruined—symbolically ridding herself of her childhood and the closeness to her mother. At seventeen, she goes abroad to study nursing, not because she wants to be a nurse, but because she needs to leave the confinement of the island. Her changed perspective forces her to search for a life outside her mother's world.

Mama by Terry McMillan

In Terry McMillan's *Mama* (1987), Mildred Peacock, twenty-seven, discards her husband Crook in the winter of 1964 and keeps her five children. Although Crook is also jealous when platinum-wigged Mildred flirts with Percy Russell, he has had a long-standing affair with another woman, Ernestine, and has beaten Mildred when inebriated. In the economically deprived town of Port Haven, Michigan, Mildred finds a variety of ways to support her children. She works in a salt factory and a spark plug plant, cleans houses, sponsors rent parties, draws welfare, and when necessary, engages in prostitution. She and Freda, her daughter, reveal through omniscient point of view their difficulties of overcoming the psychological distance between them.

Family members, Freda, Money, Bootsey, Angel, and Doll, and Mildred's best friend Curly Mae (Crook's sister) interact while trying to tolerate the weather and each other. A narrator reveals the attitudes of their acquaintances. "The bigger the car, the more stature you had, though a lot of the men who drove these cars lived in them, too. . . . Most black folks considered their cars evidence of their true worth. That and the gold capped over their teeth. . . . They started out simple: a gold cap. Then they moved into gold and diamonds, then stars, and last, their initials." Mildred instructs her own children about what she thinks is important. "And baby, let me tell you something so you can get this straight. That big fancy house ain't the only thang in life worth striving for. Decency. A good husband. Some healthy babies. Peace of mind. Them is the thangs you try to get out of your life. Everyting else'll fall in place."

She also reassures her children about their worth. She tells them to "always remember that you just as good as the next person," but she can protect neither them nor herself from others. Deadman, a retarded neighbor, helps Mildred clean because he has a crush on Freda. When Mildred leaves Freda alone one night, the inebriated Deadman arrives and tries to rape her. When Deadman tells Mildred much later what happened, she shoots and wounds him. He flees to Alabama. Money has to go to prison for theft. After Mildred marries the twenty-year-old Billy Callahan, he becomes unfaithful. She then marries and divorces Rufus and promises herself to a white man, Jim. But the birth of Doll's child breaks up that relationship because Mildred chooses to help her rather than remarry. Eventually Money goes to California with funds from Bootsey where he lies about his past and gets a job with a company that likes his work and sends him to school. Freda moves to New York and meets James, but his cocaine dependency ruins their relationship. Then her alcoholism almost destroys her.

Mildred adores Freda but is unable to physically express her love. The two never touch. Mildred's love for the infant Freda controls the remainder of her life. "She was so proud of Freda that she let her body blow up and flatten for the next fifty-five months. It made her feel like she had actually done something meaningful with her life, having these babies did. . . . These kids were her future. They made her feel important and gave her a sense of having come from somewhere." Freda observes Mildred's durability while trying to protect her children and herself, and it eventually helps her assume responsibility. But first, Freda has to leave home, fail, and then reject her own drug problem —alcohol. Freda leaves for California after high school, attends a community college, and then gains admittance to Stanford. But at Stanford, she meets Delbert, an epileptic who introduces her to cocaine. Mildred visits Freda in California, stays for a while, becomes bored, and leaves. After moving to New

York, Freda attends graduate school in journalism but begins drinking heavily. Not until her second telephone call to Alcoholics Anonymous can she make herself stay on the line. Then she slowly recovers, sells her first article, and decides to share her success with Mildred, the woman from whom she learned resilience. For the first time, after all their anger, misunderstanding, and trials, Mildred hugs Freda, making both of them feel accepted and loved.

Pigs in Heaven by **Barbara Kingsolver**

Barbara Kingsolver's *Pigs in Heaven* (1993) explores the relationships of two mothers and two daughters. Using omniscient point of view and a stylistic variation on present tense, she allows the characters located in different places to reveal their needs and concerns with an unnamed narrator, sometimes offering a different perspective on their actions and the possible consequences. The effective dialogue quickly exposes personalities and connections among the characters. The book, a sequel to *The Bean Trees*, follows Taylor Greer after her adoption of Turtle, the child she found on her way west when she left Kentucky. After she adopts Turtle, Oprah Winfrey invites Taylor to talk about the experience on television, and Taylor agrees. Annawake Fourkiller sees them and begins prosecution of Taylor for breaking the Indian Child Welfare Act, passed in 1978. Unknown to Taylor, she needed the full consent of the tribe before adopting Turtle, a Cherokee child. Annawake has seen the effects of nonwhite children growing up in white families including her own brother Gabe, who, after being adopted off the reservation, ended up in prison. Later Cash Stillwater tells Alice, Taylor's mother, that being Cherokee is "not like some country club or something. It's just family. It's kindly like joining the church. If you get around to deciding you're Cherokee . . . then that's what you are."

As women who prefer living alone, Alice and Taylor have a tolerant relationship. Alice's mother, Minerva Stamper, raised hogs on a farm by herself for fifty years. Alice loves Taylor but declares, "Kids don't stay with you if you do it right." She understands the importance of independence based on her relationship with her own mother. Alice prefers household silence at sixty-one and dislikes her second husband Harland's blaring television. "Alice wonders if other women in the middle of the night have begun to resent their Formica." While Alice rocks on her porch, the narrator ascertains that "she needs some proof that she's not the last woman left on earth, the surviving queen of nothing." From Alice's garden comes one of the meanings of the novel's title. Vietnamese pigs from a neighbor infiltrate her garden, her "heaven . . . crowded with bird music and border disputes and other people's hungry animals." She thinks, "the poor things [pigs] are just looking for a home, like the Boat People. She has a soft spot for refugees and decides to let them stay." Alice relinquishes this heaven after seeing Taylor and Turtle on television. She decides to leave Harland and go to Tucson to be with them. When Annawake starts her campaign to recover Turtle, Alice helps Taylor hide in Las Vegas before Taylor and Turtle flee to Seattle, and Alice departs for Oklahoma to reunite with Sugar Boss (Hornbuckle), a cousin with whom she grew up in Mississippi during the Depression, and a woman who might help her understand Annawake's intense efforts at parting Taylor from Turtle. Not only does protecting Turtle help Alice find another "heaven" in Heaven, Oklahoma, when she meets Sugar's brother-in-law Cash, but Alice also discovers that her grandma Stamper was a full-blooded Cherokee.

Taylor ironically has become a mother after leaving Kentucky to escape getting pregnant, the normal expectation of females in her high school. Turtle, abandoned in a bar, refuses to release Taylor when she holds her, and Taylor takes her to Tucson. When Taylor can find no other parent claiming Turtle, she adopts her. Although unrelated to Turtle biologically, Taylor has developed a love for her and a determination to make the rest of Turtle's life better than her first three years when she was abused. After Annawake begins her pursuit, Taylor flees Tucson with Turtle and gets a job in Seattle that she loses when she has no one to keep Turtle. Annawake uncovers Turtle's parentage and informs Alice of her discovery after Cash's hog fry. Before Cash's daughter Alma had committed suicide by driving off a bridge, she had asked her sister Lacey to take Turtle. But Lacey decided to dispose of the child and run away with the man who had abused it. Annawake fortunately consults a wise uncle about the case, and he advises her not to separate mothers from daughters they love. Annawake declares joint custody of Turtle between Taylor and Cash, and the union of mother and daughter tightens when Cash conveniently marries Alice.

For all these relationships, whether the women live with the daughters or apart, the most valuable aspect is their love for each other. Annie John's mother states it best: "How terrible it must be for all the people who had no one to love them and no one whom they loved so." Annawake lives by the concept based on the Native-American myth of boys turned into pigs for not obeying their mothers, that one should "do right by your people or you'll be a pig in heaven" (a second interpretation of the novel's title). The narrator in *Pigs in Heaven* further clarifies the importance of guidance. "In natural systems there is no guilt or virtue, only success or failure, measured by survival and nothing more. Time is the judge. If you manage to pass on what you have to the next generation, then what you did was right."

Additional Related Novels

Dorris, Michael. *A Yellow Raft in Blue Water*.
Kingsolver, Barbara. *The Bean Trees; The Poisonwood Bible*.
Kingston, Maxine Hong. *The Woman Warrior*.
Marshall, Paule. *Brown Girl, Brownstones*.
Morrison, Toni. *Beloved*.
Roth, Philip. *Goodbye, Columbus*.
Smith, Betty. *A Tree Grows in Brooklyn*.
Tan, Amy. *The Joy Luck Club; The Kitchen God's Wife*.

Multiracial Offspring

I am convinced that when the intellectual history of our times comes to be written, the idea of race, both the popular and the taxonomic, will be viewed for what it is: a confused and dangerous idea which happened to fit the social requirements of a thoroughly exploitative period in the development of Western man.

—Ashley Montagu, *Man's Most Dangerous Myth: Fallacy of Race* (1942)

Throughout Western history, children of mixed races have suffered ridicule and hostility. In *Our Nig*, Frado learns to ignore other children calling her "yeller." Son of Thomas Sutpen and a woman with black blood, Charles Bon in *Absalom, Absalom!* suffers when his father will not acknowledge his existence. Jim Loney in *The Death of Jim Loney* never feels part of his tribe because he is a half-breed Native American. Characters in *A Yellow Raft in Blue Water*, *Devil in a Blue Dress*, and *Light in August* have all suffered because of their birth parents, a condition over which they have no control.

Several terms describe people of mixed race, although some state laws in the United States have designated anyone with one drop of "black blood" as "black." The *OED* designates "mulatto" as "one who is the offspring of a European and a Black" or "anyone of mixed race resembling a mulatto." Another person of mixed race, a Melungeon, is a "member of a North American people of mixed white, black, and Amerindian descent inhabiting the southern Appalachian mountains in the eastern United States." Sir Francis Drake reported that, "by meanes of a Mulatow and an Indian, we had, this night, forty bundles of dried beife" (*Voyages*, 1595). *Chambers Cyclopedia* defines "mulatto" as "a name given, in the Indies, to those who are begotten by a negro man on an Indian woman; or an Indian man on a negro woman" (1727). The first mention of "Melungeon" occurs in an 1889 *Boston Traveller* article: "They resented the appellation Melungeon, given to them by common consent by the whites, and proudly called themselves Portuguese." H. L. Mencken describes attitudes toward them in 1948: "There are many similar groups of mixed bloods, always of low economic status . . . notably . . . the Malungeons of southwestern Virginia, eastern Kentucky and Tennessee" (*American Language*). Recent research reveals that the Melungeons may have settled America long before the Europeans and that their heritage may rewrite "modern America's earliest history" (Richard Lister, *BBC America*, 1999). Unfortunately, the characters in *A Yellow Raft in Blue Water*, *Devil in a Blue Dress*, and *Light in August* were not created in the last decade, and the scars they wear are indicative of persons with mixed blood.

A Yellow Raft in Blue Water by Michael Dorris

Of the three novels, only the character in *A Yellow Raft in Blue Water* (1987) readily admits her heritage. Ramona's mother Christine left an unnamed Plains Indian reservation for Seattle where she met Rayona's father, Elgin Taylor, in a bar on the day she heard that her brother was missing in Vietnam. They marry, but before Rayona is born, he is unfaithful. When Rayona is fifteen, her mother takes her to the Montana reservation and leaves her with her grandmother whom they call "Aunt Ida." Rayona meets Father Tom and accompanies him to a religious retreat, but after their unexpected sexual encounter, she decides not to return to the reservation. She gets a job at Bearpaw Lake Park, and the kind cook Evelyn rents her a room. When Rayona confesses to Evelyn that she has run away from home, Evelyn encourages her to return. Michael Dorris uses multiple narrators to tell the story, and each one adds more information, although none of them knows the others' stories. After Ramona narrates her story, her mother Christine reveals her past, but finally Aunt Ida's revelations provide the missing puzzle pieces.

Christine and Aunt Ida, allegedly Christine's mother, have never had a close relationship. Aunt Ida preferred her son Lee to her daughter, and Christine left home after urging Lee to go to Vietnam so that he would be better prepared to take tribal leadership. When Christine returns to the reservation for his funeral fourteen months after he was reported missing, she discovers that Aunt Ida and Lee's good friend Dayton, who was 4–A because his father died in World War II, blame her for his death. In reality, Christine had wanted to separate Lee and Dayton; therefore, she had manipulated Lee into thinking he should enlist. When Rayona is born, Christine shifts her adoration from Lee. Ramona "was a total miracle: the fact she breathed, the fact she wouldn't leave me. . . . She was the best so far, the new improved model, and whatever else I had to do, it had to do with her." Fifteen years later, Christine walks out of a hospital to take Rayona to the reservation. Christine knows that her cancer will soon kill her, and she wants to have Rayona safe with Aunt Ida. Aunt Ida then admits to Christine that she never wanted her, but she helps Christine obtain prescription Percocet from an unnamed source.

Ida's story covers her past from age fifteen to her present age of fifty-seven. "My life is a ring of mountains, close together and separated by deep chasms." Ida's aunt Clara came to help Ida's sick mother, and Ida's father Lecon impregnated Clara. Lecon sent Ida with Clara to have the baby in Denver, and Clara remained. Ida returned with the baby Christine, and Lecon made her pretend that Christine was her child outside the house. Later, Ida has an affair with Willard, a man of higher social status in the tribe who lost part of his face and fingers in World War II. She bears a son, Lee (short for Lecon), but leaves Willard when he says he likes her because she is loyal; she never tells anyone the identity of Lee's father. Thus her request for Christine to call her "Aunt" Ida has merit.

Rayona has to survive both off and on the reservation as the daughter of an African-American mailman and a Native American. She identifies her mother's color as Almond Joy, her father as Burnt Clay, and herself as Maple Walnut. When she reaches the reservation, she can speak the language, and Father Tom takes her to the God Squad. There she meets her cousin Foxy and another, but they ostracize her. The only friendly person, Father Tom, takes her to a jamboree, but on the way, he keeps asking her questions about sex. Father Tom stops near Bear Paw Lake, jumps in, and pretends to be drowning. When Rayona helps him reach the yellow raft, they have sex. Shocked by his behavior, Father Tom gives her money to return to Seattle and her father so that he will not be embarrassed every time he sees her. Instead she gets work at Bearpaw Lake, moves in with Evelyn and her husband Skye, and pretends she has a wonderful life with parents who love her. On July 4, Evelyn discovers Rayona's secret and tells her she will drive her home because someone should have done it for her when she was a teenager. On the way, they stop in Havre for a rodeo and to find Christine. Instead Rayona sees an inebriated Foxy who wants her to take his place in bronco riding. With only four horseback riding lessons in her past, she stays on her horse and wins a prize before revealing that she is female. When she spots Dayton, he informs her that her mother is staying at his house and that her Uncle Lee was the best bronco rider in eastern Montana. Rayona never acknowledges that her mother is dying and tries to ignore her mixed blood and her unfaithful father. But the reader cannot forget that Ramona also pretended that she had a secure home with parents who adored her.

Devil in a Blue Dress by Walter Mosley

In *Devil in a Blue Dress* (1990), Walter Mosley presents African-American Easy Rawlins at the beginning of his detective work. Rawlins, the first-person narrator, moved to Los Angeles from Houston in 1948. He began working in a factory, but after he loses his job, the bartender Joppy connects him to the white man, DeWitt Albright, a former lawyer who wants to locate a missing white woman. Since she frequents the jazz clubs located in black neighborhoods, Albright requires someone who can search for her without being obvious. Needing the money, Rawlins agrees to the terms. The people he encounters, both dead and alive, populate the sleazy Los Angeles underground of laundered money, child prostitution, and illegal liquor. As a child of a black father and a Jewish mother, Mosley probably experienced some of the feelings of his character Daphne Monet, the devil of his novel.

Easy Rawlins's doubts about his ability make him an unlikely detective. His boss at Champion Aircraft fired him because he refused to check his good work when tired. After Easy's colleague Dupree suggests that Easy reapply, Easy tells his former boss why he would not stay, and even though the man will not re-hire him, he gains respect for Easy. Easy, however, equates factory work with plantation slave labor. Thus he decides to work for Albright in order to pay his mortgage. He does not know that the wealthy Todd Carter hired Albright to find Daphne because Carter loves her even after she stole $30,000 from him. Easy describes Albright, "his grip was strong but slithery, like a snake coiling around my hand." When people Easy needs to question are murdered either before he can find them or after he has left, he calls his acquaintance Mouse in Texas and invites him to Los Angeles. Mouse had wanted to come before, but Rawlins felt guilty for the $300 he had taken from Mouse after Mouse killed his stepfather for $1,000. One day when Easy returns home, Frank Green waits to kill him, but Mouse as the deus ex machina arrives just in time. When Easy tells Mouse about his guilt and his assignment, Mouse wants to help.

During his search for Daphne Monet, Rawlins learns about the Los Angeles underground. When Albright hears that Daphne lives with Frank Green, Albright asks Easy to find him as well. After Howard Green and Daphne's friend Coretta are murdered, Daphne herself contacts Rawlins. Shocked, he meets her and admires her blue dress, and her sexuality captivates him. He concludes that Joppy gave Daphne his number and killed Howard and Coretta. Easy becomes aware, as well, that Matthew Teran had wanted to run for mayor, but that Carter had stopped his quest, most likely because Teran liked the young boys Richard McGee, a friend of Daphne's whom Junior Fournay eventually kills in alleged self-defense, supplied for him. When Joppy tries to betray Easy, Mouse kills him. As soon as Mouse sees Daphne, he recognizes her as Ruby Hanks from Lake Charles, Louisiana, and knows that Frank Green, actually her brother, murdered their father for molesting her. Daphne has the invisible scars that affect many mulattoes. Mouse says, "All them years people be tellin' her how she light-skinned and beautiful but all the time she knows that she can't have what white people have. So she pretend and then she lose it all. She can love a white man but all he can love is the white girl he think she is." Then he adds, "A nigger ain't never gonna be happy' less he accept what he is."

Light in August by William Faulkner

Like Daphne, Joe Christmas in *Light in August* (1932) passes for white. He, however, tells everyone that he is a Negro, even though he has known no parents and has no proof of his heritage. When the sheriff searches a cabin for Joe after Joanna Burden's house burns with her in it, a young Negro nearby says that two white men lived there. Joe straddles two worlds, accepting neither, in his suppressed search for his identity. William Faulkner tells Joe's story using stream of consciousness with its abrupt changing tenses along with multiple narrators (some characters important only for what they can report). After Joe arrives in Jefferson, Mississippi, he begins working in a sawmill and eventually moves into a cabin with Joe Brown. They run an illegal liquor business. Simultaneously, Joe has an affair with Joanna Burden, an older woman happy to befriend a man announcing that he is African American. When Joanna's behavior resembles that of Joe's foster father, he kills her and burns down her house. Brown claims the reward for finding the murderer, and Joe suffers the consequences. On the August day of the fire, Lena Grove arrives in Jefferson after walking from Alabama to Mississippi for four weeks searching for Lucas Burch, the father of her unborn child. Erroneously led to Byron Bunch, she soon discovers that Lucas has taken the name of Joe Brown and wants neither her nor the child.

Almost every character in the novel becomes abandoned or forsakes another. The orphaned Lena lives with her brother six years after her parents' death, and after opening the "leanto window" for Burch to enter, realizes that leaving it closed would have been a wiser decision. Someone she asks tells her that Burch might work in Jefferson, and Faulkner describes her as a "forgotten bead from a broken strong" and a "shabby bead upon the mild red string of road." She meets Mrs. Armstid, a narrator whose function is to report seeing her and revealing that she gave Lena valuable egg money. By offering Lena the money without asking her husband's permission, even though she is the only one in her household to have raised and cared for the chickens, Mrs. Armstid conveys her unsavory opinion of all men. *"He will overlook and fail to see chances, opportunities, for riches and fame and welldoing, and even sometimes for evil. But he wont fail to see a chance to meddle."*

Gail Hightower, one of Jefferson's residents, tries to influence others' opinions of Lena, but he fails as he has in all his other endeavors. A former minister who drove his wife mad with his constant references to his grandfather's noble death during the Civil War, Hightower has lost his church. An omniscient narrator describes Hightower as unable to separate "religion and that galloping cavalry and his dead grandfather shot from the galloping horse untangled from each other, even in the pulpit." Hightower, however, continues to ride thirty miles into the country to lead a choir. The town says Hightower is "DD" or "Done Damned," and the narrator philosophies about the town's regret that Hightower fulfilled their prophecy "as people sometimes are sorry for those whom they have at last forced to do as they wanted them to." Byron Bunch, the man to whom Lena has been mistakenly sent, realizes that she may be searching for Brown. "Byron remembered that he had ever thought how a man's name, which is supposed be just the sound for who he is, can be somehow an augur of what he will do, if other men can only read the meaning in time." But, almost immediately, Burch falls in love with Lena. Hightower cautions him, suggesting that he love a virgin instead, but, already emotionally entangled, Byron recognizes Hightower's reticence to face an unknown future.

"He'll cling to trouble he's used to before he'll risk a change. . . . A man will talk about how he'd like to escape from living folks. But it's the dead folks that do him the damage . . . [the ones] he cant escape from."

Although Hightower has no idea how to minister, others realize that they must aid their neighbors. Mrs. Hines, Joe's white grandmother who has just met her grandson for the first time while he is in prison, helps Lena with the birth of her child. Burch fights Lucas for deserting Lena and the baby and then returns to help her. Joanna Burden's affair with Joe begins because she wanted to help an African American; her grandfather had left the Catholic Church because of the "frogeating slaveholders." Their affair ends after she pretends to be pregnant, points a gun at him, and makes him pray like McEachern had done.

After the torment of undeserved abuse throughout his life, Joe can no longer tolerate the cycle that began with his grandfather, continued with McEachern, and climaxed with Joanna. Doc Hines, Joe's grandfather, killed Joe's father, a circus performer most likely of African-American extraction, and let his suffering daughter die in childbirth, never answering when his wife asked, "What did you do with Milly's baby?" Calling Joe "nigger," he placed him in an orphanage where he worked in Memphis at Christmas (thus the name), and when no family chose him, Hines moved him into a foster home. McEachern adopted him, and as he matured, Joe watched McEachern's wife die a little each day. This "ruthless and bigoted man . . . hammered [her] stubbornly thinner and thinner like some passive and dully malleable metal, into an attenuation of dumb hopes and frustrated desires now faint and pale as dead ashes."

At eighteen, Joe finally breaks away from McEachern when he has an affair with Bobbie, a promiscuous waitress, and his life changes. Infuriated with Joe, McEachern fights him. Joe hits him with a chair, takes money, and runs to Bobbie. But Bobbie, a woman, and two men wait for Joe and steal his money. After the three betray him, "he entered the street which was to run for fifteen years." Joanna's lies and desire for him to better himself by attending school incite him to kill her and set her house on fire. Joe's last mile, after killing Joanna, brings him to the place he wants to be. "The air, inbreathed, is like spring water. He breathes deep and slow, feeling with each breath himself diffuse in the neutral grayness, becoming one with loneliness and quiet that has never know fury or despair. 'That was all I wanted,' he thinks, in a quiet and slow amazement. 'That was all, for thirty years. That didn't seem to be a whole lot to ask in thirty years.'" Yet he knows, "I have never got outside that circle. I have never broken out of the ring of what I have already done and cannot ever undo." Doc Hines encourages Jefferson's citizens to lynch Joe for his crimes (brought about by Hines's bigotry) while his wife visits Joe in prison and tells him how Byron Burch suggests he escape. Joe escapes, but the lynchers find him. One person says about Joe, "He never acted like either a nigger or a white man." And the omniscient narrator, in describing Joe's death, notes, "Upon that black blast the man seemed to rise soaring into their memories forever and ever."

In these three novels, characters must cope with the burden of their births, an event over which they have had no control. Their lives are, as Byron Bunch thinks about Joe Christmas, "a lot of people performing a play and that now and at last they had all played out the parts which had been allotted them and now they could live quietly with one another." But, in many cases, they do not live quietly. They continue age-old hostilities, not allowing each other to be individuals worthy of honor and respect.

Additional Related Novels

Faulkner, William. *Absalom, Absalom!*
Gaines, Ernest J. *The Autobiography of Miss Jane Pittman.*
Larsen, Nella. *Passing.*
McMillan, Terry. *Mama.*
Stowe, Harriet Beecher. *Uncle Tom's Cabin.*
Welch, James. *The Death of Jim Loney.*
Wilson, Harriet E. *Our Nig.*

Nature

Man masters nature not by force but by understanding.
—Jacob Brownowski, *The Starry Messenger* (1977)

Humans often lament separation from forests and open spaces but rarely achieve contentment when they leave city surroundings because they impose artificial requirements on their environments. They usually carry mechanical artifacts into the wilderness and try to change the very condition they initially sought. The English soldiers appointed to protect Alice and Cora Munro in *The Last of the Mohicans* have no concept of clues available in the wilderness to guide their journey. On Santiago's last fishing trip, he enjoys the beauty of the sea and the creatures with which he interacts in *The Old Man and the Sea*. Henry contrasts the natural atmosphere of the forest with the horror of war in *The Red Badge of Courage*. The three novels, *Of Mice and Men*, *The Bear*, and *House Made of Dawn*, reflect the desire of humans to unify themselves with nature's power and beauty and their attempts at accomplishing it.

"Nature," a general term, can refer to landscape or humans. In the *OED*, "nature" becomes "the essential qualities or properties of a thing; the inherent and inseparable combination of properties essentially pertaining to anything and giving it its fundamental character." The word has appeared in literature since 1300. James Bryce in *American Commonwealth* spoke of Americans as leading "a solitary life in the midst of a vast nature" (1888). In the twentieth century, concern for retaining wilderness led former president Jimmy Carter to note, "It is good to realize that if love and peace can prevail on earth, and if we can teach our children to honor nature's gifts, the joys and beauties of the outdoors will be here forever" (*An Outdoor Journal*, 1988). And the twentieth-century Japanese animator Osamu Tezuka notes that "we humans are always a part of Nature, no matter how far we evolve or material civilization progresses. No advance of science can deny Nature, for that would be a negation of ourselves, as human beings" (*Earth of Glass*). The protagonists in *Of Mice and Men*, *The Bear*, and *House Made of Dawn* all desire unification with nature but must discard mechanical barriers to achieve it.

Of Mice and Men by John Steinbeck

The two protagonists in *Of Mice and Men* (1937), George Milton and Lennie Small, who search for employment during the Depression near the Gabilan mountains, have known each other since childhood in Auburn, California. The novel's title comes from Robert Burns's 1785 poem "To a Mouse" in which the speaker notes that "the best laid schemes o' Mice an' Men / Gang aft agley, / An' lea'e us nought but grief an' pain, / For promis'd joy!" Using omniscient point of view, John Steinbeck reveals that George and Lennie have plans to earn enough money to buy a small plot of land, their own piece of wilderness, with a house where Lennie can raise rabbits and relieve them from searching for work. But their plans go astray, "gang aft agley." Steinbeck begins the novel next to a creek near a ranch where the men get jobs, with Lennie and George discussing their dream, and ends at the same place with the same discussion.

George and Lennie focus on a place of their own "to look ahead to" while drifting from job to job. When they stop at a ranch and meet the boss, George tells Lennie not to talk while he discusses employment possibilities. The boss suspects something when Lennie answers none of his questions; he asks George "What stake you got in this guy?" George responds by saying that he told Lennie's "old lady" that he would look after him. But George protects Lennie, who is retarded but very strong, because Lennie cannot survive on his own. George often tells Lennie how much he could do if he left Lennie behind, but, through Lennie, George continues to have his dream of owning land. As Lennie's guardian, George hopes for a better life, or otherwise he will resemble Crooks, the lonely black stable buck not allowed in the segregated bunkhouse, who comments, "Seems like ever' guy got land in his head" but has no possibility of a different life. Even the one-handed Candy whose only solace is his dog until Carlson, another ranch hand, kills it for being old and smelly has the same desire; he even offers his savings to join George and Lennie. George summarizes their lives. "Guys like us, that work on ranches, are the loneliest guys in the world. They got no family. They don't belong no place. They come to a ranch an' work up a stake and then they go inta town and blow their stake, and the first thing you know they're poundin' their tail on some other ranch. They ain't got nothing to look ahead to."

Lennie follows George's orders, even though he cannot remember much. He barely recalls his Aunt Clara, although he collects the mice she gave him. Lennie loves to touch small, furry things but inadvertently squeezes and kills them as he did the mice. His problems on the ranch begin when Curly, the owner's son, challenges Lennie to a fight. An amateur boxer, Curly thinks beating someone larger than he will make him seem better than he is. Unwilling to fight, Lennie squeezes Curley's hand and crushes it. Sensing Curley's hostility afterward, Lennie complains to George, "It's mean here" and wants to leave. Then Lennie fondles and kills a puppy. Soon after, Curley's wife confronts Lennie in the barn and wants to talk to him. She allows him to feel her

hair, and when she starts talking too loudly, Lennie grabs her and unintentionally breaks her neck. Again feeling that something has gone wrong, Lennie
goes to the creek near the ranch like George had told him to do. George finds
him, and when George hears men coming for Lennie, George shoots him with
a gun he has taken from the bunkhouse. With Lennie's death, George loses his
dream. He will not be able to settle on a plot of land because his attempt to return to nature stops when he shoots the gun.

The Bear by William Faulkner

William Faulkner's *The Bear* (1931), a simple bildungsroman about the
boy, Isaac McCaslin, recalls Ike's yearly hunting trips from age ten in 1883 at
Big Bottom with a group of men including Boon Hoggenbeck, Sam Fathers
(son of a slave mother and Chickasaw chief father), Tennie's Jim, Major de
Spain, General Compson, Ike's cousin McCaslin, and Walter Ewell. They are
hunters "with the will and hardihood to endure and the humility and skill to
survive." On these trips, they converse about the sacredness of the land on
which they hunt and "of white man fatuous enough to believe he had bought
any fragment of it, of Indian ruthless enough to pretend that any fragment of it
had been his to convey." Each year, the men drink in honor of their religion of
hunting and commune in worship of "some condensation of the wild immortal spirit." On the last day each year, they all try to kill Old Ben, a huge bear
who has continually eluded them.

When Ike is sixteen, he learns about his family's background from reading
the family ledgers. He discovers the black blood beginning in 1832 when
Eunice, married to Thucydus, drowned herself after her daughter Tomasina
died at childbirth, begot by Carothers McCaslin, Eunice's lover and master.
Then, in 1833, McCaslin's other lover Tomy died, but her son Turl lived. With
this knowledge, Ike realizes that his family has black blood and that his grandfather refused to recognize his own son. Ike imagines himself as a contemporary Isaac, able to "repudiate immolation" because of his grandfather's
symbolic Abraham denying kinship. Ike senses that his grandfather's disloyal
deeds have freed him from having to accept the family's questionably acquired
heritage. Ike also must readjust his uncomfortable relationship to Lucas
Beauchamp, now identified as a relative. These discoveries influence Ike's re-
linquishment of land he inherits at twenty-one and perhaps his selection of carpentry as a career, like "the Nazarene." Ike also comprehends the dichotomies
underlying his decisions. Some will view his refusal to accept his father's land as
idiocy, but Ike must follow the truth that he perceives because "the heart already knows."

Also when Ike is sixteen, one of the dogs, Lion, seems like "the beginning of
the end of something" although Ike cannot identify his uneasiness. When Lion
later kills Old Ben and then dies himself, Ike thinks that "he should have hated
and feared Lion," when the dog first appeared because Sam identified the dog

as disinterested in everyone and everything. This heartless and fearless dog becomes a symbol of the progress and greed destroying wilderness life without considering or caring about the consequences. Ike, however, treasures his association with the hunt, the woods, and the enormous animal he has faithfully stalked. Faulkner undergirds the plot with questions including preservation of nature, identity, family, and truth. In four parts, the story's limited omniscient point of view from both a narrator and from Ike in stream of consciousness investigates these concepts. In the fourth section, other voices appear in the ledger that Ike's father and uncle kept about the family.

Ike learns about himself and his past through two major sources, the hunt and the family ledger. The men teach him how to hunt and, in turn, how to become a man. On his first trip at ten, he has to learn humility and patience. "He entered his novitiate to the true wilderness with Sam beside him as he had begun his apprenticeship in miniature to manhood." When Ike kills his first buck, Sam rubs blood on his face in initiation. Ike's education occurs in nature. "If Sam Fathers had been his mentor and the backyard rabbits and squirrels his kindergarten, then the wilderness the old bear ran was his college and the old male bear itself, so long unwifed and childless as to have become its own ungendered progenitor, was his alma mater."

Although the ledger gives Ike adult insight into family, his encounters with the bear shape his character. Soon after he starts hunting, he quickly realizes that "they were going not to hunt bear and deer but to keep yearly rendevous with the bear which they did not even intend to kill." The dogs yelp with "indecision and even abjectness" when they hear the bear. Ike first sees Old Ben's claws in the winter, and Sam knows that the bear will identify Ike's inexperience and attack him if the others have threatened the bear because Sam thinks Old Ben assesses the hunters for their quality. To gain knowledge of the bear, Ike goes into the wilderness without his compass or his gun. By discarding these man-made items, Ike exposes himself to the bear and to nature. On each hunt, Ike realizes that the bear enjoys the hunt, "seeming deliberately to put [his liberty and freedom] into jeopardy in order to savor it and keep his old strong bones and flesh supple and quick to defend and preserve it." Sam personifies the first dog who finally challenges the bear as "just like folks. Put off as long as she could having to be brave, knowing all the time that sooner or later she would have to be brave once so she could keep on calling herself a dog, and knowing beforehand what was going to happen when she done it." Ike watches the dog sacrifice herself, and thinks "*maybe that's what courage is.*" To Ike, Old Ben is "solitary, indomitable, and alone; widowered childless and absolved of mortality—old Priam reft of his old wife and outlived all his sons." Old Ben is mythic and immortal until he meets the amoral Lion. Ike sees the bear catch "the dog in both arms, almost loverlike." Then he watches Sam Fathers try to rescue Lion, and the scene "resembled a piece of statuary: the clinging dog, the bear, the man astride its back, working and probing the buried blade." Mortally wounded, Sam requests to be burned on a pyre, like an ancient king and a god whose kingdom no longer exists. Later when Ike and his cousin McCaslin discuss John Keats's poem, "Ode on a Grecian Urn," McCaslin identifies the speaker's topic and compares it to their yearly quest for old Ben. "*He was talking about truth. Truth is one. It doesn't change. It covers all things which touch the heart—honor and pride and pity and justice and courage and love. Do you see now?*"

House Made of Dawn by N. Scott Momaday

Without nature and tradition, Abel cannot communicate with his Native-American people in *House Made of Dawn* (1968). N. Scott Momaday begins the novel with "Abel was running" and concludes it the same way to create an unending circle. Omniscient point of view flashbacks in the middle of the novel allow the reader to see Abel as a child and discover what others have thought about him. Because Abel's mother died young as did his brother Vidal, and Abel never knew his father, an outsider, Abel's grandfather Francisco, his only family, raises him. Where he lives, "the people . . . make their living from the things that are and have always been within their reach." Francisco snares birds for their feathers, "a male mountain bluebird, breast feathers the pale color of April skies or of turquoise, lake water." And Abel as a youth sees "a strange thing, an eagle overhead with its talons closed upon a snake. . . . an awful, holy sight, full of magic and meaning." Tribal leaders agree that he should join the Eagle Watchers Society. He accompanies the medicine men who carry a sacred flute, bull and horse masks of Peco, and a little wooden statue of their patroness María de los Angeles, called Porcingula, on a journey. Abel soon catches a beautiful strong eagle but, hating to think it will live in captivity in the village, kills it. Later Abel remembers shooting geese with his brother Vidal and the beauty of the geese as they flew away. Although he is a Longhair (a true Indian), he feels separate from the others and begins to drink, the alcohol soon making him sick.

One important memory for Abel is "something strange and good and powerful" occurring when his grandmother told him stories from her past. By sharing with him, she erased the difference between their ages, making them seem as one. He sensed that she "was asking me to come directly into the presence of her mind and spirit; she was taking hold of my imagination, giving me to share in the great fortune of her wonder and delight." Through and with her, Abel had the experience "of something that was sacred and eternal. It was a timeless, *timeless* thing . . . her words were medicine; they were magic and invisible. They came from nothing into sound and meaning. They were beyond price; they could neither be bought nor sold. And she never threw words away."

After he returns from the war to his home of Walatowa, Cañon de San Diego, New Mexico, on 20 July 1945, Abel is drunk when his grandfather Francisco meets him at the bus. He attempts to communicate with his grandfather and others in his Pueblo settlement, the community that "bore a scent of earth" and feels comfortable until he soon fails at the ritual Chicken Pull. Then he feels alienated. A white married woman trying to reconcile her pregnancy present at the event lures him into a casual affair. At the subsequent Pecos Bull Dance, Abel encounters the albino, Juan Keyes, who defeated him at the Chicken Pull. The albino threatens Able, and Able kills him in alleged self-defense. After conviction for killing the albino whom Abel sees as an evil spirit permeating the community, Abel disappears into prison. Finally freed, Abel journeys to Los Angeles where his friendships with the social worker Milly and Native-American Ben Benaly do not fulfill his spiritual needs.

None of his subsequent actions help him attain the contentment he seeks. He remains ineffectual in the white world, ridiculed and abused. In Los Angeles with Ben taking peyote, Abel exclaims "Look! Look! There are blue and purple horses . . . a house made of dawn." Ben tells him stories about the old ways but knows that Abel is "unlucky" and either would never be able to change or was not yet ready. After a malicious police officer breaks his hands, Abel decides to leave the hospital unhealed and return to Walatowa to stay with his grandfather while Francisco is dying. He listens to Francisco talk about his youth each dawn for a week, and when Francisco dies, Abel calls the priest to bury him. However, Abel covers himself in ashes and runs barefooted in a race for the dead, symbolically taking his grandfather's place in the tribe. "*The moment passed, and the next and the next, and he was running still, and still he could see the dark shape of the man running away in the swirling mist, like the motionless shadow. And he held on to the shadow and ran beyond his pain.*" Not until he leaves behind the knives and shoes of the civilized does he reconnect to nature and to his past and regain his ability to pass on the oral tradition of his people to his people.

Thus the protagonists in *Of Mice and Men*, *The Bear*, and *House Made of Dawn*, all desire the completeness that unification of nature offers, but not all achieve it. Until he dies, Lennie remains close to nature, loving all animals, appreciating beauty around him, and sensing the destructive forces of the ranch. When Ike is twenty-one, he refuses the land that is his inheritance because he thinks humans cannot possess the land. He says, "Because it was never Ikkemotubbe's fathers' fathers' to bequeath Ikkemotubbe to sell to Grandfather or any man because on the instant when Ikkemotubbe discovered, realized, that he could sell it for money, on that instant it ceased ever to have been his forever, father to father to father, and the man who bought it bought nothing." Abel comprehends the ineffability of nature. "To see nothing slowly and by degrees, at last; to see first the pure, bright colors of near things, then all pollution of color, all things blended and vague and dim in the distance, to see finally beyond the clouds and the pale wash of the sky—the none and nothing beyond that. To say 'beyond the mountain,' and to mean it, to mean, simply, beyond everything for which the mountain stands of which it signifies the being." To understand nature, one must encounter it for itself rather than what one would have it be.

Additional Related Novels

Cooper, James Fenimore. *The Last of the Mohicans.*
Crane, Stephen. *The Red Badge of Courage.*
Dickey, James. *Deliverance.*
Frazier, Charles. *Cold Mountain.*
Hemingway, Ernest. *The Old Man and the Sea.*
Maclean, Norman. *A River Runs Trough It.*
Rölvaag, O. E. *Giants in the Earth.*
Twain, Mark. *The Adventures of Huckleberry Finn.*

Oppression

Many excellent people are taken in by the use of the word "liberty" at the one time, and the use of the word "order" at the other, and ignore the simple fact that despotism is despotism, tyranny tyranny, oppression oppression, whether committed by one individual or by many individuals, by a state or by a private corporation.

—Theodore Roosevelt (1913)

Even though people feel oppressed by different forces, ultimately, only humans are capable of oppressing others. Oppressed by his Chicago neighborhood, Bigger Thomas thinks that pretending to be strong and resilient will gain him success in *Native Son*. Having lived under the oppression of the wealthy, Kino and Juana are unprepared for the hostility and greed their perfect pearl evokes in *The Pearl*. Both Brother Jerome and Archie oppress the students in *The Chocolate War*, and only by refusing their demands can Jerry escape tyranny. The protagonists in *Our Nig*, *Fahrenheit 451*, and *The Bell Jar* all feel oppressed because of what others have done to them.

For this discussion, oppression means the "exercise of authority or power in a burdensome, harsh, or wrongful manner; unjust or cruel treatment of subjects, inferiors . . . the imposition of unreasonable or unjust burdens" (*OED*). Richard Hampole says that "[The] world is . . . a sted of mykel wrechednes . . . Of violence and of oppression" (*Pricke of Consciousness*, 1340). In his *Sermons*, Joseph Butler declares that "there is not a word in our language which expresses more detestable wickedness than oppression" (1729). Jeremy Bentham asserts that "the enemies of the people may be divided into two classes. The depredationists . . . and the oppressionists, whose hatred to others is stronger than their love of themselves" (1828). And Simone Weil announces: "Oppression that cannot be overcome does not give rise to revolt but to submission" (*Oppression and Liberty*, 1958.) The protagonists in *Our Nig*, *Fahrenheit 451*, and *The Bell Jar* all feel oppressed from their treatment by other humans.

Our Nig by Harriet E. Wilson

Upon publication of *Our Nig; or, Sketches from the Life of a Free Black, in a Two-Story White House, North. Showing that Slavery's Shadows Fall Even There* (1859), Harriet E. Wilson became the first African-American woman to have published a novel in English. In the novel's preface, she confesses that she needs money to support her son, George Mason Wilson, then in a foster home. Six months later when he was seven years and eight months, however, he died of a fever, and three years later, Wilson's name disappears from the Boston City Directory. Not until 1983 was the novel republished and critically recognized. In this fictional autobiography written in limited omniscient point of view, Wilson introduces each chapter with a poetry quote. In the story, the white Mag Smith falls in love and becomes pregnant. Rejected by society and deserted by the father of the child that dies while an infant, she is left destitute. Mag's comfort comes from knowing that "no one can taunt *her* with my ruin." Mag moves to another town and meets Jim, an African-American man who works as a barrel belter. He decides to marry Mag, reassuring her that he has a "white heart inside" when she expresses horror at falling farther "down the ladder of infamy." As the mulatto child of their union, Frado hears children yell at them, "black, white, yeller."

But when Frado turns six, her secure but destitute life changes. Jim dies from consumption, and his partner Seth Shipley befriends Mag. The two sell Frado as an indentured servant to the Belmont family and go elsewhere to seek their fortune. Frado never again sees her mother and becomes "our nig" to the Belmonts. Mrs. Belmont mistreats Frado but allows her to attend school with her daughter Mary. Infuriated with Frado's popularity at school, Mary tries to punish her afterward by making her cross a stream on a plank. Mary falls in instead, later claiming that Frado pushed her. Mrs. Belmont will not believe Frado's true story and beats her. Other members of the family try to protect her, including the sons Jack and James and Aunt Abby (Nab). When James returns home, he demands that Frado be allowed to sit at the dinner table with them and eat their food. James anguishes, "I have seen Frado's grief, because she is black, amount to agony. It makes me sick to recall these scenes." One day, Frado asserts that she will do no more work if Mrs. Belmont beats her again, and Mrs. Belmont resists for several months. Mrs. Belmont later tries to stop Nab from seeing the seriously ill James, but Frado informs James's wife Susan of the deception, and she summons Nab to his bedside and demands Frado's presence at the subsequent funeral. After Jack goes West to work, Mrs. Belmont sells Fido, the dog Jack gave Frado, but Mr. Belmont repurchases it. At eighteen, Frado finally fulfills her service and leaves.

The oppression Frado feels causes her to question her own worth as a human. She hides her sense of humor from Mrs. Belmont, and Mrs. Belmont remains unaware of Frado's school pranks. Frado puffs cigar smoke into her teacher's desk drawer and quickly closes it so that smoke billows when the teacher opens it. Frado confesses her problems to her one companion, her beloved dog Fido. And when Nab tries to convert her, Frado asserts that she cannot like God because he did not make her white. Mrs. Belmont says that "religion was not meant for niggers" when Frado wonders what "religion" is. Frado also has difficulty believing that a black person could go to heaven, although after hearing about it, Frado decides that if Mrs. Belmont is going, she prefers not to go. [Mark Twain might have read *Our Nig* because in *The Adventures* of *Huckleberry Finn* (1885), he has Huck feel the same way about heaven when he rejects spending an eternity doing nothing but playing a harp.] At Frado's departure from the Belmont home, she owns one dress, a Bible (her dearest possession) from Susan, and a half-dollar silver piece. Mrs. Belmont's harsh treatment continues to affect her physically for the rest of her life, and, often ill, she has trouble keeping jobs. Eventually she learns to sew and make straw bonnets, and women appreciate her excellent work in Singleton. When she meets Samuel, a fugitive slave, she marries him and has a child. But he spends almost all his life at sea. Supporting a child and ill health become too burdensome, and she has to relinquish the child to a foster home. Mrs. Belmont and Mary's oppression kept Frado in a living hell, but fortunately, a few loving humans helped her survive.

Fahrenheit 451 by Ray Bradbury

Ray Bradbury's *Fahrenheit 451* (1951) explores the oppression of a civilization that forbids its people to read books after 2022. Bradbury divides the story into three segments, "The Hearth and the Salamander," "Montag," and "Burning Bright," with limited omniscient point of view. Montag, a fireman, builds the fires that destroy books rather than save them. When Montag complains to his boss, Captain Beatty, that the Mechanical Hound, a robot programmed to detect bodily smells indicative of book abusers, has been bothering him, Beatty reaffirms their important job as "custodians of peace of mind." Beatty credits Benjamin Franklin for writing the firemen's rule book and elaborates on the history of book burning that began during the Civil War. He adds that "intellectual" eventually became a swear word. Beatty says, "not everyone born free and equal, as the Constitution says, but everyone *made* equal." He defends the firemen's importance because "we're the Happiness Boys, the Dixie Duo, you and I and the others. We stand against the small tide of those who want to make everyone unhappy with conflicting theory and thought." A world rid of all books will offend no minority.

Questions in a conversation with his seventeen-year-old neighbor Clarisse McClellan force Montag to examine his actions and his relationships. When Clarisse discovers that Montag is a fireman, she responds that many fear the firemen but that he seems unlike the others. She asks if he reads any books before destroying them. He reminds her that reading is against the law and adds that "it's fine work. Monday burn Millay, Wednesday Whitman, Friday Faulkner, burn 'em to ashes, then burn the ashes. That's our official slogan." Clarisse tells him about the sad faces on the subway and the many people her age who have been inexplicably murdered. She says "People don't talk about anything," She wants to know if he is happy, but he cannot answer. He does not know. When he returns home, ready to tell his wife Mildred about Clarisse,

Millie is comatose, having swallowed an overdose of sleeping pills. The rescue squad discloses that it has streamlined the rescue process because it has at least ten cases a night.

Thus Montag becomes aware of a problem he had not previously acknowledged. The next morning, Millie has no memory of the event, and Montag shows her the twenty books he has hidden. When he tells Beatty that he has met Clarisse, Beatty responds that the firemen have been watching Clarisse because she "was a time bomb. She didn't want to know *how* a thing was done, but *why*." And when Millie tells Montag that Clarisse is dead, Montag knows that men assigned to run over people in the streets found her. He becomes further distressed when he witnesses a woman pouring gasoline on herself and her books when the firemen arrive, saying, "We need not to be let alone. We need to be really bothered once in a while." Montag decides to contact an old English professor whom the firemen suspect of disobeying the law. The old professor Faber says, "I don't talk *things* . . . I talk the *meaning* of things. I sit here and *know* I'm alive." Later, as Montag remembers Beatty's taunting when he came to arrest Montag, Montag apprehends that Beatty wanted Montag to kill him, and Montag complied.

Montag comprehends how the oppression of censorship has negatively affected his life, and he decides to change. His discussions with Faber confirm his conviction. Faber knows that "the magic is only in what books say, how they stitched the patches of the universe into one garment for us." He believes that books give humans the right "to carry out actions based on what we learn from the interaction of [quality and leisure]." Against the advice of both Faber and Millie, Montag reads Matthew Arnold's poem "Dover Beach" to women gathering at his house with Mildred to watch the "relatives" (television screens covering three living room walls). Millie then reports Montag to Beatty, and Faber helps Montag escape by giving him clothes with unusual smells to divert the Mechanical Hound. Montag floats down the river and sees men of whom Faber has spoken in the distance surrounding a fire built for warmth and survival rather than destruction and death. They are the underground intellectuals with innumerable advanced degrees who have trained themselves to recall a book read only once. When he joins them, Montag knows that he must reject "burning of all types and sizes" and focus on a world wanting fire for rejuvenation. After all, "The sun burned everyday. It burned Time." The first section of the novel, titled "The Hearth and the Salamander," refers to the mythical salamander that can survive after burning in a fire, and, with his escape, Montag joins other salamanders warming themselves by a hearth.

The Bell Jar by Sylvia Plath

In Sylvia Plath's *The Bell Jar* (1963), the inability to follow the career that interests her in 1953 makes Esther Greenwood, the first-person narrator, feel oppressed by contemporary society. She eventually loses her ability to function mentally after winning a contest and joining eleven other young women in New York during the summer to work for the magazine. Plath herself also won a position at *Mademoiselle* magazine for a summer internship, and this fictional autobiography most likely relays some of her own experiences. Published after Plath's suicide in 1963 under the name "Victoria Lucas," the novel illustrates her poetic ability with its stark imagery and figurative language. Esther remembers after seeing a cadaver that "I felt as though I were carrying that cadaver's head around with me on a string, like some black, noseless balloon stinking of vinegar." Another time, she recalls feeling "very still and very empty, the way the eye of a tornado must feel, moving dully along in the middle of the surrounding hullabaloo."

During the seven months that lead into Esther's depression, she recollects past relationships and participates in new ones. In New York, she chooses the southerner Doreen's company because she has "intuition." Esther and Doreen go to a bar instead of a social event planned for them, and Doreen meets Lenny, a disk jockey. Esther accompanies them to Lenny's apartment where she becomes disgusted with Doreen's bawdy behavior and leaves even though the western decor in Lenny's apartment entertains her. Doreen later begs her to go on a blind date with Marco. Esther agrees but bites Marco when he tries to seduce her. Then she remembers the time that she and Buddy Willard witnessed the birth of a baby. Afterward he undressed himself and asked her to do likewise, but she had refused, unimpressed with what she saw. When Buddy later hears that Esther has had a sexual experience, he breaks their engagement, much to her relief.

After Esther returns to Boston, her mother tries to help her recover. She takes Esther to Dr. Gordon, an unlikable psychiatrist who gives Esther shock treatments for her insomia. "Whee- ee-ee-ee-ee, it shrilled, through an air crackling with blue light, and with each flash a great jolt drubbed me till I thought my bones would break and the sap fly out of me like a split plant." After Esther attempts suicide, her benefactor, the author Mrs. Philomena Guinea, funds her stay in a private hospital. Esther has no interest in the gift, although she understands that any offer of money for a getaway, whether hospital or Hawaii, would not cure her because "I would be sitting under the same glass bell jar, stewing in my own sour air." In the hospital, Dr. Nolan, a woman, gains Esther's trust and begins successful treatment. When Joan, a school friend who also dated Buddy, arrives, she shows Esther newspaper clippings about Esther's suicide attempt, and Esther soon discovers that Joan is a lesbian. After the hospital discharges them, Esther's first sexual partner rushes Esther to Joan's apartment when she starts hemorrhaging, and Joan helps her. Joan's subsequent suicide distresses Esther, but Dr. Nolan reassures Esther that she had no responsiblity for Joan's decision.

Esther's self-image comes from society's oppression. She admits, "To the person in the bell jar, black and stopped as a dead baby, the world itself is the bad dream." Distressed because her mother has said she cannot get a good job after college without shorthand, she focuses not on what she *can* do but what she cannot. She resents the idea of working for men in any way. She wants to write and mail her own letters, not someone else's. "Besides, those little short-hand symbols in the book my mother showed me seemed just as bad as let *t* equal time and let *s* equal total distance." Then she concludes that not having a job might be worse because she would have to marry and raise children, become "brainwashed" by a husband who kept her "numb as a slave in some private, totalitarian state." She thinks that all a man "wanted when the wedding service ended was for her to flatten out underneath his feet like Mrs. Willard's kitchen mat." After discovering that Buddy has had his own affair, Esther feels betrayed. "I couldn't stand the idea of a woman having to have a single pure life and a man being able to have a double life, one pure and one not." Esther's straight "As" in college amount to little in a society in which women cannot exhibit their talents and intelligence. After an "A" in physics, Esther had persuaded her dean to allow her to take chemistry without grades. Since she wrote constantly during class, the professor thought her interested, but she was actually composing poems. She bases her intelligence on her curiosity. "I liked looking on at other people in crucial situations. If there was a road accident or a street fight or a baby pickled in a laboratory jar for me to look at, I'd stop and look so hard I never forgot it. I certainly learned a lot of things I never would have learned otherwise this way, and even when they surprised me or made me sick I never let on, but pretended that's the way I knew things were all the time." During her nineteenth summer, she finally realizes that she has been unhappy for the ten years since her father died. In Boston, feeling "disgusting and ugly," she visits his grave and cries. Dr. Nolan reassures her that her loneliness, sexual thoughts, and hating her mother are acceptable responses to her grief. Then Dr. Nolan forbids Esther's mothers oppressive visits, an order freeing Esther from a distasteful social ritual. Esther seems more capable of accepting society's oppression of women after understanding that alternatives other than marriage and becoming a secretary do exist.

Only humans can oppress others or themselves. Frado barely survives the treatment of Mrs. Belmont and her daughter in *Our Nig.* When Montag in *Fahrenheit 451* understands that the oppression in which he has willingly participated has almost destroyed him, he tries to overcome it. Esther chooses death as a way to escape her perception of society's oppression in *The Bell Jar.* When people try to control others through oppression, they can destroy themselves as well.

Additional Related Novels

Alvarez, Julia. *In the Time of the Butterflies.*
Cisneros, Sandra. *The House on Mango Street.*
Cormier, Robert. *The Chocolate War.*
Ellison, Ralph. *Invisible Man.*
Flagg, Fannie. *Fried Green Tomatoes at the Whistle Stop Café.*

Gaines, Ernest J. *The Autobiography of Miss Jane Pittman; A Gathering of Old Men; A Lesson Before Dying.*
Morrison, Toni. *Beloved.*
Olsen, Tillie. *Tell Me a Riddle.*
Steinbeck, John. *The Pearl.*
Wright, Richard. *Native Son.*

Outsiders

For the Lord seeth not as a man seeth; for man looketh on the outward appearance, but the Lord looketh on the heart.

—Samuel 16:7

People often feel omitted from a group. As they watch those who seem included, they feel ostracized or isolated like an outsider. In *Bone*, Ona never
shares her feelings with her sisters or others, and her isolation leads her to commit suicide. Beginning with his experiences in college, the protagonist of *Invisible Man* remains on the periphery of the organizations with which he
associates. David in *The Rise of David Levinsky* assimilates as an American citizen, but as an immigrant, he remains an outsider around other businessmen.
In *The Age of Innocence*, *Main Street*, and *Native Son*, the protagonists either
reject the mores of the societies in which they find themselves or others keep
them outside the controlling circle of power.

An outsider remains "outside any enclosure, barrier, or boundary, material
or figurative . . . one who is outside of or does not belong to a specified company, set, or party, a non-member; hence, one unconnected or unacquainted
with a matter, uninitiated into a profession or body having special knowledge"
(*OED*). An additional definition pertains specifically to literature. An outsider
is the "archetypal artist or intellectual seen as a person isolated from the rest of
society" (*OED*). Relatively new in the language, the term first surfaced in
1800, and in 1844, George Marsh related in *Lectures on the English Language*
that "at the Baltimore convention of 1844. . . . a prominent member energeti-
cally protested against all interference with the business of the meeting by outsiders. The word, if not absolutely new, was at least new to most of those who
read the proceedings . . . and it was now for the first time employed in a serious
way." Frank Brown comments in the introduction to B. W. Aldiss's book, *Science Fiction*, that "no one knew who the Outsiders were . . . or from what far
galaxy they came" (1944). And Colin Henry Wilson comments that "he had
accepted his 'Outsider-ishness,' not as a symptom of some strange disease, but
as a sign that his healthy soul was being suffocated in a world of trivial, shallow,
corrupted fools" (1956). In *The Age of Innocence* and *Main Street*, the protagonists shift from agreeing with society to criticizing it while the protagonist in
Native Son remains an outsider all of his short life.

The Age of Innocence by Edith Wharton

In *The Age of Innocence* (1920), the protagonist Newland Archer evolves from a core member of his wealthy New York society in the 1870s to one who condemns its narrow focus after its members refuse to accept Countess Ellen Olenska into their circle for leaving her husband and running away with his male secretary. Edith Wharton tells the story through Archer's eyes using limited omniscient point of view with an unidentified omniscient narrator occasionally addressing the reader conversationally as "you." Because Archer tells the story, he cannot know Ellen's and May's thoughts about him or about each other. Just before Archer and Ellen plan to begin a serious affair, May informs Ellen that she is pregnant. Not until two weeks later does she tell Archer that she is expecting and that the doctor has confirmed her condition. Archer does not know until his son tells him after May's death when he is fifty-seven that May knew about his love for Ellen. On her deathbed, May had said that she had once asked her husband to give up what he had wanted most, and he had—Ellen. Both the reader and Archer remain unaware of that agreement or of May's strengths until May's seemingly insignificant or accidental encounters with Ellen total a full plan of interference. Their son Dallas reminds the elder Archer that he never shared anything with May, that they lived together in a "deaf and dumb asylum."

The New York society in which Archer lives and to which Ellen comes functions primarily on two tiers, but as Archer becomes reacquainted with Ellen, his opinions diverge from both of them. The Mingotts and Mansons "cared about eating and clothes and money" while the Archer-Newland-van-der-Luyden tribe loved "travel, horticulture and the best fiction, and looked down on the grosser forms of pleasure." In Ellen's first conversation with Newland at the opera, she reminds him that he kissed her when they were children. Her casual attitude about his beloved New York society offends him because he thinks it, Taste, and Family must be revered. From this first encounter, Ellen's dark hair and exotic gowns contrast to May's blondeness and white dresses. The next day, Ellen's unusual perceptions of life begin to change Archer. Society finally "welcomes" Ellen at the highly regarded van der Luyden party where she flaunts etiquette by leaving the side of a gentleman and walking unescorted across the ballroom floor to inform Archer that the Duke is a dull man. Feeling isolated as the outsider, she tells Archer that "the real loneliness is living among all these kind people who only ask one to pretend."

Archer interprets his relationship with Ellen as one of friends, but that feeling rapidly changes. Already engaged to May, Archer thinks that a quick marriage will quell his rising interest in Ellen. He even asks Ellen to encourage May to change her mind and marry quickly. Ellen agrees, and Archer and May marry much sooner than originally planned. Later, Archer tells Ellen, "I'm the man who married one woman because another one told him to." When asked by his law firm to discourage Ellen from seeking a divorce, he agrees even though he loves her. Later she tells Newland that she stayed married only because he had asked her. She also admits that she has not gone to Europe because of him. She adds, "At least it was you who made me understand that under the dullness there are things so fine and sensitive and delicate that even those I most cared for in my other life look cheap in comparison." Newland responds that, "you are the woman I would have married if it had been possible for either of us" and that each time they meet, "you happen to me all over again." Just before May tells Ellen that she is pregnant, Archer says to Ellen, "I want to get away with you into a world where words and categories don't exist. . . . nothing else on earth will matter." May's announcement stops Ellen because Ellen always treats May with kindness. But when Archer has one last chance to see Ellen in Paris after May's death, he decides not to visit. He asks his son to "say I'm old-fashioned: that's enough."

Before Archer meets Ellen, he has a high regard for himself and his society. Afterward, he becomes aware of its limitations and tediousness. "Newland Archer felt himself distinctly the superior of these chosen specimens of old New York gentility . . . but grouped together they represented 'New York,' and their habit of masculine solidarity made him accept their doctrine on all the issues called moral." But after conversing with Ellen, he becomes critical. He begins to assert that "women ought to be free." He enjoys Ellen's appreciation of literature, and he stops going to his club on a predictable schedule. May no longer distracts him, and he worries about her innocence since he has had an affair. After their marriage, he thinks, "There was no use in trying to emancipate a wife who had not the dimmest notion that she was not free; and he had long since discovered that May's only use of the liberty she supposed herself to possess would be to lay it on the altar of her wifely adoration." He thinks May only repeats what others have said and that she attracts only dull people. When he is older, Newland thinks of his past and sees into "what a deep rut he had sunk. The worst of doing one's duty was that it apparently unfitted one for doing anything else." As a gentleman, he could not be a politician or aspire to being a successful lawyer. Thus he has been a "good citizen" while missing the "flower of life." And in the end, his cowardice keeps him from seeing Ellen again, just as his cowardice had kept him away from her while they were outsiders together.

Main Street by Sinclair Lewis

In *Main Street* (1920), after Carol Milford marries Dr. Will Kennicott and moves to his home in Gopher Prairie, Minnesota, she learns what it means to be an "outsider." An orphan at thirteen, Carol has lived with her sister in Minneapolis before and during college. After college, in Chicago, she meets Will at a friend's home and marries him a year later. Although Sinclair Lewis uses omniscient point of view, Carol's perception of the town and people in it is the most prevalent. Carol has difficulty adjusting to her new home, but she tries.

When Will perceives that she is intensely unhappy, he takes her to California. After they return, and her outlook remains unchanged, she takes their son with her to Washington to work at the Bureau of War Risk Insurance. After a year, Will asks her to return, and she agrees.

Carol anticipates living in a small town until she sees the bleakness of other small towns on the train to Gopher Prairie, and, even though she says the town is "'sweet, so sweet,'" she hates it. The people do not converse; they gossip, only interested in money and social position. They condescend to the immigrant Swedes, pay them low wages as servants, and exploit the farmers. People invite her to participate—Vida Sherwin, the high school French and English teacher, wants her to teach Sunday School and join the Thanatopsis Society, but the women's discussion of British poets goes no further than a brief biography of the subject. Other women include her in the exclusive Jolly Seventeen, but she refuses to play bridge. Townspeople call Mrs. Bogart, her neighbor across the street, a "Prominent Baptist" and a "Good Influence," but Carol knows she is mainly a busybody and says "Here I'm spied on." The librarian Ethen Villets believes that "the first duty of the *conscientious* librarian is to preserve the books'" rather than interest readers. Carol suggests that the drama club present George Bernard Shaw's *Androcles and the Lion*, but another thinks it too scandalous, and they present the play, *The Girl from Kankakee*, that Carol hates. She protests, "I guess the feminine mind is too innocent to understand these immoral writers." When the war starts in Europe, the town ignores it. She detests the "vacuousness and bad manners and spiteful gossip." Frustrated, Carol "could not have outside employment. To the village doctor's wife it was taboo. She was a woman with a working brain and no work." She wants something to show herself that "I am I."

To escape from her position as an outsider, Carol tries a number of diversions. She loves art, literature, and gardening, unlike others in the town. When she goes bird hunting and visits farmers in the country, "Carol . . . found the dignity and greatness which . . . failed her in Main Street." She befriends her Swedish maid Miss Bea Sorenson and overpays her, according to the other women. She enjoys the company of the irreverent Miles Bjornstam, "The Red Swede," who makes things with his hands, and she encourages his courtship of Bea. While directing the play she despises, she berates the actors, "I wonder if you can understand the 'fun' of making a beautiful thing, the pride and satisfaction of it, and the holiness!" After Hugh's birth, Carol focuses on him for two years. She then shifts her interest to Mrs. Flickerbaugh who has loathed the town for thirty-two years and Erik Valborg, the Swedish tailor. After the California vacation, her boredom remains, but in Washington, D.C., "she had her freedom, and it was empty." She realizes that "not individuals but institutions are the enemies, and they most afflict the disciples who most generously serve them. . . . and the only defense against them, Carol beheld, is unembittered laughter." Thus when Will asks her to come home, she decides to try not to be an outsider.

Native Son by Richard Wright

In *Native Son* (1940), Bigger Thomas never has the option of being anything other than an outsider. In Chicago during the late 1930s, Bigger lives with his mother, brother, and sister Vera in a "Black Belt" efficiency. As the naturalist novel progresses, Richard Wright traces Bigger's movements using Bigger's limited omniscient point of view during the few days before and after he is arrested for two murders. Wright delineates how Bigger's fate has less to do with his actions than with his circumstances. Bigger's education limits his knowledge, and he reacts to rather than plans for events. In this bildungsroman, Bigger changes from a self-centered adolescent into an adult aware of the pain and loss his actions have caused Mary Dalton's parents and his family. Some critics refer to existentialist aspects in the novel, but Bigger shows no control over his own essence, remaining inauthentic, until he converses with his lawyer, Max. Wright's effective style in the three parts of the novel titled "Fear," "Flight," and "Fate" supports his strong story as illustrated with the parallelism that recounts Bigger's emotion in jail. "He lay on the cold floor sobbing; but he was standing up strongly with contrite heart, holding his life in his hands, staring at it with a wondering question. He lay on the cold floor sobbing; but really he was pushing forward with his puny strength against a world too big and too strong for him. He lay on the cold floor sobbing; but really he was groping forward with fierce zeal into a welter of circumstances which he felt contained a water of mercy for the thirst of his heart and brain."

Bigger's behavior affects the attitudes of those who meet him. He maltreats his sister by dangling a rat in her face, and she later reminds him that another crime will put him in prison instead of reform school. His mother worries that he will hang someday for his behavior. His acquaintances in his gang think he has become mentally imbalanced when he threatens one of them with a knife. During his interview with Mr. Dalton for a job as chauffeur, Dalton announces that he supports the National Association for the Advancement of Colored People (NAACP). Then Mary calls her father a capitalist and asks Bigger if he belongs to a union. Bigger cares nothing about the NAACP and does not know the meaning of "capitalist." Mary and her Communist boyfriend Jan patronize him by wanting to visit the black section of Chicago where he lives. Jan wants him to become a Communist and pretends to be his friend with a special handshake. Finally, the police think a black person would not be smart enough to have planned Mary's kidnaping. Not until Max talks to Bigger in prison has anyone taken time to listen to him and discuss things. For the first time, he does not feel like an outsider. And Max is Bigger's last defense when he pleads, "With every atom of my being, I beg this in order that not only may this black boy live, but that we ourselves may not die!"

Bigger has no ability to free himself from his role as the outsider. He is an outsider in Chicago, having come from Mississippi only five years before, and he is an outsider in the white section of town. He and a friend lament that they cannot become airplane pilots because they are black, but Bigger later reveals that he does not want to be a pilot. Bigger defines himself in terms of what he cannot do rather than what he wants to do. He fears everything, especially himself and his inability to control his circumstances. He fears looking foolish to his friends unless he forces them to join him in robbing Blum's deli in the nearby white section. Bigger and his buddies had always "felt that it was much easier and safer to rob their own people, for they knew that white policemen never really searched diligently for Negroes who committed crimes against other Negroes." Thus he threatens Gus with a knife when he arrives late for the rendezvous and then slashes Doc's pool table felt before leaving. He objectively mutilates Mary's body and stuffs it into the furnace after accidentally smothering her. Thus he, like Mrs. Dalton, is blind and without perception. He becomes irritated at his lack of control, and by slamming Bessie Mears, his alcoholic girlfriend, on the head with a brick and then raping her, blind actions arising from fear and a foolish pride, Bigger continues his cycle of destruction. "[Bigger] knew that the moment he allowed what his life meant to enter fully into his consciousness, he would either kill himself or someone else. So he denied himself and acted tough." Later, when he remembers Bessie, he knows that her murder killed some of the life in him. After his arrest, newspapers accuse him of rape and immorality as a black man, and he goes to see Max "to save his pride." With Max, "the word had become flesh. For the first time in his life a white man became a human being to him." He soon hears about his family's distress—Vera's shame at returning to sewing school and the arrests of his friends. He realizes that "he had lived and acted on the assumption that he was alone, and now he saw that he had not been. What he had done made others suffer." At the end, he becomes authentic from an existential stance and completes his maturation. "With a supreme act of will springing from the essence of his being, he turned away from his life and the long train of disastrous consequences that had flowed from it."

Humans shun some people and make them outsiders while others shun the group and become outsiders of their own choosing. Archer never fully understands his position in society after he meets Ellen, focusing on her instead of his compatriots, and society never wholly accepts Ellen since she avoids its criteria for membership in *The Age of Innocence*. Carol becomes an outsider when orphaned and never finds a place to charitably use her abilities in *Main Street*. Bigger, always an outsider, finally accepts his condition and acknowledges his heinous though unmotivated crimes in *Native Son*. Regardless of the effect, the road to becoming an outsider begins with a particular society's expectations for its members.

Additional Related Novels

Alexie, Sherman. *Reservation Blues*.
Alvarez, Julia. *How the Garcia Girls Lost Their Accents*.
Cahan, Abraham. *The Rise of David Levinsky*.

Doctorow, E. L. *Ragtime*.
Ellison, Ralph. *Invisible Man*.
Faulkner, William. *Light in August*.
Fitzgerald, F. Scott. *The Great Gatsby*.
Kingston, Maxine Hong. *The Woman Warrior*.
Larsen, Nella. *Passing*.
Ng, Fae Myenne. *Bone*.
Oates, Joyce Carol. *Foxfire*.
Proulx, E. Annie. *The Shipping News*.
Twain, Mark. *The Adventures of Huckleberry Finn; A Connecticut Yankee in King Arthur's Court*.
Welch, James. *The Death of Jim Loney*.
Wharton, Edith. *House of Mirth*.

Quests

There is divine beauty in learning, just as there is human beauty in tolerance. To learn means to accept the postulate that life did not begin at my birth. Others have been here before me, and I walk in their footsteps. The books I have read were composed by generations of fathers and sons, mothers and daughters, teachers and disciples. I am the sum total of their experiences, their quests. And so are you.
—Elie Wiesel, *Parade Magazine* (1992)

Every human searches for something; some have a specific goal while others want a particular state of mind. Abel searches for a reconnection with his heritage in *House Made of Dawn*. The ultimate grail for either the North or the South is winning the war and accepting the enemy's surrender in *The Killer Angels*. In *The Bear*, Ike McCaslin stalks the bear, Old Ben, and learns his way in the wilderness to find him. In *The House on Mango Street*, *All the Pretty Horses*, and *Moby-Dick*, the protagonists are on a quest for something that will fulfill their lives.

A quest is a "search or pursuit, made in order to find or obtain something" (*OED*). The word appears in literature in the 1300s. Shakespeare used it in *King Lear*, "what . . . will you require in present Dower with her, Or cease your quest of Love?" (1605). Lord George Byron speaks of *Child Harolde*, "whose desire Was to be glorious; 'twas a foolish quest" (1816). In Washington Irving, "the ghost rides forth to the scene of battle in nightly quest of his head" (*Sketches*, 1820). Edward Goulburn, speaks in *Thoughts on Personal Religion* of "eager running to and fro in quest of worldly wealth" (1862). The Dean of Admissions at Amherst College, Eugene S. Wilson, reveals his method of selecting applicants. "Only the curious will learn and only the resolute overcome the obstacles to learning. The quest quotient has always excited me more than the intelligence quotient" (*Reader's Digest*, 1968). These novels, *The House on Mango Street*, *All the Pretty Horses*, and *Moby-Dick*, show their protagonists on quests, each motivated by the desire to overcome a perceived liability.

The House on Mango Street by Sandra Cisneros

In Sandra Cisneros' *The House on Mango Street* (1984), Esperanza Cordero lives on Mango Street in a house "small and red with tight steps in front and windows so small you'd think they were holding their breath." She shares a room with her sister Nenny while her brothers and her parents live in the other two bedrooms. She fantasizes about a "real house" with a yard and trees and "three washrooms . . . like the houses on T.V." so that it becomes her quest. But intertwined in that dream is her goal for this house "quiet as snow" and clean like paper to be a place to become a writer. In first-person point of view through forty-six picaresque vignettes of prose poems and short stories, Esperanza examines the neighborhood, her family, and herself during a year in the 1960s. As a Chicana with Mexican parents, Esperanza perceives life from both American and Mexican perspectives. Esperanza consults those who might guide her, discovers that only her dying Aunt Lupe has insight, and independently forges ahead on her quest.

In this bildungsroman, Esperanza detects the attitudes of those she meets and discovers that not all of them approve of her. About herself, Esperanza thinks "I would like to baptize myself under a new name." She goes to a baptism, where embarrassed by her "old saddle shoes" with her new dress, she refuses to dance until her uncle coerces her. Then everyone claps when they finish and asks "who are those two who dance like in the movies." At her Catholic school, one of the sisters treats her disdainfully after seeing where she lives. Her friend Cathy says that her father wants to leave the neighborhood since Chicanos like the Corderos have started moving in. Esperanza has several friends, some with whom she shares the cost of a bicycle. She and her two friends pretend to have hips, and one day they prance around the neighborhood in discarded high heels. A shopkeeper suggests that they are too young for such shoes, and, in their shyness, they soon remove and hide them. She worries about her large feet, but unlike her friend Sally, Esperanza feels inadequate and ugly when placed in a sexually suggestive situation. Sally denies an interest in males, but bruises on her body betray that her father beats her and accuses her of being "bad" when she flirts. As her own body changes, Esperanza shifts from concern about what others think to what she thinks.

On her quest for a house and a place to write, Esperanza observes attitudes and behaviors in her neighborhood that she plans to avoid. Her two friends across the street use poor grammar, but she does not correct them. In her descriptions of the others, Esperanza is rarely judgmental, except to say that she likes or is fearful of someone. She knows that "Mexican men do not like their women strong," but seeing Earl lock up his beautiful wife Raphaela and college student Alicia's agreeing with her father's false declarations convince Esperanza that she will not subject herself to such treatment. About males, she thinks that "one day you wake up and they are there. Ready and waiting like a new Buick with the keys in the ignition." Esperanza's mother tells her that she could have done anything, but, instead, she left school because she was ashamed of her clothes—her mother who can "speak two languages . . . can sing an opera . . . [and] knows how to fix a T.V., [but] doesn't know which subway train to take to get downtown." The treatment of faceless immigrants anguishes her and hearing about someone hit and killed by an unidentified driver gives her pain. Her sympathy for others who suffer lead Esperanza to decide that she will have a place for the homeless in her new home. Elenita, the witch woman, reads Esperanza's future in the cards, saying she will have "a home in the heart." But the goal of Esperanza's quest is a real home where she can make up stories about her actions. She wants a friend, "one I can tell my secrets to. One who will understand my jokes without my having to explain them. Until then I am a red balloon, a balloon tied to an anchor." She knows that she must leave Mango Street on her quest and that "one day I will pack my bags of books and paper" although she will "have gone away to come back. For the ones I left behind. For the ones who cannot out."

All the Pretty Horses by Cormac McCarthy

Sixteen-year-old John Grady Cole, in Cormac McCarthy's *All the Pretty Horses* (1992), leaves home in quest of a ranch and discovers that his real quest is something different. "I was seeking to discover . . . a thing I'd always known. That all courage was a form of constancy. That it was always himself that the coward abandoned first." The limited omniscient point of view traces Cole's departure from his home in 1949 after his mother announces that she will sell the family ranch purchased in 1866. His parents divorce after his father returns from World War II, and, having blindly signed papers, his father retains no control over the dispersal of property. But his father understands John Grady's love of horses and his Christmas gift of a Hamley formfitter saddle pleases his son. The form of the novel resembles a medieval romance as Cole begins his quest journey. He has adventures unrelated to his quest that deter his path, but he eventually reaches his goal.

On his journey, John Grady has several tests and trials. He and his friend Lacey Rawlins enter Mexico where a young boy riding a stolen horse and carrying a gun joins them. They want Jimmy Blevins to leave, but he stays until he gets into trouble. The other two continue to the Hacienda de Nuestra Señora de la Purísima Concepción on the edge of the Bolsón de Cuatro Ciénagas in Coahuíla. When the owner, Don Héctor Rocha y Villareal sees how well Cole handles horses, he hires him as a trainer. John Grady fails his first test by falling in love with the don's daughter Alejandra, seventeen, an elegant rider. When he sees her, his world changes "forever in the space of a heartbeat." She soon rides with him at night and begins staying in the barn with him until morning. Soon Alejandra's grandaunt and godmother, Dueña Alfonsa, invites him to the house to play chess and talk about the family. She begins instructing him that "scars have the strange power to remind us that our past is real. The events that cause them can never be forgotten, can they?" When the don discovers that John Grady has been seeing Alejandra, he allows the corrupt law men from Encantadas to arrest him and Lacy as possible murderers after Jimmy Blevins kills a man. Before guards beat them in the Saltillo prison, they murder

Blevins in the woods. When Pérez, the jailkeeper, says they must buy their freedom, they cannot pay. John Grady fortunately passes his next trial by stabbing the man hired to kill him with a knife he bought from another prisoner. Soon money arrives from Dueña Alfonsa to free them. When Alejandro refuses to revive their relationship, John Grady knows he must leave. Ranch hands express concern about Rawlins, but understand that "a man leaves much when he leaves his own country." They believe that fate or predeterminism has placed humans in specific countries because "the weathers and seasons that form a land form also the inner fortunes of men in their generations and are passed on to their children." On the way home, they have a final adventure when John Grady tries to retake the horse Blevins stole. He succeeds, but someone wounds him by piercing his leg with a bullet.

John Grady uses his knowledge and learns much about himself and the behavior of others on his quest. On the first night in Mexico, he and Rawlins wonder about dying and heaven and hell. When one wonders if a person can believe in heaven without accepting the concept of hell, the other responds that persons should be able to think as they wish. When Rawlins asks Grady if horses had their own special heaven, Grady asserts that horses did not need a heaven. John Grady loves horses like the *vaquero* who say "that if a person understood the soul of the horse then he would understand all horses that ever were." John Grady learns that he can kill a man in self-defense and understands that he has responsibility for himself. After Grady leaves, Alfonsa asks him not to see Alejandra again. She recalls her misfortunes many years before when her love Gustavo lost an eye and she two fingers on her left hand because they were betrayed. Gustavo had said "that those who have endured some misfortune will always be set apart but that it is just that misfortune which is their gift and which is their strength and that they must make their way back into the common enterprise of man for without they do so it cannot go forward and they themselves will wither in bitterness." John Grady returns home only to find that both the family's servant of fifty years, Aubela, and his father have died. Before he leaves again, riding into nothingness, "he held out his hands as if to . . . slow the world that was rushing away and seemed to care nothing for the old or the young or rich or poor or dark or pale or he or she. Nothing for their struggles, nothing for their names. Nothing for their names. Nothing for the living or the dead." And indeed, as Alfonsa told him, "those whom life does not cure death will. . . . He thought the world's heart beat at some terrible cost and that the world's pain and its beauty moved in a relationship of diverging equity and that in this headlong deficit the blood of multitudes might ultimately be exacted for the vision of a single flower." John Grady does not find his ranch, but he does discover something more valuable, fidelity to himself.

Moby-Dick by Herman Melville

The famous first line of *Moby-Dick* (1851), "Call me Ishmael," immediately establishes the first-person narrator as an unpretentious man wanting to be friends with the reader, even addressing the reader informally as "you." Ishmael decides to go to sea to renew himself after a variety of jobs, including teaching. He says of the water, "there is magic in it. . . . It [the sea] is the image of the ungraspable phantom of life; and this is the key to it all." Before embarking on the journey, Ishmael meets Queequeg, a kind savage who offers half of his wealth, and they enlist for the same ship, the *Pequod*. Herman Melville reveals enormous knowledge and even more research though Ishmael's narration about the whaling ship, including segments on the ship's rigging and the value of ambergris, that was for Ishmael "my Yale College and my Harvard." A good student, his survival techniques later keep him alive to tell the story of Ahab's mad quest for the white whale. Melville's story recalls the tale of Mocha Dick, a sperm whale that sank ships in the 1840s and 1850s, but Melville adds complex themes indicative of American romanticism including the pain of self-discovery, the juxtaposition of good and evil, and the search for truth. Additionally, he draws from literary traditions including the epic, picaresque novel, travelogue, and allegory as he traces Ahab's quest for the whale.

Not until the *Pequod* has been at sea for several days does the crew discover its true destination. The captain, Ahab, finally appears and begins his watch for Moby Dick, the white whale. At fifty-eight, Ahab has been whaling for forty years and wears a scar on his face and a leg carved from the jawbone of another whale. Ishmael views this Ahab as a "grand, ungodly, god-like man" while knowing that the Ahab of the Bible was an evil king. Ishmael remembers Elijah warning him earlier not to sail on the *Pequod*. Ahab later announces that he is "madness maddened." When Ahab tells the men that they have shipped to find the white whale, Starbuck wonders why Ahab wants vengeance on a dumb brute, even though the whale has amputated Ahab's leg. The other men anticipate the chase, especially when Ahab offers a piece of gold to whoever first sights the white whale. When the initial whale chase begins, the crew discovers that Ahab has stowed away five men for his boat, led by Fedallah, the Parsee. After Ahab hears from the captain of the *Sammy Enderby*, who also lost a limb to Moby-Dick where the captain last saw the whale, he rushes to the site. So focused on his quest, Ahab's inhumanity surfaces when he will not pause to help the *Rachel*'s captain search for his sons lost overboard. Before the official quest of Moby-Dick, Ahab baptizes his new harpoon with blood from his three chosen harpooners in the name of the devil. Fedallah, both seer and sailor, comforts Ahab with the prediction that he will not die until he has seen two hearses—one not made by mortal hands and another with visible wood grown in America. He prophecies that only hemp can kill Ahab but that he Fedallah will die first. In the three-day battle with Moby-Dick, however, the Parsee becomes entangled in ropes around Moby-Dick, and crewmen spot him mangled and tied to the belly of the whale. Ahab wounds Moby-Dick, and the enraged whale attacks and sinks the American-made wooden ship. When Ahab laments that Starbuck and Stubb will die, he regains his humanity, but in a second vicious lunge toward the whale, Ahab's harpoon rope rebounds and strangles him. Ahab's fatal pride blinds him to the weakness of humans in the face of God and nature.

As the crew and Ishmael observe Ahab and his singular quest of the white whale, they soon understand that they are sailing on a voyage like no other. The mat-maker notes that it "seemed as if this were the Loom of Time, and I myself were a shuttle mechanically weaving and weaving away at the Fates." In a typhoon off the coast of Japan, the blazing masts lit like three candles in front of an altar by lightning underscore their feelings of participating in an other-worldly event. However, the mates "worship" Ahab and receive food from him like "alms." The men refer to the "big white god," and Ishmael wonders if its albino whiteness symbolizes something pure or spiritual. In their first en-counter with the white whale, Ahab falls into the sea, but the crew retrieves him. On the third day, Ahab demands to be lowered into the sea to fight the whale, but sharks surround the boat, waiting for him. Starbuck laments the scene and wonders "Is my journey's end coming?" As Moby-Dick charges the ship, he seems "combinedly possessed by all the angels that fell from heaven," the followers of Lucifer. Ishmael reports that "retribution, swift vengeance, eternal malice were in his whole aspect." The only survivor, Ishmael, floats on the coffin built for Queequeg during his illness until the *Rachel* rescues him. While searching for its lost children, the ship "only found another orphan." And as the only survivor, Ishmael fulfills his purpose of telling the story of Ahab and his singular quest to others.

Each of these protagonists participates in a quest. In *The House on Mango Street* Esperanza wants a home in which she can become a writer. John Grady Cole also longs for a home, albeit a ranch, where he can raise his beloved horses in *All the Pretty Horses*. And Ahab wants to regain his manhood by conquering the white whale, Moby-Dick. Not one of them reaches the goal, but Esperanza and John Grady have the possibility of succeeding beyond the confines of the fiction. Ahab, however, chooses the defeat of a symbolic god as his quest, and, fortunately, he loses.

Additional Related Novels

Cahan, Abraham. *The Rise of David Levinsky.*
Faulkner, William. *The Bear.*
Fitzgerald, F. Scott. *The Great Gatsby.*
Frazier, Charles. *Cold Mountain.*
Hurston, Zora Neale. *Their Eyes Were Watching God.*
Kincaid, Jamaica. *Annie John.*
O'Brien, Tim. *Going after Cacciato.*
Pynchon, Thomas. *The Crying of Lot 49.*

Rejection

Psychoanalysis . . . shows the human infant as the passive recipient of love, unable to bear hostility. Development is the learning to love actively and to bear rejection.

—Karl Stern, *The Pillar of Fire* (1951)

People feel rejected when they think that others are ignoring or excluding them. Most often what they want is just someone to appreciate them for their own uniqueness. After society rejects him as a "hog," Jefferson has no self-esteem until Grant talks to him in *A Lesson Before Dying*. In *A Member of the Wedding*, Frankie searches for friendship, only to find rejection. The Nedeed wives of *Linden Hills* endure the rejection of their husbands, who focus solely on their sons, money, and community control. All of Ellen's relatives in *Ellen Foster*, including her father, reject her before she finds comfort in a foster home. In *The Rise of Silas Lapham*, *Washington Square*, and *The Bluest Eye*, each protagonist experiences rejection, some of it conspicuous and some covert.

To suffer rejection is to be "to be set aside or [thrown] away as useless or worthless" (*OED*). In psychology, a parent denies a child of a loving relationship. In William Whiston's works about the Roman Josephus, he notes that "the young men were entirely [*sic*] rejected from any hopes of the kingdom" (1737). John Milton advises Samson "not to reject the penitent, but ever to forgive (*Samson Agonistes*, 1671). Joseph Butler suggests that "the whole method of government by punishments should be rejected as absurd" (*The Analogy of Religion Natural and Revealed*, 1736). And Arthur Janov contends "to feel really rejected means to . . . feel utterly alone and unwanted as that child" (*Primal Scream*, 1973). The three novels, *The Rise of Silas Lapham*, *Washington Square*, and *The Bluest Eye*, show protagonists who feel varying degrees of rejection from society as a whole or an individual.

The Rise of Silas Lapham by William Dean Howells

The opening of William Dean Howells' *The Rise of Silas Lapham* (1884) informs that newly monied Silas Lapham, fifty-five, manufactures the mineral paint his father discovered on their land in 1860. Bartley Hubbard's newspaper interview also includes family details about his wife, Persis, a former schoolteacher; Irene, his lovely redhaired and blue-eyed daughter disinterested in studying; and Penelope, an olive-skinned book lover. Although Mrs. Lapham and Irene want to establish themselves in Boston's Brahmin society, they have "no skill or courage to make themselves noticed." Most of Boston's self-assured society subtly rejects them as Tom Corey's father would like but cannot because of Tom's interest in one of Lapham's daughters. In the year after Hubbard's interview, wealth almost corrupts Lapham, but financial ruin intervenes. In his essay "Criticism and Fiction" (1891), Howells determined that art should reveal the superiority of reasoned and civilized human nature as opposed to the primitive and ignorant. He thought the writer should disagree with any absolute standard of morality by truthfully portraying characters in careful detail with an emphasis on their motivations, ethics, and social problems. Using omniscient point of view, Howells illustrates in this novel his philosophy of realism.

After Lapham becomes wealthy, Persis tries to circulate their daughters in society. One day Irene and Persis meet Harvard graduate Tom Corey, whose perfect manners make Persis "feel as if we had always lived in the backwoods." To no longer be physically isolated from Corey and others, Lapham and Persis decide to build in New Land, their highly desirable Boston property. Not understanding the exclusivity of those with "old money," Lapham thinks that all money equates with society. He announces to Tom Corey, "I've got the best architect in Boston, and I'm building a house to suit myself. And if money can do it, I guess I'm going to be suited." Corey's father Bromfield, a painter too wealthy by Boston standards to sell his work so he no longer paints, warns Tom. "suppose you know what you are about, Tom. But remember we are Essex County people, and that in savor we are just a little beyond the salt of the earth. I will tell you plainly that I don't like the notion of a man who has rivaled the hues of nature in her wildest haunts with the tints of his mineral paint; but I don't say there are not worse men." Tom, however, wants to join Lapham in business, and Lapham finally agrees. After all, Tom is "an energetic fellow, a little indefinite in aim, with the smallest amount of inspiration that can save a man from being commonplace." After the agreement, Bromfield visits Lapham and invites his family to dinner, but for this, their first social engagement, Penelope refuses to attend. At dinner, the guests surprise Lapham with their candid conversation about literature, where, as support for Howells's own theories, the minister Sewell declares that "the novelists might be the greatest possible help to us if they painted life as it is, and human feelings in their true proportion and relation, but for the most part they have been and are altogether noxious." Lapham drinks excessively and begins boasting, two actions that annoy the Brahmin social circle. The next day, Lapham apologizes to Tom, who politely dismisses his behavior. Bromfield, however, compares entertaining the Laphams to art: "They will probably come here every Sunday night to tea. It's a perspective without a vanishing point." Soon, Lapham's business dealings, investments, and bad loans leave him bankrupt; his new house burns the week after the insurance runs out; and he has to leave Boston. Although always rejected by society, Lapham retains his integrity, even though his compassionate support of a former business partner ultimately ruined him, and regains his happiness when he returns to Lapham, the place he loves.

While society rejects the Laphams, Penelope rejects society and Tom Corey. The entire family has suspected that Corey loves Irene, and she has imagined herself loving him. When Corey first meets Penelope, he briefly discusses *Middlemarch* with her, and later when he sees Irene without Pen, he talks solely about Pen. Tom has told his mother that "she's everything that's unexpected," and his mother also thinks he speaks of Irene. Although Mrs. Lapham realizes at the Corey dinner that Tom does not love Irene, she has no idea that he might care about Penelope. Tom, however, rushes to the Lapham house the following day to profess his love to Pen. Pen rejects him, horrified what Irene might think. Pen's news shocks her mother, and Pen declares, "You never thought of me!' . . . with a bitterness that reached her mother's heart. 'I was nobody! I couldn't feel! No one could care for me!' The turmoil of despair, of triumph, of remorse and resentment, which filled her soul, tried to express itself in words." Silas and Persis consult Sewell about the situation, and he advises them to support the marriage. He thinks that three suffering instead of one is a waste of effort and energy. Irene leaves for Lapham, and Pen tells Corey she will marry him. Lapham's business fails soon after, however, and Pen and Corey marry and leave for South America while the Laphams return to Lapham. Although Penelope finally accepts Corey, she never acquiesces to the whims of Boston's society.

Washington Square by Henry James

Both father and suitor reject Catherine in *Washington Square* (1881). With an omniscient and a first-person narrator, Henry James introduces Catherine Sloper, daughter of physician Dr. Austin Sloper. When Dr. Sloper was twenty-seven in 1820, he married Catherine Harrington, a woman with an income of $10,000. Their first child, a boy, died at three, and two years later Catherine was born. Mrs. Sloper, however, died within a week of Catherine's birth. When his sister Lavinia Penniman became a widow, Dr. Sloper invited her to stay with them. Although Catherine was twelve, her father had enough time to make Catherine feel inferior and eliminate any self-worth that she might have developed.

Dr. Sloper rejects Catherine because he thinks she is dull and "abnormally deficient" in intelligence. Very proud of his own intellect and social position with a house on Washington Square, he thinks Catherine's function should be to make his life comfortable. Mrs. Penniman asks him, "Do you think it is better to be clever than to be good?" He responds, "You are good for nothing unless you are clever." Catherine seems commonplace to him, and her purchase, after she turns twenty-one, of an inappropriate red satin gown trimmed in gold fringe for a cousin's engagement party annoys him. At the party, Catherine meets and admires Morris Townsend. Sloper disapproves and investigates Townsend, discovering that his widowed sister supports him and her five children. Mrs. Montgomery implores Dr. Sloper, "Don't let her marry him!" Dr. Sloper announces that he will cut off Catherine's inheritance and takes her to Europe, but she refuses to reject Morris, knowing her inheritance from her mother will suffice. When her angry father abandons her in Switzerland, Catherine experiences his further rejection and unkindness.

Encouraged by Mrs. Penniman, Morris waits for Catherine's return. Hearing, however, that she will be disinherited, he postpones their wedding. He explains to Catherine that "it isn't of the mere material comfort I speak; it is of the moral comfort, of the intellectual satisfaction." He informs Mrs. Penniman, "A man should know when he is beaten. . . . I must give her up!'" When Catherine first met Townsend, she was surprised at her loquaciousness when dancing with him. Then "it had become vivid to her that there was a great excitement in trying to be a good daughter. She had an entirely new feeling, which may be described as a state of expectant suspense about her own actions. . . . It was as if this other person, who was both herself and not herself, had suddenly sprung into being, inspiring her with a natural curiosity as to the performance of untested functions." But after Townsend rejects her by vanishing from New York, Catherine returns to Europe, refusing again to promise her father that she will not marry Townsend after her father's death. That her father changes his will, leaving only one-fifth of his money to her, pleases Catherine. She admits, "I like [the will] very much. Only I wish it had been expressed a little differently." Encouraged again by Mrs. Penniman twenty years later, Morris arrives at Catherine's door expecting her to welcome him. But she tells him never to return. Townsend "was the man who had been everything, and yet this person was nothing. How long ago it was—how old she had grown—how much she had lived! She had lived on something that was connected to *him*, and she had consumed it in doing so. This person did not look unhappy . . . he had made himself comfortable, and he had never been caught. But even while her perception opened itself to this, she had no desire to catch him; his presence was painful to her, and she only wished he would go." Once Catherine's father and suitor have rejected her, she loses the will to love either, and in turn, renounces them.

The Bluest Eye by Toni Morrison

In *The Bluest Eye* (1970), the protagonist Pecola can only overcome the pain of rejection by becoming a schizophrenic. Toni Morrison's style incorporates the oral tradition in the African-American community with changing points of view, although Claudia most often functions as narrator. Claudia the adult remembers the time in 1939 when she was nine and Pecola lived with her family. Hitler had begun invading Europe, and the monstrosity of his crimes against millions mirrors the treatment of Pecola by her family and the community. Morrison further emphasizes the connection by naming the three prostitutes Poland and China (two invaded countries) and Marie, called the Maginot Line, for the besieged France. The reader knows something unfortunate happens to Pecola from the beginning because Claudia says that "quiet as it's kept," everyone knows about Pecola. Visiting other houses to sell seeds, Claudia and her sister Frieda hear adults whispering, and they know that Pecola is having a baby.

Morrison's shifts in point of view allow the reader to know Pecola's pain and how the childhoods of her parents, Pauline and Cholly, directly affect it. Pecola thinks that if she has blue eyes like Shirley Temple, people will see her (she feels invisible) and love her. She eats Mary Jane candies with the blonde and blue-eyed girl on the wrapper and visits the local fortune-teller Soaphead Church for help. To emphasize this contrast between the blackness of Pecola and the others, Morrison begins the novel with a passage from the old Dick and Jane primer implying that children should emulate white middle-class life.

The ugliness that Pecola, her mother Pauline, and her father Cholly feel permeates their household and strangles any possibility of normal family love. Lame since two, Pauline left home at fifteen with Cholly for Lorain, Ohio, but there the women condemned her old clothes and southern accent. Since Cholly would not give her money, she went to work. When she lost a tooth sitting in a Jean Harlow movie while pregnant, she no longer cared about her appearance. After her children were born, she began working for a white family, where any tenderness she might have for her own children, who called her "Mrs. Breedlove," she granted to the little white girl, who called her "Polly." When Claudia and Frieda visit Mrs. Breedlove with Pecola one day, they drop a blueberry pie in the kitchen, and while Mrs. Breedlove chastises Pecola, she comforts the girl, saying, "Hush. Don't worry none." Pauline never instructs Pecola about the oral traditions of their family or the coming changes in her body, thus Pecola thinks she has done something bad when she begins menstruating. Mrs. MacTeer, Claudia's mother, has to explain Pecola's condition to her. After Cholly impregnates Pecola, Pauline blames and beats her instead of acknowledging the anguish that Pecola feels.

Cholly sees Pecola when he is drunk and imagines she is the Pauline of his youth. He has become an alcoholic, emasculated by events throughout his life. Cholly's twelve-year-old mother, reputed to be insane, abandoned him when he was four days old; his father had already left. His Great Aunt Jimmy raised him, and when he found his father, Samson Fuller, after her death, his father, having forgotten that he had a son, simply ridiculed and then ignored him. Two white hunters had interrupted Cholly's first sexual experience on a riverbank and laughingly commanded him to finish while they watched. Cholly refuses to be faithful to Pauline and may have murdered three men. As a father, he despises Pecola because he feels undeserving of her love. When he rapes her, "The rigidness of her shocked body, the silence of her stunned throat, was better than Pauline's easy laughter had been. The confused mixture of his memories of Pauline and the doing of a wild and forbidden thing excited him, and a bolt of desire ran down his genitals. . . . Again the hatred mixed with tenderness. The hatred would not let him pick her up, the tenderness forced him to cover her." Soon after, Cholly tries to burn down the house, the ultimate sin because everyone fears "being put outdoors." The actions of Pecola's parents emphasize the irony of their name. The "Breedloves" only create hate and ugliness.

The community, except for the MacTeers, also rejects Pecola. The MacTeers welcome her into their loving and compassionate but meager home after her family disintegrates, although Mrs. MacTeer declares, "Folks . . . just dump they children off on you and go on 'bout they business. . . . What kind of something is that?" When their boarder Mr. Henry tries to molest Frieda, Mr. MacTeer evicts him and worries about Frieda, the opposite reaction from Pauline's treatment of Pecola after Cholly rapes her. The girls play with Pecola, seemingly unaware of her ugliness, unlike other peers. Teachers ignore her, and classmates use Pecola's name to insult each other. A group of boys taunt Pecola with the worst affront, "black." Others also condemn her blackness, including a light-skinned black girl, Maureen Peal. A new student, Maureen, announces to Claudia, Frieda, and Pecola, "'I am cute! And you ugly! Black and ugly black.'" When cream-colored Geraldine movies to Lorain with her son Junior, she fears that Junior will become like Pecola and encourages him to play with white children. Geraldine "had seen this little girl all of her life. Hanging out of windows over saloons in Mobile . . . sitting in bus stations holding paper bags and crying to mothers who kept saying 'shut up!' " When Junior kills their black cat with blue eyes that fascinates Pecola, Geraldine blames her. When Frieda identifies Pecola's bleeding as "ministration," she tells Pecola she can now have babies, Pecola asks how. Frieda says, "Somebody has to love you." Pecola's next question stuns Claudia. "How do you do that? I mean, how do you get somebody to love you?" When others want Pecola's baby to die, Claudia remembers, "more strongly than my fondness for Pecola, I felt a need for someone to want the black baby to live just to counteract the universal love of white baby dolls, Shirley Temples, and Maureen Peals." Pecola's baby dies, and she goes mad.

Each of the protagonists of these novels experiences rejection by the community or from someone they love—Silas by the upper class, Catherine by father and suitor, and Pecola by the community. One cannot underestimate the unnecessary pain that rejection causes, especially when the rejected one often has no idea what to do, if anything might be possible, to change the situation. What seems most alarming is that this behavior seems commonplace throughout families and communities.

Additional Related Novels

Buck, Pearl S. *The Good Earth*.

Cather, Willa. *My Ántonia.*
Chopin, Kate. *The Awakening.*
Crane, Stephen. *Maggie: A Girl of the Streets.*
Ellison, Ralph. *Invisble Man.*
Faulkner, William. *Absalom, Absalom!*
Fitzgerald, F. Scott. *The Great Gatsby.*
Gaines, Ernest J. *A Lesson Before Dying.*
Gardner, John. *Grendel.*
Gibbons, Kaye. *Ellen Foster.*
Hawthorne, Nathaniel. *The Scarlet Letter.*
McCullers, Carson. *A Member of the Wedding.*
Naylor, Gloria. *Linden Hills.*

Responsibility

Respect for intellectual excellence, the restoration of vigor and discipline
to our ideas of study, curricula which aim at strengthening intellectual fi-
ber and stretching the power of young minds, personal commitment and
responsibility—these are the preconditions of educational recovery in
America today; and, I believe, they have always been the preconditions of
happiness and sanity for the human race.
                                  —Adlai E Stevenson, *New York Times* (1958)

When one takes responsibility for oneself or for another, one promises protection and concern for well-being. After his father dies in *April Morning*, Adam
knows that he must assume responsibility for his family. Charlotte Temple's father in *Charlotte Temple* takes responsibility, not only for himself but also for
those who have greviously wronged him. Although Miss Bess wants to ignore
Tommy, she soon ascertains that to save his life she must take responsibility for
him in *The Hiding Place*. In *Death Comes for the Archbishop*, *Fools Crow*, and
Fried Green Tomatoes at the Whistle Stop Café, each protagonist eventually
takes responsibility for the welfare of the people in the community.

Being responsible means that one is "morally accountable for one's actions;
capable of rational conduct [and] of fulfilling an obligation or trust; reliable"
(*OED*). Daniel Waterland espouses that "willing or not willing, every man is
responsible, at last, for the doctrines he teaches" (*Doctrine of the Trinity versus
Works*, 1823). Arthur Vogel explains that "there can be no true response without responsibility; there can be no responsibility without response" (*The
Christian Person*, 1963). Dorcas Hardy notes that "the one with the primary
responsibility to the individual's future is that individual" (*Christian Science
Monitor*, 1987). *Death Comes for the Archbishop*, *Fools Crow*, and *Fried Green
Tomatoes at the Whistle Stop Café* each illustrate the immeasurable value and
personal reward of taking responsibility for both oneself and others.

Death Comes for the Archbishop by Willa Cather

In *Death Comes for the Archbishop* (1927), Willa Cather traces the establishment of the Catholic Church in the territory of New Mexico during the
mid-nineteenth century. Using actual letters of the first bishop, Archbishop
Lamy, Cather creates the story of Father Jean Latour, a French missionary

priest of thirty-five, appointed the new bishop of Santa Fe. By the time Bishop Latour becomes an archbishop, he has gained status among the people, and the episodic story takes on the attributes of an epic—a hero identified with a particular nationalistic attitude. In 1851, during his travels from Ohio to New Mexico, Latour loses his worldly goods in Galveston Bay, overturns in a wagon, and almost dies from lack of water. After almost a year, he arrives, but the local priest refuses to recognize him. Following an additional 3,000 mile journey to Durango, Latour returns with the papers certifying his authority. Latour's dear friend, Father Vaillant (based on Lamy's friend Father Macheboeuf), helps him gather the parishes scattered around the area into one whole. Additionally, Cather incorporates the history and oral tradition of the region through tales and objects such as the bell reminiscent of Rome and Jerusalem, dated 1356. The novel resembles Father Vaillant's special Christmas meal, " a soup . . . the result of a constantly refined tradition. There are nearly a thousand years of history in this soup." When Vaillant is reassigned to Denver after the two have grown older and they know they will be too far apart to meet again, he reminds Latour, "We have done the things we used to plan to. . . . To fulfil the dreams of one's youth; that is the best that can happen to a man. No worldly success can take the place of that."

While serving, Bishop Latour makes difficult decisions that affect life and death. One day he helps a woman escape after six years of marriage from Buck Scales who has murdered their three children and four travelers. Bishop Latour reports Scales to authorities, and a jury convicts and hangs him. His wife, grateful for her freedom, first stays with Christóbal (Kit Carson's wife) and then begins working for newly arrived nuns in Santa Fé. When Father Gallegos in Albuquerque tells the bishop that he will not go to faraway Ácoma to say Mass because the people will not attend, the bishop goes. The glorious landscape to Ácoma captivates him: "From the flat red sea of sand rose great rock mesas, generally Gothic in outline, resembling vast cathedrals." Since the people had moved to the top of the mesa for safety, he reflects that "the rock . . . was the utmost expression of human need . . . the highest comparison of loyalty in love and friendship. Christ Himself had used that comparison for the disciple to whom He gave the keys of His Church. And the Hebrews of the Old Testament . . . their rock was an idea of God, the only thing their conquerors could not take from them." But on top of the rock, the huge church with sagging roof resembles a fortress. Latour concludes that in 1600, the Fray Juan Ramirez had built for his own glory rather than God's when he had made men carry stones and huge beams to the top of the mesa. Latour understands that the people support the church rather than the opposite and decides to replace Father Gallegos with Father Vaillant who will give the people religion instead of rumor. In Taos, Latour visits Padre Martínez, dictator of all northern New Mexico parishes. When seven Indians were unjustly accused of murdering whites, they asked for his intervention. Martínez told them to deed their land to him and left town on hanging day. Latour lets the padre and his fat student

Trinidad Lucero, son of another priest, stay until the next year, after he returns from Rome with additional priests for his diocese. He commands Martínez to resign, and, when he desists, Latour strips him of the privileges of priesthood.

Bishop Latour and his colleagues also take responsibility for the more pleasant aspects of his position. When looking for water in the desert soon after his arrival, he finds Hidden Water, where a young girl, ecstatic to see a priest, exclaims, "Such a thing has never happened to us before; it must be in answer to my father's prayers." Since 1790, when families arrived in the area, no priest had appeared to baptize the children or to consecrate the marriages. Bishop Latour fulfills their wish. When the rich Mexican ranchero, Don Antonio Olivares, dies, his third wife Doña Isabella refuses to admit that she is fifty-two instead of forty-two and her stepsons challenge his will, saying that she is too young to have the daughter she claims. Latour's one ambition, to build a cathedral in Santa Fé, makes him convince her to admit her real age and thereby obtain funds for the church. Vaillant anticipates going to Tucson to save the Indians where "faith, in that wild frontier, is like buried treasure; they guard it, but they do not know how to use it to their soul's salvation." Father Joseph comforts the illiterate Sada, a Mexican slave to lower-class Protestants who have forbidden her to attend Mass, by giving her an image of faith. Latour consoles Eusabio, an influential Navajo, after the death of his only son. Upon hearing that Vaillant has died in Denver, Latour retires outside Santa Fé to raise fruit trees, remembering Pascal's comment that "man was lost and saved in a garden." Before his death, Latour expresses pleasure in the government having freed the slaves and returned the Canyon de Chelly to the Navajos with its sacred Shiprock rising into the sky. When Latour dies at sunset, people have already gathered. The narrator says, "In those days . . . death had a solemn social importance . . . as a dramatic climax, a moment when the soul made its entrance into the next world; passing in full consciousness . . . to an unimaginable scene."

Fools Crow by James Welch

In *Fools Crow* (1986), the Blackfeet protagonist White Man's Dog comes of age, takes the name of Fools Crow, and accepts his responsibility for himself and for his Lone Eaters band of Pikini (Piegans) during the events leading to the Marias River Massacre of 1870. James Welch of the Blackfeet and Gros Ventre tribes uses omniscient point of view and Native-American elements in his novel, including dreams and animals as symbols. Although Fools Crow has dreamed about the massacre prior to its occurrence, he has no ability to prevent it. Instead, he continues to assume his responsibility by marrying and raising a family while preparing to become the tribe's medicine man. When Yellow Kidney does not return after the Crow raid, his wife mourns, but after three days, she says that he is still alive because he came to her in a dream. In a dream that Fools Crow has when he goes on a seven-day journey, he sees the destruction of his people but also detects that he and his family will survive.

A danger to the tribe's survival is the refusal of one of its members to accept responsibility. When the Pikini men decide to raid the Crow under Bull Shield, Yellow Kidney chooses the participants. He knows that Fast Horse is reckless but must include him because his father keeps one of the only three Beaver Medicine bundles in the Blackfeet tribes. Inside the enemy camp, the boastful Fast Horse, wearing the old war shirt once belonging to the brave Head Carrier, speaks aloud. After Bull Shield captures Yellow Kidney and cuts off each of his fingers, Yellow Kidney returns to the Pikini and tells what happened. Fast Horse, however, refuses to accept responsibility for Yellow Kidney's mutilation. Instead, he joins the renegade Owl Child, and they carelessly steal from the Napikwans (white men) when wiser men have told them of the trouble it will cause. After Fast Horse leaves, Yellow Kidney admits that he entered a tent in the Crow compound before he was caught and raped a girl who had the "white-scabs disease" (smallpox). He knows that he was punished because he too ignored his responsibility to others and broke "one of the simplest decencies by which people live. In fornicating with the dying girl, I had taken her honor, her opportunity to die virtuously. I had taken the path traveled only by the meanest of scavengers." After his story, White Man's Dog knows that Yellow Dog has lived his scary dream about a "white-faced girl" desiring and leading him to death. No longer feeling comfortable with his family, Yellow Kidney decides to join the Spotted Horse people, but a white man shoots him, probably in retaliation for other killings. Fast Horse finds the dead Yellow Kidney and takes him home for burial. Owl Child, also infected with the "white-scabs disease," kills near the white camps, and mourners respond by murdering Fast Horse. White Man's Dog's brother Running Fisher also shirks responsibility by sleeping with his father's third wife, an act demeaning to his father and his other wives.

When White Man's Dog turns eighteen and wants to marry Red Paint, Yellow Kidney's daughter, he realizes that he must accept his responsibilities in the tribe. He performs well at the Crow raid and becomes an informal apprentice to Mik-api, the medicine man. He has an experience with Raven and, after freeing a wolverine, believes that the wolverine is his symbolic animal from which he will take his courage. He visits other tribal groups to ask permission for Heavy Shield Woman to become the medicine woman, and then he makes his own sacrifice of flesh at the Sun Dance to the Sun Chief for allowing him to return alive from the Crow raid. On another raid of the Crow, in retribution for Yellow Kidney, the warriors witness an eclipse, although they do not know what it is. They see it as a sign of catastrophe but keep their plan to attack at dawn. White Man's Dog fools Bull Shield into thinking he is dead so that Bull Shield will come close enough to kill. When White Man's Dog returns with Bull Shield's scalp, the tribe renames him "Fools Crow." Feeling responsible for his friend's family, Fools Crow agrees to find Fast Horse and bring him home, but when he finds him, he knows that he and Fast Horse will never be friends again. He realizes that Fast Horse enjoys being with Owl Child because of the "freedom from responsibility, from accountability to the group." Fools Crow becomes a responsible leader of his family and of his people, trying to help them have a better life.

Fried Green Tomatoes at the Whistle Stop Café by Fannie Flagg

In *Fried Green Tomatoes at the Whistle Stop Café* (1987), Fannie Flagg combines two plots using omniscient point of view. Depressed and overweight, Evelyn Couch chats with Mrs. Ninny Threadgoode at the retirement home when she comes to visit her mother-in-law, and Ninny narrates the story of Idgie Threadgoode and her friend Ruth Jamison, residents of Whistle Stop, Alabama, near Birmingham. Each Sunday, Evelyn hears more about them, courageously combating racism and helping those in their community. Before long, Evelyn decides to take responsibility for herself and not blame others for her sorry mental and physical state.

Ninny was Idgie's next door neighbor for many years and observed her life from the time Idgie was twelve when a train ran over her brother. "You never saw anybody hurt so much. I thought she would die right along with him. It would break your heart to look at her. She ran away the day of the funeral. Just couldn't stand it." Ruth comes to stay with the family for a summer when she is twenty-one and Idgie is fifteen, but she then leaves to marry Frank. Idgie sits outside the church and blows her car horn during the entire service, and after four years, Ruth needs to be rescued because Frank beats her. Idgie's father gives Idgie money to open the Whistle Stop Café so that she can support Ruth. Idgie's good friends include Sipsey and her cooks, Big George (Sipsey's adopted son), and his wife Onzell. When their daughter Naughty Bird is too ill to eat, she wants only to see an elephant in Birmingham. Her parents cannot take her because the Ku Klux Klan will attack them. Idgie defeats the elephant's trainer playing poker, and the elephant comes to Whistle Stop instead. About the racist white men, Idgie says, "They're terrified to sit next to a nigger and have a meal, but they'll eat eggs that came right out of a chicken's ass." One day Ku Klux Klan members stop at the café, and Ruth recognizes Frank's shoes under the robes. Later police ask if anyone has seen Frank because he disappeared after visiting the café. Ruth soon dies from colon cancer, relieved by the morphine that Onzell has carefully saved for her, and Idgie is tried for murdering Frank. The entire town, including the preacher Reverend Scroggins, lies that Idgie was attending a revival meeting at the time of Frank's death. Hoboes whom she has been feeding during the Depression in her disguise as Railroad Bill, a thief who throws supplies off trains to the indigents below, also protect her. Idgie, however, did not kill Frank. Sipsey hit him with a sledgehammer when he came back and tried to take Stump, his son. Then she chopped off his head, and Big George added him to the barbeque served later to Frank's friends.

Before Evelyn meets Ninny, she feels a "quiet hysteria and awful despair . . . that nothing was ever going to change. . . . She began to feel as if she were at the bottom of a well, screaming, no one to hear." She tells Ninny that she's "too young to be old and too old to be young" and considers suicide. But after she hears about the responsibility that Idgie accepted, she changes. When a boy calls her names, she becomes angry rather than embarrassed as in previous times. At forty-eight, she imagines things to do and begins her secret life as Towanda the Avenger. "Towanda was able to do anything she wanted. She went back in time and punched out Paul for writing that women should remain silent. Towanda went to Rome and kicked the pope off the throne and put a nun there, with the priests cooking and cleaning for her, for a change." On *Meet the Press*, she "debated everyone who disagreed" and wanted to give "teachers and nurses . . . the same salary as professional football players." One night her husband Ed yells to her in the kitchen for another beer, and she replies, "Screw you, Ed." Soon she understands that having "balls" allows one to act bravely; "no wonder she had always felt like a car in traffic without a horn." When teens take a space at the grocery store for which she has waited patiently, she destroys their car. She diets and sells enough Mary Kay cosmetics to win the pink Cadillac. After Mrs. Threadgoode dies, Evelyn retrieves things left for her and thinks, "My God, a living, breathing person was on this earth for eighty-six years, and this is all that's left, just a shoe box full of old papers." Evelyn stops at Ninny's grave, and, after she meditates, she notices that someone has placed a note on Ruth's grave. Idgie alone remains, selling honey at a roadstand, her sense of responsibility continuing along with her.

Vaillant and Latour survive the wilds and take responsibility for the people in the diocese. Idgie lives to help others, and Evelyn gains responsibility for herself. Fools Crow, like the others, thinks, "As long as one thought of himself as part of the group, he would be responsible to and for that group." Only Evelyn has to find a group, and when she hears about Idgie and her extended family, she has one. Being responsible not only assists others but it also helps the person who accepts the responsibility.

Additional Related Novels

Fast, Howard. *April Morning.*
Morrison, Toni. *Tar Baby.*
Rowson, Susanna. *Charlotte Temple.*
Stegner, Wallace. *Angle of Repose.*
Updike, John. *Rabbit, Run.*
Wideman, John Edgar. *The Hiding Place.*

Revealing Family History

History is a relentless master. It has no present, only the past rushing into the future. To try to hold fast is to be swept aside.
—John Fitzgerald Kennedy (1960)

Storytellers in a family give its members a sense of the family's values and expectations. In *The Joy Luck Club*, the women with whom June's mother played mahjong "say" stories to their children while trying to create a continuum from the China of their ancestors to the present. Not until all the pieces of several lives fit together can Lipsha Morrissey know the identity of his father in *Love Medicine*. In *The House of the Seven Gables*, facts of Pyncheon family history reveal that Clifford Pyncheon's cousin, the judge, punished Clifford for the judge's own crime. In *Angle of Repose*, *The Hiding Place*, and *Song of Solomon*, families have secrets that, once revealed, help the protagonists choose more appropriately for their own lives.

"History" with "of" following refers to "the series of events in the life of a person or the past existence of a thing, country, institution . . . considered as narrated or as a subject for narration" (*OED*). Thus the history of a family points to the events in the life of a group of people legally related. In the anonymous poem, *Cursor Mundi*, the speaker says "in grece [{th}]an regned Preamus As ald stori telles" (c. 1300). Then in the letters of "Junius," the narrator announces, "the following story will serve to illustrate the character of this respectable family" (1771). Napoleon commented, "History is the version of past events that people have decided to agree upon" (1810). And John Kennedy posited that "we would like to live as we once lived, but history will not permit it" (ca. 1960). Finding the histories of their families in *Angle of Repose*, *The Hiding Place*, and *Song of Solomon* shows the protagonists facets of their own personalities that they may not have previously understood.

Angle of Repose by Wallace Stegner

In Wallace Stegner's *Angle of Repose* (1971), Lyman Ward finds his grandmother's papers in the old family home, Zodiac Cottage, and, while adjusting to the loss of a leg from bone disease, decides to organize them. He learns about her, about her marriage to Oliver Ward, and about himself. Stegner uses omniscient and first-person points of view to develop a novel within a novel, one about Lyman's grandparents and the other about Lyman, his family, and his caretakers. Lyman's first-person narrative begins on 12 April 1970, when he begins to sort through the materials. He tells his son Rodman, "I am cumulative, too. I am everything I ever was. . . . I am much of what my parents and especially my grandparents were . . . plus transmitted prejudices, culture, scruples, likings, moralities, and moral errors that I defend as if they were personal and not familial." Lyman recognizes the similarity between him and his grandmother, Susan Burling. "We have been cut off, the past has been ended and the family has broken up and the present is adrift in its wheelchair."

Susan Burling and Oliver came from different backgrounds, and, after their marriage, Susan never fully adjusted to the life she chose. From the East, Susan knew the literary figures of her time, "Mr. Whittier . . . Mr. Lowell . . . Mr. Holmes . . . Mr. Longfellow." Bad eyesight had forced Oliver to withdraw from Harvard, and when he met Susan the second time, five years after the first, her closest friend Amanda Drake had married their best friend Thomas Hudson, a "man of taste, intelligence, and integrity" who worked for Scribner's. But then Susan married, perhaps "stirred by Oliver Ward's masculine strength, by his stories of an adventurous life, by his evenness of disposition, by his obvious adoration," and went West in 1876 to join him at New Almaden. Pleased by the house he prepared for her, she accepts her situation and sends her articles to Hudson and to Mr. Howells at the *Atlantic*, using the money from them and her drawings, against her husband's wishes, to buy extra items for the family. Lyman's father is born, and a year later they leave when Oliver quits in protest after the manager fires a good worker. Oliver experiments with ways to make cement like that imported from Germany, and, when he succeeds, he can find no financial support. He goes to Deadwood to build a mill ditch for the Homestake silver mine, and Susan continues east. They reunite in Leadville, Colorado, and Susan meets Frank Sargent. She holds salons for the educated, including Helen Hunt Jackson, and begins a book about her grandfather. After problems there, they visit Michoacán, but Oliver says the mine will not produce, and they move to Boise, Idaho, where Agnes is born. After another move, Susan walks one day with Frank Sargent and Agnes while Oliver attends fireworks with Ollie. Agnes falls into a nearby ditch and drowns. The next day Frank commits suicide. From that point, Oliver suspects Susan and Frank of having had an affair, and for the next fifty years, the marriage remains at an "angle of repose," the geological point at which rocks cease to roll. Oliver had once told Susan, "I *believe* in trusting people, do you see? At least till they prove they can't be trusted. What kind of life is it when you can't?" As Lyman interprets between the lines, he observes that his grandfather "is the silent character in this cast, and he left no novels, stories, drawings, or reminiscences to speak for him." And although Oliver "never did less than the best he knew how," he made mistakes and suffered intensely for them.

While Lyman organizes the materials about his grandparents, he is also sorting out his own life. An award-winning history professor, Lyman has recently lost his leg, and his wife Ellen Hammond has left, unable to cope with an invalid. His son Rodman, a sociologist, "was born without a sense of history. To him it is only an aborted science." Rodman wants Lyman in a retirement home, but Lyman likes his new life in the old family home with Ada Rasmussen as his caretaker. She cooks his food and helps him bathe, and, during the day, he works. Ada's daughter Shelley becomes Lyman's researcher, and an old friend, Al Sutton, visits. In the middle of his investigation, Lyman realizes that he is writing about a marriage rather than a woman. Lyman detects that his own father Ollie left his parents' home for school with an aversion toward his mother because Ollie, many years later, had spent much time trying to create a perfect rose named "Agnes." Thus, Lyman ascertains a relationship between the two marriages—his grandparents' and his own. When Ellen Ward appears in a dream and tries to reconcile with Lyman, he imagines that she and the buxom Shelley have an argument over his care. Horrified of a change, Lyman understands that he wants to remain in his recently established life. He muses to a long-deceased Susan, "I ought to be entitled to base on the angle of repose, and may yet. There is another physical law that teases me, too: the Doppler Effect. . . . I would like to hear your life as *you* heard it, coming at you, instead of hearing it as I do, a sober sound of expectations reduced, desires blunted, hopes deferred or abandoned, chances lost, defeats accepted, griefs borne. . . . I would like to hear it as it sounded while it was passing."

The Hiding Place by John Edgar Wideman

In *The Hiding Place* (1981), John Edgar Wideman uses the voices of Clement, Bess, and Tommy to narrates six chapters in the two parts of the novel whose title comes from a spiritual, "went to the Rock to hide my face / Rock cried out, No Hiding Place." When police unjustly accuse Tommy of murder, he runs to the only place he thinks might be safe, his great-aunt's shack on Bruston Hill. Bess at first refuses to help, but then she acquiesces and brings him inside from the freezing air where they both unexpectedly begin to be of benefit to each other. The narrator Clement, a retarded boy, gives an objective view of what is happening outside the shack. He skates to Miss Bess's home with deliveries, but when Miss Bess tells him that he does not see Tommy, Clement pretends not to and never tells anyone. He hears Miss Bess tell Tommy how to plant things, and Clement knows from overhearing Tommy's Aunt Violet in the Brass Rail that Tommy's mother is upset at his disappearance and that Tommy takes his baby to see Aunt Aida. Clement also notices that one of the patrons has eyes like Tommy's (his brother).

When Tommy, twenty-five, decides to go to Bess's, he gains not only time but also an understanding of the importance of the past. His foul language offends Bess, but he tells her that he did not murder Chubby, and she knows he tells the truth. He calls her "Mother Bess," and she declares that she is no one's mother. A sniper unaware that World War II had ended shot Mother Bess's only son, born late in her life, on Guam. After receiving the telegram, she kept waiting for his return, not believing what she had been told. Tommy thinks she looks like an old squaw and that "she is . . . older than anything in Pittsburgh." He tells her about his wife Sarah whom he met at his grandfather's funeral. He had called his grandfather Mr. Lawson, and Mr. Lawson called him Thomas Edgar because his grandfather wanted to remedy the loss of black men's names to white men. Sarah realizes that Tommy is angry, and she suggests that "maybe that's why you did so much wrong. So somebody could feel sorry, so somebody could forgive." His criminal behavior causes Sarah much grief, and as he talks to Bess, Tommy becomes aware of his disastrous decisions.

When Miss Bess decides to help Tommy, she has no idea that he will also assist her. As an old woman living like a hermit, refusing to return to Homewood, and saying she is no longer a Christian, Bess's companions are her memories and all those who have died. She remembers Tommy's Aunt Aida and songs from her childhood, especially one in which she thought the singer was saying "father along" before seeing "farther along" in a white's hymnal. To her, photographs are not real and only remind her that both her husband and son are dead. At first, Bess thinks that Tommy is a "snake with frog's legs sticking out" from his pants and berates herself for not emptying the slop jar on his head. Instead, she offers him soup and reminds him that the past is why he is sitting at her table. Tommy denies any connection to the past, "all that old time stuff don't make me no nevermind. Wasn't even born yet." Bess corrects him. "Wasn't for that crazy May wouldn't be no Lizabeth and you wouldn't be sitting here neither." Because May saved the baby Lisabeth's life, she grew up and gave birth to Tommy. After a time during which Bess teaches Tommy the satisfaction of planting a seed and having one's efforts help it grow, Tommy begins to see his connection to the past as a way to understand the present. He dreams of walking on a beach with his son Clyde, "and the story ain't just words. More like it is in them old songs. What made the story so good was that other me listening too. Watching over me and my son." Tommy gains perspective about his choices, and decides to return to town, although he is fearful of death. At the same time, Tommy helps Bess to see that her isolation on Bruston Hill is also an escape. She understands that if she does not leave the hill to defend him in Homewood, Tommy will die. To take the police off of Tommy's trail and give her time to leave, she burns the shack. Tommy learns to accept the importance of the past while Bess learns to use it rather than to live in it. The indeterminate ending, however, never discloses if the burning house sidetracks the police.

Song of Solomon by Toni Morrison

In *Song of Solomon* (1987), "Milkman" can only free himself from unseen influences after learning the history of his family. Toni Morrison uses omniscient point of view in the story of Macon Dead III, born to Macon Dead II and Ruth Foster and sibling of Lena, thirteen, and First Corinthians, fourteen. Macon's father dislikes his sister Pilate and refuses to have contact with her. At twelve, Milkman admires Pilate's seventeen-year-old granddaughter Hagar's behind. His interest in her back rather than her face or her personality symbolizes his attitude toward everything. He focuses "on things behind him . . . as though there were no future to be had." Hagar falls in love with him, an "anaconda love," so that " she had no self left, no fears, no wants, no intelligence that was her own." She says to Ruth when asked not to kill Milkman for not loving her, "He is my home in this world." When Pilate later shows Milkman a bag with her inheritance, Milkman tells both his father and his friend Guitar that it holds gold. The subsequent collective greed of the three males propels their story.

The attitudes and actions of Macon's nuclear family and his friend Guitar influence his decisions. For his sisters and Ruth, "the way [Macon the father] mangled their grace, wit, and self-esteem was the single excitement of their days. . . . Ruth, began her days stunned into stillness by her husband's contempt and ended them wholly animated by it." Corinthians attended Bryn Mawr and spent her junior year in France but cannot get a job or have a relationship with anyone other than a day laborer who rents a room in one of her father's boarding houses. At forty-two, she becomes a maid. Ruth has a watermark that she examines several times a day to reassure her "that she was alive somewhere, inside, which she acknowledged to be true only because a thing she knew intimately was out there, outside herself." She continues to nurse her son until his legs dangle, and, when Freddie the janitor sees them, he starts calling the child "Milkman." Later, Milkman's father Macon tells him about his childhood on his father's land at Lincoln's Heaven and that he had seen Ruth kissing her dead father's fingers. Milkman follows Ruth one night to her father's grave. She admits to Milkman that her father was unpleasant, "but he cared whether and he cared how I lived, and there was and is, no one else in the world who ever did.'" Milkman then discovers that Guitar is one of the Seven Days, a group of militant blacks who randomly choose a white to kill every time someone kills a black. Guitar asks Milkman, "What good is a man's life if he can't even choose what to die for?" Milkman responds, "Nobody can choose what to die for." Guitar disagrees, "Yes you can, and if you can't, you can damn well try to."

Pilate's unconditional love for living things and her association with flight (her name seems to be a variation of "pilot") guides Milkman. Milkman discovers that Pilate kept Ruth from getting the abortion that his father wanted, thus saving him. Because Pilate has no navel, she seems "other" worldly, with no visible connection to an earthly mother. As a young girl, Pilate watched the Butler family murder their father when he would not cede his land to them, and she still talks to him. Pilate tells Milkman that bones fill the green bag, not gold, and they are those of a white man that Macon killed after their father's death. She tells Milkman, "You can't take a life and walk off and leave it. Life is life. Precious. And the dead you kills is yours. They stay with you anyway, in your mind. So it's a better thing, a more better thing to have the bones right there with you wherever you go." When Milkman travels to Danville, Pennsylvania, for information about the family, the old woman Circe tells him that the Butlers are "dead now. Every one of 'em. . . . Things work out, son. The ways of God are mysterious . . . you see that it always works out. Nothing they stole or killed for did 'em a bit a good." When she tells him that his grandmother's name was "Sing," he identifies her as "Singing Bird," part Native American and part white through the Byrd family, with light skin and straight hair. Circe sends him to Shalimar, Virginia, and there, at Solomon's General Store, he learns that his great-grandfather Solomon flew away from slavery, leaving his wife Ryna and twenty-first son Jake. Milkman hears children singing Solomon's song for the first time, "O Solomon don't leave me." Guitar had told him, "wanna fly, you got to give up the shit that weighs you down." Milkman finds out that "if you surrendered to the air, you could ride it." The knowledge of Solomon's achievement frees Milkman. "He didn't need no airplane. He just took off; got fed up *All the way up*. No more cotton! No more bales! No more orders! No more shit! He flew, baby!" Almost simultaneously with Milkman's insight, Guitar arrives to kill him, still thinking Milkman has gold. When Guitar shoots, he hits Pilate instead, and Milkman's response is to "fly" toward Guitar at the edge of the mountain in retribution for killing the embodiment of love.

By examining his grandmother Susan's life, Lyman begins to understand some of his choices and wishes he could have experienced the process of her life rather than reviewing it after its end. By learning about the past, Tommy decides that he wants to change his direction by first saving his life. And Milkman no longer focuses on money after learning about his great-grandfather's accomplishments. As William Faulkner has said, "The past is not dead, it is not even past."

Additional Related Novels

Baldwin, James. *Go Tell It on the Mountain*.
Erdrich, Louise. *Love Medicine*.
Faulkner, William. *Absalom, Absalom!*; *The Sound and the Fury*.
Hawthorne, Nathaniel. *The House of the Seven Gables*.
Naylor, Gloria. *Mama Day*.
Tan, Amy. *The Joy Luck Club*; *The Kitchen God's Wife*.
Tyler, Anne. *The Accidental Tourist*.

Search for a Father

Becoming a father is easy enough / But being one can be rough.
—Wilhelm Busch, *Julchen* (1877)

When sons lack a supportive father who loves them, they often seek a male who can give them guidance about the proper way to mature. Tommy in *Seize the Day*, unable to communicate with his own father, selects a surrogate father who soon deceives him. In *Go Tell It on the Mountain*, Johnny Grimes feels guilty for hating his father until he discovers that Gabriel is not his biological father. Gene Henderson thinks that playing his deceased father's violin will allow them to communicate in *Henderson, the Rain King*. In *The Adventures of Huckleberry Finn*, *The Death of Jim Loney*, and *Absalom, Absalom!* the protagonists each search for a father.

One who searches "explores" or "examines thoroughly" (*OED*), and a father is "one by whom a child is or has been begotten, a male parent, the nearest male ancestor" or "one who exercises protecting care like that of a father; one who shows paternal kindness" (*OED*). "Father," long a term in the English language, appears in early literature. In the *Anglo-Saxon Chronicle*, a speaker notes "Hine [{asg}]eces [{th}]a to f:der [father] and to hlaforde Scotta cyning" (ca. 1000). William says in *Palerne*, "a kowherde, sire . . . is my kynde fader" (c. 1350). In *The Voyage and Travels of Sir John Mandeville*, the narrator declares, "I . . . have . . . cerched manye fulle straunge places" (ca. 1400). The speaker in John Malcolm Brinnin's poem declares it most succinctly, "I seek a father who most needs a son" (*Oedipus: His Cradle Song*, 1963). In these three novels, *The Adventures of Huckleberry Finn*, *The Death of Jim Loney*, and *Absalom, Absalom!* the biological fathers all deny their sons the "paternal kindness" that they crave.

The Adventures of Huckleberry Finn by Mark Twain

Mark Twain's picaresque historical fiction, *The Adventures of Huckleberry Finn* (1885), takes place in 1835 during the slavery era, a time when Huck and Jim would have a reason to escape on a Mississippi River raft. Separated from his indolent father who "used to always whale me when he was sober" and a deceased mother, Huck gives his money, found at the end of *Tom Sawyer*, to the Judge so his father cannot legally claim it when he reappears. Huck's father instead kidnaps Huck from Miss Watson's house, takes him to a cabin, and locks him inside. Huck frees himself, encounters Jim, and the two raft for Cairo, Illinois, and freedom. While on the river, they stop for information or food until two swindlers sell Jim, and Huck must search for him on shore. Huck discovers Jim at Tom Sawyer's aunt's house, and, coincidentally, Tom arrives and wants to help Huck free Jim. After this endeavor, Huck returns to the woods because the deceptions of the "civilized" disillusion him. Twain early establishes Huck as a reliable narrator through his vernacular speech. "You don't know about me, without you have read a book by the name of *The Adventures of Tom Sawyer*. . . . That book was made by Mr. Mark Twain, and he told the truth, mainly. . . . which is mostly a true book; with some stretches." Although the river setting occurs in the Romantic tradition, Huck beholds inhumaneness on shore representative of realism.

In the novel, Twain develops many thematic strains, including outsider, insufferable religion, superstitious beliefs, civilization versus primitivism, and humans maltreating humans. Huck, outcast and poor because of his sluggard father, wants acceptance from Tom Sawyer and the boys with whom he plays robbers. After Miss Watson tells him to pray for what he wants, Huck unsuccessfully requests fish line and hooks. "I asked Miss Watson to try for me, but she said I was a fool. She never told me why, and I couldn't make it out no way." Huck questions why Providence would want him, "seeing I was so ignorant and so kind of low-down and ornery." When Miss Watson tells him "about the bad place," he wishes "I was there." Going "around all day long with a harp and sing[ing], forever and ever" has no appeal for Huck, especially with Miss Watson watching.

But Huck and Jim understand each other's foibles, and they see import in many different occurrences. Those that seem unlucky they try to control by throwing salt over their shoulders. Each time Huck goes ashore, "civilization" chills him while the primitivism of the river consoles both. "The sky looks ever so deep when you lay down on your back in the moonshine; I never knowed it before." He adds, "It's lovely to live on a raft. We had the sky, up there, all speckled with stars, and we used to lay on our backs and look up at them, and discuss about whether they was made, or only just happened." Huck comments, "We said there warn't no home like a raft, after all. Other places do seem so cramped up and smothery, but a raft don't. You feel mighty free and easy and comfortable on a raft." Huck and Jim do not wear clothes on the raft, a symbol of the Edenic cleanliness they feel. It contrasts with the family feud between the Grangerfords and the Shepherdsons on shore and the duke and the dauphin's bilking of audiences with their "performances." Although Huck feels unkindly toward these men after they force themselves aboard the raft, when people finally tar and feather the two, Huck reflects that "human beings *can* be awful cruel to one another." Huck also sees Colonel Sherburn murder Boggs and brazenly blames those watching for being a pitiful mob.

Huck avoids his father because "he tanned me so much," and, when his father reappears, he demands "You git me that money to-morrow—I want it," accuses him of being a "big-bug," and berates Huck for learning to read. He says, "If I catch you about that school I'll tan you good. First you know you'll get religion, too." After Huck escapes, Jim becomes Huck's surrogate father. Jim's kind treatment of Huck, perhaps the first Huck has ever had, and his anguish over Huck's subsequent inconsiderateness awakens Huck's own ability to care for another. Jim says, "When I got all wore out wid work, en wid de callin' for you, en went to sleep, my heart wuz mos' broke bekase you wuz los',' en I didn' k'yer no mo' what become er me en de raf' . En when I wake up en fine you back again,' all safe en soun,' de tears come en I could a got down on my knees en kiss' yo; foot I's so thankful. En all you wuz thinkin' bout wuz how you could make a fool uv ole Jim wid a lie. Dat truck dah is *trash*; en trash is what people is dat puts dirt on de head er dey fren's en makes 'em ashamed."

Shocked, Huck realizes that he will always protect Jim. "It made me feel so mean I could almost kissed *his* foot to get him to take it back. . . . I didn't do him no more mean tricks, and I wound't done that one if I'd a knowed it would make him feel that way." Huck, however, still feels guilty for not reporting Jim to authorities because he is breaking the law. "People would call me a low down Ablitionist and despise me for keeping mum—but that don't make no difference. I ain't agoing to tell, and I ain't agoing back there anyways.'" Huck eventually admits that he will go to hell if that is the consequence for protecting Jim. Tom Sawyer's offer to free Jim shocks Huck, but when Huck discovers that Jim was free all along, he feels better about Tom's involvement. After Jim discovers his freedom, he confesses that the dead man floating down the river was Huck's father, but Jim's affection helps Huck avoid the pain of being an orphan.

The Death of Jim Loney by James Welch

In James Welch's *The Death of Jim Loney* (1979), Jim Loney searches for his identity first by reconnecting with his absent father and choosing how he will die. Loney's Gros Ventre mother Eletra left when he was one, and when he was eight or nine, his white father Ike "went out drinking one night and didn't return for twelve years." Loney attended mission school in southern Montana where he played basketball, helping to win a state championship. The omniscient point of view reveals what others think about Loney as well as his own insecurities. Russell, a Native-American bartender, calls Loney "The Lone Ranger" but decides while serving him bourbon that "what he hated in Loney, [was] the fact that he didn't seem to care." Kenny, another bartender, discloses that Eletra went insane after leaving the family. Loney's affair with Rhea ends when he declines to move to Washington state with her, and after agreeing to go deer hunting with Pretty Weasel, he mistakes Weasel for a bear and kills him. After Loney's fascination with death reminds him of a Bible verse, "Turn away from man in whose nostrils is breath, for of what account is he?" he leaves Rhea, tells his father about Weasel, and decides that tribal policemen will kill him in Mission Canyon. He lures them to the site and deliberately faces his death.

Loney has had three valuable relationships in his life—Rhea, Kate, and a surrogate mother named Sandra. Rhea, a schoolteacher, had come to Montana two years before after visiting a museum with a Texas boyfriend where "an old dissatisfaction hit her like a mistral wind and she felt quite empty." Loney tells her, "Rhea, you're the only friend I've got in the whole world," and she proves it by writing his sister Kate with concerns about his behavior. Kate knows that "he saw things strangely, yet clearly" and notes that he has a "face like a wolf, so canny and innocent." Loney feels disengaged because "he couldn't think of a way in the world to be good enough." When he imagines a woman behind a Catholic church searching for her son, he wants to help; yet when he dreams of birds, they never show him how to fly. The third important relationship was with a woman he thought was an aunt who fed him cocoa and celebrated Christmas and Easter with him. His father finally tells him that Sandra was a social worker who stayed after coming to investigate the children. Loney remembers, "Of all the women in his life, she was the one he had tried hardest to love." Throughout his life, Loney has tried to create a background for himself, "something that would tell him who he was."

At twenty, Loney discovers his father's identity and avoids him, but at thirty-five, Loney realizes he has "no real love in his life" and approaches his father, who has never admitted his parentage, to ask about his mother. Ike tells him that she is a full-blooded Gros Ventre named Eletra Calf Looking, but he does not admit that she has become insane. (One must compare Loney's fascination with "the blue veins on the backs of his neighbor's legs" with his desire to know his mother, Eletra "Calf Looking.") Ike also tells him about Sandra. Loney then understands that "it was he [Loney] who was guilty, and in a way that made his father's past sins seem childish, as though original sin were something akin to stealing candy bars." Loney dreams that his father hands him a gun, and after telling his father that he has killed Pretty Weasel, Ike actually does give him a gun. Loney shoots at his father's porch light before leaving, knowing that shards of glass in his face will make Ike report Loney's actions to the police. At Mission Canyon, Loney searches for the "possibility of spirit," accepting the place as a door to his eternity, while waiting for the police to kill him. Because "his father had never instructed him in anything" and he has had no kindness from a male, Ike has had the benefit of neither biological nor surrogate father.

Absalom, Absalom! by William Faulkner

In *Absalom, Absalom!* (1936), Charles Bon wants his father Thomas Sutpen to recognize his existence. Sutpen ("man-horse-demon" with a "faint sulphur-reek") disappears from Bon's life and creates Sutpen's Hundred on 100 square miles of land purchased in 1833 from Ikkemotubbe. He then captures a French architect and coerces him along with a band of unruly men to build and landscape the house and grounds in two years. Using four unreliable narrators, William Faulkner weaves the plots of Sutpen's past, his two families (one acknowledged and Charles Bon's that he "put aside"), and Quentin at Harvard in this gothic examination of the sins of the forefathers in the South. Faulkner's style, incorporating stream of consciousness and historical layers, re-creates the heat of Rosa Coldfield's stagnant summer and Sutpen's singular vision. The biblical title refers to King David's lament at the death of his son Absalom, "O my son, Absalom, my son, my son Absalom! Would I had died for you, O Absalom, my son, my son!" (2 Samuel 18:33). Absalom had attempted to usurp his father's throne after being exiled for the murder of his half-brother Amnon for raping his half-sister Tamar; Absalom failed.

Four narrators piece together this epic puzzle—Mr. Compson (Quentin's grandfather), Quentin Compson, Shreve McCannon, and Rosa Coldfield. Rosa, dressed in black at forty-three, invites Quentin, twenty, to her home in September 1909 before he leaves for Harvard, telling him that she wants him, as an aspiring writer, to know how Sutpen "tore violently a plantation." She tells about Sutpen's marriage to her sister Ellen and his children, Judith and Henry. After Ellen's death and the Civil War, Sutpen asks Rosa to have his child and promises marriage if she bears a son. She refuses, and Sutpen instead impregnates Wash Jones' fifteen-year-old granddaughter. When the child is female, Sutpen rejects Milly. Wash Jones kills them both. Then Rosa asks Quentin to go with her to Sutpen's Hundred where Sutpen's daughter by a slave, Clytemnestra, allegedly hides Sutpen's son Henry, come home to die. Quentin must reason why Rosa chose to tell him the story. He finally surmises that he is the storyteller, the one Rosa chose "*so that people whom she will never see and whose names she will never hear and who have never heard her name nor seen her face will read it and know at last why God let us lose the War: that only through the blood of our men and the tears of our women could He stay this demon and efface his name and lineage from the earth.*"

Quentin tells his version of the story to his Canadian roommate at Harvard. Shreve extrapolates and analyzes the information on 10 January 1910, the day Quentin receives the letter telling him that Rosa has died, probably of "outrage," four months before Quentin's suicide (*The Sound and the Fury*). Shreve concludes that Sutpen wanted a grandson. But, more important, Shreve tries to understand the South, asking "What is it? Something you live and breathe in like the air? A kind of vacuum filled with wraithlike and indomitable anger and pride and glory at and in happenings that occurred and ceased fifty years ago?" Quentin responds, "You can't understand it. You would have to be born there." When Shreve asks Quentin why he hates the South, Quentin vehemently denies it: "I don't hate it I don't. I don't."

As Sutpen's only friend, Mr. Compson explains Sutpen's motivation—being refused entry by a Negro servant to the front door of a plantation house at fourteen when he did not know houses had two doors. Sutpen determined that his retaliation for this indignity would be to own a plantation with a mansion and begat a family dynasty. When Judith takes the letter found on Charles Bon's dead body to Quentin's grandmother, Mr. Compson learns about her need for affirmation. Judith says of the letter that it is something that can mark her presence on earth. "And so maybe if you could go to someone . . . and give them something—a scrap of paper—something, anything, it not to mean anything in itself and them not even to read it or keep it, not even bother to throw it away or destroy it, at least it would be something just because it would have happened." For her entire life, Judith lived in the shadow of others, only to discover that she had based her life on a fabrication, a past that never was and a future that could never be.

Sutpen discards his first wife when he discovers she is black rather than Spanish, and along with her, he denies his son Charles Bon. But Bon does not forget Sutpen; too old for the university, he attends anyway and befriends Sutpen's son Henry. Henry brings him home, and Charles thinks *"so at last I shall see him, whom it seems I was bred up never to expect to see, whom I had even learned to live without."* Ellen decides that her daughter Judith will marry Charles Bon, and the two become engaged. Sutpen never acknowledges Bon, his son, saying, "—He must not marry her, Henry. His mother's father told me that her mother had been a Spanish woman. I believed him; it was not until after he was born that I found out that his mother was part negro." When Henry confronts Charles, he says "—So it's the miscegenation, not the incest, which you cant bear. Henry doesn't answer." Henry does not want to murder Bon and says "—You are my brother. Charles goads Henry,—No I'm not. I'm the nigger that's going to sleep with your sister. Unless you stop me, Henry." Thus Charles Bon is "the son who widowed the daughter who had not yet been a bride." Sutpen's legacy traces not through Judith and Henry but through Charles Bon's son from an earlier liaison who comes to Sutpen's Hundred in 1871, marries a black, and bears a retarded child named Jim Bond who has no issue. The ultimate inhumanity of denying his progeny defeats Sutpen's desperate dynasty.

A father who renounces his son abnegates his own future. In Martin Buber's existentialist terms, the fathers of Huck, Jim Loney, and Charles Bon have treated their sons as an "It" rather than a "Thou," as things to be used rather than as humans to be loved. These men suffer for their transgressions while their sons struggle for not having a father acknowledge their value as human beings.

Additional Related Novels

Baldwin, James. *Go Tell It on the Mountain.*
Bellow, Saul. *Henderson, the Rain King; Seize the Day.*
Erdrich, Louise. *Love Medicine.*
Johnson, Charles. *Middle Passage.*
Kerouac, Jack. *On the Road*
Kesey, Ken. *One Flew Over the Cuckoo's Nest.*
Malamud, Bernard. *The Assistant.*
Ng, Fae Myenne. *Bone.*
Plath, Sylvia. *The Bell Jar.*
Warren, Robert Penn. *All the King's Men.*

Search for Identity

No price is too high to pay for the privilege of owning yourself.
—Friedrich Nietzsche, *Thus Spake Zarathustra* (1883)

Thoughtful humans usually try to find their true identity—through realistic expectations of themselves. Perhaps one of the largest barriers to their discovery is the inability to overcome their perception of others' attitudes toward them. In *Passing*, both Clare Kendry and Irene Redfield must decide whether they associate with blacks or whites. Fools Crow in *Fools Crow* earns his name and a reputation for courage by fooling and killing the Crow chief, Bull Shield. Having interest in little other than movies, Jack Bolling in *The Moviegoer* eventually chooses an identity that his aunt suggests for him. In *A Separate Peace*, Gene cannot escape the shadow of Finny's death until he returns to the scene of their 1942 summer exploits while Oedipa Maas, in *The Crying of Lot 49*, wanders through a maze of places and people, incapable of answering even one question about her beliefs. In the novels, *The Awakening*, *I Am the Cheese*, and *The Joy Luck Club*, the protagonists find their identities, but the results are very different.

In the *OED*, "identity," since the early seventeenth century, has referred to "the sameness of a person or thing at all times or in all circumstances; the condition or fact that a person or thing is itself and not something else; individuality, personality." In 1638, Francis Bacon said "the Duration of Bodies is Twofold; One in Identity, or the selfe-same Substance; the other by a Renovation or Reparation" (*History Naturall and Experimentall of Life and Death*). In 1690, John Locke commented, "consciousness always accompanies thinking. . . . in this alone consists personal Identity" (*An Essay Concerning Human Understanding*). And by 1969, Robert Terwilliger claimed that "committing yourself is a way of finding out who you are. A man finds his identity by identifying. A man's identity is not best thought of as the way in which he is separated from his fellows but the way in which he is united with them." In the novels, *The Awakening*, *I Am the Cheese*, and *The Joy Luck Club*, the protagonists must first discover what makes them different from others before they can understand themselves, but only one has the opportunity to enlarge "identity by identifying."

The Awakening by Kate Chopin

The protagonist of *The Awakening* (1899), Edna Pontellier, vacations with Creoles on Grand Isle in Jefferson Parish, Louisiana, each summer. Edna, twenty-eight, stays with her two young sons during the week at Madame Lebrun's cottages while her forty-year-old husband returns to New Orleans. Originally from Protestant Kentucky, outsider Edna is surprised at the Catholic Creoles' "entire absence of prudery." She eventually becomes friends with Adèle Ratignolle, a mothering woman who has born three children in six years and expects another. She also becomes acquainted with Madame Lebrun's son Robert. The way Kate Chopin depicts Edna's relationship with Robert and her resulting awareness of her own interests and identity caused critics to denounce the novel, and not until the mid-twentieth century did it gain the acclaim it initially deserved.

During the summer, Edna's unequal relationship with her husband begins to burden her. She resents him, knowing that "her marriage to Léonce Pontellier was purely an accident, in this respect resembling many other marriages which masquerade as the decrees of faith." During the week, he sends boxes of sweets from New Orleans, and the other women declare him "the best husband in the world." After Edna meets Robert, Léonce comes home late from his club, awakens her for his sexual pleasure, and goes to sleep, while "an indescribable oppression, which seemed to generate in some unfamiliar part of her consciousness, filled her whole being with a vague anguish." When Léonce takes her back to New Orleans, she realizes that she is no more than property to him, and Mr. Pontellier "greatly valued his possessions, chiefly because they were his."

Edna becomes aware of her discontent when she notices how much she enjoys Robert's attention and how much her husband treats her like an asset. At first, "Robert talked a good deal about himself. He was very young, and did not know any better." Her interest in him increases gradually, "when some pretext served to take him away from her, just as one misses the sun on a cloudy day without having thought much about the sun when it was shining." Under Robert's tutelage, Edna learns to swim and allows herself to react emotionally to the beauty of Mademoiselle Reisz's piano performances. In the early fall, Robert suddenly leaves for Mexico, and Edna's life clouds. Edna eventually visits Mademoiselle Reisz, who reads Robert's letter to her saying he is coming back. Edna " was already glad and happy to be alive at the mere thought of his return." Later, she meets Robert and informs him, "I am no longer one of Mr. Pontellier's possessions to dispose of or not. *I give* myself where I choose." When she asks Robert to wait for her return from the birth of Adèle Ratignolle's fourth child, he instead writes a note and slinks away.

Edna's change surprises her husband and acquaintances. At first, she is unaware of her developing identity. "That she was seeing with different eyes and making the acquaintance of new conditions in herself that colored and changed her environment, she did not yet suspect." She refuses her husband's summons to his bed, and, in New Orleans, she stops receiving her Tuesday guests. Distressed that she did not observe "*les conveyances*" (conventions) of society, Léonce believes, "it's just such seeming trifles that we've got to take seriously; such things count.'" Angry at Léonce, she takes "off her wedding ring [and flings] it upon the carpet." To Edna, "It seemed to her as if life were passing by, leaving its promise broken and unfulfilled." Her father arrives from Kentucky to coerce her into attending her sister's wedding, but she refuses. While Pontellier travels on business to New York, she goes to the horse races with Alcée Arobin and Mrs. Highcamp and decides to ask Mme. Ratignolle to evaluate her sketches. Léonce, shocked by her independence, asks Dr. Mandelet for advice, but he can offer none because Edna "reminded him of some beautiful, sleek animal waking up in the sun."

Edna decides to use money from her inheritance, winnings at the track, and the sale of her sketches to support herself in a small house, but, before she leaves, Léonce contrives to send the children to his mother's home and redecorate his house so no one will suspect their separation. Adèle warns her not to forget her children, but, after Robert deserts her, Edna can only focus on her inability to fulfill her "awakening." Mlle. Reisz had warned her, "The bird that would soar above the level plain of tradition must have strong wings. It is a sad spectacle to see the weaklings bruised, exhausted, fluttering back to earth." Edna returns to Grand Isle where, "beside the sea, absolutely alone, she cast the unpleasant, pricking garments from her, and for the first time in her life, she stood naked in the open air." She walks into the ocean, preferring the seduction of "the voice of the sea" to an existence based on society's acceptance of gender inequality. Edna searches for and finds her identity, but no one will acknowledge her as herself.

I Am the Cheese by Robert Cormier

Instead of committing suicide, Adam Farmer in *I Am the Cheese* (1985) faces possible extermination after he discovers his true identity. Robert Cormier uses parallel plot lines, each with indeterminate endings. In one, Adam's first-person point of view describes his seventy-mile bike ride from Monument, Massachusetts, to Ruttenburg, Vermont, where his father is a hospital patient. Alternating chapters in limited omniscient are question-and-answer sessions in which Brint, either a psychiatrist or a government official, interrogates Adam about details of his life before the ambush during which his mother was murdered and his father either escaped or died. Adam recalls very little.

Not until he is fourteen does Adam discover his past and that his real name is Paul Delmonte. His friend, Amy Hertz, telephones him and invites him to meet a newspaper editor visiting from Adam's old hometown of Rawlings, Pennsylvania. The man knows no Farmers and none of the people that Adam names. Wondering why, Adam secretly searches his father's locked desk and discovers two birth certificates for himself, one dated for February 14 and the other, July 14. He hears his mother make her Thursday night telephone call to a Martha as she has for years, and he sees the "gray man," Mr. Grey, accompany his father to their fortified basement. Sensing Adam's suspicion, his father tells him that the family had to enter a federal re-identification program after he testified against Mafia criminals in Washington. Adam, or Paul, was three when the family disappeared in the middle of the night, and Adam's father shows him an article in the paper announcing their deaths. Soon after Adam hears the story, someone contacts them and tells them to leave home for a few days. The family sees someone following, feels relieved to recognize the car's occupants, and stops to enjoy a vista. The driver speeds toward them and kills Adam's mother while his father escapes in the woods.

Since this occurrence, someone has kept Adam drugged and confined to a hospital. The peculiarities of Adam's discovery about his identity emerge during the interrogation chapters. Some of the questions make Adam think that Amy and her father were involved in the plot to destroy the family rather than Amy merely supplying comic relief to Adam's life with her pranks. Adam remembers little, having never questioned why the family had no relatives or friends in Monument except for Amy. His questioners have not yet been given the authority to terminate him, but if he remembers something, one expects the order to rapidly follow. In the last few pages of the novel, Cormier reveals that Adam's long bicycle ride is actually a circuit of the hospital grounds. On his route, he encounters terrors that are literally bullying patients and a barking German shepherd. Throughout his cycling, he sings "The Farmer in the Dell," a comforting song that he often sang with his father. Adam asserts, "I am the cheese" because "the cheese stands alone." Adam does stand alone, against an organization, either private or government, that will dispose of him after it has finished with him. His true identity threatens his life, and he can never reunite with his past.

The Joy Luck Club by Amy Tan

In *The Joy Luck Club* (1989), finding identity threatens the characters psychologically instead of physically. Amy Tan allows June (Jing) to be the thread of continuity among the seven voices in the sixteen first-person point of view chapters. The event precipitating the reflections of three mothers and four daughters is a meeting of the Joy Luck Club after June's mother dies unexpectedly from a cerebral aneurysm. The four mothers formed the club as a way to survive in Japanese-occupied China. "We weren't allowed to think a bad thought. . . . And each week, we could hope to be lucky. That hope was our only joy. And that's how we came to call our little parties Joy Luck." June, "always tardy," has been invited to take her mother's place at the table. During the game, the mothers ("aunties" to June) disclose their plan that she will go to China using money they invested in the stock market. They tell her that in response to her mother's many letters to China about the children she had to leave there, a letter arrived just after her death with information. The aunties expect June and her mother's second husband to meet the two daughters in China.

While reflecting about their experiences in China, the mothers reveal a depth of culture, heartache, and courage. A wealthy man betrayed An-Mei Hsu's widowed mother, and she had no choice but to become his concubine. Banished from An-Mei and other family, she commits suicide on the day of the lunar new year when "all debts must be paid, or disaster and misfortunes will follow," because Wu Tsing will then honor her children, An-Mei and Syaudi. An-Mei's daughter, Rose Hse Jordan, feels guilty, thinking she allowed her four-year-old brother Bing to drown. When Rose becomes an adult, her mother warns her that she should think for herself rather than allowing others to decide for her. After her mother's accusation, Rose surveys the progress of her marriage and thinks about its disintegration. "I had seen the signs . . . but I just let it happen." Rose begins to understand her mother's intense faith as she reflects, "that fate is shaped half by expectation, half by inattention. But somehow, when you lose something you love, faith takes over. You have to pay attention to what you lost. You have to undo the expectation." Initially dependent on psychiatry, Rose suddenly frees herself from her own indecisions and refuses to leave the home she loves or take her husband's money.

Betrothed at two, Lindo Jong leaves her own family at twelve and marries at sixteen. On her wedding day, "I wiped my eyes and looked in the mirror. . . . I had on a beautiful red dress, but what I saw was even more valuable. I was strong. I was pure. I had genuine thoughts inside that no one could see, that no one could ever take away from me." Feeling comfortable with her own identity at an early age, Lindo extracts herself from the marriage by accusing her immature, impotent husband of impregnating a servant girl, and of her own dreams that she will kill him. Frightened, Lindo's mother-in-law dissolves the marriage. About her own daughter, Waverly, she laments, "It's my fault she is this way. I wanted my children to have the best combination: American circumstances and Chinese character. How could I know these two things do not mix." But Waverly has learned from her mother. Waverly remembers, "I was six when my mother taught me the art of invisible strength. It was a strategy for winning arguments, respect from others, and eventually, though neither of us knew it at the time, chess games." She becomes a national chess champion by age nine, but, irritated at her mother's admonishments about her game, quits five years later. Waverly, however, wants her mother's approval for her marriage to Rich, a Caucasian.

Ying-Ying St. Clair remembers a celebration during her childhood when she made a wish. "It is my earliest recollection: telling the Moon Lady my secret wish. And because I forgot what I wished for, that memory remained hidden from me all these many years." As she gets older, she remembers how the day reflected her life, "the same innocence, trust, and restlessness, the wonder, fear, and loneliness. How I lost myself." But finally, she recalls "what I asked the Moon Lady so long ago. I wished to be found." Ying-Ying was a wild child whose marriage to an older man was arranged. While she was pregnant, he abandoned her for an opera singer, and she decided to kill her child before its birth. She remarried only after his death. She visits her daughter Lena and her husband Harold and thinks, "All around this house I see the signs. My daughter looks but does not see. This is a house that will break into pieces. How do I know? I have always known a thing before it happens." While Harold has been usurping the architectural business they created, Lena has not interfered. When a table falls in Lena's guestroom, her mother makes no apology. Lena says "I knew it would happen." Attempting to give Lena some of her own tiger strength, Ying-Ying responds, "Then why you don't stop it?" Lena agrees, knowing "it's such a simple question."

Although Suyuan can no longer tell her story, insights about her life appear in Jing's narratives. Jing does not want to go to China without the sisters knowing that her mother is dead. She says, "They'll think I'm responsible, that she died because I didn't appreciate her." Auntie Lindo's sad expression helps Jing begin to understand. Always defiant of her mother's wishes, Jing has either disobeyed or ignored her. In China, relatives tell Jing that her mother, weak with dysentery, left her twin daughters with all her money and jewels beside the road as she escaped from Chungking because she had no strength to carry them. Her husband dead and her children gone, she began a new life. When June meets the two sisters, they take a Polaroid, and "although we don't speak, I know we all see it: Together we look like our mother. Her same eyes, her same mouth, open in surprise to see, at last, her long-cherished wish."

All of the daughters assert themselves, reject their mothers, and then come to understand that only by accepting all aspects of their identities can they be strong. The wisdom of their Chinese mothers is embodied in Ying Ying's concern about Lena: "All her life, I have watched her as though from another shore. And now I must tell her everything about my past. It is the only way to penetrate her skin and pull her to where she can be saved." These mothers all know from their own lives that "your mother is in your bones!" and that daughters cannot and should not try to deny their complete identities. Not until each daughter realizes the value of her mother's wisdom can she proceed to a fuller life.

Finding one's identity is a painful process. It involves discarding cherished ideas of oneself, exposing oneself to others, and refusing to accept their expectations instead of one's own. In these three novels, the protagonists all come to the understanding that they are not who they thought and that they must build anew on a different foundation. Edna in *The Awakening* has no strength to continue. In *I Am the Cheese*, Adam has lost everything, but drugs help him forget some of the pains of identity. And in *The Joy Luck Club*, the daughters find themselves much better prepared for happiness with their integrated identities intact.

Additional Related Novels

Anaya, Rudolfo. *Bless Me, Ultima*.
Barrett, William E. *The Lilies of the Field*.
Bellow, Saul. *Henderson, the Rain King; Seize the Day*.
Cahan, Abraham. *The Rise of David Levinsky*.
Cormier, Robert. *After the First Death; The Chocolate War*
Crane, Stephen. *Maggie: A Girl of the Streets*.
Dickey, James. *Deliverance*.
Doctorow, E. L. *Ragtime*.
Dorris, Michael. *A Yellow Raft in Blue Water*.
Ellison, Ralph. *Invisible Man*.
Flagg, Fannie. *Fried Green Tomatoes at the Whistle Stop Café*.
Gaines, Ernest J. *The Autobiography of Miss Jane Pittman; A Lesson Before Dying; A Gathering of Old Men*.
Kingston, Maxine Hong. *The Woman Warrior*.
Knowles, John. *A Separate Peace*.
Lewis, Sinclair. *Main Street*.
Malamud, Bernard. *The Fixer*.
McCullers, Carson. *The Heart Is a Lonely Hunter*.
McMillan, Terry. *Mama*.
Momaday, N. Scott. *House Made of Dawn*.
Morrison, Toni. *The Bluest Eye; Tar Baby*.
Olsen, Tillie. *Tell Me a Riddle*.
Percy, Walker. *The Moviegoer*.
Potok, Chaim. *The Chosen*.
Proulx, E. Annie. *The Shipping News*.
Pynchon, Thomas. *The Crying of Lot 49*.
Roth, Philip. *Goodbye, Columbus*.
Silko, Leslie Marmon. *Ceremony*.
Smith, Betty. *A Tree Grows in Brooklyn*.
Styron, William. *The Confessions of Nat Turner*.
Turner, Nancy E. *These Is My Words*.
Twain, Mark. *The Adventures of Huckleberry Finn*.
Walker, Alice. *The Color Purple*.
Warren, Robert Penn. *All the King's Men*.
Welch, James. *The Death of Jim Loney*.
Wharton, Edith. *House of Mirth*.

Storytelling

[The art of the novel] happens because the storyteller's own experience of men and things, whether for good or ill—not only what he has passed through himself, but even events which he has only witnessed or been told of—has moved him to an emotion so passionate that he can no longer keep it shut up in his heart.

—Murasaki Shikibu, *The Tale of the Genji* (ca.1000)

As the gatekeepers of a society, storytellers relay the values and expectations that a community has for its members. In *The Joy Luck Club*, the mothers "say" stories to their daughters. A narrator hears the unhappy story of Ethan, Zina, and Maggie from his landlady and retells it in *Ethan Frome*. In *The Things They Carried*, the narrator details the items and their significance that the soldiers carry in the Vietnamese jungle while fighting guerilla warfare. A writer who wants to tell about World War II becomes the narrator of *Slaughterhouse-Five* and fuses fact with fantasy in the character of Billy Pilgrim. In *The Autobiography of Miss Jane Pittman*, recording the story of Jane's life becomes the frame for retelling it. In *Their Eyes Were Watching God*, *The Woman Warrior*, and *Ceremony*, the protagonists each belong to different cultural backgrounds, but within each, the oral tradition guides the development of their lives.

The *OED* defines "story" as "a narrative, true or presumed to be true, relating to important events and celebrated persons of a more or less remote past; a historical relation or anecdote." A person who relates these narratives is "one who tells stories" or a storyteller. The Greek word "mythos" means "story," and myths along with legends, fables, and folk tales constitute the oral tradition. A speaker in *Ancien Riwle* suggests, "tellen ou [{th}]eos storie uor hit were to long to writen ham here" (1225). John Richardson comments that "professed storytellers . . . are of early date in the East" (*A Dissertation on the Literature and Languages of Eastern Nations*, 1777), and Thomas Lynch in *The Rivulet* recognizes "the powers of ancient story" (1855). The authors of *Their Eyes Were Watching God*, *The Woman Warrior*, and *Ceremony* all appreciate the power of story and weave them into their narratives about African Americans, Chinese Americans, and Native Americans.

Their Eyes Were Watching God by Zora Neale Hurston

In *Their Eyes Were Watching God* (1937), Zora Neale Hurston uses a frame story with omniscient point of view to tell about Janie Crawford in Florida during the 1920s. Other important devices include metaphors and symbols emblematic of her three communities such as the pear tree, guitar, headrag, and overalls; dialect; folklore; Bible stories; and folk games. Janie's mother, raped by a white schoolteacher, disappeared when Janie was four, and Janie's former slave grandmother raised her with white children so that she did not know she was black until she saw a picture of herself at age six. Her grandmother wanted security for Janie and married her to Logan Killicks and his sixty acres. Janie had dreamed after watching bees copulate on a pear tree that marriage would bring love, but after marrying Logan, she realizes that marriage gurrantees nothing. The narrator marks the occasion; "Janie's first dream was dead, so she became a woman." Logan treats Janie like hired help, and she leaves with the well-dressed Joe Starks, settling in the all-black town of Eatonville where Starks becomes the mayor and store owner. After Joe dies, Vergible Woods, twelve years younger and known as Tea Cake, comes into the store, asks her to play checkers, and falls in love. She wears a blue silk dress to Jacksonville, marries him, and returns eighteen months later wearing overalls. When the women begin gossiping that Tea Cake took her money and disappeared, Janie's good friend Phoeby Watson comments that "an envious heart makes a treacherous ear. They done 'heard' 'bout you just what they hope done happened." Janie tells Phoeby about her "journey to the horizon and back as a delegate to de big 'association of life.' "

Even though Janie initially ignores neighbors, community plays a significant part in her life as it gathers on the porch. Joe first meets with the Eatonville men on a porch, and later, he forbids Janie to speak on the porch. After meeting Tea Cake, Janie sits on the porch and watches the moon's "amber fluid . . . drenching the earth, and quenching the thirst of day." Personification makes "the porch laugh" and metaphor makes it "boil." From the porch, Joe's purchase of a maltreated mule makes him look magnanimous. He rules from the porch with his loud voice, and Janie watches the townspeople agree with him because he is wealthy and has power. Then she understands that they have allowed him to amass the things that they seem to admire. Janie knows that Joe's money makes him like the whites. "You have tuh have power tuh free things and dat makes you lak uh king uh something." On the porch, Joe also plays the dozens, a folk game of verbal insults. After Janie marries Tea Cake, their doorstep in the Everglades near Lake Okeechobee becomes the porch, and Janie finds her voice for storytelling while Tea Cake communicates with the community through music. From the "porch," however, Tea Cake mistakenly discounts the Seminoles' departure before a storm. He does not understand the signs in nature that would alert him about the intense hurricane waiting to attack while "dead day was creeping from bush to bush watching man." As the wind begins to blow, Janie, Tea Cake, and Motor Boat gape at the door and "seemed to be staring at the dark, but their eyes were watching God." When Tea Cake tries to save Janie from drowning, a mad dog bites him. After he is "pressed into service to clear the wreckage in public places," burying black victims in a mass grave and whites in coffins, he and Janie decide to leave. But rabies craze Tea Cake, and in his madness, he tries to murder Janie, and she has to use her new shootipng skill to kill him. After her jury acquittal, she returns to Eatonville with her memories and an appreciation of the efficacy of nature.

Throughout, Janie becomes more autonomous. Her Nanny says, "De nigger woman is de mule uh de world so fur as Ah can see. Ah been prayin' fuh it tuh be different wid you." Janie wants men to speak in rhymes rather than through mules, but neither Logan nor Joe understand. "Joe spoke out without giving her a chance to say anything and it took the bloom off of things," and he tells her when she makes a measurement mistake in the store, "Somebody got to think for women and children and chickens and cows." When Janie reaches thirty-five, she first defies Joe's hostility. She tells him, "Sometimes God gits familiar wid us womenfolks. . . . He told me how surprised . . . y'all is goin' tuh be if you ever find out you don't know half as much 'bout us as you think you do. It's so easy to make yo'self out God Almight when you ain't got nothin' tuh strain against but women and chickens. She accuses him, that after twenty years, "you don't half know me atall." Then one day, she plays the dozens and calls him Methuselah. Shocked, "his vanity bled like a flood . . . robb[ing] him of his illusion of irresistible maleness." She leaves, and on his death day, she tears off the despised headrag to symbolize her freedom. For his funeral, she "starched and ironed her face . . . and herself went [privately] rollicking with the springtime." Tea Cake arrives, and for the first time, someone admires her hair, her mouth, and her eyes. He reminds her of Love and, the "bee to a blossom. . . . He was a glance from God." When Janie returns to Eatonsville after Tea Cake's death, she tells Phoeby, "love is lak de sea. It's uh movin' thing, but still and all, it takes its shape from de shore it meets, and it's different with every shore." Janie concludes that "two things everybody's got tuh do fuh theyselves. They got tuh go tuh God, and they got tuh find out about livin' fuh theyselves."

The Woman Warrior by Maxine Hong Kingston

Although published as nonfiction, *The Woman Warrior* (1977) blends autobiographical elements with fiction as Maxine Hong Kingston relates the stories of her mother, the family, and her need to find her American self. She uses first person to relate the talk-stories of her mother and extrapolate from them how the subject might have responded. Her own imagination and metaphor combined with her mother's memory make them her stories. She also includes myth, legend, family history, and ghost tales. She says, "Night after night my mother would talk-story until we fell asleep. I could not tell where the stories left off and the dreams begin." Of the five parts, "No Name Woman," "White

Tigers," "Shaman," "At the Western Palace," and "A Song for a Barbarian
Reed Pipe," the second and fifth parts relate directly to Kingston as Chinese
trying to find identity in America, and the other three reveal her mother and
her family as they adjust to unpleasant circumstances.

Brave Orchid, the narrator's mother, instructs her daughter through her
stories. Her husband's sister who drowned herself and her baby in the family
well after the villagers destroyed the family's home because "adultery is extrav-
agance" warns the narrator about the consequences of pregnancy out of wedlock. The narrator speculates that her aunt would have welcomed a male child,
but her mother tells only what is "powered by Necessity, a riverbank that
guides her life." The narrator wonders if the woman had been raped or if she
had consented to the tryst. "His demand must have surprised, then terrified
her. She obeyed him; she always did as she was told," even though the man
might have been in her own household. The narrator knows, however, that the
worst punishment would be the family's denial of her existence so that her
ghost would have no place to rest.

Brave Orchid's husband left her in China for fifteen years, and after losing
both her children, she attended medical school. She observes that "the Revolution put an end to prostitution by giving women what they wanted: a job and
a room of their own." Her mother was a physician until the Japanese came, but
in America, she is a laundry worker who bore six children after turning
forty-five. Brave Orchid wants all her children to live at home because she left
her own mother. They reject her wishes, and the narrator comments, "Before
we can leave our parents, they stuff our heads like the suitcases which they
jam-pack with homemade underwear." The narrator hears the story of Moon
Orchid, Brave Orchid's sister arriving in America thirty years later to find her
husband, from her sister who heard it from her brother. Moon Orchid's "misplaced spirit" left her incapable of facing her younger Americanized husband
and his wife after his continued financial support, and the only place she feels
safe from imagined Mexican ghosts is in an asylum.

The narrator's own life involves overcoming the oppression she feels as a
Chinese woman in America. Her aunt's story causes her to avoid making herself "American-pretty" and possibly attractive to non-Chinese males. One of
Brave Orchid's talk-stories tells of Fa Mu Lan, a warrior woman who invented
white crane boxing. She left her family to receive training from two elderly
people so that she could save the Hans. She learns to be quiet, and, at
twenty-two, although she cannot fly like a bird, she "could point at the sky and
make a sword appear, a silver bolt in the sunlight, and control its slashing with
my mind." During her training, she copied the tigers but "needed adult wisdom to know dragons." The warrior woman knows that "it is more profitable
to raise geese than daughters." And the narrator hears this message constantly.
Her uncle entertains the boys on Saturday, not the girls. She says, "I would
have liked to bring myself back as a boy for my parents to welcome with chickens and pigs." And she adds, "There is a Chinese word for the female *I*—which

is 'slave.' " As a girl no one would purchase, "When I visit the family now, I wrap my American successes around me like a private shawl; I *am* worthy of eating the food."

She continues to sort through the talk-stories, trying to understand what is real and what is not. Blood Orchid tells her about the knot-maker whose knot was outlawed for its difficulty. The narrator declares, "If I had lived in China, I would have been an outlaw knot-maker." But she lives in America, and instead, she cruelly taunts a girl for not talking. Her penance lasts eighteen months, the time to recover from an illness that infects her immediately after the incident. She warns, "Be careful what you say. It comes true. It comes true. I had to leave home in order to see the world logically, logic the new way of seeing. I learned to think that mysteries are for explanation. I enjoy the simplicity." She sees herself in Ts'ai Yen, who, captured by a Barbarian, listens to music and starts singing her own songs—or telling her own stories, creating her own identity before returning to her people.

Ceremony by Leslie Marmon Silko

Living the story becomes the only way that Tayo can save himself in Leslie Marmon Silko's *Ceremony* (1977). Tayo, a Laguna, volunteers for the armed forces with his half-cousin. In the Philippines, Rocky dies and Tayo becomes a Japanese prisoner. Tayo returns to the United States thinking himself invisible and fearful that he killed a Japanese soldier. He is admitted to a Los Angeles hospital to recover. Silko weaves story with story as Tayo recalls the disappearance of his white father and his mother Laura and his shame at the treatment of white women who loved his uniform but lost respect when he disrobed and became nothing more than an Indian. "They [the Indians] blamed themselves for losing the new feeling; they never talked about it, but they blamed themselves just like they blamed themselves for losing the land the white people took. They never thought to blame white people for any of it; they wanted white people for their friends. They never saw that it was the white people who gave them that feeling and it was white people who took it away again when the war was over." After he reappears on the reservation, his "Auntie stared at him . . . reaching inside him with her eyes, calling up the past as if it were his future too. . . . They both knew then she would keep him and take care of him . . . because he was all she had left. Many years ago she had taken him to conceal the shame of her younger sister."

Since the Los Angeles hospital staff failed to cure Tayo, Auntie finally summons a medicine man. When Ku'oosh also fails, he enlists Betonie's aid. Betonie sees that Tayo's "sickness was only part of something larger, and his cure would be found only in something great and inclusive of everything." He helps Tayo learn that part of his own ceremony for reclaiming his spirit involves finding cattle that belonged to his beloved Uncle Josiah, who once told him,

"This is where we come from. . . . This sand, this stone, these trees, the vines, all the wildflowers. This earth keeps us going."

Betonie tells Tayo that, for his ceremony, he should have a vision of stars, cattle, a woman, and a mountain. Where he had last seen the cattle, Tayo encounters a woman, Ts'eh Montaña, and spends the night with her, remembering a similar experience with Uncle Josiah's lover, the Mexican Night Swan who had seduced him. Tayo then detects a pattern of stars in the north, follows it to Mount Taylor, and finds the cattle. Texans rush to stop him, but, fortunately, a mountain lion diverts their attention. Ts'eh keeps the cattle, feeding and watering them until Tayo returns with a truck. During the summer, he meets Ts'eh again and stays with her while she instructs him and advises him to remember all that she has said. She is an extension of the mythological Grandmother Spider, a creator and Thought-Woman who introduces the novel, and as she sits "in her room . . . whatever she thinks about appears." After his ceremony ends, Tayo "finally see[s] the pattern, the way all the stories fit together—the old stories, the war stories, their stories—to become the story that was still being told."

The importance of stories is the core of *Ceremony*. Tayo enacts the traditional sacred story by entering sacred time and ascending Mount Taylor, a spiritually significant Laguna landmark. In an interview (*Suntracks*), Silko said, "that's how you know, that's how you belong, that's how you know you belong, if the stories incorporate you into them. There have to be stories. It's the stories that make this a community. . . . In a sense, you are told who you are, or you know who you are by the stories that are told about you." But one story Tayo learned misled him. "He had learned the lie by heart—the lie which they had wanted him to learn, only brown-skinned people were thieves; white people didn't steal, because they always had the money to buy whatever they wanted. The lie." Tayo's former friends, Emo, Pinkey, Leroy, and Harley, cannot escape the lie. Tayo detects their trap and escapes before they can victimize him. They literally kill each other until only Emo survives. Then the tribe exiles him. Thus Tayo is a story-in-the-making who relies on stories already known to reunite himself with his spirit and with the land. The success of his ceremony keeps him alive and entrusts him with a future.

The value of dreams and stories becomes clear in these three novels. Janie creates her own story and incorporates it into that of the community in *Their Eyes Were Watching God*. In *The Woman Warrior*, Maxine couples the Chinese stories with her own experience. Finally, Tayo becomes the story in *Ceremony*. They all find themselves by accepting the past as part of their present.

Additional Related Novels

Alexie, Sherman. *Reservation Blues*.
Gaines, Ernest J. *The Autobiography of Miss Jane Pittman*.
Momaday, N. Scott. *House Made of Dawn*.

O'Brien, Tim. *The Things They Carried*.
Tan, Amy. *The Joy Luck Club*.
Vonnegut, Kurt. *Slaughterhouse-Five*.
Welch, James. *Fools Crow*.
Wharton, Edith. *Ethan Frome*.

Suicide

Suicide is the end result of the process, not the process itself.
—J. Zubin, *The Prediction of Suicide* (1974)

For a human to commit suicide indicates that that person has faced an impenetrable wall with no pinpoints of light. That person must plan, however, and commit the act that will achieve the goal—death. In *The Sound and the Fury*, Quentin cannot tolerate Caddy's marriage or survive the legacy of the South, and he commits suicide on a day in June at Harvard. After her family and her lover reject her, Maggie in *Maggie: A Girl of the Streets* loses her will to live and drowns herself. In *The Bell Jar*, Esther Greenwood unsuccessfully attempts suicide, depressed at the enslavement of intelligent women as secretaries and housewives. In each of the novels, *The Folded Leaf*, *Bone*, and *Reservation Blues*, a character chooses suicide over survival.

A suicide is "one who dies by his own hand; one who commits self-murder" (*OED*). References to suicide occur very early in Western history. Martial recounts that "while fleeing from an enemy, Fannius killed himself. Is not this, I ask, madness—to die to avoid death?" (*Epigrams*, C.E. 85). In *London Magazine*, a writer concludes that "the Suicide owns himself . . . [and is] unequal to the Troubles of Life" (1732). In a 1996 document, the National Center for Injury Prevention and Control of the National Institute for Mental Health reports that "suicide is the ninth leading cause of death in the United States, with 31,204 deaths recorded in 1995. This approximates to around one death every seventeen minutes." The novels, *The Folded Leaf*, *Bone*, and *Reservation Blues*, present possible answers as to "why" suicide becomes the only option for some people in distress.

The Folded Leaf by William Maxwell

In William Maxwell's *The Folded Leaf* (1945), the protagonist Lymie Peters unsuccessfully attempts suicide. Maxwell uses omniscient point of view in this bildungsroman of four parts ("The Swimming Pool," "Partly Pride and Partly Envy," "A Cold Country," and "A Reflection from the Sky") with the symbolic title taken from an Alfred Lord Tennyson poem, "in the middle of the wood / The folded leaf is woo'd from out the bud . . . and there / grows

green and broad" (1833). In 1923, new student Charles Latham (Spud), reluctantly transplanted from Wisconsin to Chicago, saves Lymie from drowning during a school water polo game. Lymie and his alcoholic father live in a
kitchenette, and during the four years since Lymie's mother's death, have
eaten dinner each night in the Alcazar restaurant. Spud and Lymie, both dis-
contented with their homes, become friends, although the two seem an incon-
gruous pair—intellectual Lymie and Spud who cannot answer questions in
English class ("a sentence appeared, one word at a time, like a string of colored
scarves being drawn from a silk hat"). During high school, they become more
independent from their families; "The rites of puberty allow the father to punish the son, the son to murder his father, without actual harm to either." And
they become aware of others like the girls visiting the nearby bakery—"the
girls at LeClerc's were like wonderful tropical birds, like the ibis, the cockatoo,
and the crested crane." Lymie and Spud then attend college (Lymie's relative
Miss Georgiana Binkerd pays half his tuition) in 1927, meeting new people,
including the older Reinhart, a former reform school attendee and fellow
boarder at Mr. Dehner's. However, new friends and opportunities separate
them.

Lymie and Spud's friendship cements when a high school fraternity recruits
Spud for athleticism and Lymie for a higher academic average and continues in
college. At first, they spend afternoons in a condemned basement apartment
furnished with abandoned furniture collected by the high school fraternity.
"In a primitive society . . . the dark impulses of envy, jealousy, and hate, are tolerated and understood and eventually released through public ritual, through
cutting with crocodiles' teeth, burning, beating, incisions in the boy's penis. . . .
high school boys . . . torture . . . and the novices are convinced that, as a result
of running the gauntlet and being switched with nettles, they will have muscle
and bone, they will grow tall and broad in the shoulders, their spirit will be
warlike, and they will have the strength between their legs to beget many children." In college, Lymie first meets Hope Davison and Sally Forbes in Professor Severance's English class, and Lymie introduces Sally to Spud. But Spud
and Lymie share everything until Spud wants to join a fraternity. Since Spud
has no money, Lymie secretly arranges for Reinhart to give Spud $100 for ini-
tiation, Lymie's summer wages. But the fraternity does not satisfy Spud. He
wonders "*why was he here where he didn't want to be? Who made him do it?*" He
soon returns to the rooming house and Lymie.

But the two become estranged. Lymie spends time studying with Sally
when Spud also wants to be with her. After Spud loses a Golden Gloves tourna-
ment, Spud's family, Sally, and Lymie return to the Latham apartment. Lymie
had expected to feel excluded on his first visit there six years prior, but not until
this time does that occur. "Everything that he had thought would happen then
was happening now. He had been wrong only about the time." Lymie's subsequent effort to kill himself makes them all reassess their relationship. While
Lymie recovers in the hospital, Spud kisses him on the mouth; "He had never

done this before and he was never moved to do it again." Without words, they finally confirm their long friendship. And "when [Lymie] woke he went on looking at the wildflowers with all the strength of his eyes, and the narrow world he had lived in so long began to grow larger and wider. The world began to take on its own true size."

Lymie's experiences with death begin when his mother dies in 1919 and climax when he chooses to kill himself. Each year he and his father visit the grave of his mother, and the unhappy experience of one visit on a cold, windy March day when Lymie loses his return train ticket and the flowers will not remain arranged on the grave makes him feel guilty for his mother's death. Lymie's English professor, Dr. Severance, invites him to dinner, and Severance's mother dies soon after. When Mrs. Lieberman, an auditor in Professor Severance's class, observes Lymie, she decides that he needs someone to love him. Spud's commitment to Sally, however, makes Lymie feel completely alone. Pursuing life no longer interests him because "to live in the world at all is to be committed to some kind of a journey." He first attempts suicide by drinking iodine but regurgitates instead. After he slashes his wrists and throat, Reinhart finds him and rushes him to the infirmary. When Lymie's father arrives, they converse for the first time, and, when Spud affirms their friendship, Lymie realizes "seeing clearly is everything." Lymie fortunately finds a reason to live—he discovers that others do love him.

Bone by Fae Myenne Ng

In Fae Myenne Ng's *Bone* (1993), Ona's suicide occurs before the story begins, and each member of her family feels responsible. "First Girl" Leila (Lei), a schoolteacher in San Francisco, uses first-person point of view to search for possible answers as to why "Middle Girl," twenty, jumped from the thirteenth floor of a housing project. Also grieving are their mother, Dulcie (Mah) Leong; Lei's stepfather and Ona's father, Leon Leong; and Lei's younger stepsister Nina Leong, "End Girl." Lei's own father Lyman Fu has disappeared, and she has married Mason Louie, an automobile mechanic. Lei, however, loves Leon as much as a biological father because he tells her that regardless of what other Chinese think, having three girls is not unlucky. He believes that "it's time that makes a family, not just blood." During her parents' marriage, Leon was often at sea working two shifts. Leon says, "Life was work and death the dream." As Lei pieces together their lives, she uncovers information about her parents and examines her own relationship to family and community. Lei remembers that "the oldtimers believe we have a heavenly weight, and that our fates can be divined by the weighing of our bones." Thus the title refers to the remains of a body and its value after all else has been stripped away.

Contemplating the effect of immigration on the family reveals Lei's own need to find an identity separate from the group. Her mother often sucked on pigeon bones, saying they were tasty while actually sacrificing for her children.

After Ona's suicide, Leon moves away from Mah, and Lei helps him apply for Social Security by locating identity documents to support his claim. She opens a suitcase containing his papers and discovers all of his aliases for survival. He entered the country using someone else's documents and, as necessary, changed his name or his situation to obtain what he needed. She realizes, "I'm the stepdaughter of a paper son and I've inherited this whole suitcase of lies. All of it is mine. All I have is those memories, and I want to remember them all." She understands for the first time that Mah had married Leon for his green card and they had "toil[ed] together" so that Lei's generation could marry for love. They, therefore, expected the girls to return their intense loyalty. Nina, however, rejects the family by moving to New York and becoming a leader for groups going to China. Lei escapes family expectations by visiting Nina and marrying Mason in New York rather than at home with a traditional Chinese banquet. Both choices disturb Mah. Ona, however, chooses the most drastic departure from the culture.

Although the police indicate that Ona was taking "uppers" when she jumped, the family looks elsewhere for reasons. Lei considers "blood and bones. The oldtimers believed that the blood came from the mother and the bones from the father. Ona was part Leon and part Mah, but neither of them could believe that Ona's unhappiness was all her own." Leon blames himself because he did not return to China with Grandpa Leong's bones as he had promised. Leon cannot retrieve Leong's bones because they have been disinterred and mixed with other family bones to create additional space in the cemetery. Because Leon had not fulfilled his commitment, he blames himself for Ona's suicide. Mah thinks that she has caused the family's misfortunes because of an affair with her boss, Tommy, during one of Leon's trips. Additionally, Leon and Mah invested their money in a laundry business with a partner. He later betrayed them, taking their money, and, after Ona fell in love with his son Osvaldo, Mah and Leon forbade the relationship. Then Lei wonders about her own lack of understanding and thinks that she should have rescued Ona from her parents, forcing them to leave Ona and Osvaldo alone. And even though a non-Chinese would not understand, Ona might have commited suicide because of her family position. "In Chinatown, Ona was the middle girl and she felt stuck in the middle of all the trouble." When Lei remembers that Leon thought "*the heart never travels,*" she reflects: "I believe in holding still. I believe that the secrets we hold in our hearts are our anchors, that even the unspoken between us is a measure of our every promise to the living and to the dead. And all our promises, like all our hopes, move us through life with the power of an ocean liner, pushing through the sea." She knows that "inside all of us, Ona's heart still moves forward. Ona's heart is still counting, true and truer to every tomorrow."

Reservation Blues by Sherman Alexie

In *Reservation Blues* (1996), one of the characters commits suicide. The omniscient point of view, combined with first person, allows the reader to know the discouragement that Junior Polatkin feels as part of a group that fails. Sherman Alexie uses a collection of dreams, newspaper articles, journal entries, a story within a story, name symbolism in Phil Sheridan and George Wright, and magic realism in his ten chapters, each beginning with blues lyrics, to tell about a group of young Spokane Indians from Wellpinit, a town created on the Spokane Indian Reservation in 1981. "Junior had learned from Freud and Jung that dreams decided everything. He figured that Freud and Jung must have been reservation Indians, because dreams decided everything for Indians too." After Robert Johnson appears and gives Thomas Builds-the-Fire his guitar, Victor Joseph destroys the guitar, but it restores itself overnight. Thomas, Junior, and Victor then start a band calling themselves Coyote Springs. At their first performance, they meet and invite Flathead Reservation residents Chess and Checkers Warm Water to join them. Soon they recognize that "Buddy Holly wasn't a Spokane Indian" and start writing their own lyrics. Thomas maintains the oral tradition because his "stories climbed into your clothes like sand, gave you itches that could not be scratched. If you repeated even a sentence from one of those stories, your throat was never the same again." Thomas's stories and the self-playing guitar lead to Alexie's stylistic use of synaesthesia and metaphor. The reservation "opened its mouth and drank deep because the music tasted so familiar." Tribal leaders, especially David WalksAlong (Thomas's father Samuel defeated him in high school basketball) and his nephew Michael White Hawk (just released from jail) dislike having a rock band representing them. But the group performs, first in Seattle where they become involved with the white women Betty and Veronica, and then in New York at an audition for a record contract. Their abilities disintegrate, and after they return to the reservation, Junior commits suicide. After his death, Chess and Thomas move elsewhere.

In addition to the band, Alexie incorporates the Faust legend, religion as delineated through the characters of Big Mom and Father Arnold, and horses as symbols. When Robert Johnson arrives in Wellpinit, he is searching for Big Mom who may "save" him from the Gentleman. "The Gentleman held the majority of stock in Robert Johnson's soul. . . . Since 1938, the year he faked his death by poisoning and made his escape, Johnson had been running from the Gentleman, who narrowly missed him at every stop." The Gentleman took Johnson's soul in return for freedom and guitar expertise. Thomas tells Johnson that "Big Mom" does not let anyone go up the mountain to see her unless she summons them, but she invites Johnson. When the band needs assistance preparing for their audition, Big Mom sends a letter offering her help. She knows that a priest molested a younger Victor and that Chess and Checkers are actually Eunice and Gladys. She tells the band that she can help them, but she has no power to control what they do. Victor chastises Thomas for "admitting that Big Mom ain't God." "'It's not blasphemy,' Thomas said. 'There is no god but God. She's just part of God. . . . We're all a part of God, enit? Big Mom is just a bigger part of God.'" Father Arnold, however, seems more rooted to the earth; while fighting against a physical attraction for Checkers, he represents the Catholic god. Checkers thinks, "I looked at Big Mom and thought that God must be made up mostly of Indian and woman pieces. Then I looked at Father Arnold and thought that God must be made up of white and man pieces. I don't know what's true." Big Mom also recalls the slaughter of Indian horses 147 years before Johnson's arrival after which she carved a flute to play daily from the ribs of the most beautiful horse as a reminder. At important moments in the tribe's life, the horses respond. When Johnson and the Gentlemen agreed, the horses screamed. They also scream when the band leaves for New York. Thus the horses, unless shadows, seem to represent the tragedies in life. When Checkers and Thomas leave the reservation, the benevolent shadow horses protect them.

Of the band members, Junior, the only one to have attended any college and to have had a job, commits suicide. He can no longer save either himself or the others. He cannot overcome the long hours of cold in the car while waiting for his parents to drink in a bar, the ignominy of the band, or the refusal of his white college girlfriend to marry after she became pregnant with his child. He can no longer laugh, the one weapon that the Spokanes use against failure. Father Arnold "was impressed by the Spokanes' ability to laugh. He'd never thought of Indians as being funny. What did they have to laugh about? Poverty, suicide, alcoholism? [He] learned to laugh at most everything, which strangely made him feel closer to God." Chess's and Thomas's appreciation of the beauty on the reservation, "the way a honey bee circled a flower," does not transfer to Junior. Yet Chess fears for half-breed children: "No matter what he does, he'll never be Indian enough" or white enough. Junior delivers water on the reservation, an act of preservation for both him and the inhabitants, yet he chooses to shoot himself on top of the water tower. Thus the miscegenation, the alcoholism, the government, the empty fascination of whites for things Indian, and the pessimism all overcome Junior. But Alexie adds another reason. The guitar asks Victor to sacrifice the most important thing to him in order to play well; he continues the Faustian tradition by choosing Junior.

Suicide seems like a remote, unremarkable act. Lymie survives, but Ona and Junior will never answer the questions of those who feel rejected. The narrator in *The Folded Leaf* summarizes the situation. "The horror may be . . . that all people share, in some degree, the impulse toward self-destruction; and when some one person actually gives way to it, all are exposed to the common danger. Or perhaps the horror stems from something else, something much less complicated. The suicide doesn't go alone, he takes everybody with him."

Additional Related Novels

Clark, Walter Van Tilburg. *The Ox-Bow Incident.*

Crane, Stephen. *Maggie: A Girl of the Streets.*
Faulkner, William. *The Sound and the Fury.*
Guest, Judith. *Ordinary People.*
Knowles, John. *A Separate Peace.*
Plath, Sylvia. *The Bell Jar.*

Survival

Victory at all costs, victory in spite of all terror, victory however long and hard the road may be; for without victory there is no survival.
—Winston Churchill (May 1940)

To overcome personal and natural catastrophes, people must find survival skills within themselves. Fran Benedetto in *Black and Blue* continually tries to placate her husband so that he will not beat her, but, to survive, she must physically remove herself from his sight. In *The Grapes of Wrath*, the Joads think that traveling west to California will help them find security, but instead they must search for food and survive a flood. Chiyo in *Memoirs of a Geisha* must learn how to survive without benefit of family or friend in the hostile world of geisha politics. In *Giants in the Earth*, *These Is My Words*, and *Fallen Angels*, the protagonists must also survive in new surroundings.

The term "survival," incorporated into the language around the sixteenth century, implies that "something . . . continues to exist after the cessation of something else." In the *Origins of Civilization and the Primitive Condition of Man*, Sir John Lubbock says that "the use of stone knives in certain ceremonies is evidently a case of survival" (1870). Andrew Carnegie comments that "while the law [of competition] may be sometimes hard for the individual, it is best for the race, because it ensures the survival of the fittest in every department" (*Wealth*, 1889). Robert R. Marett states that "folklore, usually defined as the study of survivals, needs to conceive its object in a dynamic, not a static way" (*Psychology and Folklore*, 1920). And, in a speech, Wendell Berry said that "to cherish what remains of the Earth and to foster its renewal is our only legitimate hope of survival" (1983). Survival to the characters in *Giants in the Earth*, *These Is My Words*, and *Fallen Angels* involves braving nature's foibles and the evils of other humans.

Giants in the Earth by O. E. Rölvaag

In O. E. Rölvaag's *Giants in the Earth* (1927), the Per Hansa family moves from Fillmore City, Minnesota, to the Dakota Territory, where they survive violent weather, hazards, unfertile soil, grasshopper plagues, Indian threats, and claim disputes. This pioneer novel, in ominiscient point of view, covers the lives of Per, his wife Beret, children Ole, Hans Kristian, and Ánna-Marie. On the way, they have wagon problems and have to separate from their wagon train. Per Hansa tells the family that he is following the sun: "The sun is a sure guide, you know!'" His son believes him; "To Store-Hans the truth of them seemed as clear as the sun itself; in the first place, because dad had said it, and then because it sounded so reasonable." Yet Per actually discovers the path in the middle of the night, and they appear five days later to join Syvert Tönseten and his wife Sörine and Hans Olsa and his wife Kjersti. Then the Irish Solum brothers arrive, Henry and Sam. The brothers eventually want to leave, but the Norwegians convince them to remain and teach them English. Beret, with no one to discuss her fears, becomes jealous of Per's friendship with Hans Olsa. Another woman who comes to the settlement wants to return to her son who died on the trail and bury him. Stopped in the day by her husband, she awakens in the middle of the night and takes Beret's child as a replacement.

Per Hansa's preparations on the farm protect his family. He loves the area, and his "heart filled with a deep sense of peace and contentment. . . . Was he really to have his friends for neighbors, both to the north and to the south—folks who cared for him and wanted to help him out in every way?" He works constantly at projects questioned by the others and experiments with crops. He builds a large house containing both a house and a barn and finds woods to cover the roof, although others think he cannot. He develops trading relationships with the Trönden and Helgelander tribes. The others are fearful of storms and Indians, but when left with the women while the other men go to town, Per Hansa visits Indians camped on a nearby hill and helps cure a wounded man. As appreciation, one of the Indians delivers a saddled pony to his door. When the cows disappear, he takes the advice of one of the wives and finds them with a bull so he rents a bull from the Trönden folk and satisfies the cows. When he finds two land stakes with names on them on the corner of his friends' land, he destroys them. He feels guilty, not understanding that his claim would have been denied had their deeds been legal. He becomes the first to sell produce, potatoes and vegetables, to German pioneers passing through, and he whitens his house. He watches his wife become quieter and more forgetful, before renaming the family "Holm"("island" in Norwegian). He trades with the Indians during the winter, jeopardizing his health but paying down his debts. When he plants his wheat in the early spring, Tönseter calls him foolish when it snows soon after; however, the wheat grows beautifully throughout the season. Per's last errand is to summon the minister for his dying friend, but he cannot survive the fierceness of the storm that freezes him in a haystack.

Throughout the arrival of plagues and storms ("giants in the earth"), Beret becomes more mentally imbalanced. She hates the place and constantly fears terrible things will happen, beginning with the discovery of a graveyard on Hansa land. To her, "the broad expanse stretching away endlessly in every direction, seemed almost like the ocean—especially now, when darkness was falling. It reminded her strongly of the sea, and yet it was very different. . . . . This formless prairie had no heart that beat, no waves that sang, no soul that could be touched . . . or cared. . . .Here no warbling of birds rose on the air, no buzzing of insects sounded. . . . Could no living thing exist out here in the empty desolate, endless wastes of green and blue?" She laments their decision to come; "They had sold off everything that they had won with so much toil, had left it all like a pair of worn-out shoes—parents, home, fatherland, and people . . . and she had done it gladly, even rejoicingly! . . . Was there ever a sin like hers?" She feels even more guilty because she conceived her first son out of wedlock, and her subsequent parents disapproved of her marriage to Per. While expecting her last child, Beret thinks that she will die at its birth, and she tells Per to bury her in her grandfather's chest. When the child is born on Christmas with a caul, Per Hansa thinks he is destined for good fortune and names him with what Beret thinks is a blasphemous name. Fortunately, a minister stops at the settlement and convinces her that her guilt is groundless. But she subconsciously kills her husband by demanding that he leave during a blizzard to get the minister when his seriously ill friend Hans Olsa wants to repent his sins. Per Hansa's frozen body lies undiscovered until spring.

These Is My Words by Nancy E. Turner

A second pioneer novel is Nancy E. Turner's *These Is My Words: The Diary of Sarah Agnes Prine 1881–1901 Arizona Territories* (1998). Turner's great-grandmother's diaries, beginning on 22 July 1881, reveal the difficulties that Sarah survives during ten years. Turner's comment was that "if I hadn't met Sarah Agnes, I would have sworn that my mother had made her up." Sarah, her parents and four brothers, Ernest, Albert, Harland, and Clover, travel to San Angelo with a wagon train. A snake bites her youngest brother Clover, and he dies on August 13. Soon after, Apaches attack, take the horses, wound her father, and break Ernest's leg so that he must have it amputated. When men rape Ulyssa, one of the four Quaker sisters on the journey, Sarah kills the men, but Ulyssa's family will no longer speak to her because they do not condone murder. After Sarah cries in anguish while beheading a chicken, the girls decide to disobey their father and stop shunning her. Then her own father dies soon after they reach San Angelo. Jack Elliott, the wagon train leader to Tucson, lets her use extra horses and take books from an abandoned wagon. Ernest joins the cavalry and soon writes that he has begun shoeing horses, job he does well. When finally exhausted, she confesses all to Elliott and promptly becomes ill. Caring for Sarah helps her mother regain her own sanity and overcome the depression following her husband's death. After Sarah recovers, Albert and Mama ride ahead to Tucson to make claims for land near Cienega Creek. There, two men, Captain Elliott and Jimmy Reed, a ranch hand the family had known before San Angelo, show interest in her. She marries Jimmy who never says "I love you," and after she becomes pregnant, no longer sleeps with her.

When Jimmy dies the next year, Albert tells her that Jimmy has always loved someone else, stole horses, and had often visited Tucson brothels. One day Sarah rescues Captain Elliot, who, while chasing Indians and Geronimo nearby, becomes pinned under a horse. The plotting of her brothers and Jack succeeds, and Sarah eventually marries him, understanding that being quiet with someone can mean you are in love. When Jack is killed, Jack's father Chess moves in with Sarah and her children.

While on the trail or settled in the untamed west, women were always prey for men. Men rape Ulyssa, and another cuts Savannah's throat before Sarah can kill them. Her bravery also impresses peaceful Indians because one brings her scalps from the men she kills and gives her a horse. After Jimmy dies, the vile Moses Smith returns to her home to rape her and hurt her daughter April, but Jack appears and saves them. Jack takes Moses to town, and when Jack uncovers Smith's past of train robber, murderer, and horse thief, Smith hangs. Sarah also has to endure additional other insults from arrogant males. She, however, beats the braggart Mike Meyers at shooting but astutely returns his rifle, claiming it is too heavy. Another serious enemy of survival is childbirth. A woman on the wagon train has a stillborn and then dies herself. Sarah's second child arrives before Savannah and Mama can appear at her door, she has a stillborn, and another child dies of a fever. A physician revives the hemorrhaging Savannah after twins with the new technique of transfusion by taking Sarah's blood to replace that lost by Savannah. Since Savannah has eight children and great difficulty with their births, Sarah has to tell her how to avoid having a ninth.

On the wagon train and after she arrives in Tucson, Sarah learns ways to survive both physical and mental anguish. She makes soap using perfume and coloring found in an abandoned wagon and begins selling it in town. She notices the kindness of Indians when they give her a horse, and Jack tells her he was married to one who had disappeared six years before. After Jack kisses her, Savannah dispels Sarah's fears of being promiscuous by saying kissing is permissible for those betrothed. Sarah wants an education desperately, and Jack, who attended West Point, supports her. He tells her, "education doesn't keep a person from being a fool, and the lack of it doesn't keep a person from being intelligent." When she takes the test to pass her high school work, she admits that "taking a school test is a new way to be afraid, and takes the knees right out from under you. If I'm riding a horse and get thrown, it's just a matter of getting back on. And if I'm fighting for my life, there's only living and dying to choose from. But taking that test, that's like showing other people the inside of your thoughts; and just waiting for them to say, wrong, wrong, wrong, and you can have a thought that seems right but since you never went to school, maybe it isn't." But she makes ninety-four, higher than her brother Harland. After Jack dies, she still wants to learn. "It seems there is always a road with bends and forks to choose, and taking one path means you can never take another one. . . . It's just that I want everything, my insides are not just hungry, but greedy. I want to find out all the things in the world and still have a family and a ranch." Thus Sarah learns through survival to pursue a more fulfilling life.

Fallen Angels by Walter Dean Myers

In Walter Dean Myers' *Fallen Angels* (1988), Richie Perry hones his survival skills long before he leaves for Vietnam. Richie's first-person narrative describes his school years in New York living with his mother Mabel and his brother Kenny. His father had disappeared when Kenny was four, and his mother had started drinking. Richie graduated from high school and wanted to attend college to learn to write like James Baldwin, but City College "hadn't made sense anymore." He kept trying to remember what his English teacher, Mrs. Liebow, had told him when "I would feel a pressure to give in, to let a rebound go over my head, to take the outside shot when I knew I had to take the all inside. . . . Mrs. Liebow . . . said that it was what separated heroes from humans, the not giving in, and I hadn't understood that." Instead of "giving in," he substitutes Vietnam for college and leaves on 15 September 1967. He makes friends with Peewee, another African American, and meets Jenkins. His first challenge becomes the environment—the heat, insects, and intermittent deafening artillery noise. "The noise was terrible. Every time a mortar went off, I jumped. I couldn't help myself. The noise went into you. It touched parts of you that were small and frightened and wanting your mommy." His second adjustment is his new home of Chu Lai where he must face the enemy named Charlie, Victor Charlie, or Vietcong. His experience and that of the other men makes them want to return home safe and soon.

Richie tries to help others while facing racial prejudice and the war's propaganda. He sends money to his brother Kenny for clothes to keep him in school. He sends him a birthday present at Thanksgiving and more money to join a basketball team. Later he sends Kenny his Purple Heart. Richie's mother writes to his friend Peewee, and Richie writes her. When Lieutenant Carroll dies, Richie writes his wife a letter to say how much they liked and respected him. But, simultaneously, white officers ignore Richie's concerns for others by selecting him for the most conspicuous and vulnerable assignments. The government's misinformation, including exaggerated body counts of the Viet Cong, spread to make Vietnam sound like a successful campaign also dismays him. Additionally, Richie watches soldiers entertain villagers with Walt Disney movies while announcements assert that the soldiers are shooting jets out of the sky.

The pain of Vietnam permeates Richie's life with its "hours of boredom and seconds of terror." As soon as he arrives, Jenkins steps on a land mine and dies. Soon after, they shoot at another company in their platoon. Then Richie himself kills a man. "All I had thought about combat was that I would never die, that our side would win, and that we would all go home somehow satisfied.

And now all the dying around me, and all the killing, was making me look at myself again, hoping to find something more than the kid I was." Richie asks Peewee why he killed a Cong and wonders if self-defense is an adequate response. Peewee thinks he needed to "think about killing the Congs before they killed me. That had better be my reason, he had said, until I got back to the World. Maybe it was right. But it meant being some other person than I was when I got to Nam. Maybe that was what I had to be. Somebody else." Richie does not want to change, but after hearing about a woman who mined a child and handed him to a soldier so that the child and he exploded, he wants to discuss the situation. "The war was different now. Nam was different. Jenkins had been outside of me, even the guys in Charlie Company had been outside. Lieutenant Carroll was inside of me, he was part of me. Part of me was dead with him. I wanted to be sad, to cry for him, maybe bang my fists against the sides of the hooch. But what I felt was numb." After four months fighting, Richie is hit and evacuated from the front with Peewee and Monaco. Their intense struggle unites them more closely than any casual conversation. Thus Richie's survival allows him to recall the horrors of his experience and his suspicions of anyone who wanted to stay longer in Nam than required.

The Hansa family battles the weather and its inner turmoil in *Giants in the Earth*. Sarah negotiates with other people in *These Is My Words*, and Richie dodges mortar shells of the body and mind in *Fallen Angels*. They know, however, that only their direct involvement can improve their precarious situations. Thus they learn and develop skills appropriate to survive for another day.

Additional Related Novels

Alvarez, Julia. *In the Time of the Butterflies.*
Cather, Willa. *My Ántonia; O Pioneers!*
Crane, Stephen. *The Red Badge of Courage.*
Dickey, James. *Deliverance.*
Flagg, Fannie. *Fried Green Tomatoes at the Whistle Stop Café.*
Golden, Arthur. *Memoirs of a Geisha.*
Heller, Joseph. *Catch-22.*
Hemingway, Ernest. *A Farewell to Arms; For Whom the Bell Tolls; The Old Man and the Sea.*
McCarthy, Cormac. *All the Pretty Horses.*
McMillan, Terry. *Mama; Waiting to Exhale.*
Naylor, Gloria. *The Women of Brewster Place.*
Oates, Joyce Carol. *Foxfire.*
O'Brien, Tim. *Going after Cacciato; The Things They Carried.*
Quindlen, Anna. *Black and Blue.*
Silko, Leslie Marmon. *Ceremony.*
Steinbeck, John. *The Grapes of Wrath.*
Tan, Amy. *The Joy Luck Club.*
Wideman, John Edgar. *The Hiding Place.*
Wilson, Harriet E. *Our Nig.*

Trials

Equal and exact justice to all men, of whatever state or persuasion, religious or political . . . and trial by juries impartially selected . . . guided our steps through an age of revolution and reformation.
—Thomas Jefferson, *First Inaugural Speech* (1801)

When someone has allegedly committed a crime, a judge or a jury usually questions that person to determine guilt or innocence. In *Foxfire*, a judge finds Legs guilty of stealing a car and sentences her to a prison term. In *A Gathering of Old Men*, the characters face a self-appointed jury planning to convict and kill without facts. A schoolboy mock trial condemns Gene for harming Phineas in *A Separate Peace*. Claggett in *Billy Budd* sentences Billy Budd to death without knowing all of the facts and immediately hangs him. Clifford Pyncheon serves thirty years in prison, victim of an unscrupulous judge in *The House of the Seven Gables*. Not all trials occur in a courtroom, and not all of them end fairly since people live by hidden codes not written into law, situations clearly illustrated in the novels *The Ox-Bow Incident*, *To Kill a Mockingbird*, and *Snow Falling on Cedars*.

According to the *OED*, a trial is an "inquiry or investigation in order to ascertain something." In legal terms, it is "the examination and determination of a cause by a judicial tribunal; [or the] determination of the guilt or innocence of an accused person by a court." In *The Leviathan*, Thomas Hobbes noted, "in the ordinary trialls of Right, Twelve men of the common People, are the Judges" (1651). In Greece, Connop Thirlwall recounts, "He was brought to tria, [and] Theramenes, lately his intimate friend, became his accuser" (*A History of Greece*, 1838). Lloyd Paul Stryker notes that "a trial is still an ordeal by battle" (1955). In these three novels, three trials occur, one without an investigation in *The Ox-Bow Incident*, one with evidence of innocence not accepted by the jury in *To Kill a Mockingbird*, and one with incomplete, circumstantial evidence in *Snow Falling on Cedars*.

The Ox-Bow Incident by Walter Van Tilburg Clark

The action in Walter Van Tilburg Clark's *The Ox-Bow Incident* (1940) occurs in one day, after the first-person narrator Art Croft and his partner Gil Carter come from the winter range to Bridger's Wells, Nevada, in 1885. They stop at Canby's bar, where the only activities available are to "eat, sleep, drink, play poker or fight. Or . . . shoot some pool . . . [on the] new table in the back room." Cattle rustlers are the latest news in town, and Greene brings that problem and another into the bar when he announces that someone has killed Jeff Farnley's buddy, Kinkaid. Farnley urges the men present to find and punish the killer.

Some of the men desist, wanting to defer a manhunt until the local judge legalizes a posse. Davies tells them that the judge has "time, precedent, and the consent of the majority that he shall act for them." Croft and Greene search for Judge Tyler, and when they encounter Mapes (the deputized sheriff who likes to make quick decisions), Greene refuses to tell him the problem. The judge comes to the bar and asks the men to be reasonable. But when Mapes enthusiastically supports a posse, Davies encourages the group to wait. News arrives, however, that three men have been spotted and are probably guilty. The headstrong Mapes prevails.

The men who do not listen to either Judge Tyler or Davies think justice will not be served if the judge holds a trial. The rancher Bartlett asks, "What is justice? . . . Judge Tyler . . . says we have to fold our hands and wait for his eternal justice? Waiting for Tyler's kind of justice, we'd all be beggars in a year." Tetley, a former Confederate soldier and the valley's tallest man, agrees. He decides that he and his son (whom he thinks is effeminate) will lead the posse. But young Tetley, Gerald, says sarcastically, "That's the hunting we like now, our own kind." He tells one of the men during their ride that "we're [riding] in the pack, because we're afraid not to be in the pack." The black man Sparks views the event as "man takin' upon himself the Lohd's vengeance." He admits that at the age of six, he saw his own brother lynched.

After the self-appointed posse finds the three men, the men deny the murder. Gil agrees that one of the men, Martin, should appear before the judge because his story that he neither killed Kincaid nor stole the cattle surrounding him at Ox-Bow seems reasonable. No one other than Davies supports him. The Mexican with Martin pretends not to speak English at first and then admits to knowing ten other languages, all the while showing his courage. After Davies reads the letter that Martin writes to his wife, he is certain that Martin is innocent. Martin, however, will not let Davies read the letter to the others. Martin says that he bought the cattle from Drew, who planned to mail the bill of sale to him at a later time. None of the men wants to wait so they lynch the three suspects. On their way home, the group meets the sheriff, Drew, the judge, and Kincaid—who is not dead. Davies chastens the men, "Most of you couldn't help it. Most men can't; they don't really think. They haven't any conception of basic justice." Croft realizes that Tetley was "cold crazy" and could only have been stopped from lynching if someone shot him. Overnight, Gerald commits suicide, and, when his father finds out, he kills himself. After the experience in town, Gil and Art, like Huckleberry Finn, are ready to leave town and "civilization." Men who declare themselves both judge and jury in a mock trial often make deadly mistakes.

To Kill a Mockingbird by Harper Lee

Harper Lee presents a number of juries in *To Kill a Mockingbird* (1960), only one of them in a courtroom. Six-year-old Scout (Jean Louise Finch), the first-person narrator, lives in the small town of Maycomb, Alabama, with her father Atticus Finch and brother Jem (ten) during the mid-1950s. Scout's father (whom she calls Atticus) has raised his children with the help of Calpurnia since his wife died when Scout was two. Scout approves of Atticus's actions. She notes that "he played with us, read to us, and treated us with courteous detachment." But each year, she becomes more aware that Atticus, a lawyer, views life differently from their community. From her conflicts with others, she contemplates, "There's four kinds of folks in the world . . . the ordinary kind like us and the neighbors . . . the kind like the Cunninghams out in the woods, the kind like the Ewells down at the dump, and the Negroes." Jem thinks education makes a difference. "I think it's how long your family's been readin' and writing.' . . . Somewhere along when the Finches were in Egypt one of 'em must have learned a hieroglyphic or two and he taught his boy." Atticus reminds them that background is how one treats others. "As you grow older, you'll see white men cheat black men . . . but . . . don't you forget it—whenever a white man does that to a black man, no matter who he is, how rich he is, or how fine a family he comes from, that white man is trash."

Scout's unusual upbringing causes problems in her community. Anticipating school, she is dismayed when her first-grade teacher does not want her to read or write, two things she has long been able to do. Atticus advises her, "You never really understand a person until you consider things from his point of view. . . . until you climb into his skin and walk around in it." Scout must also cope with her Aunt Alexandra who was like "Mount Everest . . . cold and there." On the other hand, Scout likes her Uncle Jack. He chastises her for using "damn" and "hell" and teaches her and Jem to use the air rifles her father gave them for Christmas. Only when Atticus grabs a gun to kill a rabid dog do they discover that he can shoot and that his nickname used to be "One-Shot Finch." Cal warns Scout about her relationships, "It's not necessary to tell all you know . . . When they don't want to learn there's nothing you can do but keep your mouth shut or talk their language."

The Cunninghams, Boo Radley, and Dill become an integral part of the trials in Scout's everyday life. Scout and Jem bring young Walter Cunningham home for lunch after the teacher embarrasses him because he has no money. Dill's imagination fills Scout's and Jem's summers when he comes from Mississippi to stay with his aunt. He interests them in Boo Radley, the next-door neighbor who never goes outside; his family is ostracized for not attending church and for Mrs. Radley's "never join[ing] a missionary circle" or taking a coffee break with the neighbors. The Radleys, therefore, like Sula in *Sula*, "were responsible for every bad thing that happened in town." Boo never appears, but he leaves soap carvings for them to find—like mockingbirds they must not harm because they only sing and do good things. Scout and Jem watch the neighbors, including Mrs. Maudie with her false teeth and colorful azaleas. Atticus admonishes them for anger at Mrs. Duboses's insults, saying that he has never seen a braver woman because she overcame her morphine habit before she died. When Scout and Jem attend church with Calpurnia, they see her son Zeebo lead the "lining" so that the illiterate congregation can sing the hymns he first reads aloud.

The legal trial involves Atticus's defense of Tom Robinson, a black man of twenty-five with no left hand, whom Robert E. Lee Ewell declares has raped his daughter, Mayella. In actuality, the lonely, friendless Mayella tried to seduce Tom while her father, who had sexually abused her, watched. Atticus informs Scout that he will lose the case, but "simply because we were licked a hundred years before we started is no reason for us not to try to win." Miss Maudie tells the children that the Judge knew that Atticus would do the best job when he appointed him, and, even though many malign him, Atticus refuses to abandon it. Atticus says, "Scout, I couldn't go to church and worship God if I didn't try to help that man." He adds, "The one thing that doesn't abide by majority rule is a person's conscience." When a mob goes to the jail attempting to lynch Tom, Scout unknowingly halts it when she sees Walter's father and starts asking him questions. Atticus notes, "It took an eight-year-old child to bring 'em to their senses. . . . That proves something—that a gang of wild animals *can* be stopped . . . you children last night made Walter Cunningham stand in my shoes for a minute. That was enough." Later, however, the white male jury convicts Tom, the mockingbird. On Halloween, Boo Radley, another mockingbird, pushes Ewell on top of his own knife when Ewell tries to stab the children. Thus Scout and Jem serve as either defender or prosecutor in their private and communal trials of maturation.

Snow Falling on Cedars by David Guterson

The action in *Snow Falling on Cedars* (1994) centers on the trial of a Japanese American, Kabuo Miyamoto, for murdering Carl Heine on Carl's boat, the *Susan Marie*, during the night of 16 September 1954. Art Moran, the county sheriff, and his deputy, twenty-four-year-old Abel Martinson, find Heine, a gill-netter for salmon, caught in his net with his skull crushed above the left ear and drag him from Puget Sound. For the December trial during a severe snow storm, Miyamoto's lawyer, Nels Gudmundson, is seventy-nine, almost blind, and suffering from neurasthenia. The prosecutor, Alvin Hooks, represents the townspeople, and David Guterson's use of omniscient point of view enables the reader to know how many of these characters feel about Miyamoto, Heine, and the alleged crime. The educated Ishmael Chambers, a local reporter who went to school with Kabuo and Kabuo's wife Hatsue, provides much of the description.

Throughout the trial, the people judge Kabuo on his past actions and his present demeanor. Although Carl and Kabuo were best friends during school, animosity between them began during World War II when Kabuo's family had to go to Manzabar. Carl's mother sells land the Miyamotos were buying from the Heines at a profit, saying that they had missed their last two payments. The new buyer Ole Jurgensen decides to sell, and Carl quickly negotiates to buy before Kabuo has the opportunity. Thus the townspeople think that Kabuo has a motive for murdering Carl. Because his parents have taught him to hide his emotions, Kabuo seems unconcerned about the trial's proceedings. But Kabuo reveals to the reader that he thinks he is suffering for the crimes he committed during the war, when he served in the U.S. Army. As a Buddhist who must abide by the laws of karma and pay for those he killed in war, he expects the death penalty. Because Kabuo trained to be a good soldier (his great-grandfather had been a samurai) by learning kendo from his father, he is condemned instead of praised for his skill. During the trial, that Art Moran arrested him on circumstantial evidence involving his past rather than the present becomes clear.

As the witnesses appear on the stand, they disclose their prejudices. The coroner Horace Whaley comments to Art, that "if he were inclined to play Sherlock Holmes he ought to start looking for a Jap with a bloody gun butt—a right-handed Jap, to be precise." This jest reminds Art of Kabuo. The gash over Carl's ear reminds Horace of the war, and he thinks of kendo. "The Japanese field soldier, trained in the art of kendo, or stick fighting, was exceptionally proficient at killing in this manner." Horace also recalls that many Japanese killed by hitting their victims above the left ear with their right hands. But Carl died from drowning, and Nels notes that Carl could not have died of a head wound because he was breathing underwater. The jury notes that Kabuo was "not like them at all, and the detached and aloof manner in which he watched the snowfall made this palpable and self-evident." Yet Whaley remembers that Carl seemed to have few friends and, although polite, always worked by himself. Nels Gudmunsson, the old lawyer, remarks in conclusion to the jury, "What I see is again and again the same sad human frailty. We hate one another; we are the victims of irrational fears. . . . Will you contribute to the indifferent forces that ceaselessly conspire toward injustice? Or will you stand up against this endless time and in the face of it be truly human? In God's name, in the name of humanity, do your duty as jurors." Only when Ishmael discovers that an enormous freighter came through the fishing grounds on September 16 but went unreported because the two men on duty transferred stations the next day can Kabuo go free. This legal jury would have never released him otherwise.

An important subplot in the novel surfaces when Ishmael and Hatsue see each other and remember their past relationship. Even though the Japanese had lived in the area since 1883, their neighbors betrayed them after Pearl Harbor, 7 December 1941. By March, Hatsue and her family were interned at Manzabar, and there she realized that she could never marry Ishmael, her teenage love. She wrote him and "confessed to experiencing a moral anguish over meeting him so secretly and deceiving her mother and father." Hatsue's mother had taught her Japanese beliefs. "The whites, you see, are tempted by their egos and have no means to resist. We Japanese, on the other hand . . . understand that by ourselves, alone, we are nothing at all, dust in a strong wind." Ishmael illustrates the difference because he focuses on himself after he goes to war and loses his arm. "It seemed . . . that the world was thoroughly altered. . . . People appeared enormously foolish to him. He understood that they were only animated cavities full of jelly and strings and liquids. He had seen the insides of jaggedly ripped-open dead people." He is self-conscious about his missing arm and thinks "that his existence in the world made others nervous." At the trial, Hatsue asks for Ishmael's help, but when he finds the truth that will free Kabuo, he almost refuses to reveal it. Then he realizes that he could not live with himself or with Hatsue if he neglected to free her husband from prejudice and false accusation. He remembers that his father, when alive, "hoped for the best from his fellow islanders . . . and trusted God to guide their hearts, though he knew them to be vulnerable to hate." While he writes his article for the newspaper, he understands "that accident ruled every corner of the universe except the chambers of the human heart."

Trials, supposedly based on law, are sometimes unfair. Clark felt that *The Ox-Bow Incident* illustrated fascist terrors and was himself concerned with political power abusing individual rights. As Ishmael writes his article about Kabuo's trial in *Snow Falling on Cedars,* he realizes that "the heart of any other, because it had a will, would remain forever mysterious." People are the judges and the juries of other humans, and their attitudes, formed as children, often taint their decisions. Too many times, people retain membership in an anonymous mob, so vilified by Mark Twain in *The Adventures of Huckleberry Finn*, and illustrated in each of these novels for a number of reasons, including lack of education or fear of being excluded from community or family for being different. Seeing people as individuals requires the strength of an Atticus—either Atticus Finch in *To Kill a Mockingbird* or Atticus (109–32 B.C.E.), the Roman preserver of truth.

Additional Related Novels

Gaines, Ernest J. *A Gathering of Old Men.*
Hawthorne, Nathaniel. *The House of the Seven Gables.*
Knowles, John. *A Separate Peace.*
Melville, Herman. *Billy Budd.*
Oates, Joyce Carol. *Foxfire.*

Value of Land

The ground is holy, being even as it came from the Creator. Keep it, guard it, care for it, for it keeps men, guards men, cares for men. Destroy it and man is destroyed.

Alan Paton, *Cry the Beloved Country* (1948)

As a limited commodity, the value of land usually rises, and investors, whether homeowners or farmers, often feel gratified with its appreciation. People who have saved money and deprived themselves of material goods so that they can buy land know that land, carefully tilled, always remains when other things have disappeared. In *Giants in the Earth*, Per Hansa revels in the pleasure of owning land and trying to make it produce food. The Nedeed family in *Linden Hills* purchases allegedly fallow land in 1837 and begins a dynasty by creating a cemetery and adding houses in nearby areas. George and Lenny in *Of Mice and Men* think that owning a small plot of land will give them stability and happiness. In the novels, *The Good Earth*, *Barren Ground*, and *O Pioneers!*, the protagonists borrow money to buy as much land as they can, knowing that no one can steal it from them.

Land is "ground or territory as owned by a person or viewed as public or private property; landed property" while value is "a standard of estimation or exchange; an amount or sum reckoned in terms of this; a thing regarded as worth having" (*OED*). William Langland mentions "laborers that haue no lond." (*Piers Plowman*, 1362). William Jevons notes that "some one will say that he is beyond question rich, who owns a great deal of land" (*Political Economy*, 1878). Louis J. Glickman says that "the best investment on earth is earth" (*New York Post*, 1957). Louise Erdrich makes a strong statement about land and its importance: "In our own beginnings, we are formed out of the body's interior landscape. For a short while, our mothers' bodies are the boundaries and personal geography which are all that we know of the world. . . . Once we no longer live beneath our mother's heart, it is the earth with which we form the same dependent relationship, relying . . . on its cycles and elements, helpless without its protective embrace (*New York Times*, 1985). In the novels, *The Good Earth*, *Barren Ground*, and *O Pioneers!*, the protagonists appreciate the value of land.

The Good Earth by Pearl S. Buck

In Pearl S. Buck's *The Good Earth* (1931), the peasant Wang Lung slowly gathers land and wealth. He describes his life in limited omniscient point of view from the day he marries O-lan, a slave who costs less than other women, until his death. He brings O-lan to live with him and his father (Old Man), and she does their housework and helps in the fields. Although disappointed that O-lan's feet have not been bound, Wang Lung finds her reasonably attractive and soon wants "this woman of mine" to like him. She bears him five children and then another child during her illness that she strangles. Wang Lung buys eggs and dyes them red to proudly announce his sons' births, but not for the girl, the "slave." They live frugally, with O-lan carefully repairing broken items and Wang Lung's hard work earning him money to buy land. Famine eventually overtakes them, however, and rather than sell the land, they leave for the city where they beg for food. When they return to the farm, Wang Lung's prosperity increases, but, during his idleness, while his fields are flooded, he visits a brothel, falls in love with Lotus, and brings her home. Because O-lan ignores her, Wang Lung must build another kitchen for her and her maid Cuckoo. After O-lan's death, Wang Lung's two oldest sons await his demise, planning to sell the land. When he hears their discussion, he discourages it. " 'It is the end of a family—when they begin to sell the land,' he said brokenly. 'Out of the land we came and into it we must go—and if you will hold your land you can live—no one can rob you of land—.'And the old man let his scanty tears dry upon his cheeks and they made salty stains there. And he stooped and took up a handful of the soil and he held it and he muttered, 'If you sell the land, it is the end.' "

As a woman, O-lan has a subservient role in Wang Lung's life, but her talents help the family endure. She rises at dawn to light the fire, cleans, and sews. After their first son is born, she asks Wang Lung for money to dress the child for a visit to the House of Hwang where she was once a slave. When O-lan takes the money, she says that she has never before touched silver. That their third child is a girl or "slave" upsets Wang. Crows, evil omens, appear at her birth, and later they call her "Poor Fool" because she is feebleminded. When the family has to survive in the city, O-lan makes huts from mats and teaches her children to beg, both skills she learned as a child. She also suggests to Wang Lung that they sell their daughter, but he refuses. When enemy troops invade the city, O-lan steals jewels from the houses of the wealthy and hides them. After Wang Lung brings Lotus and Cuckoo to live with them, O-lan rejects them, saying, "I am not slave of slaves in this house at least.'" O-lan has her daughter's feet bound, and Wang Lung asks the child at ten why she has not wept from the pain. She responds, "My mother said I was not to weep aloud because you are too kind and weak for pain and you might say to leave me as I am, and then my husband would not love me even as you do not love her." Thus O-lan knows Wang Lung's true feelings and will not burden him with her own troubles, including her final sickness. Wang Lung realizes what O-lan has done for his family and shows her that she will be cared for in death by buying her a coffin. Old Man dies soon after, and Wang Lung buries the two of them at the same time.

Wang Lung's generally frugal decisions throughout his life help him buy his land and raise his family. He rarely exhibits extravagant behavior until his old age. He bathes only on his wedding day to prepare for a new life because water is scarce. After marriage, he no longer has to rise early and light the fire or prepare meals for himself and his father and begins to consider that work is a luxury. But his unexpected interest in O-lan shames him because "she was, after all, only a woman." He plants grain, onions, and garlic and sells his wheat in winter when the price is higher. His money "had come out of the earth, this silver, out of his earth that he ploughed and turned and spent himself upon. He took his life from this earth; drop by drop by his seat he wrung food from it and from the food, silver." As time passes, he feels more confident in his financial status and decides to buy Hwang's land, even though it is far away. At first he regrets his decision but then he decides to buy more.

Wang Lung wants to help those who have aided him, but his undeserving uncle's family begins to take advantage of his wealth, wanting him to support them. When he refuses, villagers break into his house to find his money. Since he has spent it on land, he has none. In the city during the famine, a naked man gives him gold with which he restarts his farm. Since Ching gave him beans during the famine, he shares the gold with him. He buys more Hwang land and Ching's land, asking Ching to become his steward. Wang Lung makes his sons work in the fields, while O-lan, wife of a wealthy man, stays in the house. He tries to store enough food for survival during the next famine of flood, drought, or locusts expected in a cycle of seven or eight years. When his uncle, aunt, and worthless son reappear, he must welcome them because his uncle controls a band of robbers. To keep them occupied, Wang Lung's son induces him to give them opium. After Ching's death, Wang Lung becomes less interested in visiting his land, and, as his age advances, he asks Pear Blossom, his young slave, to look after Poor Fool when he dies, knowing that his sons and eleven grandchildren will ignore her and destroy the family by selling its valuable land.

Barren Ground by Ellen Glasgow

Ellen Glasgow uses limited omniscient in *Barren Ground* (1925) to present Dorinda Oakley's point of view toward the land and the people around her. Dorinda lives in Pedlar's Mill, Virginia, a small town where the "Presbyterian faith sprang up and blossomed like a Scotch thistle in barren ground," and she has to walk two miles to work at Nathan Pedlar's country store. Her own mother overworks, looking after Rufus and Josiah, and suffers from "religious depression." Dorinda has observed her father Joshua become a slave to the land, unsuccessfully trying to make things grow, but she has never heard this overworked, unfulfilled man openly complain about his fate. Dorinda becomes engaged to Jason Greylock, but he marries someone else after she is pregnant. She leaves home and takes the train to New York where a carriage hits her soon after her arrival. While in the hospital for two weeks, she loses her baby, but the doctor hires her to work for his family. She stays for two years until her father dies and then returns to Pedlar's Mill to run the family farm. She marries Nathan but dedicates herself to amassing land and cultivating it with the help of Nathan's son, John Abner, although he, like all males, has "the masculine instinct to domineer over the opposite sex."

As Dorinda interacts with the people around her, she wonders about her prospects. When objectively analyzing herself, she realizes that she can escape neither her past nor her future. The land and the people she knew held her like "invisible wires of steel." She wonders as she helps Rose Emily, Nathan's sick wife, if the ordinary things happening every day were the essence of life, all that it could offer her. When she falls in love with Jason, physician son of dissipated Dr. Greylock, she becomes amazed that "not one of them [the women that she knows] had ever betrayed to her this hidden knowledge [the glory of love], which was the knowledge of life." For a moment, she escapes the mundane, but an omniscient narrator interjects that Jason seems unstable. Jason confesses to Dorinda, "Father . . . always gets his way with me. He's thwarted everything I ever wanted to do as far back as I can remember. For my good of course. I understand that. But you can ruin people's lives—especially young people's lives—from the best motives." Dorinda ignores the warning and spends money saved to buy a cow on a blue dress for Easter after Jason tells her she would look lovely in blue. Jason then appears at church escorting Geneva Ellgood and ignores Dorinda. Dorinda begins to question, "Was love, like life, merely a passing from shock to shock, with no permanent peace?" Dorinda's mother tells her that love is "just the struggle to get away from things as they are." And Dorinda worries, "Was this all there was in her feeling for Jason; the struggle to escape from the endless captivity of things as they are? In the bleak dawn of reason her dreams withered like flowers that are blighted by frost." She avoids Jason for two weeks after the Easter disappointment, and, when he sees her, he proposes marriage. She forgets her doubts, and "for the first time in her life she had ceased longing, ceased striving. She was as satisfied as Almira [Josiah's girlfriend] to drift with the days toward some definite haven of the future."

Although Jason soon deceives her, Dorinda survives, eventually dedicating her life to the land. Jason impregnates her before eloping with Geneva, and when Dorinda appears at his door with a gun, he tries to placate her by blaming his father. And Dorinda, "with a piercing flash of insight . . . saw him as he was, false, vain, contemptible, a coward in bone and marrow. He had wronged her; he had betrayed her; he had trampled her pride in the dust; and he had done these things not from brutality, but from weakness." Two years later, after she returns from New York, she sees Jason at her father's funeral and rebuffs him.

She decides to marry the recently widowed Nathan and care for his children, especially John Abner with the clubfoot. Simultaneously, Geneva commits suicide, unhappy living with the alcoholic Jason. Dorinda's life continues to change after Nathan takes the train to Richmond to see the dentist. On his return, the train wrecks and he escapes, but when he rushes into a burning car to rescue others, he dies. Burying him first like a hero, people then collect money to create a monument for him. In contrast to Nathan, Jason needs Dorinda to rescue him from the woods so that he can die in the warmth of her home, and those who attend his funeral do so out of curiosity. Although the steady Nathan offered none of Jason's sexual attraction, Dorinda realizes how fortunate she was to have married Nathan instead.

Dorinda knows that "the one thing . . . immutable and everlasting . . . [is] the poverty of the soil, " and it, like life, is "just barren ground where they have to struggle to make anything grow." People at first think Nathan strange, but he appreciates the land's need for renewal through crop rotation just as humans need to participate actively in their lives to find contentment. Old Matthew says, "Thar's one thing sartain sure, you've got to conquer the land in the beginning, or it'll conquer you before you're through with it." In New York, Dorinda studies dairy farming, and when her father dies, she borrows money to buy cows on her return home. She inherits the farm, makes money, and, pays off the loan when she is thirty-three. She begins to understand that "you can't have everything," but she enjoys her work. After World War I ends, she owns both the Greylock farm and Five Oaks, the Ellgood farm that Nathan bought for her at auction. She accepts that, without the love she had once wanted, like Old Matthew had said, "the land is the only thing that will stay by you." Although both she and the ground are barren, she cultivates herself and it as best she can. After her death, the ground will become her legacy.

O Pioneers! by Willa Cather

Willa Cather's *O Pioneers!* (1913) celebrates the spirt of Alexandra as she nurtures her family's farm on the prairie in Hanover, Nebraska. Cather takes her title from Walt Whitman's poem, "Pioneers! O Pioneers!" as she personifies the land that "wanted to be let alone, to preserve its own fierce strength, its peculiar, savage kind of beauty, its uninterrupted mournfulness." To both Cather and Alexandra, "the great fact" of prairie life "was the land itself." The Swedish immigrant Alexandra arrives when "the little town of Hanover was trying not to be blown away," with her brother Emil. There she meets Carl Lindstrom when he is fifteen. After Carl helps her rescue their cat, they begin a friendship. Then Carl becomes Alexandra's best friend after she takes over the family farm at her father's death. Her brothers Lou and Oscar never relished farming like Alexandra, and her father asks the three to keep the land together until marriage and then divide it three ways. Alexandra feels that she is part of the land because she understands it.

Although Alexandra loves the land, she also relates well to people in the town. She consults Crazy Ivar, a hermit other people shun and whose knowledge Alexandra respects, about hogs. Her brothers dislike experimenting with either animals or plants, but she knows that they must for the farm to function. Carl feels unproductive, but Alexandra reassures him. "It's by understanding me, and the boys, and mother, that you've helped me. I expect that is the only way one person ever really can help another." Later, Alexandra assists others when she is financially secure. After her father has been dead sixteen years, Alexandra sends Emil to college. She supports Ivar who loses his farm through mismanagement. She sponsors Swedish men and women who have wanted to immigrate to the area and then hires them to work for her. Mrs. Lee, Alexandra's sister-in-law's mother, loves visiting Alexandra for relaxation in December.

Although Alexandra has success with her land, she copes with unhappiness and personal tragedy. When Carl returns to town and stays with Alexandra for a month after they become adults, her brothers complain, but Alexandra says "people have to snatch at happiness when they can, in this world. It is always easier to lose than to find." Carl, however, resents the criticism and immediately departs for the West. Emil has adored Marie, wife of the jealous Frank, since he met her when they were very young. After Emil's best friend Amédée dies from appendicitis the week after Amédée's son is baptized, Emil professes his love. Emil has tried to escape from it and Marie by going to Mexico, but he cannot erase his feelings. Frank finds them and, enraged, kills them both. Alexandra mourns Emil, but helps Frank get a release from prison, saying that Emil and Marie were wrong. Carl reads about the trial and comes to Alexandra. Although she has passed her fortieth birthday, they decide to marry and enjoy what happiness might be left.

Alexandra thinks of the land as "beautiful . . . rich and strong and glorious." She tames the land that defeated her father by making it "ben[d] lower than it ever bent to a human will before," and Alexandra's creativity appears in "the joyous germination in the soil." After three years of drought, when people, including Carl's family, leave the area, Alexandra buys their land. From the day that Alexandra decides to keep her family's farm rather than investing in a river farm, she realizes that "the history of every country begins in the heart of a man or woman." However, she also discounts the role of humans in the land's history. She tells Carl, "we hadn't any of us much to do with it. . . . The land did it." Even after she marries Carl, she yearns to unite with the land while the personified land hopes to "one day . . . receive hearts like Alexandra's into its bosom, to give them out again in the yellow wheat, in the rustling corn, in the shining eyes of youth!" Alexandra, therefore, loves the land and understands its power to regenerate and its value for humans.

These protagonists, Wang Lung in *The Good Earth*, Dorinda in *Barren Ground*, and Alexandra in *O'Pioneers!*, all know that land, even seemingly barren land, has intrinsic value beyond mere pieces of silver. They invest their energy in cultivating the land not only for themselves but for those who would inherit it. They know that land, carefully tilled land, offers family stability and hope for the future. Its value defies rootlessness and impermanence.

Additional Related Novels

Cather, Willa. *My Ántonia.*
Faulkner, William. *Absalom, Absalom!*
Marshall, Paule. *Brown Girl, Brownstones.*
Naylor, Gloria. *Linden Hills.*
Rölvaag, O. E. *Giants in the Earth.*
Steinbeck, John. *Of Mice and Men.*

Appendix A: Additional Selected Themes and Topics

Each theme or topic is followed by a list of American novels in which it occurs.

African Americans

Absalom, Absalom!
The Adventures of Huckleberry Finn
The Autobiography of Miss Jane Pittman
The Bear
Beloved
The Bluest Eye
The Color Purple
The Confessions of Nat Turner
Devil in a Blue Dress
Fallen Angels
Fried Green Tomatoes at the Whistle Stop Café
A Gathering of Old Men
Go Tell It on the Mountain
The Hiding Place
Invisible Man
A Lesson Before Dying
Light in August
The Lilies of the Field
Linden Hills
Mama
Mama Day
Middle Passage

Native Son
Our Nig
Passing
Ragtime
Song of Solomon
The Sound and the Fury
Sula
Tar Baby
Their Eyes Were Watching God
To Kill a Mockingbird
Uncle Tom's Cabin
Waiting to Exhale
The Women of Brewster Place
A Yellow Raft in Blue Water

Bildungsroman

All the King's Men
All the Pretty Horses
Annie John
April Morning
The Bean Trees
The Bear
Bless Me, Ultima
The Bluest Eye
Brown Girl, Brownstones
The Catcher in the Rye
Ceremony
The Chocolate War
The Chosen
Cold Sassy Tree
Deliverance
Folded Leaf
Fools Crow
Foxfire
The Great Santini
The House on Mango Street
How the Garcia Girls Lost Their Accents
The Human Comedy

Invisible Man
A Member of the Wedding
The Moviegoer
Native Son
A River Runs Through It
Sister Carrie
To Kill a Mockingbird
A Tree Grows in Brooklyn
A Yellow Raft in Blue Water

Chinese and Chinese Americans

Bone
The Good Earth
The Joy Luck Club
The Kitchen God's Wife
The Woman Warrior

Dreams and the Supernatural

Angle of Repose
Bless Me, Ultima
Ceremony
Fools Crow
Going after Cacciato
The Great Gatsby
The Heart Is a Lonely Hunter
House Made of Dawn
The House of the Seven Gables
Love Medicine
Mama
Mama Day
Reservation Blues
Slaughterhouse-Five
Tar Baby

Fathers and Daughters

Absalom, Absalom!
The Bell Jar
The Bluest Eye
Bone
Brown Girl, Brownstones
Charlotte Temple
Cold Mountain
The Color Purple
Ellen Foster
Foxfire
The Good Earth
The House on Mango Street
How the Garcia Girls Lost Their Accents
In the Time of the Butterflies
The Poisonwood Bible
The Rise of Silas Lapham
The Shipping News
Song of Solomon
A Tree Grows in Brooklyn
To Kill a Mockingbird
Washington Square

Fine Arts and Education

The Accidental Tourist
The Age of Innocence
Angle of Repose
The Awakening
The Bell Jar
Brown Girl, Brownstones
The Chosen
Cold Mountain
Deliverance
Fahrenheit 451
Foxfire
The Heart Is a Lonely Hunter
The House on Mango Street
Main Street

Mama
Memoirs of a Geisha
The Moviegoer
The Poisonwood Bible
Ragtime
Reservation Blues
A River Runs Through It
The Shipping News
Sister Carrie
Slaughterhouse-Five
Snow Falling on Cedars
These Is My Words
A Tree Grows in Brooklyn
Winesburg, Ohio
The Woman Warrior

Frontier Life

Angle of Repose
Death Comes for the Archbishop
Fools Crow
Giants in the Earth
The Last of the Mohicans
My Ántonia
O Pioneers!
The Ox-Bow Incident
These Is My Words

Hispanic and Caribbean Extraction

All the Pretty Horses
Annie John
Bless Me, Ultima
Brown Girl, Brownstones
The House on Mango Street
How the Garcia Girls Lost Their Accents
In the Time of the Butterflies
The Pearl

Infidelity

The Age of Innocence
All the King's Men
Angle of Repose
The Awakening
Brown Girl, Brownstones
Ceremony
The Color Purple
The Crying of Lot 49
Ethan Frome
Fools Crow
The Good Earth
The Great Gatsby
Mama
Rabbit, Run
The Scarlet Letter
Seize the Day
Sister Carrie
Sula
Tender Is the Night
Waiting to Exhale
A Yellow Raft in Blue Water

Judaism

The Assistant
The Chosen
The Fixer
Goodbye, Columbus
The Rise of David Levinsky
Tell Me a Riddle

Marriage

The Age of Innocence
Angle of Repose
The Awakening
Black and Blue
Bone
The Color Purple

A Death in the Family

Dinner at the Homesick Restaurant

Fahrenheit 451

Giants in the Earth

The Good Earth

In the Time of the Butterflies

The Kitchen God's Wife

Main Street

Mama Day

Ordinary People

Passing

The Pearl

The Poisonwood Bible

Rabbit, Run

Ragtime

The Rise of Silas Lapham

The Shipping News

Song of Solomon

Tar Baby

Tell Me a Riddle

Their Eyes Were Watching God

These Is My Words

A Yellow Raft in Blue Water

Native Americans

The Bean Trees

Ceremony

The Death of Jim Loney

Fools Crow

House Made of Dawn

I Heard the Owl Call My Name

The Last of the Mohicans

Love Medicine

Pigs in Heaven

Reservation Blues

A Yellow Raft in Blue Water

Religion

The Adventures of Huckleberry Finn
The Assistant
Bless Me, Ultima
The Catcher in the Rye
Ceremony
The Chosen
Cold Mountain
Cold Sassy Tree
The Color Purple
The Confessions of Nat Turner
Death Comes for the Archbishop
The Fixer
Go Tell It on the Mountain
The Great Santini
House Made of Dawn
I Heard the Owl Call My Name
Light in August
The Lilies of the Field
The Poisonwood Bible
Reservation Blues
A River Runs Through It
The Scarlet Letter
Slaughterhouse-Five
Uncle Tom's Cabin
A Yellow Raft in Blue Water

Slavery

The Adventures of Huckleberry Finn
The Autobiography of Miss Jane Pittman
Beloved
The Bridge of San Luis Rey
The Confessions of Nat Turner
A Connecticut Yankee in King Arthur's Court
The Good Earth
Killer Angels
Memoirs of a Geisha
Middle Passage

Uncle Tom's Cabin
The Woman Warrior

War

April Morning
A Bell for Adano
Catch-22
Ceremony
Cold Mountain
Fallen Angels
A Farewell to Arms
Fools Crow
For Whom the Bell Tolls
Going after Cacciato
The Human Comedy
In the Time of the Butterflies
The Joy Luck Club
Killer Angels
The Last of the Mohicans
Memoirs of a Geisha
The Poisonwood Bible
The Red Badge of Courage
Shiloh
Slaughterhouse-Five
The Things They Carried

Appendix B: Guide to Suggested Themes in 150 American Novels

This guide provides an alphabetical listing of the 150 American novels discussed. Each title is followed by a list of themes for discussion. Those examined in the essays are marked by an asterisk.*

Absalom, Absalom!

African Americans, Family, Fathers and Daughters, Fathers and Sons, Multiracial Offspring, Rejection, Revealing Family History, Search for a Father,* Value of Land

The Accidental Tourist

Bereavement,* Death, Fine Arts and Education, Revealing Family History

The Adventures of Huckleberry Finn

Abandonment, African Americans, Community, Friendship, Nature, Journeys, Male Behavior, Oppression, Outsiders, Religion, Search for a Father, *Search for Identity, Slavery

After the First Death

Alienation,* Betrayal, Cultural Conflict, Death, Duty, Fathers and Sons, Search for Identity

The Age of Innocence

Compassion, Cultural Conflict, Fine Arts and Education, Independent Women, Marriage, Infidelity, Outsiders*

All the King's Men

Being and Becoming, Betrayal, Bildungsroman, Community, Corrupting Power,* Friendship, Infidelity, Love, Search for a Father, Search for Identity

All the Pretty Horses

Betrayal, Bildungsroman, Cultural Conflict, Hispanic and Caribbean Extraction Imprisonment, Injustice, Journeys, Male Behavior, Quests,* Survival

Angle of Repose

Betrayal, Compassion, Dreams and the Supernatural, Disabled, Family, Fine Arts and Education, Frontier Life, Infidelity, Loss, Love, Marriage, Responsibility, Revealing Family History*

Annie John

Bildungsroman, Hispanic and Caribbean Extraction, Mothers and Daughters,* Quests

April Morning

Absurdity of War, Bildungsroman, Death, Family, Loss,* Responsibility

As I Lay Dying

Being and Becoming,* Death, Duty, Family

The Assistant

Alienation, Imprisonment, Judaism, Loneliness,* Male Behavior, Search for a Father, Search for Identity, Religion

The Autobiography of Miss Jane Pittman

African Americans, Multiracial Offspring, Independent Women,* Injustice, Oppression, Search for Identity, Slavery, Storytelling

The Awakening

Fine Arts and Education, Being and Becoming, Independent Women, Infidelity, Love, Marriage, Rejection, Search for Identity*

Barren Ground

Compassion, Courage, Independent Women, Loneliness, Loss, Love, Search for Identity, Value of Land*

The Bean Trees

Bildungsroman, Friendship,* Immigrant Life, Independent Women, Journeys, Mothers and Daughter, Native Americans

The Bear

African Americans, Bildungsroman, Courage, Loss, Nature,* Quests

A Bell for Adano

Absurdity of War, Community, Compassion,* Duty

The Bell Jar

Bereavement, Disabled, Fathers and Daughters, Fine Arts and Education, Oppression,* Search for a Father, Suicide

Beloved

African Americans, Injustice, Love,* Mothers and Daughters, Oppression Slavery

Billy Budd

Compassion, Duty,* Trials

Black and Blue

Battered Women,* Marriage, Survival

Bless Me, Ultima

Being and Becoming*, Bildungsroman, Compassion, Dreams and the Supernatural, Hispanic and Caribbean Extraction, Healers,* Religion, Search for Identity

The Bluest Eye

African Americans, Bildungsroman, Corrupting Power, Disabled, Fathers and Daughters, Rejection,* Search for Identity

Bone

> Chinese and Chinese Americans, Community, Family, Fathers and Daughters, Immigrant Life, Loneliness, Marriage, Outsiders, Search for a Father, Suicide*

Breakfast at Tiffany's

> Friendship, Independent Women, Loneliness, Masquerading*

The Bridge of San Luis Rey

> Journeys, Loneliness, Love,* Slavery

Brown Girl, Brownstones

> Bildungsroman, Fathers and Daughters, Fine Arts and Education, Hispanic and Caribbean Extraction, Immigrant Life,* Infidelity, Mothers and Daughters, Value of Land

Catch-22

> Absurdity of War,* Corrupting Power, Loss, Survival

The Catcher in the Rye

> Alienation, Bereavement,* Bildungsroman, Compassion, Death, Knowableness of God, Loneliness, Loss, Religion

Ceremony

> Abusurdity of War, Bildungsroman, Cultural Conflict, Dreams and the Supernatural, Healers, Infidelity, Native Americans, Religion, Search for Identity, Storytelling,* Survival

Charlotte Temple

> Abandonment, Betrayal,* Family, Fathers and Daughters, Healers, Responsibility

Chocolate War

> Bildungsroman, Corrupting Power,* Fathers and Sons, Oppression, Search for Identity

The Chosen

> American Dream, Bildungsroman, Duty, Family, Fathers and Sons, Fine Arts and Education, Friendship,* Judaism, Religion, Search for Identity

Cold Mountain

> Absurdity of War, Compassion, Death, Fathers and Daughters, Fine Arts and Education, Greed, Independent Women, Journeys,* Loss, Love, Nature, Quests, Religion

Cold Sassy Tree

> Bildungsroman, Community, Family, Knowableness of God,* Religion

The Color Purple

> African Americans, Battered Women,* Fathers and Daughters, Friendship, Infidelity, Love, Marriage, Search for Identity, Religion

The Confessions of Nat Turner

> African Americans, Imprisonment,* Injustice, Knowableness of God, Loss, Religion, Search for Identity, Slavery

A Connecticut Yankee in King Arthur's Court

> Absurdity of War, Corrupting Power, Injustice,* Outsiders, Religion, Slavery

The Crying of Lot 49

> Infidelity, Journeys,* Quests, Search for Identity

The Day of the Locust

> Alienation, Grotesques,* Loneliness, Masquerading

A Death in the Family

> Bereavement, Bildungsroman, Death,* Family, Fathers and Sons, Loneliness, Marriage

Death Comes for the Archbishop

> Death, Friendship, Frontier Life, Religion, Responsibility*

The Death of Jim Loney

> Abandonment, Alienation, Death, Loneliness, Multiracial Offspring, Native Americans, Outsiders, Search for a Father,* Search for Identity

Deliverance

> Bildungsroman, Death, Fine Arts and Education, Journeys Male Behavior,* Nature, Search for Identity, Survival

Devil in a Blue Dress

> African Americans, Courage, Greed, Love, Multiracial Offspring*

Dinner at the Homesick Restaurant

> Abandonment,* Betrayal, Family, Fathers and Sons, Marriage

Ellen Foster

> Battered Women, Death, Emotional Abuse,* Family, Fathers and Daughters, Independent Women, Loneliness, Rejection

Ethan Frome

> Being and Becoming, Disabled,* Infidelity, Loneliness, Love, Marriage, Storytelling

Fahrenheit 451

> Absurdity of War, Fine Arts and Education, Marriage, Oppression*

Fallen Angels

> Absurdity of War, African Americans, Death, Survival*

A Farewell to Arms

> Absurdity of War, Death, Loss,* Love, Survival

The Fixer

> Imprisonment,* Injustice, Judaism, Religion, Search for Identity

The Folded Leaf

> Bildungsroman, Friendship, Journeys, Suicide*

Fools Crow

> Absurdity of War, Bildungsroman, Community, Courage, Dreams and the Supernatural, Frontier Life, Infidelity, Native Americans, Responsibility,* Storytelling

For Whom the Bell Tolls

> Absurdity of War, Courage, Duty,* Love, Survival

Foxfire

> Alienation,* Bildungsroman, Community, Fathers and Daughters, Fine Arts and Education, Imprisonment, Independent Women, Injustice, Loss, Outsiders, Survival, Trials

Fried Green Tomatoes at the Whistle Stop Café

> African Americans, Battered Women, Bereavement, Community, Compassion, Death, Courage, Family, Friendship, Healers, Independent Women, Love, Loss, Oppression, Responsibility,* Search for Identity, Survival

A Gathering of Old Men

> African Americans, Community,* Injustice, Oppression, Search for Identity, Trials

Giants in the Earth

> American Dream, Community, Compassion, Courage, Frontier Life, Immigrant Life, Loneliness, Marriage, Nature, Survival*

Go Tell It on the Mountain

> African Americans, Battered Women, Knowableness of God,* Male Behavior, Religion, Revealing Family History, Search for a Father

Going after Cacciato

> Absurdity of War,* Dreams and the Supernatural, Duty, Quests, Survival

The Good Earth

> Chinese and Chinese Americans, Family, Fathers and Daughters, Greed, Infidelity, Marriage, Rejection, Slavery, Value of Land*

Goodbye, Columbus

> Compassion, Cultural Conflict,* Judaism, Love, Mothers and Daughters, Search for Identity

The Grapes of Wrath

> American Dream, Betrayal, Family,* Journeys, Survival

The Great Gatsby

> Alienation, American Dream,* Greed, Grotesques, Infidelity, Loneliness, Masquerading, Outsiders, Quests, Rejection

The Great Santini

> Bildungsroman, Family, Fathers and Sons,* Male Behavior, Religion

The Great Train Robbery

> Betrayal, Greed,* Masquerading, Trials

Grendel

> Disabled, Grotesques,* Loneliness, Rejection

The Heart Is a Lonely Hunter

> Alienation, Community, Disabled,* Dreams and the Supernatural, Grotesques, Imprisonment, Loneliness, Loss, Fine Arts and Education, Search for Identity

Henderson, the Rain King

> Alienation, Being and Becoming,* Healers, Journeys, Quests, Search for Identity, Search for a Father

The Hiding Place

> African Americans, Alienation, Loss, Responsibility, Revealing Family History,* Survival

House of Mirth

> American Dream, Alienation, Betrayal, Greed, Masquerading,* Outsiders, Search for Identity

House Made of Dawn

Courage, Dreams and the Supernatural, Loneliness, Native Americans, Nature,* Religion, Search for Identity, Storytelling

The House of the Seven Gables

Betrayal, Corrupting Power, Dreams and the Supernatural, Greed,* Family, Revealing Family History, Trials

The House on Mango Street

American Dream, Bildungsroman, Fathers and Daughters, Fine Arts and Education, Hispanic and Caribbean Extraction, Oppression, Quests*

How the Garcia Girls Lost Their Accents

Bildungsroman, Cultural Conflict,* Family, Fathers and Daughters, Hispanic and Caribbean Extraction, Immigrant Life, Outsiders

The Human Comedy

Absurdity of War, Bildungsroman, Community, Compassion, Death,* Family, Grotesques, Love

I Am the Cheese

Betrayal, Corrupting Power, Loneliness, Masquerading, Search for Identity*

I Heard the Owl Call My Name

Community, Compassion,* Cultural Conflict, Death, Friendship, Native Americans,* Religion

In the Time of the Butterflies

Absurdity of War American Dream, Betrayal, Bildungsroman, Family, Fathers and Daughters, Hispanic and Caribbean Extraction, Imprisonment, Injustice,* Marriage, Oppression, Survival

Invisible Man

African Americans, Alienation, American Dream, Being and Becoming, Betrayal, Bildungsroman, Emotional Abuse,* Oppression, Outsiders, Rejection, Search for Identity

The Joy Luck Club

Absurdity of War, Chinese and Chinese Americans, Cultural Conflict, Death, Immigrant Life, Masquerading, Mothers and Daughters, Revealing Family History, Search for Identity,* Storytelling, Survival

The Jungle

Alienation, American Dream, Family, Immigrant Life,* Injustice

The Killer Angels

Absurdity of War, Duty,* Loss, Slavery

The Kitchen God's Wife

Battered Women,* Chinese and Chinese Americans, Cultural Conflict, Family, Immigrant Life, Marriage, Masquerading, Mothers and Daughters, Revealing Family History

The Last of the Mohicans

Absurdity of War, Community, Courage,* Frontier Life, Native Americans, Nature

A Lesson Before Dying

African Americans, Death, Friendship, Injustice, Imprisonment,* Oppression, Rejection, Search for Identity

Light in August

African Americans, Alienation, Emotional Abuse, Multiracial Offspring,* Religion

The Lilies of the Field

African Americans, Journeys, Love,* Religion, Search for Identity

Linden Hills

African Americans, Battered Women, Corrupting Power,* Family, Greed, Rejection

Love Medicine

Community,* Dreams and the Supernatural, Family, Greed, Native Americans, Revealing Family History, Search for a Father

Maggie: A Girl of the Streets

Abandonment,* Immigrant Life, Loneliness, Rejection, Search for Identity, Suicide

Main Street

Alienation, American Dream, Community, Cultural Conflict, Fine Arts and Education, Immigrant Life, Imprisonment, Loneliness, Marriage, Outsiders,* Search for Identity

Mama

African Americans, Community, Family, Fine Arts and Education, Independent Women, Infidelity, Loneliness, Mothers and Daughters,* Multiracial Offspring, Search for Identity, Survival

Mama Day

African Americans, Community, Death, Dreams and the Supernatural, Family, Healers,* Marriage, Love, Revealing Family History

A Member of the Wedding

Alienation, Bildungsroman, Death, Loneliness,* Rejection

Memoirs of a Geisha

Abandonment,* Absurdity of War, Family, Fine Arts and Education, Grotesques, Love, Slavery, Survival

Middle Passage

Abandonment, African Americans, American Dream, Greed, Grotesques, Imprisonment, Injustice,* Journeys, Knowableness of God, Male Behavior, Search for a Father, Slavery

Moby-Dick

Corrupting Power, Friendship, Journeys, Quest,* Religion

The Moviegoer

Alienation,* Bildungsroman, Family, Search for Identity, Fine Arts and Education

My Ántonia

American Dream, Friendship, Frontier Life, Immigrant Life,* Independent Women, Rejection, Survival, Value of Land

Native Son

African Americans,* Alienation, Bildungsroman, Oppression, Outsiders*

The Natural

    Betrayal,* Corrupting Power, Disabled, Greed

Of Mice and Men

    Emotional Abuse, Friendship, Loneliness, Male Behavior, Nature*

The Old Man and the Sea

    Bildungsroman, Compassion,* Death, Friendship, Nature, Survival

On the Road

    Alienation, American Dream, Being and Becoming, Friendship, Journeys,* Search for a Father

One Flew Over the Cuckoo's Nest

    Betrayal, Community, Disabled, Healers,* Male Behavior, Search for a Father

O Pioneers!

    American Dream, Community, Frontier Life, Immigrant Life, Survival, Value of Land*

Ordinary People

    Bereavement,* Death, Family, Fathers and Sons, Marriage, Suicide

Our Nig

    Abandonment, African Americans, Disabled, Emotional Abuse, Loneliness, Multiracial Offspring, Oppression,* Survival

The Ox-Bow Incident

    Corrupting Power, Frontier Life,* Injustice, Suicide, Trials*

Passing

    African Americans, Marriage, Masquerading,* Multiracial Offspring, Outsiders

The Pearl

    Community, Hispanic and Caribbean Extraction, Family, Greed,* Male Behavior, Marriage, Oppression

Pigs in Heaven

    Immigrant Life, Injustice, Mothers and Daughters,* Native Americans

The Poisonwood Bible

    Absurdity of War, Emotional Abuse, Family, Father and Daughters, Fine Arts and Education, Knowableness of God,* Marriage, Religion

Rabbit, Run

    American Dream, Betrayal,* Bereavement, Infidelity, Marriage, Male Behavior, Responsibility

Ragtime

    African Americans, Alienation, American Dream,* Courage, Family, Fine Arts and Education, Immigrant Life, Injustice, Marriage, Outsiders, Search for Identity

The Red Badge of Courage

    Absurdity of War, Bildungsroman, Courage,* Death, Nature, Survival

Reservation Blues

    Abandonment, Alienation, Betrayal, Dreams and the Supernatural, Family, Fine Arts and Education, Knowableness of God, Loneliness, Native Americans, Outsiders, Religion, Storytelling, Suicide*

The Rise of David Levinsky

> American Dream,* Immigrant Life, Judaism, Loneliness, Outsiders, Quests, Search for Identity

The Rise of Silas Lapham

> Family, Fathers and Daughters, Love, Marriage, Rejection*

A River Runs Through It

> Bildungsroman, Death, Family, Fathers and Sons,* Fine Arts and Education, Nature, Religion

The Scarlet Letter

> Being and Becoming, Emotional Abuse,* Infidelity, Love, Rejection, Religion

Seize the Day

> Alienation, Death, Fathers and Sons,* Greed, Infidelity, Loneliness, Love, Rejection

A Separate Peace

> Bildungsroman,* Death,* Friendship, Male Behavior, Search for Identity, Suicide

Shiloh

> Absurdity of War, Male Behavior*

The Shipping News

> Being and Becoming,* Community, Compassion, Disabled, Duty, Fathers and Daughters, Fine Arts and Education, Independent Women, Loneliness, Marriage, Outsiders, Search for Identity

Sister Carrie

> American Dream, Being and Becoming, Betrayal, Bildungsroman, Fine Arts and Education, Independent Women,* Infidelity

Slaughterhouse-Five

> Absurdity of War,* Alienation, Dreams and the Supernatural, Fine Arts and Education, Knowableness of God, Religion, Storytelling

Snow Falling on Cedars

> Community, Cultural Conflict, Death, Fine Arts and Education, Immigrant Life, Injustice, Loneliness, Love, Trials*

Song of Solomon

> African Americans, Family, Fathers and Daughters, Friendship, Greed, Loneliness, Marriage, Revealing Family History*

The Sound and the Fury

> African Americans, Disabled, Family,* Grotesques, Revealing Family History, Suicide

Sula

> African Americans, Betrayal, Friendship,* Independent Women, Infidelity

The Sun Also Rises

> Betrayal, Disabled, Infidelity, Male Behavior*

Tar Baby

> Abandonment, African Americans, Cultural Conflict,* Dreams and the Supernatural, Fine Arts and Education, Loneliness, Marriage, Masquerading, Responsibility, Search for Identity

Tell Me a Riddle

> Death, Family, Imprisonment, Judaism, Loneliness,* Loss, Marriage, Oppression, Search for Identity

Tender Is the Night

> Disabled,* Emotional Abuse, Greed, Healers, Infidelity, Masquerading

Their Eyes Were Watching God

> African Americans, Battered Women, Emotional Abuse, Love, Marriage, Quests, Storytelling*

These Is My Words

> Bereavement, Death, Family, Fine Arts and Education, Frontier Life, Independent Women, Marriage, Search for Identity, Survival*

The Things They Carried

> Absurdity of War, Bereavement, Courage, Death, Friendship, Loss,* Storytelling, Survival

To Kill a Mockingbird

> African Americans, Bildungsroman, Fathers and Daughters, Fine Arts and Education, Injustice, Trials*

A Tree Grows in Brooklyn

> Bildungsroman, Family,* Fathers and Daughters, Fine Arts and Education, Independent Women, Loneliness, Mothers and Daughters, Search for Identity

Uncle Tom's Cabin

> African Americans, Betrayal, Compassion, Courage,* Love, Religion, Slavery

Waiting to Exhale

> African Americans, Community,* Friendship, Love, Independent Women, Infidelity, Survival

Washington Square

> Betrayal, Fathers and Daughters, Greed, Rejection*

Winesburg, Ohio

> Being and Becoming, Fine Arts and Education, Grotesques, Loneliness

The Woman Warrior

> American Dream, Chinese and Chinese Americans, Cultural Conflict, Family, Fine Arts and Education, Mothers and Daughters, Outsiders, Search for Identity, Slavery, Storytelling*

The Women of Brewster Place

> Abandonment, Bereavement, African Americans, Death, Healers, Independent Women,* Loss, Love, Survival

A Yellow Raft in Blue Water

> African Americans, Bildungsroman, Emotional Abuse, Infidelity, Marriage, Mothers and Daughters, Multiracial Offspring,* Native Americans, Religion, Search for Identity

Author/Title Index

Main entries appear in **boldface type**.

Subject and Character Index

About the Author

LYNDA G. ADAMSON is Professor of Literature and Chair of the English Department at Prince George's Community College. She has taught American, Children's, and Comparative Literature courses and has been honored with the Senate Faculty Excellence Award. She has previously written ten reference books including *Notable Women in American History* (Greenwood 1999), *Literature Connections to American History* (1998) and *Recreating the Past: A Guide to American and World Historical Fiction for Children and Young Adults* (Greenwood 1994).